The Anglosphere
Challenge

The Anglosphere Challenge

Why the English-Speaking Nations Will Lead the Way in the Twenty-First Century

James C. Bennett

ROWMAN & LITTLEFIELD PUBLISHERS, INC.
Lanham • Boulder • New York • Toronto • Oxford

ROWMAN & LITTLEFIELD PUBLISHERS, INC.

Published in the United States of America
by Rowman & Littlefield Publishers, Inc.
A wholly owned subsidary of The Rowman & Littlefield Publishing Group, Inc.
4501 Forbes Boulevard, Suite 200, Lanham, Maryland 20706
www.rowmanlittlefield.com

PO Box 317
Oxford
OX2 9RU, UK

British Library Cataloguing in Publication Information Available

Library of Congress Cataloging-in-Publication Data
Bennett, James C., 1948–
  The anglosphere challenge : why the English-speaking nations will lead the way
in the twenty-first century / James C. Bennett.
    p. cm.
  Includes index.
  ISBN 0-7425-3332-8 (cloth : alk. paper)
  1. Commonwealth countries—Politics and government. 2. Civil
society—Commonwealth countries. 3. Democracy—Commonwealth countries. 4.
Science—Political aspects—Commonwealth countries. 5. Technology—Political
aspects—Commonwealth countries. I. Title.
  JN248.B46 2004
  300'.917'521—dc22
                            2004008433

Printed in the United States of America

⊗ ™ The paper used in this publication meets the minimum requirements of
American National Standard for Information Sciences—Permanence of Paper
for Printed Library Materials, ANSI/NISO Z39.48–1992.

To

C. William Bennett

Contents

ACKNOWLEDGMENTS   xi

INTRODUCTION   1
- Three Questions about the Future: Answers from the Past   2

1 THE INTERNET ERA—AND BEYOND   9
- Beyond the Information Revolution: The Singularity   11
- Thinking about the Revolutions of the Singularity   12
- Bounded and Unbounded Visions   13
- Bounded and Unbounded Problems: The Space Development Example   14
- Y2K as the Opposite Case: Mistaking Bounded for Unbounded Problems   18
- Death and Taxes: Extending Lifespan, and Its Consequences   20
- Taking a Possibility Seriously   21
- How to Think about the Effects of These Revolutions: The "Pessimistic Scenario"   23
- Industrial Goods as Software: The Next Phase of the Information Revolution, and Its Implications   25
- Civil Society and the Hazards of the Singularity Revolutions: The Case of Nanotechnology   29
- Civil Societies and the Economy of the Singularity   31
- After the Economic State: The Civic State and the Network Commonwealth   39

- Hobbes and Rousseau in Cyberspace — 40
- Limits to the Breakdown of Big Governments — 42
- The Growing Worldwide Market in Sovereignty Services and the Decline of the Monopoly of the Economic State — 44
- Linux as a Foreshadowing of the Economics of the Singularity: The End of Capitalism and the Triumph of the Market Economy — 47
- The Civic State: On the Nature and Limits of Governments in the Era of the Singularity — 55
- Building the Network Commonwealth: The Power of Self-Assembly Protocols — 61
- Political Self-Assembly Protocols: A Tool for the Singularity Revolution — 62
- A Call for Civilizational Construction — 65

2 THE ANGLOSPHERE AND ITS REVOLUTIONS — 67
- The Anglosphere and the New Understanding of the West — 72
- Reconvergence and Culture: Why the Information Revolution Is Drawing the Anglosphere Closer Together — 75
- What Is the Anglosphere? — 79
- The Fundamental Structures of the Anglosphere: States, Regions, and Cultural Nations — 82
- Cultural Nations—The Invisible Understructure — 83
- Cultural Nations and Regions: What's the Difference? — 84
- Becoming a Self-Aware Civilization: The Anglosphere Perspective — 89
- Memetic Plagues of the Anglosphere — 93
- Coming Home to the Anglosphere — 100

3 TRUST, CIVIL SOCIETY, GOVERNMENT, AND CYBERSPACE — 109
- One World through the Internet? The Role of Trust, Cooperation, and Cultural Commonality — 113
- Trust and Civil Society — 114
- Trust, Reform, and the Three Gateways — 117
- One World, Many Marketplaces — 122
- The New Amphibians: Living Simultaneously in Cyberspace and the Physical World — 124
- Better Communications and the Rise of Nationalism — 126
- Space and Power: Geopolitics and the Topology of Information Space — 129
- Hanseatic Leagues in Cyberspace — 132
- The New Understanding of the Market: Rules of Thumb for Intervention — 135
- The Anarcho-Capitalist Debate and Other Red Herrings — 138
- Civic States and Large-Scale Federations — 141

- Coherent Noncontiguous States 142
- What Will Become of Big Government Establishments? 143

4 THE CIVIC STATE AND THE NETWORK COMMONWEALTH 146
- The Sinews of the Network Commonwealth:
  Evolving New Forms from Existing Elements 148
- Trade, Security, and Technology Intersect: The Case of
  Anglosphere Defense Cooperation 159
- Who Will Control the Commonwealth? Popular Control
  of Transnational Institutions 167
- Commonwealth or Tribalism 169
- Network Commonwealths around the World 172
- United Nations—or Associated Commonwealths? 179

5 THE ANGLOSPHERE AS A UNIQUE CIVILIZATION 181
- The Anglosphere Constitutional Tradition and War 185
- Five Civil Wars: Union and Secession in the Anglosphere 193
- Preserving the National Voice in a Decentralized World 197
- The Anglosphere's History as the History of Its Cultural
  Nations 199
- American Cultural Nations and Their Histories 199
- The Relationship between Cultural Nations and
  Nation-States 211
- Cultural Nations in Actuality: North America 213
- Cultural Nations Elsewhere in the Anglosphere 223
- Regions, Civic States, and Scale 224

6 THE ANGLOSPHERE CENTURY 227
- 1776: Divergence and the End of the First Empire 228
- Convergence in Politics: The Dilemma of the
  Second Empire 230
- Potential Roadblocks to an Anglosphere
  Network Commonwealth 233
- Postimperial Identity Questions in the
  Commonwealth States 237
- The African Special Relationship: American Africans, the
  Caribbean, and Africa 238
- Embedded Cultures, Native Nations, and
  Pan-Anglosphere Minorities 240
- What's at Stake: Uses of the Network Commonwealth 242
- Controlling Dangers, Maintaining Freedoms:
  Constitutional Traditions and the Technologies
  of the Singularity 248
- Common Law and Common Markets: Harmony without
  Homogenization 250

- The Anglosphere Debate   251
- Moving toward an Anglosphere Network Commonwealth   257
- Doing Their Part: Leadership and the Emergence of the
  Network Commonwealth   257
- Devolution and the Neverendum in Scotland and Quebec   258
- African America: The Stalled Transition to High Trust   261
- Prospects for the Anglosphere   263
- Canada and *Le Projet Trudeau*   264
- Quebec and the Nine Provinces: Two Nations and Two
  Network Civilizations   266
- Britain: Scotland and the West Lothian Question;
  The Euro and the Westphalian Question   268
- The United States and the Anglosphere:
  From Post–Cold War Reorientation to the
  Challenge of the Singularity   274
- South Africa: What Form of Union?   277
- Australia and New Zealand: Identity in Oceania   278
- Ireland: What Price the EU?   280
- Trade and Defense Drivers for the
  Network Commonwealth   283
- The Anglosphere as the "Offshore Island"   285
- The Anglosphere and the Challenge of the Singularity   287

ANNOTATED BIBLIOGRAPHY   291

INDEX   321

ABOUT THE AUTHOR   337

Acknowledgments

I would particularly like to thank Baroness Margaret Thatcher, whose critique of an early presentation of these ideas at a Hudson Institute conference was both sympathetic and acute, contributing substantially to their refinement and further evolution.

Additionally, special mention is merited to three people whose support, in various way, was essential to the production of the book: my wife, Karen, for her belief in me, and her forbearance of the inevitable annoyances of living in the vicinity of the writing process; my mother, Marion Bennett Rodger, for her lifelong support and belief in me; and finally, John O'Sullivan, who has been an extraordinary champion of this work.

Finally, I would like to acknowledge the assistance, advice, criticism, comment, review, and encouragement of the following people as enormously helpful to the writing of this book:

Carol Adelman, Charles F. Bacon, Howard Baetjer, Xavier Basora, Peter Brimelow, Greg Burch, Tom Burroughes, Grenville Byford, Bill Cash, Chris Champion, Geoffrey Charlish, Robert Conquest, Conyers Davis, David Davis, Alan Dayton, Joanne Dayton, Perry de Havilland, Brannon Denning, Andrew Ian Dodge, K. Eric Drexler, Charles Evans, Mark Frazier, Gerald Frost, Dan Fylstra, Gay Hart Gaines, Stanley Gaines, Jeff Gedmin, Daniel Hannan, William Anthony Hay, Edna Heird, Carl Helmers, Scott Hicks, John Holt, Michael Howard, Neil Hrab, John Hulsman, Justin Jackson, Lindsay Jenkins, Dana Johnson, Barbara Johnson, George Jonas, Sam Karnick, Jonathan Kay, Jason Kenney, Yasuhiko Kimura, Norman Lamont, Eli Lehrer, John Lloyd, Herb London, Michael J. Lotus, Spencer MacCallum, Gerald Malone, Patrick Minford, Iain Murray, Scott Pace,

Suman Palit, Malcolm Pearson, Christine Peterson, Madsen Pirie, Stephen Pollard, Bob Poole, Richard W. Rahn, John Ray, William Rees-Mogg, Glenn Reynolds, Karina Rollins, Alexander Rose, David Justin Ross, Enrique Salgado, Neil Seeman, Frank Sensenbrenner, Jon Sisk, Joseph Skelley, James M. Smith, Leif Smith, Marni Soupcoff, Nathan St-Armand, Courtney Stadd, Irwin Stelzer, Ira Straus, John Tate, Greg Treverton, Ricardo Valenzuela, Claudio Véliz, Patricia J. Wagner, Robert West, Russell Whitaker, Scott Wickstein, John S. L. Williamson, Gareth Young.

Any virtues the book may have are undoubtedly due in part to their participation; all of its faults are due entirely to me.

Introduction

In the year of my birth, Harry Truman was president of the forty-eight United States; George VI was King of Great Britain and had just ceased to be emperor of India; and Joseph Stalin was the dictator of something called the Union of Soviet Socialist Republics. Airliners were driven by piston engines and could not cross the Atlantic without refueling in Newfoundland; and computers were the size of a large room and ran on vacuum tubes. A transatlantic telephone call was booked in advance and cost a good day's wage for a three-minute call; and if you produced a document (by pecking it out on a typewriter), you could only have a copy if you had placed a sheet of carbon paper under the original. The first commercial photocopy machine was to be sold that year. A secret U.S. government project was figuring out how a satellite might be launched into space to take photographs of the earth; and two scientists named Watson and Crick were figuring out that a molecule called deoxyribonucleic acid (DNA, for short) might contain the "genes" that Mendel had predicted.

As a young boy in the 1950s, I consumed enormous amounts of low-grade science fiction, mostly in comic-book form. These presented an intriguing, if not necessarily convincing vision of a twenty-first century that seemed unimaginably distant, in which we would have flying cars, cities of soaring towers connected by aerial ramps, routine flights to colonies on other planets, atomic robots cleaning our houses, and gigantic computers the size of skyscrapers capable of conversing in natural language. As I grew older, I gradually became aware of not how rapidly things were progressing, but rather how slowly. The launch of Sputnik held the promise that space would soon be available as an arena for human activity. By the time of the moon landings, it became clear that space travel as actually practiced was extremely costly and was only being addressed by ponderous governmental bureaucracies. A life spent in the space program would not be spent jaunting to other planets, but mostly sitting at grey metal desks in government buildings creating endless viewgraph presentations about programs that would mostly be canceled before they ever cut metal.

Internal combustion engines were replaced first with turboprops and then with jet aircraft. The first supersonic airliners never developed beyond the handful of Concordes kept aloft as political symbols, limited by high costs, sonic booms, and environmental concerns. Nuclear power became a political disaster rather than a source of cheap, unlimited power. Far from becoming the Radiant Cities of the future, cities seemed to be turning into urban wastelands prowled by bands of thugs. Mad Max seemed to be replacing George Jetson as the citizen of the future.

Today, at the start of the twenty-first century, it is clear that some of the promises of the future will never be kept, while other things not readily imagined in the first half of the twentieth have already come to be. The Information Revolution has gone from a miracle to a cliché without really being understood by a fraction of the people who toss around the term with familiarity. It was touted as an economic miracle by people who could not tell a good venture from a bad one, and is now being dismissed, equally ignorantly, by people (often the same ones) who cannot tell a bad venture from good.

THREE QUESTIONS ABOUT THE FUTURE: ANSWERS FROM THE PAST

In the course of writing this book, three questions came to me. The first was: "Will the revolutions of the Singularity* mean the end of the nation-state and (as many prophesy) the advent of the borderless world?" As we will see, the answer that gradually emerged was that we would indeed have a borderless economy, but not a borderless world. The concept of the nation-state as an economic state is indeed at an end, but the civic state, based not on the illusion of economic sovereignty but on the realities of

---

* The *Singularity* is a term, taken from mathematical science, which refers to a dramatic statistical discontinuity. Writer Vernor Vinge (who defined it as "the point where a rising trend line on a graph turns completely vertical") used the term to describe the effect of a number of scientific, technological, and social revolutions coming together at the same time and as a result of their mutual interaction. Observers see the Singularity unfolding as numerous parallel events driven by rapid progress in various fields begin interacting and supporting each other at a rate previously never experienced.

commonalties in language, culture, and shared narratives, would emerge as the basic organizing form of the new era.

The second question was, "Where will these changes first arise?" They will arise first in the United States (where indeed these changes are substantially advanced) and almost simultaneously in the rest of the English-speaking, Common Law-based nations of the world—the Anglosphere. Shortly thereafter they will spread through the rest of the developed world, more or less in the order of the strength of their civil societies. Thus, Scandinavia very quickly, some of the Latin and Mediterranean countries, less quickly.

The third question was, "Why has the Anglosphere been the leader of the scientific-technical revolution uninterruptedly from the start, and how deep-seated are the characteristics which have enabled this leadership?" The answer to the first part of the question is complex, and I will discuss it at greater length later in this book, but it can be summarized by saying, "The Anglosphere developed a strong civil society early, and it grew least hindered here while its counterparts elsewhere (seemingly equally promising) were smothered or destroyed."

The answer to the second part is more intriguing. Chasing the answer to this question became a detective story in history, trying to determine the departure point at which English-speaking society became substantially distinct in this fashion from its Continental neighbors. It took me further and further back, through the Industrial Revolution, back to the American Declaration of Independence, back to England's Revolution of 1688, then to the English Civil War—and beyond. Every time I thought I had found the departure point, I found evidence that significant changes existed even further back in time. Magna Carta played a part, but Magna Carta came about because English society had already acquired a broad class of surprisingly literate, surprisingly individualistic, surprisingly outspoken civic participants—hardly the passive, oppressed peasants depicted in bad historical novels and movies. They were aware of the concept that they had rights under law and were accustomed to acting together to defend those rights.

This led me to reexamine what has been called, broadly, "Whig history"— a school, now discredited in academia, which interpreted the history of England as an inevitable process or progression of society to greater freedom. Although one could readily demonstrate that the element of inevitability was indeed more in the mind of the historian than inherent in history, the Whig narrative was what we might call emergently true; that is, even when its specific points are obviously wrong, the overall picture it presents still discloses useful patterns in history.

There is an element of cultural evolution visible in the history of the Anglosphere, of a variation of social forms combined with selection of those forms most compatible with the self-organization of society into increasingly complex patterns. These organized themselves using larger and larger amounts of energy, tying together larger and larger areas of the globe. Whig history, in order to be useful today, must be shorn of its assumptions of inevitability; corrected for its blind spots in ignoring or misunderstanding Ireland, and other anomalies; and must be based on a more sophisticated understanding of cultural evolution. Given these updates, however, an understanding along the broad outlines of Whig history—call it Whig History Version 2.0, if you will—emerges as a useful way of looking at the history of strong civil society, and of the Anglosphere in particular.

These patterns become clearer once certain veils, which have served to obscure, have been parted by time and growing understanding. The veil of Marxism, which unsuccessfully tried to fit all phenomena into a Procrustean bed of materialist determinism, labor theory of value, and Hegelian mysticism, has largely fallen by the wayside. The declinist theories of Spengler and his various acolytes have largely been disproven by events and by more sophisticated analysis. Such theories saw our civilization as subject to a set of patterns of rise and fall which may have been valid for preindustrial civilizations dependent on slave labor, but have never been demonstrated to have validity for industrial or postindustrial cultures. Rome may have been dependent on the surplus wheat produced by Egyptian peasants, but Industrial England and America fed themselves by free labor. If slavery was the principal critical factor in financing the Industrial Revolution, then Portugal and Spain, the great slave masters of the Atlantic world, should have industrialized first, and America and Britain should have grown poorer after abolition, rather than immeasurably richer.

Imperialism theory, the bastard offspring of Marx and Spengler via Lenin and Stalin, has similarly fallen to superior historical analysis. It is sometimes difficult to recall that Marx predicted that the industrial working classes of the West would grow progressively poorer through the end of the nineteenth century, rather than, as was the fact, much more prosperous. Imperialism theory was an attempt to extend the lifetime of Marxist prophecy by introducing ever-more-complex cycles and epicycles. But in the end it proved no more useful than its parent. Finally, the narrow nationalist narratives of America and Britain alike, as well as the recent narratives of other Commonwealth nations, which have served to distort the proper perception of the Anglosphere as a distinct civilization, are beginning to fall away as well. The return of a renewed Whig history in a new form is relevant to a more sophisticated understanding of the issues of the Singularity Revolutions.

This new Whig history should not shy away from a clear-eyed discussion of slavery, colonialism, or internal oppression of minorities. However, it should place them in a realistic historical context. The Anglosphere is not remarkable for having traded in or kept slaves, but it is remarkable for having given birth to the philosophy of abolition, and the practical movement which eventually accomplished it. The Anglosphere is not unique in having maintained exploitative land practices in Ireland and elsewhere, long after their abolition in England, which maintenance (while not ignoring other things) was certainly the leading contender for the root cause of the Irish famine. English-speaking society is unique in having moved beyond feudalism in its core lands so early in history, transitioning from a society with an illiterate peasantry to one based on a free and essentially independent, literate, rights-protecting yeomanry long before the Industrial Revolution.

It may even be possible to have a realistic examination of the history of the British Empire, neither the celebration of it common in the Victorian era nor the demonizations of it which have dominated historiography for the past half-century. (The recent work of David Cannadine and Niall Ferguson may be considered a start in this direction.) Indeed, the later episodes of British colonial practice have interesting similarities to the "humanitarian interventions" of recent times, in that a similar mixture of genuine humanitarian sentiment, media sensationalism, *raison d'etat*, and short-term interest has driven the dispatch of British gunboats then and American helicopter gunships now to distant corners of the world. In fact, British colonialism may be preferable to United Nations humanitarian intervention, in that, once the Union flag was run up and a governor installed, Britain acquired some accountability for the results of its actions before its citizens' eyes, while responsibility in the case of recent humanitarian interventions has typically been somewhere between diffuse and nonexistent.

Similarly, much criticism of British colonial practice was formulated on the idea that Britain was exploiting surplus value from native populations for its own benefit, and that once independence was established, the colonies would be richer and freer, and Britain poorer and more insignificant. Orwell loved to predict that Britain minus India would have to subsist on "herring and potatoes," yet a stroll around London today suggests that the diet has evolved more toward sushi and Chardonnay. In fact Britain has become much richer since it shed its colonies, and its former colonies have had a mixed experience. A few, such as Singapore, have in fact become richer while many (particularly in Africa) have become poorer and more despotic. We called the Amritsar events of 1919 a massacre, and rightly so, but today many Third World police forces would just call it a good day's work.

I suspect an independent and objective analysis would show that relatively few colonial schemes were profitable to the British state and people, when all net costs were counted. Some were highly profitable to individual persons and companies, and it might be possible to see much colonialism as an elaborate cross-subsidy scheme by which British taxpayers were subsidizing British colonial profiteers, with the actual colonized populations randomly benefiting or suffering. Certainly much of the geopolitical thinking that motivated later British imperialism was illusionary. There was no point in formally colonizing land to control overseas mineral resources, when (for example) it was naval supremacy which determined whether the minerals of Africa would be available to Britain or Germany in World War I, not the formalized control of the land upon which the minerals were found.

In fact, the Achilles' heel of the Second British Empire may have been its self-identity as empire. The British administrators of the late nineteenth century were lulled by classical educations into revering the Roman Empire, and seduced by the antiquity and persistence of the Chinese and other non-European empires. In constructing the Indian Empire in particular, they did not stop to ask whether a preindustrial model of administration (and one which rested on a profoundly nondemocratic mentality) should serve as the template for even a part of an Industrial Era polity. If they can be faulted, it must be for an insufficient confidence in the Indians as pupils (and thus, in themselves as teachers) in constructing a modern industrial society. Every aspect of the Indian Empire—its tax policy, its Civil Service based on the Chinese model, its willingness to retain existing preindustrial Indian political models (benign in intent, but already betraying a growing self-doubt over their own social achievements), demonstrated either an expectation that India would never become modern, or a demonstration that the British had lost the appreciation of the causes of their own success.

These issues are not idle intellectual curiosity, but are key in understanding the roots of the Anglosphere as the cradle of the scientific-technological revolution, and in attempting to construct the institutions to deal with the next phase of that revolution. For example, it is inevitable that some will brand Anglospherism as an attempt to reconstruct the British Empire. This is precisely the reverse of reality: it is rather the Second British Empire which can now be seen as an early and overly backward-looking attempt to create an international polity connecting the English-speaking world. The very name empire discloses its weakness in looking to past imperial models, a weakness which had much to do with its demise. As Indian author Nirad Chadhauri pointed out, the final logic of empire required that either the Indian remained subjugated to the English, no matter how well-assimilated he became, or that ultimately the center of gravity of the empire would shift to India. Anglospherists are constructing neither an empire nor a state, but rather what I discuss in this book under the name of a network commonwealth. In such a commonwealth, should the Indians choose to engage it, it may well be that Bangalore becomes a major center of the Anglosphere in thirty or fifty years' time. Anglospherists do not fear this, knowing that just as London is still great today because it shares an Anglosphere with New York and Los Angeles, it and the American metropolises will be great tomorrow partly because they might share it with Bangalore.

The Anglosphere Challenge is more than a bit Janus-like, looking simultaneously ahead to the challenges of the Singularity and the culmination of the Scientific-Technological Revolution, and backward into the foundation of the Anglosphere in the mists of time. It is certain that technologically oriented readers may question the relevance of the history, and historically oriented readers may be puzzled at the introduction of radical speculation about the shape of the near future. Yet if there is a particular value to this book, it is precisely in its attempt to look backward and forward with equal interest. Technologists' speculations about the future often incorporate assumptions about the history of technology and society which are simplistic, ill-informed, and quite often unexamined altogether. Many still contain assumptions of an ability to rationally plan and program human events far in excess of any demonstrated capability to that effect, and now in the face of numerous disastrous attempts in that direction. At the same time, historians who venture into speculation about the future are often hampered by equally uninformed assumptions about technological change, its pace, and its ability to bound the limits of human action.

The viewpoint underlying this work rejects determinism of all varieties, whether the economic determinism of Marx, the geographic determinism of Haushofer, the genetic determinism of the more extreme sociobiologists, or the technological determinism of numerous utopians. Yet it acknowledges that each of these factors form certain circumscriptions within which human efforts must play their parts. Understanding these bounds is critical to understanding the menu of options from which we as moral individuals must choose.

This work is furthermore distinct in not presenting itself as a work of detailed research, nor a blueprint for future action. It is rather a series of linked essays on the nature of the scientific-technological revolution, its relationship to the emergence of constitutional freedom, and its common roots in the emergence of a strong civil society. These interests lead to an examination of the Anglosphere as the cradle of all three phenomena in the modern world, the arena in which their precursor institutions survived challenges which defeated their analogues elsewhere. It goes on to discuss the rise of the network commonwealth as the emergent political form in the coming era, and the particular prospects for the emergence of the first network commonwealth in the Anglosphere.

I have striven to refrain from specific blueprints or deterministic predictions. These chapters are intended to be suggestions for a framework for new research, not the results of that research. Similarly, I have tried to give enough examples of what network commonwealths might be, and how they might arise, to serve as starting points for discussions about whether and how to pursue such opportunities. It is clear that I write as an advocate of an Anglosphere Network Commonwealth, and that I feel that the creation of such is the best course for all in the Anglosphere. It is also the best course for the well-being of the world, for I believe that any possible solutions to the challenges of the Singularity must come from the toolkit of strong civil society. The Anglosphere Challenge is a challenge to the Anglosphere, to learn from its successes and failures in order to deal with the coming issues of the future.

At the same time, the book is intended as a challenge to those outside the Anglosphere. Certainly some will call it a work of English-speaking triumphalism, or a call for the universalization of English-speaking culture. That would be a misunderstanding. In fact, the more the roots of the Anglosphere's successes are understood, the more it must be realized that Anglosphere institutions cannot be copied blindly in cultures with far different histories and circumstances. What is universal is the need for strong civil society. Each culture must learn for itself how to achieve these characteristics, and how to evolve its own institutions to such ends.

Any book containing new ideas or new outlooks is by necessity a letter in a bottle, tossed into the ocean of future possibilities. It is my hope that it will be found and read by those who will find it a stimulus to thought, a rule of thumb for judging options, and an outline of future courses of action. The Anglosphere debate has already begun. I offer this as my contribution.

1

The Internet Era— and Beyond

We are . . . very much in the middle of an English Industrial Revolution that is scarcely more than two centuries old and shows no symptoms of weakness or decline. On the contrary, vigorous, relentless change remains the characteristic sine qua non of the modern industrial ambit, and the resulting immense flow of major and lesser innovations ceaselessly adds complexity and diversity to the leading countries of a world that is certainly not tottering on the brink of dissolution.

—Claudio Véliz, *The New World of the Gothic Fox:
Culture and Economy in English and Spanish America* (1994)

Modern civilizations often seem to have the peculiar characteristic of loving to contemplate their own demises. Every decade, some new book appears to warn of the impending global predominance of some other ideology or nation. In the early 1990s we heard much of the neo-Confucian model exemplified by the Four Tigers of East Asia, winning through work ethic and family values. Before that it was Japan, Inc., dominating world commerce through the samurai-like dedication of its corporate salary men and their collusion with the godlike Ministry of International Trade and Industry. In the 1960s, Europe was similarly horrified by Jean-Jacques Servan-Schreiber's *The American Challenge*, which predicted that American corporations would crush European business through their superior corporate technique and aggressive marketing.

Of course, these works were primarily devices by which authors preached to their own countrymen. Their picture of the foreign challenger has usually borne only a slight resemblance to reality, and often the virtues of the supposed competitive threat bore a curious inverted mirroring of the flaws the author detected in his own countrymen. Americans of the 1980s and early 1990s used the Japanese and East Asian models to decry the indiscipline, lack of cohesion, and declining values they saw in their own lands. Likewise, Servan-Schreiber's book was more about the backwardness and lack of modernity he feared in his own country than any actual virtues of General Motors or U.S. Steel, both of which were about to get their clocks cleaned by foreign competition.

I titled this book *The Anglosphere Challenge* in a sort of tangential homage to Servan-Schreiber. Unlike the works described earlier, I do not discuss an overseas competitor that I fear is about to overtake America, or more properly, the Anglosphere, the entirety of English-speaking civilization. Rather I argue that the current gap in technological, military, and financial leadership enjoyed by America and its Anglosphere cousins over the rest of the world is likely to increase over the next twenty years. I believe this increase will take place in the context of a rapid acceleration of genuine technological revolution, one in which entrepreneurial innovation and rapid adaptation will play an increasingly large part in commercial, financial, technological, and national success.

Although I will inevitably be accused of triumphalism, I in fact warn that this success has not been due to any inherent superiority of Anglosphere language or peoples. Rather, it is the result of a long series of developments, more than coincidence but less than foreordained fate. These developments resulted in the Anglosphere nations having a particularly strong and independent civil society; openness and receptivity to the world, its people, and ideas; and a dynamic economy.

There is no reason to believe that other cultures cannot develop their own versions of these characteristics, nor that the Anglosphere cannot lose the advantages it now has. The Anglosphere experienced the creation of the Industrial Revolution, modern constitutional democracy, and the Information Revolution, first in Britain, and then in America. The Anglosphere and the institutions it created have led throughout.

It is now creating the next set of scientific-technological revolutions, which some are beginning to speak of as the revolutions of the Singularity. If the Anglosphere can retain the openness and dynamism that allowed it to lead in the past, it will remain among the leaders of the future. If it loses those characteristics, it will at last be overtaken.

Therefore, the challenge of *The Anglosphere Challenge* is of the Anglosphere to both itself and the rest of the world. To itself, the challenge is to understand the sources of its strength and to maintain and expand upon them. It must also understand its own failures and their causes, and to cure them before they overtake and undo its successes. To the rest of the world, the challenge is likewise to understand the reasons for the Anglosphere's successes and failures, and to use that knowledge to cure their own failures and expand upon their own successes. In doing so, mere imitation of Anglosphere institutions and practices will not be sufficient; in fact, it may even be harmful. More important is to understand the deep roots of strong civil society, constitutionally bound civic states, and dynamic, open cultures. The greater challenge for the rest of the world is to examine the roots of their own societies and move them toward their own version of those virtues.

I begin this book with a look forward to some of the possible revolutions of the Era of the Singularity. I follow this with a discussion of how these developments might affect the social and political environment. Then I look to the past, to the newly emerging appreciation of the Anglosphere as a distinct world civilization, child of Western civilization but no longer defined within those bounds.

I discuss at greater length the assertions made earlier about its relationship to the leadership of the technological and political revolutions of the past three hundred years.

BEYOND THE INFORMATION
REVOLUTION: THE SINGULARITY

Over the previous decade there was much talk about the Internet Era. Few really understood it. What was least understood may have been two things: the first, how early on into it we then were, and how much more there was still to come; and the second, that the Information Revolution, and the Internet Era it appeared to be generating were not the main events. Rather they are the warm-up act, the advance guard of a related series of scientific-technical revolutions that, when taken together, will have a more startling cumulative effect on our daily lives than the Industrial Revolution.

The end result of these revolutions will make the comic-book futures of the past century look pale and unimaginative. The Singularity, a term taken from mathematical science, describes an abrupt discontinuity: a point where a rising trend line on a graph, for example, turns completely vertical.

Writer Vernor Vinge appropriated it to describe the effect of numerous scientific, technological, and social revolutions coming together at the same time and interacting with each other. The term has since gained currency in futurological parlance. What we are talking about, then, are the effects of not just the Information Revolution, but of the revolutions of the Singularity.

This book is an exploration into the world of the Singularity Revolutions and the English-speaking civilization—the Anglosphere—which, for better or worse, is leading the move into that world. Readers may be surprised to find that the book talks more about the nature of government, culture, and society than about molecules, bytes, or rockets, and draws more on history than on mathematics.

That is because science and technology, as fundamental as they are in affecting the future, cannot tell us what the world will be like in twenty years, nor how we will live our lives, or how we will think and feel about our lives. It can only put upper and lower bounds on our options, and often cannot describe those bounds very well. History, however imprecise and changing its interpretation, is in effect one of the most important databases available to help us understand the changes we face and to suggest how we may respond to the challenges to our benefit.

In facing the Singularity and its consequences, a vital lesson we have learned from the failures of the past is to reject Utopia as a goal. This lesson reflects the end of the idea that technological progress, or social progress, or any other arrangement of human affairs can establish universal human happiness. We know that technological and social changes have removed specific causes of unhappiness, and the world is better off for it. A key example is the worldwide end of slavery as a direct consequence of the Industrial Revolution. Whatever the subsequent unhappiness of a liberated slave, a patient cured of tuberculosis, or a woman able to bear a child she once would have lost, it is rare to find people relinquishing those benefits of change.

The Singularity revolutions promise to alleviate scarcities, pollution, diseases, ignorance, and even the fixity of life span. What they do not promise is that, having delivered those benefits, humans will then be happy. Happiness will remain the realm of religion and philosophy. But in facing the Singularity, we must at least remove one additional cause of misery, which is the harm that utopian philosophies have caused in attempting to engineer the perfect society. Coming into an era which is likely to be marked by unprecedented abilities to affect our condition in the world, it is all the more important to do so without the illusion that such changes, however great and however desirable, will bring perfection.

THINKING ABOUT THE
REVOLUTIONS OF THE SINGULARITY

What is the nature of the Era of the Singularity? It is a new technological, social, and economic period, comparable at least in effect to the Industrial Revolution but accelerating faster. This era appears to be emerging since the Singularity revolutions began to accelerate in the 1990s. They promise to explode in the first decades of the twenty-first century. It is currently fashionable to view the Internet-enabled stock explosion of the late 1990s as a tulip-mania exercise. This ignores the genuine great improvements to productivity added by information technologies, even in their current immature form. Yet this increase in value added is itself merely a forerunner of the economic changes of the next phases.

My aim is not to take readers on a technological tour of these revolutions, but instead to show ways to think about these revolutions using general knowledge rather than narrow expertise in any field. In doing this, I will mention five revolutions, not an exhaustive list of the possible revolutions by any means. I will talk about biotechnology, a new generation of space capabilities, significant life extension, molecular manufacturing (also known as molecular nanotechnology or MNT), the possibility of commercially exploitable petroleum of abiogenic origin, and advanced information technologies, including strong computer-integrated manufacturing.

I write as a commentator, not a prophet, and make no claim that any of these revolutions are bound to come true, although several seem hard to avoid. That said, I would be amazed if none of them came true in any way, or if we did not experience at least one other revolution that I neglected entirely. That is the real point of Singularity—that we have gone beyond hope of anticipating all of the major changes that we will encounter in the coming years. That is why this book will devote its attention not to any particular revolution per se, but to the characteristics of the kind of societies that have generated such revolutions and the social institutions that promise to deal best with the consequences.

BOUNDED AND UNBOUNDED VISIONS

I introduced this book by describing the vision of the futurists at the end of World War II, as filtered through the popular media to a boy of that day. This vision was driven by the awesome scientific developments unveiled in the closing years of that war—radar, computers, long-range rockets, jet aircraft, and above all, the atomic bomb. In their own way, the science fiction writers and denizens of the first think tanks such as the Rand Corporation envisioned a scientific-technical revolution as sweeping as the Singularity; but unlike the Singularity as it is now envisioned, they believed it could be predicted, anticipated, and planned with substantial precision. They had enormous faith in the powers of operational analysis and planning, and that faith seemed justified. Robert McNamara and his staff, the original Whiz Kids, used these methods to plan U.S. wartime bomber production with brilliant success.

Later, as defense secretary to John Kennedy and Lyndon Johnson during the Vietnam era, McNamara attempted to apply these methods to the "rationalization" of the Defense Department and the conduct of the Vietnam War, but with disastrous results.

What was little appreciated at that time, outside of the then-arcane world of Austrian, or Hayekian, economics, was the distinction between "bounded" and "unbounded" problems. The former are the sort typical of engineering problems, having a finite and definable number of elements and a predictable set of significant interactions. The latter, which include the issues of predicting and understanding very large systems such as the weather, natural ecologies, or complex human economies, are characterized by extremely large numbers of elements and near-infinite sets of possible significant interactions. Methods such as McNamara's operational analysis, which produced wondrous results applied to even complex bounded problems, failed miserably when applied to unbounded problems. Why did space and atomic energy, although they produced real but limited benefits, not produce the results predicted in the science fiction and techno-optimism of the 1950s? The answer is that many of the problems which had to be overcome were unbounded problems, while that era tried to deal with them having only a tool set useful for bounded problems. The Singularity is above all an unbounded problem, and therefore the history of the 1950s and 1960s provides a cautionary tale of great significance.

BOUNDED AND UNBOUNDED PROBLEMS:
THE SPACE DEVELOPMENT EXAMPLE

The history of space exploration offers a very clear example of how inability to make this distinction between bounded and unbounded problems is at the heart of the difference between triumph and failure. It is likewise the key to understanding why we are on the verge of a new revolution in space and aviation. The first rocketry and space projects were wartime emergency defense mobilizations—the German V-2 project; the Soviet intercontinental ballistic missiles (ICBM) project; the American defense rocketry and space projects; the Atlas, Thor, and Titan ballistic missiles; and the first American reconnaissance satellite project, launched as a consequence of the Project Feedback design study. The last led to the true start of the American space program in 1954.

These were bounded, closed-ended projects—build a rocket that can carry x kilograms y kilometers, build a satellite that can take photos of the earth. Their methodology was an extension of the successful approaches used by the defense industry in World War II, and carried out under similar circumstances—as government projects with strong national commitments, good access to national resources, and few if any cost constraints.

In 1957, the Soviets used some assets from their ballistic missile program to establish a demonstration space program for propaganda purposes, an extension of the 1930s Soviet practice of record-setting aviation feats. The embarrassed U.S. government created what became the National Aeronautics and Space Administration (NASA) on a similar basis and, under Kennedy, began the Apollo lunar program, which was taken forward by Johnson with the additional agenda of serving as an economic development tool for Texas and politically allied Southern states. These programs also addressed bounded problems, albeit very challenging ones, and enjoyed the same access to policy support and national resources. On those terms, they were also brilliant successes.

The prevailing overconfidence of the 1960s led U.S. political authorities to begin applying techniques used successfully on bounded problems to address unbounded problems. The question "If we can put a man on the moon, why can't we X?" became a trap for authorities, because the true answer, not well understood at the time, usually was, "Because putting a man on the moon was a bounded problem, and X is an unbounded problem." Seeking a new role for NASA after the success of Apollo, the Nixon administration and NASA developed the Space Shuttle project. This took NASA out of the field of narrow-focused projects like the lunar landings, and put it into the operation of routine transportation for paying customers in a competitive field. The new task was accompanied by a novel set of constraints—tight budget limits with uncertain and wavering support.

NASA's structure, personnel, and administrative practices were all inappropriate to these tasks. Long-term management issues, which had been swept under the rug during the Apollo days, emerged to haunt the agency. (One of the founders of a major systems consulting firm explained to me that the original NASA center managers, inherited from its minuscule research-oriented predecessor, the National Advisory Council for Aeronautics, were academics "barely competent to procure a box of pencils." This led to a pattern of less-competent agency managers relying on programmatically more sophisticated contractor personnel to tell them, in effect, what they should buy from them.)

To make the shuttle work politically, NASA's leadership disastrously committed themselves to an unachievable cost target, which led them to assume an insupportable flight rate that far overstressed the available technology. The loss of the shuttle *Challenger* was a predictable consequence of using inappropriate approaches for an unbounded problem—creation of a cost-effective space transportation capability.

After *Challenger*, the U.S. government was pressured by the nascent commercial space industry to adopt a policy that shifted the routine provision of launch services to the private sector, returning NASA to research and development (R&D) and exploration. This was appropriate and realistic—the marketplace is effectively an unbounded phenomenon, and the private sector is one of the best-adapted means for addressing unbounded problems. However, the transition, although it established a competitive international launch services industry, has remained stuck in a regime of high costs and relatively unreliable service using for the most part spin-offs of existing military designs. At current launch costs, most of the projected uses of space, from relatively mundane ones such as space manufacturing to exotic dreams such as tourism and colonization, remain earthbound. The only sectors which have established themselves at all have been information-sector initiatives: telecommunications, location and navigation services (the Global Positioning System), and digital imagery from space—"remote sensing" or satellite photography. Even there we have seen stagnation and massive business miscalculations, such as the bankruptcy of Motorola's Iridium venture. The only thing that we can really afford to import from space at this time is information.

Yet the 1980s, the 1990s, and even more the current decade have become a time of great entrepreneurial ferment in the space field. Although none of it has borne fruit yet in any area other than information technology, a nontrivial amount of private capital was raised and poured into R&D in the fields of space launch, space tourism, and human-inhabited space infrastructure. A wide variety of for-profit and nonprofit organizations have been started, a substantial number of which have survived. In particular, the field has begun to attract the participation of a number of highly successful entrepreneurs, mostly from the information industry, who seem willing and able to make the commitment of long-term, patient capital the field has lacked to date.

A number of factors exist which, in combination, have the potential to push the entrepreneurial space field into an economic takeoff mode. Many of the other Singularity revolutions discussed here (but particularly molecular nanotechnology) have the potential to rapidly accelerate the rate of that development. Space development has been promised for such a long time that it has acquired an aura of permanent overpromise. This has masked the reality that breakthrough into space is potentially quite close at hand. Even the revolution in computation has begun to have an effect on the cost of access to space, as the type of calculation that once required expensive computers and exotic software can be performed on ordinary desktop machines and in some cases with open-source free software. Linux, with its robustness and widespread technology base, may become an excellent operating system for space-based hardware.

The revolution in computer-aided design and manufacturing now in progress promises to greatly lower the time and cost of the development of space hardware of all sorts. Molecular nanotechnology, the ultimate enabling technology, could enable a great explosion of activity into space, making the entire solar system readily available, and even inhabitable, in short order.

The path of development into space is likely to take a rather different path in the Singularity Era than previously anticipated. Much of the literature of space development from the late 1940s through the early 1990s anticipated the gradual evolution of a human-crewed space infrastructure. This infrastructure would have initially built on communications, through materials processing and space manufacturing, and led to the eventual production of massive space power facilities which might then beam power back to Earth. Human presence would arise as a sort of company town like the mining towns of the American West or the employees' towns of the Panama Canal Zone.

In fact, it is now more likely that the first substantial nongovernmental human presence in space will be for purposes often regarded as frivolous: tourism and entertainment. Acting to change the picture is the general growth of wealth, led by the discretionary incomes of a nontrivial segment of the developed world's population and the production budgets of massive entertainment projects. These climb on the graph, while the costs of creating tourism and entertainment facilities in space have fallen. The set of the movie *Titanic* cost more than some projected private space facilities; sooner or later some producer will take a flyer based on that logic. The economics of the science- and technology-driven entrepreneurial sector have created the business template upon which such ventures will eventually form and finance themselves. Singularity-minded entrepreneurs may well become the "angels" needed to provide the seed funding for such space ventures, a trend that has already, as noted above, begun to happen.

Eventually, somewhere on the other side of the Singularity, the real attraction of space will likely be—space. That is, its fundamental attraction will be the availability of physical space for humans to settle, inhabit, and experiment with different approaches to the issues of society, morality, and ethics. Each new technology will, after all, create options for such moral and ethical issues, ones which may become impossible to settle by compromise, and on which people will have strong convictions. (Consider human cloning as one possible example. One person's Frankenstein technology may be another person's dearly sought-after infertility treatment or incurable-disease cure.) There will be a premium for space for people who cannot abide the consensus in their home societies. Nanotechnology and biotechnology could make space settlements not the claustrophobic tin cans of cheap science fiction, but places people could validly think of as home. The ongoing need for human social diversity and the likely persistence of strong moral and political positions will create a need for living space for differing groups.

As with every other such Singularity Revolution, the real issues will ultimately be human and social, rather than technological. Existing space law was based upon a series of United Nations treaties and founded on several premises, which have subsequently been undercut by emerging reality. The treaties assumed almost all parties in space would be governmental; but it is becoming likely that most will be private. It assumed that human presence would be scarce and transitory, consisting of government employees carrying out scientific missions or mining extraterrestrial resources for return to Earth. It is more likely now that when humans go into space in large numbers, they will go as private individuals, and that the natural resources we once imagined them mining will have been rendered of little importance by the advancing revolutions of the Singularity. If diamondoid materials produced by nanotechnology become the principal structural materials of the future, mining metals becomes a small matter. At the same time, international treaties designed to control a few scientists become ill-suited to the needs of large emerging communities of private parties. The Anglo-American common-law tradition, which facilitated the replication of dozens of free polities in the settlement of North America and Australasia, becomes a more relevant set of experiences.

Technology may set the bounds for human action, but they will be wide bounds, within which human choice will determine the outcomes. Most important in determining how people will live, on Earth or elsewhere, will be the social and political arrangements they create. The technologies unleashed by the Singularity revolutions will have both creative and destructive potential; and we must find means to constrain the dangers while reaping the benefits, while preserving the valuable aspects of our societies—above all, hard-won human freedoms. The answers to these challenges lie primarily in the histories of the societies that have created and led the Scientific-Technological Revolution, of which the Singularity revolutions will be only the latest expression.

Y2K AS THE OPPOSITE CASE: MISTAKING
BOUNDED FOR UNBOUNDED PROBLEMS

As we have seen, mistaking unbounded problems for bounded ones arose partly from the great successes of modern systems engineering and problem solving in addressing highly complicated, bounded problems, but even more from the inability to understand the difference between the two. The scientists and engineers of midcentury America have often been accused of hubris by later commentators.

But this hubris did not consist of pride in their achievements; rather, it came from assuming that their techniques had become so powerful that all problems could be reduced and addressed by their systems engineering techniques.

The 1970s and 1980s brought a general reaction to and skepticism about the problem-solving ability of science and technology. Unfortunately, this skepticism was for the most part no more understanding of the bounded/ unbounded distinction than of the engineers and planners it criticized. This led to a throwing out of the baby with the bathwater: a belief that no problems could be successfully addressed by science or engineering.

The last few years of the 1990s brought a massive public phenomenon displaying exactly this mistake: concern over the century date change in the worldwide computer network, better known as the Y2K Crisis. Specifically, this was the problem of modifying computer software worldwide to ensure that all older programs expressing dates using a two-numeral date field (i.e., writing 1-1-99 for January 1, 1999) could properly function after January 1, 2000. Computers needed to correctly interpret the change from 1999 to 2000 as an increase rather than a decrease. Failure to do so would create a substantial disruption in many automated or computer-aided processes.

I first became aware of this issue in the early 1970s when I took an elementary programming course and understood how dates were handled in computers.

At that time, nobody was concerned about the issue, because they assumed that the computers of the late 1990s would have software written from scratch shortly before, and that the problems would have been dealt with. Much to my surprise, and nearly everybody else's, by the mid-1990s large amounts of "legacy" software (programs little or not at all modified since first written in the 1960s or 1970s) were still widely in use, and many new programs still used two-year date fields. Furthermore, little to no work had been done to update software to deal with this problem.

As anybody who was not living as a hermit now knows, the media became filled with cries predicting that the world would grind to a halt on January 1, 2000. At first, most people dismissed such cries as alarmist, but gradually, more sober analysis began to reveal that indeed there was a real problem, very little had in fact been done about it, and that it was difficult to assess the scope of the problem.

This alarm was particularly compounded by the fact that many of the systems that people might be most concerned about, like nuclear weapons command and control systems, were highly classified, and no open public examination of the issue was possible.

I myself must be counted, if not as a Y2K alarmist, at least as an observer who leaned toward the side of concern. In my column in *Strategic Investment* newsletter, a financial publication with between 60,000 and

100,000 readers during the 1995–2000 period, I repeatedly called attention
to the open questions regarding Y2K, and, in the initial years, suspected
that there could be substantial financial impact from the event. Between
1997 and 2000, I gradually became convinced that the United States, and
most of the other stronger civil societies, had started to address the Y2K
issue to the extent that there would be no major disasters, and that the financial impact, although real, had been adequately discounted.

I still overestimated the impact in the weaker civil societies and was
mildly surprised to find that there were no major problems, worldwide,
throughout New Year's Day 2000 and beyond.

In retrospect, it is now clear that the Y2K problem was not one huge unbounded problem beyond the ability to address or control. It was instead a
parallel set of many bounded problems, each addressable by the same
means, and in which problems in one area could be contained and prevented from spilling over into other areas. One of the lessons of the Y2K
episode is that the degree of society's dependence on computers, and the
degree of computers' interdependence on each other, was overestimated.
Y2K was not solved by any "silver bullet" cure. It was solved by large numbers of programmers working long hours, carrying out tedious remediation
work, usually fixing or working around each date field individually.

In the end it was successfully addressed by the same system management approaches that built the bomber fleets of World War II, ran the
Manhattan Project, and took Apollo to the moon. Such approaches are in
fact increasingly effective in addressing the appropriate kinds of problems, because of the advent of powerful computerized management tools.

In approaching the Singularity, both the successes and failures of the
managerial and planning techniques of the twentieth century must be understood. Adequately understanding the nature of a problem is the first
step in fixing a problem.

Mistaking an unbounded problem for a bounded one can be fatal; the
Y2K experience suggests that the opposite is true as well. The Singularity
itself is undoubtedly an unbounded problem as a whole; but at least some
of its component problems will turn out to be addressable by classic engineering means. We need an overall framework which allows each approach to be applied as needed.

DEATH AND TAXES: EXTENDING
LIFESPAN, AND ITS CONSEQUENCES

Uncertain as the revolutions of the Singularity are, those triggered by
biotechnology and life extension are most likely to come to pass in the
next twenty years.

These revolutions are in themselves a convergence of a number of advances.

Advances include improvements in microscope technology (particularly scanning tunneling microscopes, which can resolve individual atoms); falling costs and increasing power of computing; and the sheer critical mass of knowledge about the molecular structure of organisms, the nature of genetics, and the evolutionary drivers of medical phenomena.

Some of these advances will be the result of the Human Genome Project and other genome research. Some will be advances in medical understanding unrelated to genetic research, such as the recent growth in emphasis on infectious causes for diseases that were once thought to have other causes. (Some, like stomach ulcers, are now understood to be curable through antibiotics; others such as heart disease are the subjects of such investigation.) New approaches to molecular design of drugs and alternatives to traditional invasive surgery are improving the ability to treat many diseases and conditions. Potential advances in neurosurgery and other treatments begin to hold hope for curing previously incurable conditions, such as spinal cord injuries. Cloning technologies hold out the possibility of replacing organs without reliance on donors and immunosuppressive treatments.

Beyond these advances, which are themselves startling, are more radical potential advances. Molecular nanotechnology promises the ultimate molecular medicine—repairing, maintaining, and rebuilding the body from the inside, molecule by molecule, under full control. Equally radical in its own way is the current research into telomeres—the bits on the end of chromosomes which serve to control the starting and stopping of cell division, and thus have the potential to control the aging process as well as provide a generic treatment for cancer.

TAKING A POSSIBILITY SERIOUSLY

Which of these paths will work, and which may be blind alleys, is beyond the scope of this discussion. There is no way to tell for sure whether any of these approaches will happen or will bear fruit. However, we must have some way of knowing whether these prospects are in fact things we must anticipate, concern ourselves about, and take into account in our planning. The whole impact of disease-reducing and life-span-increasing technologies is so complex that assessing and predicting its impact on society is a classic unbounded problem. Since it cannot be effectively addressed by precise forecasting, the best thing we can do at this point is introduce some basic rules of thumb. Experience suggests that the following indicators, when taken together, offer a reasonably good chance that a revolution will in fact be upon us in the next one to two decades. Such indicators include

- *Genuine increase in knowledge.* We know not just more, but far more about living organisms, how they work, and how they reproduce themselves, than we did a decade ago, or even a few years ago. One of the key drivers of the Singularity is the achievement of a sheer critical mass of knowledge and understanding, such that each year's worth of new understandings breeds not just a little more knowledge, but a lot more.
- *Multiple visible paths of attack.* One visible path of attack, no matter how promising, always has the prospect of being derailed by unknowns. This has indeed happened many times in the history of science and technology. When multiple paths are visible, the likelihood that at least one will succeed is much higher. The Manhattan Project, for example, pursued simultaneously two separate paths to production of a working atomic bomb, a decision justified by the outcome.

  As we have seen, there are not one or two, but a plethora of paths available to gaining control over disease, disability, and life span. This makes the likelihood of success by at least one means substantially more realistic.
- *Absence of fundamental scientific barriers to implementation.* Many people not involved with either science or technology make the mistake of confusing the two. The title of British scientist C. P. Snow's novelistic musings on the intellectual gap between science and the humanities, *The Two Cultures*, would be equally appropriate to a discussion of the gap between scientists and engineers.

  Understanding this difference is critical to understanding whether the obstacles to realizing a vision are ones of fundamental scientific principle or engineering difficulty. It is a waste of time to devote ingenuity in design or improvement of tools to try to propel a spaceship faster than the speed of light, for example. If you wish to do that, you must attempt to improve upon the theory of relativity. On the other hand, if you wish to manipulate atoms in order to advance toward nanotechnology, it is well worth your while to improve scanning tunneling microscopes and develop better grasping tips for them.

  The interesting questions then become those in which one cannot be sure whether a fundamental scientific barrier exists. However, in listening to a debate about the possibility of a proposed goal, it is critical to determine whether people are saying, "It flatly contradicts known scientific principles that x is possible," or that "It hasn't yet been demonstrated in theory that x is possible," or that "We accept x

is possible in theory, but the practical obstacles to realization are enormous." No fundamental theoretical objection to the feasibility of nanotechnology has ever been generally accepted by the scientific community; a debate exists regarding the theory, and almost everybody accepts that the obstacles are substantial. The fact is that none of the approaches for medical progress are in the category of violating fundamental laws of science; most are in the second or third categories. This is a good indication that at least some of them will bear substantial fruit.

- *Better tools are coming along.* Once it is accepted that a proposed advance is theoretically feasible and there are plausible avenues of approach for dealing with implementation issues, the next thing to look for is what new tools and enabling technologies are becoming available. If there is a rapidly improving set of tools, materials, techniques, or capabilities which might become usable in overcoming the practical obstacles to implementing technologies, it becomes reasonable to assume the technology is on the way to deployment. The airplane is an interesting example. Much of the theoretical aerodynamics of heavier-than-air flight was worked out well before the Wright brothers actually flew. There were learned societies and journals of aerodynamics throughout the latter nineteenth century. What was needed to move the dream from vision to reality was simply an improvement in the tools needed to produce engines light and powerful enough to make the airplane fly. The achievement of the Wright brothers was to combine an understanding of the scientific principles of aerodynamics with the tools and materials necessary to designing a practical internal combustion engine with sufficient weight-to-power ratio to permit powered flight. In the case of advanced biotechnology and nanotechnology, a powerful stream of computational, investigative, and operational tools began to become available throughout the 1990s, and promise to increase both in power and availability in the coming decade. This improvement in and increasing availability of tools is another powerful indicator that these revolutions are moving from theory to reality.

HOW TO THINK ABOUT THE EFFECTS OF THESE REVOLUTIONS: THE "PESSIMISTIC SCENARIO"

The total effect of these changes is to promise an affordable, generally applicable set of treatments that will prevent or cure most debilitating diseases and conditions and extend active, healthy life spans beyond (perhaps well beyond) the century-and-a-bit that seems to be the inherent limit today. The manner in which these changes are advancing is typical of the Singularity—progress is advancing along so many different fronts that it is difficult to say which will arrive and which won't, or on what schedule. What is also typical of the Singularity is that timid straight-line projections of current reality are the least useful means of addressing these issues.

Most observers seem to believe that the application of technology is increasing medical costs. In reality, technology has begun to lower medical costs, as effective treatments begin to keep people out of long-term nursing care. Every treatment approach discussed earlier will tend to have the same effect—substituting a simple, generic, and permanently effective short course of treatment for a complex, condition-specific, partly effective or palliative treatment, not to mention drastically reducing the need for extended or permanent labor-intensive care.

The political and social effects of these treatments will be a mixed lot. Programs like America's Medicare and the British National Health Service will likely be rescued from a nightmare of increasingly aging patients supported by a dwindling population of taxpaying workers. Conversely, America's Social Security system, like other taxpayer-supported state pension schemes, will be under increasing pressure as retirees continue to live on and collect their checks rather than conveniently dying. The Social Security Administration once published a set of demographic projections: the "Optimistic Scenario" showed the retirees continuing to die at the then-current rate; the "Pessimistic Scenario" showed them living longer. By this logic, the Singularity Scenario would have to be labeled the "Catastrophic Scenario."

Of course, we then must take into account the other changes likely to happen.

With an extended healthy life span, the pressure to retire and collect government-funded pensions at 65 or 70 becomes much diminished if not nonexistent.

The growth of public participation in the capital markets throughout the English-speaking world, by means of tax-sheltered plans such as the American IRA and the British equivalents, has meant that many retirees no longer look to the rather minimal state pensions as a significant source of retirement income. This is likely to continue to grow as a phenomenon. Similarly, the revolution in medicine will likely reduce the percentage of income needed to pay for health treatments, relieving the burden on the institutions responsible for payment, whether private health insurance or state insurance schemes such as the National Health Service.

Another important question is the fate of other political-social assumptions in an environment of continued economic growth combined with extended healthy life spans. The institutions that most developed nations have inherited from the mid-twentieth century were created primarily from fear. Economic regulation is driven by fear of joblessness; medical insurance systems are driven by fear of disease and premature death; and state pension systems highlight the fear of impoverishment at the end of the working life. (The remaining fear is military security, with fear of terrorist attack replacing fear of massive nuclear exchange or invasion. This fear, however, is decoupled from the classic social fears of the twentieth century.) As these fears diminish, it is likely that people will question the high opportunity cost these systems carry, and be willing to forego the relatively minimal rewards they carry in return for a more open and flexible social system.

This questioning will be accompanied and intensified by a growing need for flexibility in order to deal with the consequences of multiple healthy, active generations within the economy and political arena. Hierarchical institutions will be under multiple pressures as a result of the changes driven by the Singularity revolutions.

They will be forced to reform or retrench when the seniority principle creates greater strains on their systems. Either they will have to force senior members to retire when they are still active and healthy, or junior members will suffer long periods in lower ranks while waiting for the seniors to leave and open up spaces.

An entrepreneurial economy, in which all members expect to change the relationships of their work life every few years, makes it easier to give young people early entry into responsibility while permitting older people to remain active. The Singularity revolutions will have other interesting effects, such as permitting women to postpone childbearing until much later in life, which will likely increase the birth rate among intelligent, educated, ambitious women substantially (while being more than offset by a general drop in the birth rate as general prosperity increases). The political ramifications of having more than the four current generations active in political life at one time also remain an open question.

As we will see, each Singularity revolution brings its own set of questions, all equally complex. The interactive nature of each of these changes makes planning harder and raises the relative value of a flexible and reactive social, political, and economic system.

INDUSTRIAL GOODS AS SOFTWARE: THE NEXT PHASE OF THE INFORMATION REVOLUTION, AND ITS IMPLICATIONS

Few concepts have been misunderstood as much as that of the Information Age.

In popular misconceptions, it is imagined that in America and the other advanced countries people will sit and peck at computers, while manufacturing will be done somewhere in the Second or Third World, in factories which resemble existing facilities. This is a complete misconception of the transition from the Industrial to the Information Age. Consider the parallel transition from the Agricultural to the Industrial Age. When Britain and America became industrialized, they did not cease producing food. In fact the United States became the greatest food exporter in the world because it mastered the Machine Age early. Those who master information technology will likewise hold mastery over manufacturing.

Consider the production of the U.S. Air Force's B-2 bomber, a very significant milestone in this transition. The B-2 bomber was the first large artifact to be designed entirely in software and subsequently downloaded to manufacture directly, never having been printed out in paper blueprint form. Northrop Grumman, its manufacturer, created the design of the B-2 in the computer, downloaded it to the plant, and began producing it. One reason for its extremely expensive development costs was the need to develop the capability to do this directly.

With this capability, the future design-to-manufacture process of aircraft or other industrial artifacts ultimately becomes cheaper. It is another example of technology and automation investment lowering costs in the long run. The B-2 bomber, a large stealth aircraft, could not have been produced except by this mode of design and manufacture, because it is too complex an artifact to produce in any other fashion.

One could compare the impact of the ability to perform this mode of integrated computer-aided design/computer-aided manufacturing to the ability to build a steel battleship in 1880 or 1890. The implications of this for military supremacy should also be obvious, as forces equipped with such ships cut through those equipped with wooden battleships like the proverbial hot knife through butter. This will also be the case in high-technology production of the future.

This complete integration of manufacturing, production, and design over the Internet will eventually become the principal mode of production. As a consequence, the current wage advantages of the Second and Third Worlds will be of reduced importance. Manufacturing supremacy will go to the countries that have the best information technology. The United States, being the current leader in information technology while still possessing a large manufacturing base, is likely to be the primary beneficiary of this process. Concerns over the current outflow of manufacturing to lower-wage countries expressed by observers such as Kevin Phillips and Patrick Buchanan are therefore misplaced. Such commentators fear that the entire assembly-line base of manufacturing will eventually migrate to lower-wage or higher-subsidy areas of the globe, and thereby undermine American military or economic strength. This is like fearing that the advent of steel-hulled warships in the nineteenth century would undercut British or American naval might, because it made irrelevant those nations' mastery of wooden ship technology.

The implications of this revolution, however, go far beyond the issues of military supremacy and national manufacturing dominance. This phenomenon is properly named a revolution because it will require a very substantial adjustment in the employment and economic situations of people throughout the globe.

Adjustment will involve an intensification of some, but not all, existing trends, and the emergence of other entirely new patterns. The traditional blue-collar job—a place in a mass workforce employed as wage workers on assembly lines in centralized facilities—will dwindle into obscurity, if not entirely disappear. Some workplaces may retain vestiges of these patterns—shipyards, possibly—and analogous employment patterns will linger in some fields such as transportation. But for the most part, mass employment in manufacturing is likely to come to an end.

Government workforces, which have already become the mainstay of traditional labor organizing, may continue to retain similar characteristics. Mass service organizations, such as hotel chains, may also continue to be mass employers.

But the dominant economic activity in the world of the Singularity revolutions will continue to be information-based work of one form or the other. As I discuss in the section titled "The End of Capitalism and the Triumph of the Market Economy," the information-based economy is evolving beyond the corporate forms which dominated the nineteenth and twentieth centuries. Rather than monolithic organizations carrying out long-term plans, the network economy of the Information Revolution will likely be characterized by network organizations linking shifting combinations of entrepreneurs, financiers, and marketers.

In this environment, labor cost and the capital cost of the production facility become minor components of the value of an item. Marketing and distribution via Internet cut the cost of those components substantially. The marketing advantages of traditional brand names continue to be worth something, but even that will be relentlessly driven down by competition. Internet business has already accustomed us to considering a brand name "established" if it has been in the marketplace for only three years, and this may extend fairly easily to the branding of material goods as well. True open-source approaches may emerge in areas like aircraft and automobiles, where there already exist large communities of technically skilled enthusiasts willing to collaborate on designs and production software without immediate pay. It may not be much of a stretch from existing companies which offer blueprints and assembly kits for aircraft hobbyists, to become companies which offer aircraft built from open-source designs and assembled in highly automated manufacturing facilities.

Observable trends suggest that the answer to "what will people do when manufacturing is automated?" lies in greater reliance on entrepreneurship and self-employment, including the classical services sectors and a large proliferation of niches of design and prototyping of goods and devices to be manufactured via these software-based industrial capabilities. This is consistent with the shift in employment from the Agricultural to the Industrial Era and its movement from farm to city. Many migrants to the cities capitalized on mechanical skills learned while working on farm machinery, yet retained vestiges of rural lifestyle habits such as recreational fishing and hunting, gardening, and pastimes such as baseball (or cricket) and horse racing. Some skills will require upgrading, such as computer literacy (but not programming, which will become largely automated at the submodular level) or, for industrial design, some mathematics and engineering skills (again aided by design software). But the rural migrants to the cities also had to acquire higher educational skills than they previously enjoyed.

As the Information Revolution aspect of the Singularity revolutions progresses, increasingly advanced issues come into play. Moore's law— the geometric improvement in the performance of computers, combined with the geometric reduction of their cost—has continued to accurately describe the progress of computing hardware. New technologies, like nanotechnology, promise to continue this progress even after the ultimate physical limits of integration on silicon chips have been reached. As computer performance continues to improve, previously unseen—and somewhat spooky—phenomena will begin to emerge. Already, work at the Santa Fe Institute has established the reality of "e-life"—the creation of software constructs that act in accordance with the laws of evolution.

Several different approaches promise to create computers within the next twenty to forty years which may be able to pass the Turing Test—that is, to be capable of an exchange which a human observer cannot distinguish from a conversation with another human being. At what point should such entities be considered truly intelligent and possessing of rights?

Later in this book, I discuss the nature of this emerging society as "amphibious"—existing partly in cyberspace and partly in the physical world. Advanced computer interface devices bring the prospect of some humans living increasingly in the cyberspace environment. This trend will probably start among persons having severe physical disabilities, who can experience a comparatively unencumbered existence within cyberspace, but eventually embracing persons who choose it for other reasons.

Ultimately, these developments will create new social and political issues, the impact of which cannot be well predicted or effectively addressed from this side of the Singularity. What we can understand is the way past frameworks have accommodated radical technology-driven social change and the relative successes of the various approaches. I believe these offer hints about the nature of the framework in which the solutions to the challenges of the Singularity can be met.

CIVIL SOCIETY AND THE HAZARDS OF THE SINGULARITY REVOLUTIONS: THE CASE OF NANOTECHNOLOGY

Molecular manufacturing, or molecular nanotechnology (MNT), involves physically manipulating individual atoms and molecules to create materials, structures, and machines. In essence, MNT proposes constructing things from the atom up, assembling larger and larger modules until the desired structure and scale are achieved, but without necessarily using biological materials or the self-replicating capabilities of natural systems. First proposed by K. Eric Drexler in the early 1980s, MNT has never required any overturning of scientific principles—it is, rather, the ultimate challenge of engineering, one which will give an enormous mastery over physical devices.

Ironically, MNT and related Singularity technologies seem to be passing in the eyes of some from being the object of unsupported ridicule to the object of irrational fear without any intervening period of rational consideration. In the March 2000 issue of *Wired* magazine, software entrepreneur Bill Joy published a long, pessimistic essay in which he considered the effect of three revolutions within the bounds of what is discussed here—genetics, nanotechnology, and robotics. He speculated they would either cause an unintended catastrophe that could wipe out all life on Earth, or lead in the relatively short term to the emergence of artificial intelligence much more powerful than the human mind. In this scenario, we would eventually become obsolete and therefore either reduced to the status of pets, or extinct. Joy ended his article with a call to establish Draconian measures to end or greatly inhibit technological progress, and to establish what would effectively become a static, totalitarian society.

Joy himself has subsequently moderated his position, still being wary of the downsides of the Singularity, but also realizing the hazards of a relinquishment strategy. However, his article and the alarm it raised has taken on a life of its own. Many who dismissed the prospect of MNT for two decades, and who ignored the real work being done on the dangers of nanotechnology (which are real, if not as extreme as Joy represented in his article) and advocated measures that forego the potential enormous benefits of this technology. In the end, such a relinquishment regime as Joy originally advocated is both intolerable in its effects and ineffective in combating the hazards it seeks to avoid. His list of solutions included a call for international controls of MNT and other technologies, on the model of proposals for the "internationalization" of atomic energy made in 1945. Unfortunately, the history of international systems for technology controls, even when dealing with cruder, less concealable technologies in eras without the formidable information technologies of the Web, is poor. It would require either the creation of a global empire under the control of "trusted" nations and individuals, with the implementation of a pervasive totalitarian regime of surveillance and control (which would create grave "Who watches the watchers?" problems), or, in a truly international regime, cause enormous problems from the linking of civilizations with extremely different concepts of civic duty and the function of the state.

In facing the real challenges of the Singularity, we must draw on the experiences of technological societies. We must consider two issues. Firstly, we must ask which social characteristics are typical of the societies most open to the rapid development of new technologies, because in reality, the rules of dealing with the new technologies will be set by the society that first produces them. Secondly, we must ask which constitutional systems permit effective control of real hazards in a regime that does not create incentives to take research and production underground.

I have studied and discussed these issues for the past two decades. At the same time, I have been active in the entrepreneurial sector of two of the key technologies discussed earlier. The conclusions I have derived from this work are that the key to controlling the hazards of the Singularity lies in the same phenomenon that has made it possible—the strong civil society that created both the Industrial Revolution and constitutional democracy. The strongest and most prolific of the strong civil societies at the center of the Industrial Revolution have been and remain those of the English-speaking world—the Anglosphere. Any hope of realizing the benefits of the Singularity requires an understanding of the Anglosphere and its unique features. Any hope of dealing effectively with the hazards of the Singularity likewise will be found in its past successes.

Military analysts sometimes use the term "come-as-you-are party" to describe the opening phases of a war, or a short war in its entirety. The term refers to the fact that in these short time frames, combatants cannot count on any resources—troops, weapons, or supplies—that do not already exist. In a long war, they must take into account the possibility that new troops will be enlisted and trained, new weapons will be developed and deployed, or new supplies can be obtained. In the near-term time frame, the emphasis has to be on making do with what exists.

The time frame of the Singularity revolutions is likely to be very short by the standards of social and political change and will cause major changes in livelihood and life in the space of a decade or two. The social challenge of adaptation must be treated as a come-as-you-are party. There will be no time to experiment with and test novel social arrangements, philosophies, or institutions once the Singularity begins. This may seem counterintuitive to many people. Surely novel technological capabilities require novel social institutions, don't they? The experience of the past century argues that the opposite is the case. Institutions tend to be modified more than replaced, institutions tend to not die out unless they demonstrate actual and substantial harm, and institutions tend to adapt only as much as needed to provide a viable solution to pressing problems.

It should give pause to advocates of radically different and untried institutions that the same arguments, widely used to justify some of the most grotesque and deadly social experiments of human history—Adolf Hitler's Germany, Stalin's Soviet Union, and Mao Tse-tung's China—were offered as justification for well over 150 million human murders. The early twentieth century was filled with predictions that the airplane, the automobile, or the assembly line (or whatever) had made parliamentary democracy, market economies, jury trials, and Bills of Rights irrelevant, obsolete, and harmful.

Today we have already brought the Scientific-Technological Revolution to the point where spacecraft and the Internet make the technologies of the early twentieth century—its fabric-winged biplanes, Tin Lizzies, and "Modern Times" gearwheel factories—look like quaint relics. Yet all of the "obsolete" institutions derided by the modernists of that day thrive and strengthen. The true surprise of the Singularity revolutions is likely not to be the technological wonders and dangers it will bring, but the robustness of the strong civil-society institutions which will bring them forth, and which offer the best hope of exploiting and constraining them.

We are entering an unplanned and unplannable time of great promise and pressing hazard. We need to respond to these challenges by strengthening an evolving and evolvable framework, based on our best and most successful institutions, to address such issues. I will examine one strong civil society—the Anglosphere of this book's title—which has thrived on unplanned phenomena and has evolved the most successful to date of systems for dealing with the unexpected.

It is here that clues to these issues will mostly be found, and here that the hunt will primarily take place.

CIVIL SOCIETIES AND THE
ECONOMY OF THE SINGULARITY

Given that the economic climate of the coming era is likely to be dominated by a highly entrepreneurial and fast-moving economic model, which nations are going to be well-positioned to take advantage of developments? Why do some nations do well, and not others, and what does this say about the alignments and associations in international politics that we currently have?

In the past two decades, we have observed such varied phenomena as differing responses of nations to the end of communism in Eastern Europe and the former Soviet Union, collapse of the East Asian neo-Confucian bubble, and revival of entrepreneurism in Britain in the wake of the Thatcher reforms. These experiences have created a better appreciation of the link between a strong civil society and prosperity. In the emerging economy of this new Scientific-Technical Revolution, these strong civil-society values will be even more central to success.

A civil society is built of a vast network of networks. These networks start with the individual and the families, community organizations, congregations, social organizations, and businesses created by individuals coming together voluntarily.

Continuing up through the local, regional, national, and international networks, the tying together of local organizations creates civil society. Such civil societies beget civic states. These states are ones in which authority begins at the local and community level and gradually is built upward to deal with wider-scale issues. Civic states are built on community assent and a feeling of participation in a local, regional, and national community. Law is generally accepted, as are the common rules of society, and the authority of the state is not upheld by constant exercise of force but by the willingness of citizens to comply.

It is important to make clear that at the root of civil society is the individual.

People who define themselves primarily as members of collective entities, whether families, religions, racial or ethnic groups, political movements, or even corporations, cannot be the basis of a civil society. Individuals must be free to dissociate themselves from such collectivities without prejudice and reaffiliate with others in a civil society. Societies that place individuals under the permanent discipline of inherited or assigned collectivities, and permanently bind them into such, remain bogged down in family favoritism, ethnic, racial, or religious factionalism, or systems such as the "crony capitalism" which has marked in particular East Asia and Latin America.

It is likewise important to make clear that a family in a civil society is a voluntary association, even though it is built on inherited connections. It should not place loyalty to its members above moral obligations to the rest of society, such as fair dealing, and should have no power over its members, other than the sanction of withdrawal of help or association. Similarly, its individuals may choose to join associations marked by inherited ties, such as ethnic or religious organizations, but are not penalized for declining to join. Those individuals should be dealt with by the state as individuals, rather than as members of that collectivity.

Thus would-be advocates of civil society are often fooled into seeing family-dominated societies, in which membership in family networks determines one's economic, social, and political future, as civil societies, when in fact they are the opposite of such. Some also see societies in which everyone is dealt with by the state as a member of an ethnic, racial, or religious community (such as the old vilayet system of the Ottoman Empire) as civil societies. These are in fact authoritarian societies corrupted by the lack of choice.

The "family values" of a crony society are not the same as the family values of a civil society. The ethnic- or religious-based voluntary associations of a civil society are not the same as the ethnic or religious compartments of an authoritarian society. One of the quiet success stories of strong civil societies, particularly the United States, has been the manner in which the compulsory family and religious affiliations of the Old World were transformed into voluntary associations of civil society when transplanted by immigrants. These immigrants transformed themselves from members of traditional societies into self-actualized individuals in civil societies. This took place in the same generation in some families, and in two or three generations in others.

Most societies have some elements of civil society, but their strength differs greatly from society to society. Some states, generally the most peaceful and prosperous ones, are civic states, or have elements of being civic states, but others have little or no civic nature: totalitarian states, personal dictatorships, and kleptocracies. The latter are states existing primarily to permit the persons or groups in control to steal from those subject to its power. Most of the poorer and strife-wracked states of the world are in the latter category. The relationship between civil society and prosperity, like that between civic statehood and domestic peace, is not coincidental. However, the link of causality has often been misunderstood.

It is now quite clear that prosperous states are rich because of the strength of their civil society, and that peaceful states are peaceful because of the strength of their civic statehood, not the other way around. States that have inherited vast natural wealth relative to their populations have been able to spread wealth around, but this has not generally strengthened civil society or the coherence of the civic state. When Saddam Hussein invaded Kuwait, the sons of the rich Kuwaitis fled to Cairo, while their parents negotiated the price of Western intervention. This is not a strong civic state.

Also misunderstood are the concepts of democracy and the market economy.

Democracy, modern market economies, and civic states are effects of a strong civil society, not causes. Over the past century, there has been a misdirection of attention to the surface mechanics of democracy, to nose-counting, rather than with the underlying roots of the phenomenon. It is clear now that a society containing the strong networks of association which characterize a civil society also develops means of expressing the interests of those networks to the state. It is the need for effective means of expression that gave rise to the original mechanisms we now call democratic. Later, intellectuals in societies that did not have a strong existing civil society, particularly pre-Revolutionary France, looked at societies that did, particularly England, and attempted to derive an abstract theoretical construct which captured the essence of that experience. They called this thing democracy, but they subsequently focused attention on their model (and its misunderstandings) rather than the essence of the thing they actually admired.

England's strong civic state had its roots in the local expressions of civil society in the civic realm, a process which may or may not have had roots in pre-Norman Conquest days but was certainly well-rooted by the fourteenth century. These include the grand and petit jury systems, the election of various aldermen and other local officials, and the quasi-official roles of many civil-society institutions. Selecting members of the House of Commons was one of many different mechanisms by which local communities gave or withheld their consent to the state.

Today we look back and focus on the ways in which those days differed from today—the restricted franchise, the "rotten boroughs" which elected members of Parliament with a handful of voters, the lack of a mass party system, and the open sale of votes for money or favor. We see those characteristics as not very democratic, but it is a mistake to ignore the many ways in which England's system created a far more effective means of assent and dissent compared to other state systems of the times. The lesson from English history has been repeated many times over, up to and including contemporary events in Taiwan and South Korea. When civil society reaches a certain degree of complexity, democracy typically emerges. Absent that civil society, importing the mechanisms of democracy—the forms and rituals—results only in creating one more set of spoils for families and groups to fight over at the expense of the rest of society.

Similarly, the market economy is more than the absence of socialism. It is more than the absence of interventionist government; it is the economic expression of a strong civil society, just as substantive (rather than formulaic) democracy is the political expression of a civil society and civic state. Majoritarian mechanisms no more create civil society than wet streets cause rain. There is theoretically no reason why democracy needs a market economy, or vice versa—but in practice they are almost always found together. This is a clue. Entrepreneurship in business uses and requires the same talents and often the same motives that go into starting a church, a nonprofit organization, or a political party. The society that can create entrepreneurial businesses tends to be able to create the other forms of organizations as well—often the same individuals start several of each form at different stages in their lives.

The market economy also requires a civil society with general acceptance of a common framework of laws, practices, and manners. Without a general acceptance of fair dealing, an agreement on what fair dealing means, and an adjudication system that can resolve and enforce resolution of disputes, a modern market economy cannot exist. Just as post-Soviet Russia's politics demonstrated that the mechanics of democracy alone cannot create a civic state, its economy demonstrated that market formulas cannot by themselves create a market economy or a civil society. They are necessary but insufficient conditions in each case.

These realizations have immense implications for the Singularity Era. It is highly likely that the innovation of the current Information Revolution will continue to spark innovation for the other Singularity Revolutions. This suggests that they will likewise emerge in an entrepreneurial environment marked by the fast creation of teams and fast capitalization through venture money and public markets. The rapid formation, deployment, and financing of enterprises typical of Silicon Valley are also an inherent characteristic of a strong civil society.

The strong role of noncompany organizations (such as professional and industry associations, and informal networks of acquaintance) in Silicon Valley also argues that this form of entrepreneurism is a strong civil-society phenomenon. In fact, I will argue in more detail that the current wave of entrepreneurism is a characteristic of a more advanced evolution of civil society now emerging, and which is part and parcel of the Singularity Revolution.

Looking at the geography of the Singularity, it is no accident that it is emerging first in the United States. Strong civil society has its roots in medieval Europe, as a result of the society being built of a mix of tribal, feudal, local, church, family, and state institutions, characterized by the lack of a single, overwhelming power which could impose its will. Gradually the different interests established negotiated relationships of power and influence, none of which involved full submission of one element to another. At first these institutions were neither free nor voluntary in nature, for the most part. However, the multiplicity of institutions eventually permitted some liberty, and eventually enabled many individuals to establish substantial freedom and independence through astute negotiation.

England, by virtue of its being an island at the periphery of Europe, was insulated from many of the more absolutist influences, driven by the needs of military competition, that eventually eradicated the complexity of emerging medieval civil society.

In particular, its insulation from effective invasion after 1066 and lack of need to maintain a large land army shielded it from the centralization of political authority into Sun King-style monarchies in the sixteenth and seventeenth centuries. Thus, it was free to continue combining medieval institutions such as Parliament, juries, and corporations into effective forms of complex civil societies. These forms were present throughout Western Europe but faded or changed into instruments of state power over civil society on most of the continent, while still flourishing in England.

The colonization of North America happened in such a way that the most useful characteristics of civil society were brought to its soil from England, while many of the less useful remnants of feudalism were left behind. In fact, Anglo-America was a particularly strong civil society from the start, especially in New England and Pennsylvania, where Puritans and Quakers, both of whom were strongly dedicated to the fundamentals of civil society, brought particularly robust institutions. In particular, both elevated the sanctity of contract and covenant to central places in their moral universe, a great advantage for dynamic entrepreneurship.

There appears to be a vital fundamental link between the entrepreneurial cultures of the Quakers of Pennsylvania and northern England, the dissenters of northern and midland England and America, and the Calvinists of New England and Scotland, to the emergence, development, and continuing dominance of the Industrial and Information revolutions. It is important to reject a triumphalist or essentialist view of the Anglo-American role in this matter. The fact that the Calvinist Netherlands originated many of the capitalist mechanisms later developed more fully in the Anglosphere is sufficient to prove that there was no inherent virtue in English-speaking people at the heart of its success. This also implies that the set of characteristics which have given the Anglosphere its leadership can be lost as well as acquired, that other cultures can (and to some extent have) acquired characteristics with similar effects. It also implies that these cultural and institutional characteristics are fairly deep-seated, and changes, negative and positive alike, usually require several generations to take full effect.

As the saying goes, "There is a lot of ruin in a nation." Thus England took more than a few generations to lose the characteristics that enabled entrepreneurial vigor, and when relatively shallow political and institutional changes reversed the climate of decline, entrepreneurial vigor quickly resurfaced there. Conversely, it will take more than "anticorruption" campaigns in low-trust cultures in the former Soviet states, Latin America, or East Asia to change a deep-rooted cultural bias toward nepotism in business and government.

The consequences of these conclusions are very significant to the specific outcome of the Singularity revolutions of the next decades. The Singularity is likely to emerge in a strong civil society—most likely, the Anglosphere. It will continue to be the center of the Singularity Revolution process for the foreseeable future. This suggests that the most important political challenge of the near future is to create close cooperative ties among groups of strong civic states, starting with the Anglosphere nations. These conclusions also suggest that one critical preparation for this process is for nations to gain an awareness of the distinctiveness of their own civilization, not in order to feel superior to others but to create a realistic basis for addressing the substantial opportunities and problems arising within this civilization. Finally, we must realize that every advance brought by the Singularity revolutions will bring a serious potential for danger and disruption. The potential solutions to such dangers must come from the strengths of the civilization from which they emerged.

For a half-century now some have advocated constructing a world government in hopes that it would control such hazards. Such a government (unless it is a disguised empire of the major powers imposed on the rest) would have to be constructed on a lowest-common-denominator basis to include a substantial collection of brutal dictatorships, rotten oligarchies, and naked kleptocracies. It may be more useful to construct a framework for cooperation starting with a small number of significant strong civil societies and to work on improving constitutional structures which can restrain harmful use of power, whether political or technological, while preserving safeguards against political abuse. Any such institution will have to draw on civil-society strengths of openness, voluntary consent and compliance, inclusion, constitutional restraint of authority, and flow of participation from the fundamental levels of society to the top. Any other approach is unlikely to be effective in achieving its goals or be tolerable to its citizens.

An understanding of the success of market economies and democratic government will lead inevitably to skepticism about ambitious, broadly inclusive international or transnational institutions. International cooperation will be essential to meet the challenges of the Singularity revolutions. But the first challenge of organizations is to attempt to link internally states with much in common. If we cannot make such forms work, there is no hope whatsoever for institutions hoping to link across different cultures, except in the most superficial ways. Thus, the first challenge is creating the institutional ties to parallel the economic realities of the convergence within the English-speaking economies.

Other areas of the world that are beginning to show similar creativity and entrepreneurship are, interestingly enough, also strong and relatively open civil societies—Scandinavia, as mentioned, and places like the Netherlands. It is no accident that a figure such as Linus Torvalds—who created the Linux language and the Linux phenomenon—is a citizen of Finland. It is also of note that he promptly moved to the English-speaking world—in this case Palo Alto, California—in order to advance his dreams.

The problem is not any lack of creativity among non-English-speaking people, nor a lack of energy or entrepreneurial drive. The problem is that when creativity does arise and ventures start, the prevailing set of social, economic, and political institutions retards their growth. In corrupt and undemocratic countries with weak civil societies, family networks permit entrepreneurs to get around these obstacles, up to a point. But they cannot expand easily beyond that. In stronger civil societies such as Germany, which have high-trust characteristics but lack openness and flexibility in their political and social systems, ventures start but can become frustrated by bureaucratic barriers. In America, start-ups draw heavily on Indian programmers and entrepreneurs. In Germany, a proposal to give visas to Indian programmers gave rise to a political slogan of "Kinder statt Inder"—"(our) Children, not Indians."

This resistance to flexibility may change. In fact, I believe it will. However, these changes will not happen overnight. The European Union (EU) will likely go through one or more rather severe crises before it changes its nature; the Japanese system is similarly rigid and slow to change. The decades it will require for these changes to take place will also be the critical decades of the Singularity revolutions.

In the short term, therefore, it is likely that the Anglosphere nations will continue to pull away from Continental Europe and Japan.

When I have presented these conclusions in public forums in places such as Silicon Valley, I have had comments from audience members—French and Italian immigrants—who have told me, "In my country, I just could not start a company. I wanted to start a software company, so I had to come to America."

Similarly, many young Continental Europeans use their EU rights to relocate to Britain because it has a more entrepreneurial culture than the continent, and they want that freedom. Free movement has been reported as a success of the EU principles, but it is very much one way. Young Continentals move to Britain and Ireland, suggesting it may be an example of the English-speaking world's continual attraction for the smart, talented, and ambitious. To be sure, there is a substantial reverse flow of British migrants to the continent, but these tend to be retirees or long-distance commuters remaining economically linked to the Anglo-sphere while enjoying continental weather, wine, and lower costs of real estate. There is a French Silicon Valley, but it does not lie in any of the planned technology centers created by the French state—it stretches along the Channel link line through the Thames Valley, where hundreds of thousands of young French men and women (including the latest model for Marianne, the incarnation of the Republic) have relocated to pursue their dreams without the high taxes and social burdens of the continent.

Immigration patterns suggest that the institutional arrangements and alignments which the English-speaking nations have pursued over the past thirty years are probably obsolete and need serious rethinking, realigning, and in some cases, abandonment. Other institutions need to emerge to take the place of the declining ones.

Much can be learned from the successes and failures of the North Atlantic Treaty Organization (NATO), the EU, the North American Free Trade Agreement (NAFTA), the North American Aerospace Defense Command (NORAD), the Association of Southeast Asian Nations (ASEAN), and the U.K./U.S. alliances.

Adapting these lessons to the needs of strong civil society and implementing the new forms of strong alliances are the political and social challenges of the Era of the Singularity.

AFTER THE ECONOMIC STATE: THE CIVIC STATE AND THE NETWORK COMMONWEALTH

Gunpowder, stagecoach roads, and sailing ships made possible the original nation-states of Europe. Railways, telegraphs, and steamships made possible the large-scale nation-states of the nineteenth and twentieth centuries. What political form will be made possible in the twenty-first century as a result of the revolutions of the Singularity?

The answer is beginning to emerge: from the Internet; the communication satellite; fast, cheap intercontinental aircraft; and all the rest. Social changes driven by the Information Revolution have begun to decentralize or break apart many existing states—particularly those I call "economic states" as opposed to "civic states."

Despite this trend, certain benefits delivered by large-scale organization remain desirable. With the waning of the economic states that first created those benefits, there will be a need for new means to achieve those gains. I have defined and named one new form, the "network commonwealth" and offer it up as a social basis for connecting civic states today. These network commonwealths are in turn built on a new, emerging pattern of culture, "network civilizations"—globe-spanning, multinational linguistic-cultural communities integrated into a unified informational space. Just as the ethnic nation was the raw material from which the classical nation-state was built, so the network civilization is the raw material from which the network commonwealth will be built.

Such network commonwealths may emerge along whatever lines of association their component states find in their interest to pursue. However, I expect they will associate primarily on the lines of cultural contiguity: groups of nations sharing language, customs, legal systems, religions, and other significant values, most specifically, trust characteristics. In the worldwide network, communication costs are unaffected by distance. Ease of cooperation will be determined by similarity in language, culture, and common institutions and practices to a greater degree than ever before, eclipsing physical proximity.

Network commonwealths will be able to provide many benefits without the costs that economic states have historically imposed on individuals and society.

People today are becoming increasingly unwilling to pay those costs, but still desire the benefits. The network commonwealth offers a way to reconcile these conflicting sentiments.

There has been little discussion about the cumulative effects of the Singularity revolutions outside of science fiction. Most discussion has centered upon the effects of the first stages of the Information Revolution—but as we have seen, that is but the leading edge of a wider and deeper transformation.

HOBBES AND ROUSSEAU IN CYBERSPACE

In discussions about these changes and their effects, two schools of thought seem to have emerged to date. One is a gloomy and apocalyptic vision of many small, essentially unconnected ministates engaged in intermittent low-level conflict and confrontation reminiscent of Hobbes's "War of All against All"—a vision of a few rich Singapores and many poor, conflict-torn Kosovos. This view is reflected in political works such as Robert Kaplan's *The Coming Anarchy*, and in futurist fiction by visions such as Neal Stephenson's *The Diamond Age*.

The other could be described as a "One World via Internet" vision of increased communication (with the implied assumption of English as the universal language), omnidirectional cooperation, and networking on a worldwide scale. Its proponents, such as the cyberfuturists of *Wired* magazine, envision that lowering the transaction costs of cooperation to a uniform level worldwide will make it equally likely for any one person anywhere to cooperate with any other person anywhere else. In many versions, less futurist, perhaps, but more typical of Hegelian-Kantian internationalists, it leads to a vision of world governance—of increasing integration into regional transnational organizations such as the EU and NAFTA, in parallel with single-purpose world-level structures such as the World Trade Organization, ultimately all merging into a mode of world governance. The universalists divide into the more optimistic libertarian internationalists such as Walter Wriston or Kenichi Ohmae who see globalization *à tout azimuth* as an inevitable product of social evolution, and those who see this world as a goal to be imposed. The latter (including most of the pro-Europeanist theoreticians such as Charles Kupchan, Will Hutton, and Paul Habermas) have been usefully categorized as "transnational progressives" by Hudson Institute scholar John Fonte (a term now shortened to *tranzi* in Weblog discourse.) The usual contrast to "Hobbesean" is "Rousseauean," which would not be invalid as a descriptor of this vision, but "Hegelian" or "Kantean" might be better, given the passion of the latter two for ideals of global governance.

If the one vision leads to a few Singapores and many Kosovos, then the other looks to a multicultural Golden Era benignly presided over by an enlightened United Nations and its international organs. Neither vision is likely to be realized. The breakdown of the old structures need not and probably will not continue infinitely. If it were to persist, the ongoing division of national communities would result in an undifferentiated and disconnected mass of ever-smaller nation-states, or more honestly said, tribal states. The dissolution of the USSR and of the Socialist Federative Republic of Yugoslavia show what the human costs of such processes can be. Equally, there is an inherent limit to the prospect of any form of universal or global governance in the near future. One need only look at the ineffectiveness of the United Nations in coping with many global and regional issues, due in large part to the substantial democracy gap between the genuine civil societies at one end of the spectrum, and the failed states at the other, to see the limits of this approach.

Network commonwealths can accomplish most of the good that global governance promises, without the dangers of instituting a universal and homogeneous state. It is a new sort of organization built on what is itself a new emerging cultural pattern, namely "network civilizations"—that is, globe-spanning, multinational linguistic-cultural communities. Just as the ethnic nation was the raw material from which the classical nation-state was built, so the network civilization is the raw material from which the network commonwealth is being built. A network civilization is a group of nations sharing language, customs, history, legal systems, religions, and other significant values—most specifically trust characteristics. This facilitates the movement of people, goods, and services across borders, forming and strengthening shared cultures (both elite and popular) and experiences—for example, common publications read by the publics of all of the nations of a particular network civilization. In turn, this lays the foundation for greater institutional cooperation (in the form of common markets, permanent security alliances, and joint scientific and technological projects). A network commonwealth would build on these existing forms of transnational cooperation and thus emerge along existing information-oriented lines of linguistic and cultural affinity. It would be defined by close trading relationships and substantial military cooperation and intelligence-sharing among its constituent states, and a high degree of intranetwork flows of migration and investment.

Most of the mechanisms that will be used to build the network commonwealth already exist. By giving a name to the new possibility and by presenting a vision of what it might become, we may be able to light the path of the future a bit, and help avoid some of the stumbles that come from treading in the dark. I believe that these developments will unfold over the next twenty years: maybe faster, maybe slower. That is the time scale I will use in describing the path from here to the realization of the network commonwealth.

What are the trends changing the political landscape worldwide? They include the following:

- the increasing transformation of economic activity to the new technologies of the Singularity revolutions, embedded in the matrix of the Internet,
- the continually falling cost of exchanging and sharing information across geographic and political boundaries, and
- the breakdown of centralized command structures which previously made possible the now-eroding ability to control flows of information.

These trends are driven and accelerated by other developments such as instantaneous, worldwide, flat-rate communications and cheap long-range aviation.

These changes are creating a new topology of political space. In this new environment, physical proximity is no longer the most important factor in either trade or power projection. This will drive a transition from organization along lines of geographic regions to structures organized primarily along linguistic, cultural, or religious lines.

LIMITS TO THE BREAKDOWN OF BIG GOVERNMENTS

The emergence of the network commonwealth as a potential form of political, social, and economic organization is driven by three emerging realities:

The Basis of the World Economy Is Changing from Manufacturing to Information.

In this new economy, the most central, strategic, and highest-value trade is in ideas and informational products and the human minds and skills in which they are embodied. Just as agriculture remained important in the Machine Age, manufacturing (and agriculture) will remain important in the Era of the Singularity—but mastery of manufacturing will come with mastery of information, just as a mastery of agriculture passed to those who mastered machinery. Similarly, as military predominance once passed to those powers that led in industrialization, so will military predominance pass to those who best master information technology.

In the Era of the Singularity, Physical Space Is No Longer the Most Important Factor in Political Association. Cultural Space Is.

What is the result of this shift? In an Internet-mediated economy where information is the chief product, London, Toronto, Los Angeles, Capetown, and Sydney are next door to each other—while London and Paris, Toronto and Québec City, Los Angeles and Beijing, Sydney and Jakarta are all at distant poles. Deep cooperation among entrepreneurs, software architects, and artists will be needed to produce the items of greatest value. Those who share language, cultural assumptions, and attitudes of trust will cooperate best. There is always a transaction cost to be paid when attempting collaboration among people of different political structures, languages, and cultures; and enterprises burdened with such costs (particularly when such collaboration must pass through governmental structures) tend to be slower and less competitive than those without such burdens.

Cooperation Is Proportional to Communication as Complexity Increases.

Meaningful, thorough, and successful cooperation is most easily accomplished among those who can communicate most deeply and most clearly.

This is most easily done with shared language, assumptions, or behavioral standards underlying the culture expressed in the language. Although substantial multinational and multicultural cooperation does occur in business, scientific, and political circles, the focus of the cooperation is information-intensive.

Cooperation benefits from the greater utility of shared linguistic-cultural assumptions. German, American, and Japanese companies have cooperated successfully in production of automobiles, but international cooperation in motion pictures or software has most frequently been among companies rooted in the same linguistic communities.

THE GROWING WORLDWIDE MARKET IN SOVEREIGNTY SERVICES AND THE DECLINE OF THE MONOPOLY OF THE ECONOMIC STATE

The lowering of transaction costs for international financial activities in the 1960s started to allow major corporations and banks to take advantage of the lower tax and regulatory burdens of tax havens such as the Netherlands Antilles. Corporations became sophisticated consumers of "sovereignty services," in this case, venue of incorporation. In doing so, they built on a trend started by 1920s shipowners, who had increasingly sought Panamanian and Liberian registry for their ships.

Over the past three decades, these trends have accelerated enormously as the breakup of the old European empires began the process of multiplication of sovereign entities. The emergence of larger numbers of sovereign entities has created a more competitive market for sovereignty services, most particularly for incorporation but also ship registration, passports, residence permits, and other desirable items that any sovereign state has to sell. The increase in number of providers, combined with the falling cost of accessing the providers, has made sovereignty services a highly competitive market area. As devolution produces yet more sovereign states and the Internet reduces the cost of accessing the services to rock bottom, this market can be expected to flourish. The market for sovereignty services has shown great price elasticity: the users of offshore accounts, shell corporations, and trust services proliferate as the transaction costs of setting up such services fall.

Consider the ability to sell products and services on the Internet, and the decline of the corporation-employment model (seen in the practices of downsizing and delayering). Private Internet currencies based on strong encryption (cybermoney) may soon provide payment mechanisms that are not recorded in central clearinghouses and are thus beyond subpoena power. We can see that much of the actual economic activity of the coming era will pass into the transnational realm.

There, it will be beyond the full control of any particular state. Only a few decades ago, even major nations set currency-exchange rates politically, and many controlled their citizens' ability to carry money abroad. Today even the most powerful nation-states find it impossible to set currency or interest rates at will, without reference to the world marketplace. In the near future, this financial power will come to the home and office, at the family and individual level.

Nor can the economic state count on coercive solutions to counteract this trend. It cannot tax what it cannot see. One of the products of cheap, ubiquitous computing has been the growing worldwide availability of strong programs for encrypting data on personal computers. With such programs, individuals and companies can communicate and trade beyond the easy ability of governments to intercept or, if proper precautions are taken, to even be aware that the transactions exist. The entire paradigm of citizens' economic transactions being visible to the government, much less controllable, is fading.

Some may ask whether the moves against anonymous offshore banking and other privacy features in the wake of the September 11, 2001, attacks will not reverse this trend. It is true that following September 11 the pendulum has swung from a relatively high degree of governmental tolerance of data anonymity to a desire to fully eradicate anonymity. Yet the unexpected consequences of such greater transparency, including embarrassment of the political classes, particularly the consequences of a more thorough public disclosure of their own private lives, will likely create a counterdemand for renewed privacy measures. This will likely lead to a new balance in which governments abandon some of the circumstances in which they can review citizens' data in return for at least a conditional ability of some authorities (perhaps not governments, but possibly private arbitration services) to trace key data trails to enforce antifraud judgments, and for security agencies to enforce critical antiterrorism measures.

States that cling unrealistically to the models of the past will find their economies becoming more like Italy's, where a very substantial portion (over 50 percent by common estimates) of the gross domestic product (GDP) is estimated to be off the books and beyond the view (and reach) of the state. This becomes a vicious circle, as the declining collections force the state to cut services or raise the rates on those who still pay taxes— usually both at once. Cutting services causes taxpayers to question the value of their relationship with the government.

Raising rates pushes more taxpayers further into tax avoidance, as shown by the Italian model. Both further reduce the ability of the state to command the sort of revenue stream it has become accustomed to enjoying.

The reduction of the effective available percentage of GDP to taxation authorities will accelerate the existing trend toward the decline of economic states. An economic state is one whose support rests primarily on its ability to transfer resources from one sector of society to another. Such states will be subject to stronger pressures to break apart, as the ability to shift wealth declines and the social compacts they support grow weaker. Pay-as-you-go services such as Social Security in the United States and the state pension systems of Continental Europe will be placed under ever-increasing fiscal pressure. (Health systems like Medicare in the United States and the British National Health Service may have these pressures partially offset by expected gains in healthy life span and the effective treatment of debilitating diseases.) To the extent that loyalty to states depends on the delivery of such elaborate benefits, economic states will become decreasingly cohesive.

Some commentators predict that these trends will bring on "crypto-anarchy."

This is highly unlikely. There will continue to be episodes of disorder, such as the kind transitional periods and breakdown of ruling paradigms always produce. However, the decline of the economic state will mostly be a quiet and gradual affair, a revolution made of many individual decisions which, taken together, have a cumulative effect on the continued viability of economic states. A Canadian executive may take a job in the United States because the income tax burden is so much lower. Continental Europeans might move to London to start a company in order to escape the "social burden" of regulation in France or Germany, and an executive could outsource software development to India, where the workers speak English well and are cost-competitive. These are the individual decisions that will shape the emerging world.

In this world, there will still be nations and states, and they will still have vital interests. The problem will be to develop alternative means of pursuing the vital interests of the states that remain. Those that will dominate the new era will be the civic states. Civic states are those which are able to generate an essentially voluntary adherence on the part of their populations, whether for patriotic or religious reasons. They also encourage a widely shared feeling that the government is acting in the best interests of the citizens. The things of value that civic states provide to their citizens—values, identity, community—are fundamentally intangible things that, unlike economic aspects of sovereignty, cannot become commodities in the world marketplace.

Such civic states are far less likely to act as economic states. They will not likely be able (or want) to create or sustain large-area organizations with tightly integrated populations generating a consensus to pay for and share an elaborate structure of state-provided and state-mediated benefits consuming high proportions of the state's GDP. The economic state is in serious decline, but these trends will not destroy the civic state—instead, they will drive its further development. The decline, decentralization, and in some cases destruction of economic states will provide impetus to the search for newer, more flexible, and less centralized mechanisms for linking large-scale activities. This search will be driven primarily by the crises created by the breakup and threatened or attempted breakup of large economic states.

The network commonwealth would meet this need by using mechanisms drawn from existing successful forms of transnational cooperation. These include common markets, permanent security alliances, and international science and technology organizations, but all evolved into new, looser forms. These network commonwealths will likely emerge along information-oriented lines of linguistic and cultural affinity, as these commonalties will become increasingly more important to economic success than geographic proximity. They will also begin to become more important to individuals' identity, as the shared experience upon which wider identity is based becomes languagewide rather than nationwide.

The network commonwealth is to unions based on economic cross-subsidization (such as the EU) what the civic state is to the economic state. As the EU is an "economic union," a network commonwealth could be called a "civic union." Just as the developments of the Information Revolution are putting great strain on economic states, they will likewise weaken economic unions. And just as these changes benefit civic states relative to economic states, so will they give civic unions the advantage over economic unions. For these reasons, network commonwealths will rise first, and most successfully, among groups of civic states. The stronger the civil society in the constituent states, the more likely a network commonwealth will arise early.

LINUX AS A FORESHADOWING OF THE ECONOMICS OF THE SINGULARITY: THE END OF CAPITALISM AND THE TRIUMPH OF THE MARKET ECONOMY

A funny thing happened on the way to the third millennium. Capitalism ended.

At least, capitalism as defined by the man who coined the term. It is a peculiarity of socioeconomic systems that they are typically known by the names that others give to them. The knights and princes of the Middle Ages never knew that they lived under "feudalism"; this name was invented only in the modern era.

Our current era is a particular case of these peculiarities. We call our economic system "capitalism," and our political system one of democratic nation-states. Yet the term capitalism came from Karl Marx, who thought that the era of market-economy nation-states was, in the middle of the nineteenth century, about to be replaced by a world-state with a centralized command economy, which he termed "scientific socialism." He was wrong about the inevitability of the transition to a command economy, as well as the desirability of that transition. These facts have finally been generally accepted. Yet we continue to accept his term of "capitalism," and for the most part his definition of that system, and think of the "market economy" and "capitalism" as being synonymous. This is sloppy thinking.

Marx saw capitalism as a step on the road to centralization of society, economy, and the state. In his system, the relation of individuals to the means of production of material goods and services was the fundamental tool for analyzing society. Land was the principal means of production under feudalism, at a time when agriculture was the principal economic activity, and the fact that land was owned by feudal lords made them the ruling class of feudal society. He viewed capitalism as the system of the Industrial Revolution, in which industry replaced agriculture as the principal productive activity. The means of production—the industrial plants and tooling—were large, expensive machine installations and were owned by the shareholders of the corporations that arose to build them. Thus the class of shareholders became the ruling class of industrial society. Because ownership of capital—liquid, investable wealth and the industrial plants it paid for—was the characteristic of this class, he called the system capitalism.

Over the past three decades, however, an enormous transition has taken place. Industrial manufacture has declined as the dominant and characteristic activity of the economy, and has been replaced by the production, organization, and manipulation of information. The means of producing and processing information have become the principal economic activity, and the tools used in those processes—computers and information networks—have become the principal means of production. At first, this seemed not to matter to Marxists, nor to others who saw the dominance of capital as the salient feature of the economy. The production and manipulation of information seemed to require large, capital-intensive tools—computers, communications networks, and broadcasting systems—and it seemed as if large corporations could dominate this field by controlling the massive capital needed to create and operate these tools.

The rise of Microsoft to dominance seemed to validate this model. Employing thousands of "Microserfs," using its massive capital to amass software patents and enforce them, using battalions of lawyers to wear down the competition, and using its capital throw-weight to establish new products through brute-force control of advertising and distribution, Microsoft seemed to be the Standard Oil of the new industry. Yet just as Microsoft seemed to be guaranteeing the predominance of the capitalist model in the new era, several significant things were happening which suggested that, rather than being the first corporation of the new era, Microsoft was the last corporation of the passing one.

The first indication came when the falling price of computers crossed the point where the average programmer could afford to own a computer capable of producing the code from which he typically earned his living.

This meant that, for the first time since the beginning of the Industrial Revolution, the ownership of the most critical tool of production in the most critical industry of the world's leading economy was readily affordable by the individual worker. Throughout the first three decades of the Information Age, the individual worker was still dependent on his employer for his means of production, just as any textile worker in Manchester or Lawrence was in 1840. Suddenly, this changed. Now, it is as if a steelworker could afford his own blast furnace or rolling mill, an automobile worker his own assembly line. By strict Marxist definitions, capitalism ended some time in the early 1990s. This is a development that has not received adequate attention.

The second indication has been the rise of the Internet, which is taking control of the communication networks and communications media out of the hands of the large corporations that have always controlled them. It is creating the basis for a highly diversified, worldwide, real-time market in which packages of communications capability and content will be bought and sold as commodities, and in which small players will likely hold the advantage over big ones. The Internet, the computer, and broadcasting capabilities will just be arbitrary divisions within a wider, uniform medium. The cost of a facility for Webcasting is far less than the cost of a facility for television broadcasting. At some point in the relatively near future the quality of the Webcast will be as good as, if not better than, that of broadcast television, and the cost of a Webcasting facility for high-quality production will be within the range of many individuals. Just as the personal computer capable of producing first-rate software is revolutionizing the work relations of software, the personal Webcasting facility will change the nature of the broadcasting media.

It also changes the dynamics of production. Even though the tools of production can now be owned by the workers, individually and severally, there still has seemed to be a need to bring programmers together in one place and put them under the control of management. Although this remains the case in most instances, the rise of Linux and other open-source products has provided another paradigm, one that will soon grow to become the principal model of production in the principal industry of the leading economies of the planet.

The open-source software world is unlike anything described by Marx, either as present reality or future possibility. Consider Linux, the most famous open-source product. Software code is produced and distributed without direct financial compensation by a wide collection of individuals, voluntarily coordinating themselves over the Internet. Consensus is the primary decision-making mode.

Expertise and reputation are then used for marketing individuals' services as employees or as members of entrepreneurial teams. They assemble in for-profit companies (like Red Hat), taking the source code (which is available to all, free on the Internet), and turning it into commercial products to be sold and supported by those companies. The Linux world runs what amounts to a parallel economy paying in reputation, rather than cash, linked loosely to the cash economy. It is a one-way linkage; reputation can be turned into cash, but cash cannot be turned into reputation. It is remarkably free from regulation and confiscation; no government agency can take a reputation for good work away from one participant and give it to another.

The closest analogy to the Linux model of production may be that of the live theater industry. There, would-be actors perform for free or for minuscule reward to demonstrate their talents. Eventually they are accepted in a profit-making enterprise or band together with other would-be entrants to form a new company.

Once a certain breakthrough is made, the reputation of the actor becomes a reliable meal ticket, and often a means to wealth. The difference between the theater model and the Linux model is that where the demand for theatrical entertainment is capped and relatively inelastic, the demand for good software is enormous and will continue to grow because the functions of society are increasingly becoming suffused with and dependent upon computation.

The process of producing Linux seems like Marx's ultimate communism, after the supposed withering away of the socialist state—"from each according to his ability" would be a fair way of describing the production side. But the distribution side is a little different. The product is given away not "to each according to his need," at least not directly, but automatically and universally. People then take what they need. The only thing the producers get is reputation, and that is awarded on an utterly ruthless basis of merit. Meanwhile, within the larger Linux universe, a subuniverse of pure laissez-faire market relations plays out, with entrepreneurial companies acting in accordance with pure market theory.

The real evidence that this model is not a fluke but rather a harbinger of a new economic model is that open-source products compete very well against the products of traditional capitalist corporations. Apache, an open-source product, has established itself firmly in the server marketplace. The Linux server operating system has established itself against traditionally produced, supported, and marketed products. It is particularly noteworthy that the server market is commercial: more demanding and more quality-conscious than the client market, where commercial products still hold sway, for now, with less-demanding, less quality-conscious consumers. Linux holds market share against traditionally produced products because it is more reliable and more robust than its competitors. This is extraordinary. Imagine that a type of aircraft developed by amateur home-builders and produced by small entrepreneurial companies were to be bought by airlines in preference to the aircraft of Boeing or Airbus, who in turn could only compete in private aviation markets! Yet this is a good parallel to the situation in server software today.

The Linux model will not become the sole model for software production or sales, particularly on the consumer side, where branding will remain important. However, as it evolves over time, Linux will become an important model for software, and one of the dominant modes of production. It is also important to understand that "software" will come to encompass the bulk of the value of any manufactured product, as integrated design-to-automated production systems become the norm in industry. Flexible, automated, computer-controlled fabrication facilities, ultimately quite small and decentralized, will become the normal means of fabrication of goods. Time on such machines will become a commodity, which the market will force down to the lowest possible margin. The software that describes the good and commands its manufacture will constitute the greater part of the value of the good. There is no reason to believe that such software, and therefore the design of most goods, could not be produced on the Linux model.

Given the stability and reliability of open-source software compared to closed-source, it will probably be preferred for applications where reliability is important. The example of a homebuilt aircraft being preferred by airlines over Boeing products was fanciful, but in the coming world where industrial goods are mostly software, an "open-source" aircraft design might be a reality.

While Marx's "capitalism" becomes obsolete as an economic category, it is clear that the new economy is a market economy—and likely to become a purer market economy than ever seen before. What we are witnessing is the triumph of the Austrian free-market economist F. A. Hayek over Marx, not only in the political realm, but in the realm of social science as well. Hayek, a Nobel laureate, offered a particular understanding of the market economy that is becoming the underpinning of the economics and social science of the Singularity revolutions. Hayek understood that the essence of the market economy is not the ownership of the means of production per se, but the exchange process itself. The Linux model confounds Marx's rules completely, but it is entirely consistent with a Hayekian market-process understanding. If the exchange of values is voluntary, taken by a wide range of individuals, and the final product is the result of those exchanges, created by an emergent understanding of the relative value of the items exchanged, then it is a market process. The fact that the Linux model values the original inputs by the volunteer hackers only in reputation, rather than cash, does not mean that it is not a market process. Hayek's theory explains the Linux world as readily as it did the corporate world of the twentieth century in which it was formulated.

The Linux model has profound consequences for the fate of corporations, just as the Singularity revolutions do for the existing, economic states. Nobel economics laureate Ronald Coase posited in his seminal article *The Nature of the Firm* that corporations offered an advantage in the marketplace because their size allowed essential internal functions to be performed with lower transaction costs than in a comparable-sized network of individual actors. The Linux world is an example of what happens when the easy communication of the Internet, and the substitution of reputation payments for cash payments, lowers the transaction costs of an open-source network below those of competing firms. Only the small, entrepreneurial firms working within the Linux world, such as Red Hat, preserve the advantages of the corporate form as they interface with the cash-economy world. Cash- and reputation-based economies mesh readily in an overall framework of free exchange. In this new medium, we need a new "Theory of the Network" to supplement and update Coase's theory of the firm. (This new theory would not invalidate or replace Coase, any more than Einstein invalidated Newton.)

Instead, just as Einstein qualified Newton by defining the particular assumptions in which Newton's laws applied, so would a successor to Coase qualify the theory of the firm by further defining the technological and social framework within which Coase's conditions for the advantages of the firm are true.

This understanding has been largely absent from the debate over the "post-nation-state" future. Many observers seem to believe that although the Internet economy will undercut the power of the economic state, it will leave the great corporations not only intact but essentially omnipotent. This is as unlikely as the assumption that the collapse of the independence of nobility at the end of the Middle Ages would leave kings omnipotent. Although this did happen in some places for some periods of time, in general the collapse of baronial power ultimately empowered new actors: the new trading and manufacturing classes in the maritime states, and civil and military bureaucrats in the continental states.

Corporations and the established wealthy have relied heavily on the power of economic states to protect them from competition, and more important, from the instability of technological change (Joseph Schumpeter's "creative destruction").

One of the most successful public relations triumphs of the twentieth century was the selling of the idea that social democracy was forced on the unwilling rich for the benefit of the poor and working classes. Instead, social democracy has often been a device the wealthy have used to stabilize society and limit opportunities for upward mobility by forcing people through narrow, state-administered meritocratic channels. Massive taxes on new income, for example, hurt start-ups and upwardly mobile entrepreneurs far more than established wealthy families and corporations. Heavy financial and product regulations cripple new competition and protect established firms. State-mandated labor union rights and lavish mandated employee benefits present a formidable barrier to entry to new companies.

Existing family wealth can usually be sheltered in offshore trusts or other wealth-preservation devices available to those with the large existing fortunes needed to justify the transaction costs of these mechanisms.

Thus, it is no wonder that established wealthy families and their corporate empires have often supported social democratic politics. The Rockefellers in the United States, the Wallenbergs in Sweden, and the "Tory wet" class in Britain spent much of the twentieth century supporting the genteel politics of regulated capitalism and tax-supported redistribution of (some) wealth. They would have preferred that politics be a debate between their parties (the "Rockefeller Republicans" in the United States, the Christian Democrats on the continent, and the pre-Thatcher Tories in England) and the more moderate socialists and social democrats of the Left (Humphrey Democrats, the social democratic parties of the Continent, Hugh Gaitskell's Labour in the United Kingdom).

It is also little wonder that the political classes, overwhelmingly dependent on large bureaucratic institutions for their incomes, viewed voices outside this consensus with horror. Barry Goldwater, Ronald Reagan, and Margaret Thatcher in the political arena, and Milton Friedman and F. A. Hayek in the sphere of academic economics all encountered ferocious ridicule and criticism far out of proportion to the impact of the actual policies they advocated or implemented.

What sparked intense opposition was their threat to the reigning consensus. The changes introduced by the Thatcher and Reagan governments were most important as changes of direction than in what they accomplished in the short term. More important was what I have called the second gateway wave of deregulation, decontrol, and privatization introduced worldwide in the 1980s and 1990s by conservatives, liberals, and socialists alike, which resulted in substantial shake-ups to the existing corporate structures. (The first gateway is the establishment of basic rule of law, property rights, and civil peace—steps that still elude many ex-Soviet republics and failed states in Africa.) Many established bureaucracies either reformed or adapted, or vanished from the scene. This process is far from finished, but one can now see in the more advanced societies an integrated, downsized, "leaner and meaner" corporation, more networklike in its internal structure and more flexible in its response to the marketplace. Gone are many of the characteristics of the midcentury corporation, including the expectation of lifelong loyalty in either direction.

It is tempting to view the new corporation as the end point of this transition process. But the logic of the end of capitalism, or the third gateway of fluid entrepreneurism, argues that the transition is far from complete, and the end point is not even necessarily visible today. The stock markets were dazzled by companies such as Netscape, which began with a product produced by two college students in their dormitories in the early 1990s for a system, the World Wide Web, created as an open-source phenomenon. They have not really begun to understand true open-source companies such as Red Hat, with its huge (and transitory) success in the stock market. And Red Hat and its like are not the end point of this process either.

There will still be a role for corporations, including large corporations, in the network economy of the Singularity revolutions. Their economic weight and established brand names will continue to be valuable assets. However, their relation to the whole system will be very different from the role of corporations in the economy now passing. The network economy of free exchange will be a matrix; individuals, small groups, and open networks (like the Linux community) will interact with corporations without subservience. We might dub this very open and fluid environment the network marketplace.

The political question is, what will be the relationship between the state forms and the emerging marketplace forms? I have argued that the world political system of (usually) large, economic states is giving way to one of more coherent (and usually smaller) civic states linked in looser confederal forms, the network commonwealths. These will interact with a fluid network economy in which much-changed corporations, consisting largely of links between financing and research centers, will interact with a host of smaller entities in a market-economy matrix. Government intervention, as I discuss elsewhere, will be much more local and limited—specific interventions for limited ends.

The world of helpless individuals squeezed between large, powerful states and large, powerful corporations will be a dim historical memory—neither will survive in its historical, twentieth-century essence, although the forms will probably still be there. Fears of corporate domination of the network world are misplaced.

In fact, as the power of big corporations wanes, it will likely be left-wing nostalgics who mourn them the most, for it was the corporation—with its paycheck deductions, mandatory union membership, and stable markets—that made the social democratic economic state possible.

A new understanding of the market is essential to comprehending the network economy. The Marxist concept of "capitalism" has long outlived its usefulness. It was a tool for understanding power relationships in the early Industrial Revolution era; and as a tool for understanding corporations, it was rapidly superseded by Coase's theory of the firm and his understanding of the centrality of transaction costs. Capitalism, in that sense, is dead. Let us, then, move on to examine the emerging world of the network economy and the network commonwealth.

THE CIVIC STATE: ON THE NATURE AND LIMITS OF GOVERNMENTS IN THE ERA OF THE SINGULARITY

There is a school of thought—the self-described "cryptoanarchists"—who maintain that the availability of cyberspace transactions beyond the ability of the state to monitor or control will destroy the ability of the state to maintain itself. Those who adhere to this school of thought foresee an era of essentially chaotic social organization, in which market forms predominate in both the economy and in many other relationships. I believe that although many of the individual premises of that argument have some validity, the results will not be as extreme as envisioned.

Rather than ending the state, it is more likely that these changes will substantially transform the nature of the state. Most states will either adapt to those changes or cease to exist. (However, just as a small number of feudal states manage to exist even today in marginal areas of the world, some states of the current form may continue to exist well into the future.)

The essence of the new state is that it will be dependent on essentially voluntary forms for cohesion, rather than assuming its ability to command the majority of its subjects. It is true that most modern democracies are already voluntary states to some degree. Taxes are not extracted at gunpoint but usually paid voluntarily (although nobody doubts that a refusal to pay would eventually bring the tax man to your door). Military conscripts usually report voluntarily when summoned, rather than being impressed on the street and chained for transport to the barracks, as in more despotic states. Laws, if disobeyed on a sufficiently widespread basis, are often repealed or ignored (as with, in the United States, alcohol prohibition and the 55 mph speed limit). But in the larger sense, governments have been able to assume their ability to command the allegiance, money, and when needed, the lives of their subjects. This assumption has already substantially eroded throughout the industrialized world. The Singularity revolutions will see it further diminish. Coercive measures for the ordering of subjects' lives and economic affairs will be insufficient to enforce such plans.

This does not mean that states will cease to order their subjects' lives. It means that the threshold of consensus and social cohesion needed to enforce a state regime will be substantially higher than in past experience. Some states will still be able to achieve such consensus and cohesion, and many current states will not manage to do so without substantial changes. But the rules will be changed. It is likely that surviving cohesive states will have one or more of the following characteristics:

- Small populations. Consensus and coherence are easier to achieve among a limited number of people; this will favor small jurisdictions. What is small?

  That will be relative to other factors but will range from several tens of thousands (small Caribbean states, for example) to several tens of millions (author Kenichi Ohmae's "region-states"). Jurisdictions larger than that will probably be structured as federations of small, coherent, civic states.
- Relatively confined geographic spread (although not necessarily contiguous).

  Islands make coherent states, in general, although Ireland, Sri Lanka, and Fiji have not yet done so.
- A core population sharing strong ethnic or religious bonds. Religious or ethnic ties create a strong basis for cohesion. One obvious answer to the question of why Israelis put up with the inordinate fiscal and regulatory interventions of their state is that to leave Israel is to leave the community of their identity. Most will continue to support intervention in the future, provided the state makes reasonable adaptations.
- Visibly successful. Singaporeans put up with their intrusive government, even when few have any ideological, ethnic, or religious reason to do so, because it has delivered visible prosperity and security to its inhabitants over their lifetimes.
- Market-ordered economies with scope for individual enterprise. Citizens will put up with state interventions in a market economy so long as they aren't visibly harmful, they leave room for individual enterprise, and the state delivers reasonable performance in the services people require. Citizens have stayed in social democracies with state-protected corporations and heavy taxation and regulation, but they tend to flee state-socialist regimes in droves whenever possible. Swedes have always been free to leave their country, and East Germans were not, yet the latter fled in great numbers when the opportunity arose, to the ultimate demise of their state, while relatively few Swedes have exiled themselves.
- Low transaction costs for leaving. It is far easier to maintain cohesion if unhappy persons are permitted to leave, and are not heavily pe-

nalized for doing so. Exit taxes are the sign of a loser state. Nazi Germany and the Soviet Union were rightfully despised for levying one; the United States should reconsider the steps it has already taken to follow in their wake. After the malcontents have left, it should be possible for them to return. Many will leave; of them, more than a few will decide to return, and having returned, will be less discontented.

Even permanent expatriates should be encouraged to maintain family and social ties with the home country; expatriates can deliver useful business and political contacts even when they aren't paying taxes.

- Serve as the home base for a diaspora. A diaspora provides an environment for useful commercial relationships worldwide; similarly, having even a minuscule territory with sovereign characteristics, capable of issuing passports, makes life far easier for members of a diaspora. The Internet makes maintenance of personal ties and continued access to one's home culture far easier and cheaper.
- Maintain enough international associations to enjoy the security, economic, and cooperative ties formerly enjoyed only by large states. Iceland maintains a unique culture and language in a prosperous civil society with a population base of only 270,000 people. As such, it would seem to be an advertisement for the viability of very small states. It is not at all clear, however, that it would be nearly as prosperous, secure, or independent if not for its active memberships in NATO, the European Economic Area, and the Nordic Council.
- Share a positive, self-affirming narrative. Many such narratives are provided by religious, national, or ethnic identity. Political entities that do not have ethnic or religious cohesion need a sophisticated and equally compelling narrative.

The United States has a complex and compelling narrative—exemplified in the phrases, "We hold these truths to be self-evident . . ." and ". . . the wretched refuse of your teeming shores." Nations that lose the ability to sustain a positive narrative, on the other hand, lose coherence and identity, and thus voluntary citizen support. In the new environment, such nations will find it difficult to maintain revenue bases, enforce regulation, or defend their citizens.

The new states emerging in this environment will most likely have characteristics of one of three kinds of states:

- The classical-liberal civic state, which seeks to carry out most social functions through voluntary institutions of civil society rather than through the state, seeks to minimize the percentage of GDP devoted to the remaining core functions, and in general seeks to maximize the prosperity of its citizens as individuals;

- The nationalist-conservative or religious civic state, which generates a strong nationalist, religious, or ideological narrative and places duty obligations on its citizens, yet maintains a relatively open market economy;
- The social-democratic civic state, which maintains a high tax rate relative to classical-liberal states, intervenes more frequently in its market economy, delivers more elaborate social benefits, and seeks to maximize the economic and emotional security of its citizens.

Although the third example appears to contradict many of the assumptions of this work, in fact the nature of this projected civic social democracy is different from existing social democracies. Current social democratic states assume the ability to forcibly regulate their citizens' affairs, even over a wide geographic area. They are economic states—they base their justification on their ability to transfer wealth from one sector of society to another. This ability is rapidly eroding and will erode even more rapidly as the Internet economy progresses.

Small, coherent civic states that treat participation in their institutions as voluntary and can limit the number of free riders taking their benefits may well attract a sufficient number of productive participants to maintain a functioning, even thriving economy. Civic social democracies are civic states with a social-solidarity narrative, as opposed to today's social democracies, which are economic states with an egalitarian justification. So long as civic social democracies can convince their creative, entrepreneurial, high-productivity individuals to remain and contribute financially, they can survive and even flourish. Looking at Sweden and Finland, with their vigorous information sectors, one can discern a possible model for the civic social democracies of the future.

Unlike today's social democracies, such states would not seek to monitor the economic lives of their citizens intrusively. Rather they would, like other civic states of the coming era, use noninvasive forms of taxation, essentially taxes on land, fuel, and luxury items (with exemptions for lower-income persons to create a progressive character of taxation) to finance limited cross-transfer schemes and provision of general social benefits. They might even be able to have a flat income tax based on voluntary self-assessment, somewhat like tithing in medieval Europe.

Like today's Ireland, states will permit transnational ventures to locate physical-space operations there without attempting to tax them at uncompetitive rates.

These states will deduce that the indirect revenues generated by the presence of these ventures will be as much reward as it will be practical to obtain. Unlike today's socialists, who encourage narratives that identify prosperity as a marker of guilt, civic social democrats would create strong psychological rewards for their big-ticket taxpayers in the form of civic honors and titles, and would encourage a public narrative creating general respect for such contributors.

Monarchies may find it easier to create such rewards, in the form of titles—it may not be an accident that many of the more successful social democracies, such as Sweden, Denmark, and the Netherlands, are monarchies. In a world where mobility of persons and their capital will be extremely easy, social democracies must rely on people's desire for emotional and economic security and identity as high-status individuals within a small country, as the primary means of retaining the efforts of productive individuals.

In an economic environment where government revenue must be coaxed, rather than commanded, and where artists and educators are directly linked to the feedback mechanisms of taxpayers' willingness to support expenditures, the coming political evolution may tend to favor artists who support the narratives that legitimize their funding. Public education and public art subsidies in such states would support curricula, artists, and works that reinforce the national narrative. The art of such states would resemble more the U.S. Works Progress Administration-sponsored art of the 1930s than those subsidized by the current National Endowment for the Arts or that win Britain's Turner Prize.

A few years ago much was heard of Tony Blair's "Third Way" between socialism and capitalism. Although not much has been heard of the Third Way recently, its proponents may yet become the progenitors of the civic social democrats of the next generation, provided they examine their past failures honestly. The Third Way failed to capture the general imagination because it was still too enamored of the coercive side of government. Its proponents talked about civil society, but they overestimated the degree to which civil society cannot be created or led by state action, other than in the primary task of promoting honest law enforcement and adjudication. Most of the work of promoting civil society today must still consist of dismantling government activities that corrode civil society.

Similarly, conservative or religious nationalist states will retain the efforts of productive individuals by fostering intense patriotic or religious loyalties, so that such individuals will continue to pay higher taxes rather than emigrate. Again, high-ticket taxpayers might be rewarded through civic honors, titles, and ranks.

These revenues will be spent more on defense than on welfare schemes, although patriotic solidarity will usually result in a safety net for loyal citizens. These states may require universal military service, either through a conscription system like Israel's or a compulsory militia system like Switzerland's. Welfare benefits may be channeled primarily through reserve or militia structures, or through veterans' benefit systems, permitting social welfare costs to be presented as defense expenditures. Similarly, high rank in militia or reserve forces may serve as a source of social status.

Economic theory suggests that classical-liberal states will tend to predominate over time, as they will attract the bulk of the productive individuals and enterprises of the world. This will likely depend on the ability of such classical-liberal states to generate and maintain narratives accepted by their citizens and to result in their active loyalty. As I will explain in the next section, although market economies can operate despite state intervention, such intrusions come with costs, and the long-term effect of such costs will be to render interventionist states less competitive.

Classical-liberal states will hark back to nineteenth-century Britain in their expenditure levels and attitudes toward government spending, although in a context of a much different economy and society. In such states, civil-society solutions will be heavily favored for all but the most essential functions of society. For example, many might not maintain government-run schools at all, preferring voucher or other nonstate solutions. Military expenditures will also be kept low, and greater reliance will be put on voluntary militias for land defense. Many government functions may also be contracted from private providers or other governments.

Classical-liberal states would come closer to the political ideals of libertarians than any states existing today. However, such classical-liberal states, although they would be minimally intrusive and antiauthoritarian, would not have the antinomian flavor that characterizes many of today's libertarians. It is not clear whether many of today's more fervent libertarians would be able to defend such a society from external pressure. Some seem to have the mentality that a classical-liberal state that fails to privatize every last lighthouse is just as evil as, and no more deserving of defense than, its more authoritarian rivals.

In a true classical-liberal civic state, the constraints of law in the areas of manners and morals would likely be replaced by the constraints of social norms.

To form the principles for such a society, Adam Smith's *Wealth of Nations* must be read together with his less well-known *Theory of Moral Sentiments*, and his contemporary Adam Ferguson's *Essay on the History of Civil Society*.

Because of the low transaction costs of relocation from state to state in a network commonwealth framework, populations would tend to sort themselves geographically in terms of comfort with the prevailing or evolving social norms.

All of these types of coherent states will tend to seek compatible network commonwealth arrangements, as a means of retaining trade ties and assuring military security with a minimum of public expenditure. This would free revenue for favorite state projects in the nationalist and social democratic states and minimize taxation in the classical-liberal states.

BUILDING THE NETWORK COMMONWEALTH: THE POWER OF SELF-ASSEMBLY PROTOCOLS

The World Wide Web, for all the excitement it has generated, is at heart nothing but a set of self-assembly protocols: communication standards permitting computers to find and exchange complex information easily and uniformly. Millions of preexisting computers were assembled into the World Wide Web simply by adopting these protocols. What has not yet emerged is an equivalent tool set in the international political order: a clear set of protocols allowing groups of smaller political units to assemble themselves together into network commonwealths to address problems which previously required large, centralized nations or empires.

The Constitution of the United States was once such a set of protocols, in that it permitted thirteen independent states to assemble themselves into a larger entity.

As with any useful protocol, it permitted further expansion, with thirty-seven more units being added over time. The Treaty of Rome similarly served as a self-assembly protocol for creating the EU.

The U.S. Constitution was designed to lead to a united republic, albeit a decentralized one. The pressures of the times united it further than many of its founders would have expected, or wanted. The authors of the Treaty of Rome were divided between those (the majority) who wished to create a united state, and others who hoped to avoid such. The network commonwealth protocols will be written in a different era, one in which unification into a large-scale, united state is not only not the goal, but recognized as an outcome to be avoided.

For the question must be asked: Should not the network civilizations, which would be the bases of network commonwealths, anticipate becoming one nation over time, as new communications methods abolish spatial distinctions? I assume here that they should and will remain separate nations, albeit closely related ones.

The deep values in common among English-speaking nations are sufficient common ground to permit closer cooperation and quicker consensus than in a more universal organization, but there are real and important differences among the various English-speaking nations in public identity and values, differences which would make national-scale integration problematic.

We are not seeing a convergence among like-minded nations on identity and value issues; rather, we are seeing the increasing divergence on such issues within existing nations. These divisions will probably facilitate the devolution of existing nations into federations or looser unions of smaller, more coherent civic states. These divisions are also irrelevant to a network commonwealth, for there is no need to have a homogenous pan-commonwealth policy on such issues. Even larger federal states such as the United States are having an increasingly difficult time generating an internal consensus on these issues. Conservatism of evolution argues against trying to generate national-level consensus where it is not needed.

Network commonwealths may emerge more quickly than might be supposed.

The World Wide Web was created by a few people and offered as a voluntary standard that anybody could copy and adopt without charge. Nobody forced anybody to use it. No government or United Nations organization promoted its use—yet it spread around the world at the speed of light and created a global network for sharing information within a year. The political opportunity of the Singularity revolutions is the creation of analogues of the Web protocols in other areas. This will allow the civic states arising from the wreckage of the economic structures of the Machine Age to reassemble themselves in new forms according to the network paradigm. Network commonwealth mechanisms can be the equivalent of the protocols that allowed the Internet and World Wide Web to emerge.

POLITICAL SELF-ASSEMBLY PROTOCOLS:
A TOOL FOR THE SINGULARITY REVOLUTION

The network commonwealth is a means of linking together political units, at both the national and subnational level, to facilitate deep cooperation among peoples with substantial linguistic, cultural, and institutional commonalties. It differs from previous attempts at supernational organization in that it concentrates on interchange at the informational level in a tightly-linked informational space. Its goals are flow of informational products, software, and people at the most direct level possible, bypassing the gatekeeper institutions of the past. The mechanisms of the network commonwealth are familiar: trade agreements, immigration agreements, and security alliances.

The new focus is on information, taking advantage of a growing phenomenon not yet widely understood: the growing convergence within the network civilizations now emerging and the potential for a new awareness of a supernational community based on deep commonalties. The network commonwealth is based on a further evolution of existing forms of linkage to serve broader purposes, and with a stronger set of mutual shared values. Although the structures may reflect the predecessor forms such as NATO and NAFTA, they differ not only in elaboration but also in the generation of a shared narrative among their member peoples.

The network commonwealth takes its name both from the information network that enables it and the network paradigm that replaces the fading modernist machine paradigm as our tool for understanding and dealing with reality. The network commonwealth is not a nation-state of the historical type. It is not a state at all, although it has the potential to offer an alternative means for fulfilling some traditional functions of economic states. It is a means of linking smaller political communities so that they can deal with common concerns. It is a way to provide opportunities to the members of those communities—opportunities that cannot be provided by small, independent sovereignties, and for which economic states and empires exact too high a price.

The network commonwealth should learn from and imitate the successes of multinational communities such as the EU and, in a different realm, NATO, while seeking to avoid their errors. The EU has been a resounding success in increasing the effective freedom of Continental Europeans in many ways. It has abolished state monopolies, opened protected markets, and has greatly increased the average European's freedom to travel, reside, work, and compete throughout its territory. Most important, it has served to keep many of its politically more marginal members, such as Spain, Portugal, and Greece, from backsliding into dictatorship—creating an incentive for shaky Eastern European and Mediterranean democracies to join.

At the same time—and with almost uniformly disastrous results—by trying to be a larger, federal-state-like entity, the EU has increased the amount of bureaucracy, planning, and intervention in many areas of life. Additionally, it has replaced some of the barriers with which small states attempt to insulate themselves from economic reality with larger, Union-wide barriers such as customs tariffs, quotas, and subsidy programs, which have the same equally futile goal in the world economy. At its worst, the EU is a backward-looking mechanism that seeks to maintain an already strained entitlement-based and dirigiste political and social model at the expense of its youth and the generations to come. It will find itself under ever-increasing pressure in the decades to come because of these weaknesses.

A network commonwealth would resemble the EU in promoting free movement of people, ideas, and capital throughout its internal area. It would seek to promote cooperation in all areas where existing commonalties permit greater cooperation between similar cultures. It would seek, as far as possible, to create a common economic, informational, and residency space for the citizens of its member nations. It would differ from the EU in not attempting to dictate the social policies of its member nations, not attempting to relocate executive agency power in community-wide bodies, and not maintaining large cross-community subsidies to help member governments resist needed restructuring.

"Harmonization" campaigns would be minimal or entirely unnecessary because the economic, legal, and social systems of the candidate nations for a network commonwealth typically are already far more harmonized than were the EU member-states before harmonization. A community focused on trade in information-based products and services needs fewer common standards, many of which are already in place.

Language is the most important standard for an information-based economy.

Given the emergence of transmission control protocol/Internet protocol (TCP/IP) as the universal standard for Internet communications, and of hypertext markup language (HTML) as the document standard (both of which were accomplished without international governmental mandates), it is not clear that any further harmonization is needed at all. Each of the member nations can happily maintain its current standards for wall plugs, paper, telephone jacks, or whatever, as the continued evolution of manufacturing toward computer-aided systems, and the consequent versatility of production means that many goods will increasingly be manufactured in multiple versions to satisfy local standards anyway. For this reason the benefits of harmonization in physical-goods standards are beginning to diminish relative to their costs of implementation. The network commonwealth would consist of overlapping sets of institutions, alliances, agreements, and standards aimed primarily at easing and facilitating the interchange of information and information-related goods and services among political communities. These communities would be linked by bonds of language, customs, attitudes, practices, and human relationships, and aiding in the defense and security of those member communities. It would affirm those special links and ties without denying others that some communities might have with other networks. In fact, metaconnections between networks will be an essential feature of the network commonwealth world.

Arrangements might include trade agreements, especially in informational goods and services; agreements permitting citizens of commonwealth members to travel, visit, study, work, and immigrate freely; and the development of common political institutions. Network commonwealths may also form the main armature of permanent security alliances.

A CALL FOR CIVILIZATIONAL CONSTRUCTION

The Singularity will require a great deal of flexibility from society in response to new technologies and the unprecedented individual and social options they will present. The history of the developed world since the onset of the Scientific-Technological Revolution has been a matter of searching for a new equilibrium following the creative destruction of the old order. From the moment the cannons of the centralizing monarchs of the Renaissance destroyed the castles of the feudal lords, to the contemporary cry of the various monopolists discomfited by the Internet, we have seen the recurrent but futile desire to ensure that the new technologies do not disrupt the existing social order. The world of the Singularity will be another forum for this contest.

This time, however, we may be able to avoid, after such bitter experience, the utopian temptation, and construct an adapted civilization firmly on the roots of the strong civil society we have inherited. The twentieth century brought many failed attempts at utopian social construction; we live yet among their ruins. It also brought many attempts to reinstitute the values of previous eras or (in many cases) imagined versions of previous eras. None of these returns to the past were ultimately successful, although new generations often look back to previous generations' revivals as nostalgic models. Thus, the Eisenhower era's rather timid attempts to reconstruct earlier American eras have themselves become an object of nostalgia.

In the following chapters, I will discuss the Anglosphere and its relation to the characteristics of the strong civil society that will form the basis of whatever solutions emerge to the challenges of the Singularity. I will discuss the need for an Anglosphere network commonwealth as a response to these challenges. It must be clear that this is not a nostalgic call for restoration of old forms. Nor is it a call for a conservative opposition to social change. On the contrary, it is a call for civilizational construction on a new, non-utopian basis. It demands that we repair the roots of civil society where they have been eroded. It calls for the construction of civic states to replace the failing institutions of the economic state. It requires civilizational self-awareness, not to create a new civilization but to see and accept the reality of what is already emerging.

These tasks will no doubt seem tame to those who long for exotic and wholly novel forms of human society. However, the construction of a civilization that can lead humankind through the challenges of the Singularity without repeating the disasters of the twentieth century is not a trivial piece of work. It is a task that will fully occupy even a young person facing a very long lifetime. For those whose lives have been occupied with preventing or repairing the disasters of failed utopian visions, the turn to construction, and away from opposition or remediation, will require a major change of mentality. Above all, it requires in young and old alike the recovery of self-assurance. It requires us to understand that we are the standard-bearers of a civilization that has defeated much evil (including that generated by our own wrong decisions) and now stands poised to lead us, step by step, through the travails of yet more change, to the stars.

2

The Anglosphere
and Its Revolutions

It was far less its Parliament, its liberty, its publicity, its jury, which in fact rendered the England of that date so unlike the rest of Europe than a feature still more exclusive and more powerful. England was the only country in which the system of caste had not been changed but effectively destroyed. The nobles and the middle class in England followed together the same courses of business, entered the same professions, and what is much more significant, intermarried.

—Alexis de Tocqueville, *L'Ancien Régime*

Increasingly during the past few centuries, the English-speaking world has been the pathfinder for all of humanity. English-speaking civilization generated the first modern nation-state, the first liberal democratic state, the first large secular republic, and the first industrialized society, and is now generating the first information economy. It will be the heart of the Singularity revolutions. As the network commonwealth becomes the characteristic political form of the emerging era, it will probably emerge first in the Anglosphere.

I say this not so that we can feel good about ourselves, but to be realistic. Being the pathfinder also means experiencing the problems of the new era first, problems often traumatic and without obvious solution. Like most new political developments, the network commonwealth will probably arise from crisis. Other nations may watch our crisis, and because it is not yet upon them, think that the ways in which their own societies differ from ours will save them from such problems. They will be wrong.

Already, the social democracies of Continental Europe are trying to respond to the threatened collapse of their Industrial Era institutions. Unfortunately, their attempted solution is to strengthen the very features that are causing the collapse.

Some crony capitalists in East Asia similarly hope to preserve their collapsing systems by blaming outsiders and resisting reforms. They too are fooling themselves.

Other nations will benefit by watching and learning from our experiences.

To deny that such change may come to them, willingly or not, is self-deception.

The Anglosphere is serving as the mine canary for the world in these things. What hits us first will likely hit others as well.

Throughout the Anglosphere, politicians are placing their hopes in various supranational blocks, such as North Atlantic Free Trade Agreement (NAFTA) or the European Union (EU), seeking to join geographic neighbors. These are of limited value at best, and at worst do harm when they attempt to homogenize nations with substantially different characteristics.

The Anglosphere has the potential to generate a more real, vital, and ultimately more useful common political, economic, and defense structure than any geographically defined region.

The Anglosphere is an emerging network civilization out of which such a structure—a network commonwealth—could emerge. The various nations of the Anglosphere had been growing apart in terms of self-awareness, national feeling, and political ties for the past two centuries. However, the coming together of people speaking common tongues in communication space is now causing the tide to flow the other way. What is sometimes described as a flood of "American" popular culture, is in reality something much more complex—a multidirectional cross-current.

We have always had a lot in common—and the common parts are growing. A network commonwealth for the English-speaking nations would draw on the shared deep values of Anglo-American constitutional, legal, cultural, and political traditions.

People are already asking whether political entities based on geographical proximity and trade in physical goods—the EU, a NAFTA expanding only into Latin America, or proposed Asian affiliations for Australia and New Zealand—are the most useful or desirable of unions.

When agricultural produce and manufactured goods were the most important objects of international trade, a common trade area including, say, Canada, Australia, and the United States would have been of limited interest. Many of Canada's and Australia's products—cattle, sheep, wheat, timber, ore—competed with U.S. exports, while their principal customers lay elsewhere. Furthermore, the amount of cultural common ground needed to sell wheat or iron ore is minimal.

The degree to which cultural commonality improves the chance of marketing such goods is similarly minimal. The campaign by some Australians to reidentify their country as "Asian," to take a case in point, is therefore futile. Worse yet, it is silly. Even if Australians were, en masse, to memorize the Analects of Confucius and adopt rice as their principal dietary item, it wouldn't raise or lower the price of the iron ore they sell to Asians by even a penny a ton. The goods that will count in the future will be such things as value-added information content, applications software, advanced technical designs incorporated into computerized manufacturing instructions, and sophisticated entertainment. These are culturally dependent to a much greater degree and are products on which companies from English-speaking cultures can collaborate more readily than companies from diverse civilizations.

Our explorations of civil-society characteristics—trust and openness—as attributes of a civilization can provide some clues to why the English-speaking nations have established and maintained a leadership position in so many areas.

They help explain why the gap between English-speaking nations and others seems to be widening, rather than narrowing, in recent times. The Anglosphere's leadership in the political, economic, industrial, and information realms appears to be a product of a set of characteristics variously described as high trust, or civil-society attributes. Over the past few decades, historians such as William McNeill, David Landes, William Sowell, and David Gress have been generating what has broadly been called a "macrohistorical" analysis. This analysis blends history, economics, and anthropology to generate a long-term, broad-perspective view of history seeking to explain "how the West grew rich" and "the causes of the wealth and poverty of nations," to borrow from the titles of some of their books.

This body of work offers a better explanation of who we are and how we got this way than the Marxist, multiculturalist, declinist, or race-gender analysis explanations which have been popular in academia during recent decades. It presents a picture of particular areas of the globe developing, through particular circumstances, characteristics that set them on a path to increasing prosperity and freedom. It correctly attributes to the workings of social evolution what scholars in past eras had mistakenly attributed to religion or race. These developments of social evolution created a virtuous circle—each development made further advances possible, and each advance set those societies further apart from those around them that failed to develop such characteristics. It also shows that many societies began to develop such characteristics but, through historical circumstances, short-circuited that development and slipped back into poverty and despotism.

England, because of its position offshore from the European continent, was able to avoid enough of the pitfalls (particularly those of domination by a garrison state) and retain its advantageous developments while others lost theirs. England maintained these advances while spreading its social template widely around the globe. As a result of these developments, English-speaking civilization became the only high-trust one to become an open-template civilization also. Its high-trust characteristics made it richer and freer than most around it. Its openness and template characteristics allowed it to draw people from cultures around the globe, give them the ability to liberate their talents and energies, and create the critical mass of population needed for economic, political, and military leadership on the planet.

Britain in the nineteenth century, and America in the twentieth, exercised this leadership. It is possible that, by creating a network commonwealth, the emerging English-speaking network civilization could exercise leadership through the twenty-first—the Anglosphere Century. This, in short, is what is at stake.

Past narratives have hindered understanding. Their creators' social and political agendas led them to emphasize irrelevant or surface characteristics and to misunderstand the underlying causes of wealth versus poverty, and freedom versus despotism. Sociologist Max Weber popularized the term "Protestant work ethic," but Protestantism (more specifically Calvinism) may have been as much effect as cause. The growth of high-trust civil societies in pre-Reformation Germany, the Netherlands, and England created strains within the church-state relationship inherited from the late Middle Ages, even though this relationship was what allowed the emergence of civil society in the first place. The split of society into church-ruled and state-ruled spheres created enough free space between the two that individuals began to attain some autonomy. Church-related but lay-run voluntary devotional and mutual aid societies became the seeds of the independent organizations of civil society.

Ultimately, the growth of this independent sector of society, one ill-served both by the feudal legal system and by the anticommerce attitudes of the Church, created the pressures leading to the Reformation and the emergence of the nation-state.

Many, but not all, of the emerging high-trust societies embraced Protestantism.

In doing so, they identified Protestantism with freedom and prosperity.

In the era of religious sectarian strife, English Whig historians associated high-trust values with Protestantism and low-trust values with Catholicism, and identified English and Scottish Protestantism as a source of freedom and prosperity. (The "Orange Toast" of Ulster Protestants identified "brass money and wooden shoes"—symbols of inflation and poverty—as the fate from which William of Orange saved them in prevailing over Catholicism in 1689.) Yet Catholic societies such as northern Italy and Austria displayed high-trust characteristics. Japan, never Christian, also developed a unique high-trust civilization. This misidentification of Catholicism with low-trust societies per se reinforced Catholic disenfranchisement in the United Kingdom until the 1830s. This failure hindered the integration of Ireland into that union, and thereby began the process of unraveling it. It similarly led to anti-immigrant movements in the United States in the mid-nineteenth century that likewise hindered the assimilation of Catholic immigrants, fortunately not permanently.

In the same manner, the growth of modernist scientific narratives in the late nineteenth century led to bogus analogies between social and biological evolution, and misunderstood biological evolution as well. These misunderstandings led to the idea that the characteristics of Anglosphere civilization were innate and genetic. This narrative held that there was an "Anglo-Saxon race" which had somehow retained its genetic purity throughout the centuries since Hengist and Horsa landed on the Saxon shore, and was passed on to America and Australia as well. A religious offshoot of this doctrine held that the Anglo-Saxons were a lost tribe of Israel and therefore God's true chosen people, a doctrine that survives today in the "Identity Christianity" movement.

These doctrines precisely invert reality. The strength of Anglosphere culture has been its ability to serve as a high-trust template that immigrants over the centuries have been able to adopt. This enabled them to become increasingly empowered members of society. This ability has allowed first Britain, and later the English-speaking nations of North America and Australasia, to grow rapidly and gather in the talents of capable individuals of all races and cultures. There are two essential parts to this process: the willingness of the host society to offer the template and the willingness of immigrants to accept it.

Where the high-trust template was imposed on an unwilling society, as in the case of a colonial regime, it seldom worked as well. Only a minority of the colonized people adopted the template willingly or wholeheartedly. The colonizing power usually preached the virtue of its customs and institutions but withheld full membership and acceptance from the colonized individual who adopted those values.

Where the society was marked by slavery, as in the American South or the West Indies, there were similar barriers to acceptance for the slaves after emancipation.

The Anglosphere has been strongest when and where the high-trust template has been allowed to operate most freely. This ability has often been undermined at different periods of Anglosphere history by nativist, racial, and religious prejudices. Only by appeal to core Anglosphere values, as was done by Frederick Douglass and Martin Luther King Jr., have these prejudices been defeated.

Most recently, the multiculturalist ideology, in attacking the assimilationist paradigm, has worked to deny the immigrant from low-trust societies the means of adapting to the demands of life in a high-trust civil society as anything but a menial laborer, a government transfers recipient, or a gangster. The problems posed by the existence of large numbers of immigrants and internal minorities within the Anglosphere include poverty, crime, alienation, and other attributes of low-trust cultures. The solutions lie in bringing such people into the circle of trust and the web of associations of a strong civil society, from which they are now wholly or partly excluded.

THE ANGLOSPHERE AND THE NEW UNDERSTANDING OF THE WEST

The experience of Eastern Europe and the former Soviet states since the fall of the Berlin Wall has driven home the fact that market-economy formulas cannot be merely dropped into societies like airlifted famine rations. In countries where civil-society institutions were once strong, they are blooming again. Where they were weak or nonexistent, the societies have remained mired in poverty and corruption.

Within that understanding, attention is now focusing on the particular role of English-speaking societies in creating the strongest, freest, and therefore most advanced of civil societies in early modern Europe. The role of Britain as the cradle of both the Industrial Revolution and parliamentary democracy is no longer understood as a fluke of history—it is understood as the logical consequence of the strong institutions of British civil society built over the preceding two centuries.

Most Western European societies had medieval parliaments and chartered companies of merchants. Why did England's Parliament rise to challenge the power of the Crown while its Continental counterparts shriveled into impotence?

Why did English law develop and retain institutions for resisting the arbitrary power of state over citizen, such as habeas corpus, presumption of innocence, and jury trials?

Why did English corporations transform themselves into flexible instruments for raising private capital and investing it in progressive enterprises, while their Continental counterparts often degenerated into instruments for collection of state-guaranteed monopoly rents? The answers are to be found in the strength and independence of English civil society.

Similarly, America is no longer seen as a new nation that sprang, like Athena fully formed from the head of Zeus, into the world in 1776. Nor is its Constitution understood as something created out of the imaginations of a group of big brains gathered in Philadelphia in an act of political creation science. A new appreciation is emerging of how deeply rooted most things American are in this particularly British (and primarily English) development of civil society. Similarly, the American Constitution is properly seen as the evolutionary product of the British Whig political tradition. This appreciation began perhaps with Alan Macfarlane's *The Origins of English Individualism* (1978). Macfarlane offers fascinating evidence that the classic characteristics of individualism—"bourgeois" nuclear families, individual rather than family landholdings, and geographic mobility—were characteristic of much of English life as early as the fourteenth century, in contrast to Continental Europe. This stands conventional history on its head. Such "modern" social characteristics were long imagined to be effects of the Industrial Revolution, and they clearly followed industrialization on the continent. Yet these characteristics also just as clearly preceded it in England. This is an important demonstration of the already-emerging distinctness of English-speaking civilization. It furthermore carries the intriguing suggestion that these social characteristics, rather than being effects of industrialization, may in fact have caused it. Perhaps, rather than the English being individualistic because they industrialized early, it happened that the English started the Industrial Revolution because they had already become individualistic.

But was English exceptionalism (the idea that England was more distinct from Continental nations than they were from each other) also the direct source of Anglosphere and above all, American exceptionalism? David Hackett Fischer's *Albion's Seed* (1991) suggests that it is, and strongly so. Fischer demonstrated the depth and persistence of British Isles cultural roots in America's development. His book particularly highlights the importance of understanding the different regions' cultural, linguistic, and religious traditions in the British Isles and their enduring role in establishing American regional cultures. Kevin Phillips's *The Cousins' Wars: Religion, Politics, and the Triumph of Anglo-America* (2000) advances and elaborates on this understanding. Underneath these regional differences, however, Britain and the other English-speaking nations have shared several fundamental characteristics, discussed below.

Ambivalence toward the Continental European Concept of the Nation-State

Classic nation-state theory holds that nation-states unite all members of any particular ethnolinguistic group in a single state entity. Yet the modern world includes a large number of English-speaking nations with healthy national identities, none of which have any great desire to become part of any other one. This is an anomaly that has been glossed over or defined away by proponents of Herderian-style blood-and-soil nation-states. (It disappears, however, if one views the civic state as the appropriate form of the Anglosphere.)

Looking more closely at our history, we see that the English-speaking world was only unified in a single state between 1707 and 1776—a mere sixty-nine years. (Not counting the transitory, isolated, and ultimately rejected episode of Oliver Cromwell's commonwealth.) I discuss why this has been so in the section "Five Civil Wars: Union and Secession in the Anglosphere."

Great Fluidity in Composing and Decomposing
States within and from Anglosphere Components

It was not decided until late in the day that New Zealand would not be part of the Australian confederation, and that Western Australia would be; Newfoundland became Canadian only fifty years ago, and very casually at that. The Southern states quickly constructed a functioning apparatus for the Confederacy in 1861, as did the Irish for their nation in 1921. Such fluidity is not exactly consistent with the idea of the state as the fundamental expression of a national essence.

Divergence and Reconvergence

George Bernard Shaw famously held that America and Britain were two countries separated by a common language.

Even fifty years ago, American and British English seemed to be on the road to becoming two separate languages; Australian probably a third. Today, culture and language are reconverging because of the modern media, and the Internet and World Wide Web will greatly increase this tendency. I discuss this further in the next section.

A Common Legal and Constitutional Tradition

The United States and the Commonwealth countries appear to have substantially different constitutions.

The United States has its division of powers, and the United Kingdom has fused powers. The United States has entrenched constitutional rights and judicial review, while the United Kingdom reveres parliamentary supremacy.

The United States has an independent, elected president, whereas the Commonwealth countries have parliamentary-selected prime ministers and ceremonial heads of state, most commonly a monarchy. However, as with related species, the superficial differences disguise a deep commonalty of cultural roots. All Anglosphere countries base their law and court procedures on the common law. Any person with a business or personal issue in another Anglosphere country already knows most of what he needs to know about the legal system of that country to deal with legal counsel and assess the situation. In comparison, a legal process in the Roman law tradition of the continent, not to mention an Islamic or Chinese proceeding, is totally alien.

Exceptionalism

As discussed earlier, both England and America have demonstrated a particular thread of exceptionalism which emerges again and again in their history. Since the advent of the Puritans, America has been the "City on a Hill," serving as a light unto the world. England has been "The New Jerusalem," in William Blake's words. Although this exceptionalism is deemed to have religious origins, Macfarlane and others have documented a general sense of English exceptionalism, a feeling that the island was freer than the continent, dating back long before the Reformation. We must at least consider the possibility that the religious expressions of English and American exceptionalism were attempts to give theological significance to an already observable sociological difference. Anglosphere exceptionalism, in contrast, seeks to understand a sociological reality that is not only perceivable empirically, as centuries of English speakers have intuited, but now demonstrable statistically. Put another way, the remarkably persistent tendency of the Anglosphere nations to cluster in most statistical treatments of the world's societies is a data set that in any other science would demand explanation.

That current political theory ignores or even denigrates the mere mention of such correspondences is a distortion of almost Lysenkoan proportions.

RECONVERGENCE AND CULTURE: WHY THE INFORMATION REVOLUTION IS DRAWING THE ANGLOSPHERE CLOSER TOGETHER

Reconvergence is an effect of the Information Revolution. Since America's secession from the British Empire, nationalist commentators on both sides of the Atlantic have consciously or unconsciously stuck to a script suggested by the evolution of Latin into the various Romance languages. American, by this script, would eventually become a separate language, as it and British English increasingly diverged. Later, this model was applied to the various colonial forms of English as well. The development of various pidgins and creoles in places such as Sierra Leone and New Guinea seemed to validate this model, as did cases from other European languages of settlement. One colonial European language, South African Dutch, was codified into a new language, Afrikaans, in the nineteenth century. Recently, attempts have been made to codify Quebec's French into a separate language with its own orthography.

But the divergence of the Latin languages required a thousand years and a Dark Age, with its deterioration of communications and transportation. The Afrikaner seed population was dumped in South Africa and subsequently isolated and ignored, as were, to a lesser extent, the ancestors of the Quebecois in Canada. English speakers in the colonies of settlement, by contrast, remained in constant communication with the metropolis and were supported by additional immigration throughout their history. And this communication became drastically improved from the nineteenth century on.

Steamships and telegraphs brought news, mail, books, and visitors across the Atlantic and Pacific in ever-increasing numbers. At first, new media such as the mass popular press, cinema, and radio seemed to confirm divergence. The United States and Britain developed their own distinct film industries, each with a distinct national voice. Each English-speaking nation developed its own mass periodicals and radio broadcast system, so that each nation became a distinct informational space.

Each generation began to experience national events through shared media experiences. Every Briton's experience of World War II included the BBC broadcasts of Winston Churchill. Every American alive on December 7, 1941, remembered not only the news of Pearl Harbor but specifically the network coverage of the event and the subsequent coverage of Roosevelt's "Day of Infamy" speech. Mass media changed professional sports from local events into national dramas. Every American baseball fan remembered the classic World Series games and the network sports announcers; every Canadian hockey fan followed the Stanley Cup playoffs and the CBC's "Hockey Night in Canada"; and every English soccer fan watched the winning of the World Cup. The development of nation-specific informational watershed events seemed to confirm divergence.

At the same time, however, the Anglosphere nations were transcending boundaries.

British and Commonwealth audiences began to hear American voices, once rare, as the talking pictures began to be exported. A lesser, but still significant, number of British films began to reach American audiences. World War I brought Commonwealth troops through England in great numbers. Many Anglo-Canadian and Anglo-Australian marriages resulted from that intermingling. World War II brought more Commonwealth troops, but also this time vast numbers of ordinary American draftees, flooding Britain, providing an instantaneous and dramatic lesson in the differences and similarities of the two nations. Although much friction resulted from this sudden and unprepared mixing, much warmth and lasting friendship did as well, including some 50,000 marriages. Popular films such as *Yanks, Hope, and Glory*, and *Hanover Street* recall the real drama of the sudden, literal reconvergence of ordinary, rather than elite, English speakers.

Subsequently, the mingling of Anglosphere peoples accelerated. By the 1960s, the popular music of Britain, the United States, and other Anglosphere nations had fused dramatically, resulting in the creation of an ongoing shared popular music space. Television and cinema became even more intermingled, as more U.S. programs were aired on prime-time British television, while the American PBS network sometimes seemed little more than a rebroadcasting facility for the BBC.

By the late 1960s, decreasing jet-travel prices began to tie the Anglosphere together in terms of personal space as well, as students and retirees joined businessmen and military personnel in frequent travel. Increasingly, English speakers began to view postings to other Anglosphere nations as not much more wrenching than a domestic transfer. Differences between the Anglosphere nations are becoming perceived as akin to regional differences within the nations, rather than fundamental differences, particularly as globalization also exposes people to startlingly different cultures. An American World War II conscript fresh out of Iowa might well have perceived England as a profoundly different place from home; today's American businessman coming back from Asia or the Middle East arrives at Heathrow or Kingford Smith feeling almost home. A few years across the Atlantic or Pacific has become part of many people's lives, and the relationships formed from those sojourns (more and more of them marriages) became ever-easier to maintain, thanks to cheap vacation travel, inexpensive overseas calls, and, now most important, the advent of the Internet.

The arts and letters of the English-speaking world, particularly at the popular level, are again converging after a long history of divergence. Popular entertainment was once highly country-specific. Now, popular music venues present performers and groups from the United Kingdom, Jamaica, Ireland, the United States, Canada, and Australia with equal enthusiasm. Films from Australia and New Zealand have begun to reach the international art circuits. Not long ago Disney felt it necessary to Americanize Christopher Robin in their cartoon series derived from *Winnie the Pooh*; today the Australian setting and character of the Wiggles, or the Koala Brothers cartoons are considered part of their charm. (A year ago only a handful of Americans could tell you what or when Australia Day was; now, thanks to the latter series, millions of five-year-olds could tell you.)

The rise of the Internet and the World Wide Web, the transition from broadcasting to narrowcasting, and the associated disintermediation of the communications industries will all accelerate the reconvergence of the Anglosphere into a common informational space. Until the advent of the Web, young Britons or Americans were still exposed to a nationally distinct mix of media. Even when they might watch each others' programs, they would be limited to the British programs chosen by American networks, or vice versa.

Within a few years, however, the Web will be the primary and universally available distribution channel for information and entertainment in the English-speaking world—and it will be fully interactive. The youth of the Anglosphere will be accustomed to drawing information and entertainment from throughout their common informational space, with less and less discrimination as to national source. Although this will increase the awareness of national differences among the Anglosphere nations, it will also put them in a more accurate perspective as people become more familiar with the thoughts and perspectives of more alien cultures. Immersion into multiplayer online games, interest groups, and other collaborative activities will give them experience in cooperation with other Anglosphereans. They will instinctively develop an appreciation for one of the main points of this book, the increased possibility for deep cooperation among persons sharing common linguistic and cultural assumptions. Childhood friendships influence educational and marriage choices, and these choices in turn influence subsequent choices of occupation, residence, and business collaboration.

As the first Internet generation reaches adulthood, the frequency of international educational, marriage, and employment choices will greatly increase. It is also likely that the majority of those choices will be intra-Anglosphere rather than translinguistic. The pan-Anglosphere ties advocated in this work—the "sojourner" provisions allowing residence and work, the provisions for easier pan-Anglosphere contract adjudication, and the general lowering of barriers to deep collaboration across the Anglosphere—will probably meet a demand that is already being generated. The sooner these arrangements are concluded, the greater the benefits that will accrue to the nations that make it happen and to their citizens.

In keeping with this trend, it is interesting to note the frequency with which intra-Anglosphere romances are represented in film and television as unremarkable.

Once, any romance between, for example, a British and an American character was treated as an exotic event, and the Anglo-American differences would be the center of the plot. Today, by contrast, Anglo-American relationships are presented almost without comment in films such as *Four Weddings and a Funeral, Nine Months, L.A. Story, Good Will Hunting, Sliding Doors, The Horse Whisperer, Mickey Blue Eyes,* and *Notting Hill,* and in television programs such as *Friends.*

The emphasis is on the particular personality interplay between the characters, with the transatlantic differences reduced to background color, plot devices primarily related to the obstacle of distance, or minor comic relief. Romances between English speakers and true foreigners, in contrast, still portray cultural differences as a principal issue between the couple, as in *French Kiss* or *Green Card,* for example.

In *Sliding Doors,* Gwyneth Paltrow, an American actress, was chosen to play an Englishwoman in a relationship with an Englishman in London, played by an English actor, whose character has an affair with an American woman played by an American actress. Yet the Americanness of his partner is not in any way an issue in the plot; she could just as well have been a Briton, just as Paltrow's character could easily have been made an American. The fact that this fungibility of Anglosphereans does not come from any Anglosphere consciousness among screenwriters or media executives, but is instead a product of the desire to draw on actors from any English-speaking nation interchangeably for casting convenience, is to my mind evidence of the strength of the trend. The film industry has spontaneously created a unified economic space in spite of obstacles (visa requirements, tax codes, and so on) placed in its way by governments. This leads to the question of how vigorous the common economic space would be if these obstacles were removed.

The reconvergence of the English-speaking cultural world is bound to have an effect on the political world as well. The EU spends substantial funds on programs to build feelings of commonality among its member citizens, yet young Britons find American, Canadian, and other Anglosphere destinations equally interesting and desirable, even though no programs exist to encourage those feelings.

These trends are likely to continue. As they continue, and accelerate, the common understandings generated will create a fertile ground for the practical political steps to encourage free movement of people, funds, ideas, and information.

WHAT IS THE ANGLOSPHERE?

The Anglosphere is more than the sum of all persons who have learned the English language. To be part of the Anglosphere implies the sharing of fundamental customs and values at the core of English-speaking cultures: individualism; rule of law; honoring of covenants; in general, the high-trust characteristics described by Francis Fukuyama in *Trust: The Social Virtues and the Creation of Prosperity*; and the emphasis on freedom as a political and cultural value. The Anglosphere shares a narrative in which the Magna Carta, Bill of Rights, trial by jury, "innocent until proven guilty," "a man's home is his castle," and "a man's word is his bond" are common themes. Two persons communicating in English but sharing the narrative and assumptions of a different civilization are not necessarily a part of the Anglosphere, unless their values have also been affected by the core values of English-speaking civilization.

An interesting characterization of the Anglosphere can be derived from the comments of French foreign minister Hubert Védrine in his book *Les Cartes de la France à l'heure de la mondialisation*, where he defined the following list of attitudes as "un-European": "ultraliberal market economy, rejection of the state, nonrepublican individualism, strengthening of the universal and 'indispensable' role of the United States, common law, Anglophone, and Protestant rather than Catholic concepts." It's clear that the word M. Védrine is searching for is "Anglospheric."

The Anglosphere, as a network civilization without a corresponding political form, has necessarily imprecise boundaries. Geographically, the densest nodes of the Anglosphere are found in the United States and the United Kingdom. English-speaking Canada, Australia, New Zealand, Ireland, and English-speaking South Africa are also significant populations. The English-speaking Caribbean, English-speaking Oceania, and the English-speaking educated populations in Africa and India constitute other important nodes.

One way to visualize the Anglosphere is as concentric spheres marked by differing degrees of sharing of the core Anglosphere characteristics. The innermost spheres are in the nations populated by native or assimilated-immigrant English speakers speaking the language at home, at work, and in government and naturally immersed in English-language media. The nations where all these elements are present are at the heart of the Anglosphere. Where any are present, the people are part of the Anglosphere.

Network civilizations are porous, imprecise, and interpenetrable. A city, region, or state can occupy a position in more than one linguistic area, and may become a member of more than one network commonwealth, but it will have to give one commonwealth's metarules priority. Here is a rough anatomy of the Anglosphere:

Innermost: states with an entirely or predominantly English-speaking population, where English is the primary or sole home language. They develop a legal system based on common law, with trial by jury. There is representative government, and the news and entertainment media are primarily in English, sharing information with the rest of the Anglosphere. This core group includes the United States, the United Kingdom, Ireland, Australia, New Zealand, English-speaking Canada, and the English-speaking Caribbean, along with assorted small islands and territories. Areas with other official languages and/or legal systems, such as Quebec, Puerto Rico, and Wales, are seen as exceptions, as they are geographically discrete subunits.

Middle: English-dominant states. These are states in which English is one of several official languages and is one of the principal languages of government administration and commerce. Significant daily media are presented locally in English, but other languages are important. English is a minority as a home language and is confined primarily to an educated elite and perhaps an urban middle and industrial class. These are placed in a more inward circle when the country is not part of a larger, non-English world civilization; in other words, one where the primary connections to the outside world are in English.

South Africa is on the borderline between the Inner Sphere and the Middle, because of its substantial, but not majority, population of first-language English speakers.

English speakers in South Africa are essentially part of the Anglosphere; Afrikaan speakers are not. Additionally, South Africa's retention of Roman-Dutch law keeps it outside the inner circle of the Anglosphere in an important dimension. Beyond South Africa and Zimbabwe, the non-Islamic, non-Indian former colonies of England in Africa, the South Pacific, and some parts of Asia are perhaps the primary examples; the Philippines might also be considered borderline.

Outer: English-using states of other civilizations. (Typically, these states have been the core of their own linguistic-cultural sphere; their Anglosphere affiliations are secondary, although often important commercially.) These consist of nations that use English as a governmental or commercial language and have significant local media in English, but use other languages in official communications, business, and media as well and identify themselves with another major world-civilization tradition. India, Pakistan, the Arab states formerly under British control, and the Islamic former colonies of Britain (Malaysia, African states) are all examples of such states. Israel is a special case, because it is the focal point of a wider relationship between the Jewish diaspora and the Anglosphere, but it probably fits better in this category than any other.

Periphery: States that use English as a language of wider communication. These include ones in which knowledge of English is widespread and English is the principal second language of the nation but is not official. These include Northern Europe, East Asia (particularly Japan, Taiwan, South Korea, and Southeast Asia), and northern Latin America. Southern Europe, Eastern Europe, and southern Latin America are moving in this direction as well, as French, German, and Russian lose their position as the principal second languages of those areas.

THE FUNDAMENTAL STRUCTURES OF THE ANGLOSPHERE: STATES, REGIONS, AND CULTURAL NATIONS

Traditionally, even those accustomed to thinking about the English-speaking world as an entity with its own reality have tended to accept that its fundamental components are the current nation-state divisions—the United States, the United Kingdom, Canada, Australia, and so on. Those with a little more sophistication may see the separate nations of Britain—England, Scotland, and Wales—as fundamental units instead of the U.K. itself. In the era now closing, in which economic states were the principal actors, this view made sense. In the era now emerging, it is worth looking at the units that may form the emerging coherent civic states. Doing so will help us understand both the structure of the Anglosphere and the role these units may play in the decomposition of the economic state structures and the emergence of network commonwealths.

In traditional preindustrial economies distinct regions were quite small and discrete. Each county of the nations of Britain formed a coherent region with its own dialect, folkways, customary legal system, local elite, and identity. These grew out of the particular geographic and ecological characteristics of the area, which in turn influenced the economic base of the region. Waves of invasion and immigration completed the complex pattern, as each corner of the British Isles experienced a different proportion of Celtic, Anglo-Saxon, Viking, and Norman settlement and influence. In the centuries leading up to the Norman conquest of England in 1066, the local fiefdoms and principalities coalesced into several kingdoms, of which England was the richest and most coherent. The Normans introduced parts of the Continental feudal system into England, Wales, and Ireland by conquest, and to lowland Scotland by influence. However, local life remained strongly autonomous; English law was not consolidated into a kingdomwide common system until the fifteenth century.

When British settlement of the Caribbean and North America began in the late sixteenth and early seventeenth centuries, the original seed populations of the colonies were drawn from strongly distinct regional cultures. Each of these seed populations became the foundation of a strongly distinct regional culture in the New World, as meticulously documented in Fischer's *Albion's Seed*. The East Anglian Puritans founded New England, the Northern English Quakers from Yorkshire and Lancashire founded Pennsylvania, the Sussex Cavalier landholders founded Virginia, and the border population of the violent Anglo-Scottish frontier populated first Northern Ireland and then, a few generations later, the Appalachian highlands of America. Each of these seed populations grew, adapted to American conditions, and was joined by immigrants who tended to settle among like-minded hosts.

CULTURAL NATIONS—
THE INVISIBLE UNDERSTRUCTURE

Historical linguists, tracking the spread of regional dialects across North America, have long been aware of the existence of major population streams that remained distinct in the movement west across the American continent. These created major population groupings with a clear correspondence to the four regional groups described by Fischer. In discussing these groupings, I have described them as *cultural nations*: entities that, although not discrete nation-states, have shown remarkable consistency over four centuries in dialect, customs, associations, loyalties, and characteristics—most of what nations (as opposed to nation-states) are about. Each of these cultural nations has subdivided itself into a number of regional cultures. These are distinguished by differing economic and ecological adaptations, and influenced in turn by the various immigrant and preexisting populations with whom they have had contact.

In addition to the four groups described by Fischer, I would add a number of additional cultural nations that have established themselves in North America.

The most distinctive of these, the Anglo-Canadians, added a strong Scottish influence to the ethnic mix, and its accent crossed the continent in its own stream from Halifax to Vancouver.

Similarly, I believe that we must ask whether the English-speaking, African-descended population of the New World must be considered as two separate, closely related, cultural nations: the African American and Anglo-Caribbean, each subdivided into many regional cultures. The claim of these peoples to cultural nationhood is difficult to deny, given the distinct dialects persisting over many centuries, the distinct folkways, and the distinct institutions, affiliations, and loyalties created through their history. The African-American cultural nation even maintained for some time an overseas colony, Liberia. Although the African-American culture was influenced by Southern folkways, and influenced them in turn, the two cultures have become distinct and remain so today, even after the legal forces of slavery and segregation have long been gone. Unlike the previously described cultural groups, the African-American cultural nation is not geographically distinct but rather exists in communities dispersed unevenly across the United States.

Although the African-American cultural nation has always defined it-self, and been defined by others, as a racial group, in fact this has never been entirely true.

From the beginning, some Africans were able to escape slavery and join Indian tribes beyond white control. The Seminole, for example, are sub-stantially African in genetic composition, but they are considered Indians. Many Puerto Ricans, Cubans, and other Hispano-Caribbean immigrants have been genetically identifiable as African, but they remained unassim-ilated into the African-American cultural nation. A nontrivial number of American Indians, Latin Americans, Asians, and whites have married African Americans and subsequently been effectively assimilated into that cultural nation. In the past few decades, it has become possible for African Americans and new immigrants of African genetic composition to assimilate into other cultural nations, usually by intermarriage. The de-scendants of these marriages, who once had no effective choice in their cultural-national identity, now do. The Anglosphere civilizational iden-tity, as a fundamental identity that transcends race, may have a particular attraction for some such individuals. Frederick Douglass used terms such as Anglo-Africans and Afro-Saxons to refer to English-speaking people of African descent. One of these terms might find new utility today.

CULTURAL NATIONS AND REGIONS: WHAT'S THE DIFFERENCE?

If, as many commentators believe, regions will emerge as significant eco-nomic agents in the Information Revolution economy, the proper defini-tion of a region becomes a significant issue for understanding the new map of the world. Ohmae adopts a primarily economic view of regions, as does Darrell Delamaide in his *New Superregions of Europe*.

In their view, a region is a coherent economic unit typically smaller than the average nation-state. The nation-state typically linked a number of such regional economic units into a national-scale economy, relying on, or creating if needed, commonalties in language. Ohmae argues that as re-gions now compete directly in the world economy, there is little function for the structures that link them together and often inflict harm, as a dom-inant region can impose on a less powerful one policies contrary to its in-terests.

Ohmae cites the Kansai region of Japan—the densely populated, entre-preneurial, economically vital area centered around Osaka and Kyoto. Throughout modern times, this region has been overshadowed and over-powered by the Kanto region of Tokyo and its vast suburbs. Ohmae ar-gues that so long as Tokyo and its interests impose, through the highly centralized Japanese economic state, policies that favor Kanto over Kansai, the latter will be crippled in its quest for success in the world marketplace. In Spain, mercantile Catalonia has similarly been overshadowed by the political-military power of Castille; one might think that cultural autonomy might satisfy the Catalans, but discovering how often a Barcelona businessman needs to travel to Madrid to obtain permissions will quickly disabuse one of that notion.

Delamaide argues that the important units of Europe are its emerging superregions—such as the arc from Barcelona through Milan, as far inland as Geneva and Lyon. Again, these superregions are defined economically, linking areas that have belonged to substantially different cultural nations. Joel Garreau's *The Nine Nations of North America* is a regionalist treatment of North America relying on an economic-ecological definition of regions. Garreau calls them "nations," although they are essentially the same sort of region-state as Ohmae posits.

This confusion between region and nation stems partly from the failure of Ohmae, Delamaide, Garreau, and other regionalists to distinguish between economic and civic states. Many of the regions described by these authors are what I term cultural nations; many of the functions of the nation-states they see as becoming obsolete in the modern economy are specifically those of the economic state. Regions can be vital cultural nations. Following the demise of the economic state, some may choose to become independent or highly autonomous civic states, while others may choose to remain bound more closely with neighboring regions in larger civic states based on mutual acceptance of a shared narrative. Northern and Southern England may in fact have some quite distinct cultural characteristics, but their history of shared Englishness is more than likely to continue binding them together into a single state with a strong civic identity.

Kansai and Kanto will still each be Japanese, and that will still constitute a strong bond. This is independent of the question of whether such large states may devolve internally and return more decision making to local and regional levels, as the trends I have discussed will urge.

Garreau does discuss cultural affinities as a secondary factor, and is particularly aggressive about crossing the east-west political boundaries on the North American continent. His New England includes Atlantic Canada; his "Foundry" includes industrial Ontario; his "Breadbasket" (essentially the Great Plains) extends from north Texas to Saskatchewan; and his "MexAmerica" includes the western Sunbelt and the northern states of Mexico. Interestingly enough, Garreau, of French-Canadian descent, defines only one region-state on primarily cultural lines, the only such region that does not cross an existing international boundary—Quebec. By dividing North America in this way, Garreau takes a position on a long-standing question of whether the north-south, or regional, ties in North America are more important than the east-west ties—those that define the current nation-state boundaries. In light of the history of the cultural nations of North America, the answer is neither and both.

North America, like the rest of the world, must be understood as a set of areas that have links among both the economic superregions of which they are part and the cultural nations from which they have sprung. Garreau's categories match the definition of economic superregion fairly well, although with some poor fits.

(Vancouver is defined as part of "Ecotopia," Edmonton and Calgary as parts of the Breadbasket—but they are clearly among the economic capitals of his resource—extraction "Empty Quarter" as surely as is Denver.) However, they are not likely to form the basis of coherent political units, either now or as the Singularity revolutions develop. This is because they are crosscut by the boundaries of the cultural nations of North America, and, as cultural commonalties will be one of the primary sources of coherence of states in the future, it is unlikely that new coherent states will form across cultural-national boundaries.

Consider Garreau's Breadbasket, for example. This stretches from north Texas through the Canadian prairie provinces. Its boundaries are defined economically and ecologically—it is the area of large-scale grain agriculture. In this Garreau is correct: the entire area shares common economic and ecological concerns.

However, the Breadbasket also cuts across several cultural-national boundaries, and the institutions and cultures of each region within the area are strongly marked by the respective cultural-national characteristics.

Now consider politics. Each region responded to similar crises, such as the deflationary economic periods between 1880 and 1940, with substantially different solutions. Texas, Oklahoma, and Kansas turned to Populism. This movement reflected the region's roots in the "Dixie" and "New Ulster" cultures. Populism relied on a heavily emotional appeal, using rhetoric and staging derived from fundamentalist religion, heavily identified with charismatic leaders like William Jennings Bryan, and targeted toward simplistic solutions—inflation via fixed-ratio, bimetallic currency, and raids on the public treasury for favored factions. The Populist Party never developed a rooted party organization; most Populists were quickly absorbed into the Democratic Party at the time of Bryan's capture of the latter party's presidential nomination.

Further north, New England-settled Minnesota and the Dakotas developed Progressive agrarian politics. Agrarian Progressivism was a more literate and well-educated movement, albeit based on erroneous assumptions. It developed a complex program advocating a mix of cooperative institutions, state regulation and sponsorship of key industries, and the development of a set of deep-rooted political institutions, such as Minnesota's Farmer-Labor Party. Just as the Populist movement echoed the fervor of a Baptist camp meeting, the Progressive movement echoed the well-regulated life of a New England Congregationalist meeting in pursuit of its vision of ordered liberty.

Further north, Canadian farmers similarly built deep-rooted political movements such as the Cooperative Commonwealth Federation in Saskatchewan, which became the nucleus of the social democratic New Democratic Party. They proposed cooperative and state-mediated solutions similar to those advocated by the Progressive movements, but incorporated some uniquely Canadian features including the use of Crown Corporations and state projects such as a railway line to Hudson Bay to lower wheat export costs. Although these measures, like Agrarian Progressivism, drew on socialist rhetoric and analysis, the Canadian solutions also included a strong measure of Tory paternalist conservatism absent from politics further south. It is no coincidence that the Western Canadian Progressive Party eventually merged with the Conservatives, rather than the Liberals.

So we see that superregional economic commonalties did not determine the political responses of the various regions; instead, cultural-national commonalties led each region to seek unique solutions based on its underlying cultural-national characteristics.

This pattern is likely to continue. The map of North America (as with the other continents) will probably continue to show two types of boundaries—economic/ecological regions, and cultural-national boundaries. The combination of the two will probably define the coherent units that emerge. One of the reasons that network commonwealth institutions will become more important in this future of emerging regions is their ability to allow linkages along several different lines simultaneously. Thus the regions will be linked along east-west lines to the cultural nations with which they share like attitudes, and in all directions to the closer geographic neighbors with which they share common economies and ecologies, including those crossing current national or state borders. They will all be linked within the network civilization in which they share fundamental values of language, common law, and common institutions.

Cultural nations in North America experience a similar gradient of regional distinctions. The New England states are distinguished from their western descendants by smaller-scale agriculture, intense industrialization and subsequent deindustrialization, and the heavy influence of the Irish, Italian, and French-Canadian immigration of the past 150 years. Minnesota, the Dakotas, and eastern Montana are marked by their economic domination by cereal agriculture and by the cultural influence of

Scandinavian immigration. The Cascadian region has a different agricultural and industrial mix and is influenced by its orientation to the Pacific and its Asian and Latin-American immigrant populations. The Mountain West was also influenced by its mining booms, which introduced highly mixed populations into mining towns. Each of these regions will probably become coherent states, sharing public policy preferences with each other but probably not much more in political ties.

Each of these coherent region-states will maintain strong ties and cooperative forms with the regions to the north and south but will probably not form into larger coherent entities with them. The New England states and the Canadian Maritimes have common interests, and even common ties of settlement. (Southern Nova Scotia was settled from New England; only the proximity of British naval strength in Halifax prevented it from joining the American rebellion.) However, as long as Canada and the United States maintain common economic and defense ties, there is little point in constructing a common political framework for the two regions. Likewise, although Minnesota and the Dakotas have strong economic similarities with areas to the north and south, their social, cultural, and political differences will likely keep them separate. Thus Canada, or at least the English-speaking part, will be a reality in some form long into the future, regardless of what constitutional form it takes. The other cultural nations may or may not form specific political structures via interstate confederations. With or without such structures, Dixie will be Dixie. North America may realign its current boundaries in a form that accommodates both cultural-national and economic/ecological boundaries. This could be done by permitting states with substantially distinct and opposed regions to divide themselves into separate states more readily than at present, and permitting confederations of the new smaller states to absorb functions from the federal governments of the United States and Canada. North America might thus evolve a complex set of arrangements among its constituent canton-states, regional confederations, and cultural nations. Its substantial commonalties in language, culture, and traditions will make these arrangements easier to negotiate and maintain.

Since the 2000 American presidential election, it has become commonplace to speak of the divide between the socially conservative "Red States" and the socially liberal "Blue States," based on the media maps of state voting results. The county-by-county map is more enlightening, showing that the "Blue" territory is primarily a few urbanized regions, plus the largely African-American parts of the South. But there has been a long-standing divide between these areas on the desirable level and function of government, one that is likely to continue. Many of these decisions could be effectively devolved to a regional level, reducing interregional political conflict. Smaller, more coherent states and regional interstate authorities could be useful tools for pursuing such a program.

BECOMING A SELF-AWARE CIVILIZATION: THE ANGLOSPHERE PERSPECTIVE

An Anglosphere perspective differs from any of the lenses through which our societies have been viewed in the past. It could not have arisen at an earlier point in time. Although aspects of the perspective may seem familiar, they are applied in new ways and combined into new synergies. The principal characteristics emphasized by the Anglosphere perspective include the following.

Historical Continuity

The Anglosphere is a relatively old social construct, with a tangible continuity reaching back at least twelve centuries. Although substantially transformed by each new human wave added to the whole, and by each invasion of ideas, the Anglosphere is recognizably evolved from Alfred's kingdom. Americans or Australians who long for depth of historical perspective ought properly to find it in the Anglosphere identity. The better we understand history, the more clearly we see that the transatlantic voyage was, fundamentally, continuity rather than new creation. This perspective has substantial consequences for our understanding of political, social, economic, military, and technological history.

Memetic, Rather than Genetic, Identity

Richard Dawkins popularized the concept of the meme, the equivalent of a gene in the process of evolution of information. Memes reproduce, spread, and evolve far faster than genes, and thus human societies are far more affected by memetic, rather than genetic, evolution. A century ago, proponents of English-speaking political unions had a primarily genetic view of the English-speaking world, seeking to reunite the British with their genetic descendants in America. This vision failed, partly because so many Americans were already of non-British descent by that time. In contrast, the Anglosphere is a memetic concept.

Those who come to use the language and concepts of the Anglosphere (and further their evolution) are the memetic heirs of the Magna Carta, the Bill of Rights, and the Emancipation Proclamation, whatever their genetic heritage.

"Innocent until proven guilty" now belongs to Chang, Gonzales, and Singh as well as Smith and Jones.

Networked, Rather than Hierarchical, Structure

The first vision of the unity of the English-speaking peoples was of rule from London. English kings from the earliest days claimed suzerainty over all of Britain. James I, a Scottish monarch, achieved a Union of the Crowns, and Anne eventually achieved an incorporating Union of all Britain, including the new universe of English-speaking colonies beyond the seas. The ideal of rule of all English speakers was contested many times by the Scots and Irish, and was eventually put beyond reach in Philadelphia in 1776. The second vision, that of Cecil Rhodes and Alfred Milner, was that of corule from London and Washington. The high-water mark of this vision was the Anglo-American high command of World War II, which merged the two militaries far more closely than a mere alliance. But this relationship was diluted into NATO and the United Nations after the war, and the vision faded. The third vision, Harold Wilson and Lyndon Johnson's plan for a NAFTA, was waylaid by the politics of the day and by the suspicion that it would have ended in rule from Washington—the burden of Vietnam and the shadow of Suez (where the United States refused to help Britain and France regain the Canal after Egypt nationalized it in 1956). The network commonwealth vision is the fourth iteration of Anglosphere cohesion. It is polycentric and collaborative, appropriate to an era where the network, rather than the plan, is the ruling paradigm. Coalitions of the willing, variable geometry, and multiple, overlapping political ties—rather than One Union, One Parliament, and One Capital—are the characteristics of the network commonwealth approach.

Emphasis on Taking Advantage of Similarities, and Recognition of Differences

Narrow racial and nationalist narratives have emphasized the differences among Anglosphere nations, and deemphasized similarities. At the same time, a superficial universalism has encouraged a suppression of appreciation of genuine differences between the Anglosphere and other civilizations.

This has led to the facile and futile attempt to impose the surface mechanisms of the Anglosphere on cultures that have not experienced a slow evolution toward a strong civil society. Kosovo cannot be turned into Kansas or Kent in two years. An Anglosphere perspective concentrates on tending and perfecting our own garden first, creating deep and strong ties between highly similar nations and cultures, and seeking to help other nations by serving as an example (and sometimes as a caution). It does not impose solutions on nations we cannot assume will benefit from them.

The English-speaking peoples are beginning to perceive their commonality.

To move forward, new mental categories must be given name and definition and brought to general attention. I noted earlier that there has been no concise term for the category of English-speaking nations. Even that clumsy phrase is imprecise, as it focuses excessively on the linguistic aspects and ignores the much wider set of shared legal, constitutional, and social values that these nations hold in common.

I have adopted the term *Anglosphere* for convenience. It is concise, it goes beyond mere linguistic commonality, and it has no racial overtones. However, it is not clear that it will become the term of the future; it has overtones of "Anglophile," which is a value not universally considered positive in the Anglosphere. The term Anglo in California has come to be identified with non-Hispanic whites, and in Canada, Anglophone now refers to non-French whites. In Ireland, the word Anglo carries overtones of England and the British political system, rather than English-speaking civilization as a whole. An Anglosphere perspective would help reclaim the term from these narrow usages and connotations.

The Anglosphere is about much more than those terms comprehend. Time will tell whether this neologism will endure. Although Anglosphere Network Commonwealth is a convenient shorthand to discuss such things, the formal title of such an entity may be more prosaic—a Community of English-Speaking States, for example—or it may reach for a more poetic form—a League of the Common Law, perhaps. It will depend on the temper of the times that bring it forth.

More generally, what is needed is an explicit recognition of a status that is "not a fellow citizen, yet not a foreigner": a middle category between the two—a fellow member of a network civilization. As the shared information-space of network civilizations becomes more and more of an everyday reality, the emergence of a wider identity based on the sharing of that space and the values promoted within it may offer a wider identity capable of serving as a basis for significant common action.

The Anglosphere, despite the intense patriotism its member nations have traditionally exhibited, has in fact been ambivalent to the concept of the nation-state in its classic, Continental European form. In its strictest form, nation-state theorists (such as Johann Gottfried von Herder) would say that the English-speaking world only attained full nation-state status in 1707, with the creation of the United Kingdom and the first British Empire, and lost it in 1776 with the independence of the American English-speaking states.

Of course, we call the United States and the United Kingdom nation-states, but from a Herderian perspective, that is inaccurate. Based on the definitions of common language, law, customs, and ancestry, Americans and Britons have redefined the nation-state several times in order to permit historians to continue using the terms (retroactively, of course). This happened once noticeably in 1707, when English and Scots began to wrestle with the question of a British nationality. It happened in 1776 when American colonists had to choose between being British, American, or Virginians (or another state identity). And it happened again in 1861 when Southern Americans had to choose between South Carolinian (or some other state), Confederate, or American identities. Since then, other English-speaking nations, most noticeably Australia, New Zealand, and (somewhat problematically) Canada, have moved toward self-definition as nation-states, but in each case stretching the definition of nation-state further. To deal with this ambiguity and fluidity of national character, I have adopted the term Grand Union to describe what the United States and United Kingdom have become—political unions of a number of cultural nations that have taken on some but not all of the characteristics of nationhood.*

An Anglosphere perspective might leave at least the Herderian concept of the nation-state behind entirely, leaving it to the French and the Japanese, who fit within it more easily. Instead, the idea of a number of historically based "cultural nations" or "cousin nations" forming sovereign civic states, whether independent or autonomous, cooperating in the framework of common civilization, distinct among the civilizations of the world, may fit reality much more closely. Similarly, the Anglosphere perspective will look to leave behind racial-based identities, particularly as the increasing frequency of intermarriage among the Anglosphere's racial and ethnic groups erodes the validity of that viewpoint. Following from this is the need for a wide pan-Anglosphere perspective, an insertion into discussions of politics, current events, and history of the commonalties and connections that increase daily.

During the perception phase, education becomes a critical area for promotion of awareness. Resources for students distributed on the Web can have a powerful impact on perceptions. American universities have begun American studies programs, but an Anglosphere studies program would make more sense. History must be taught from an Anglosphere perspective. Churchill's *History of the English-Speaking Peoples* is a good point of departure, although as it reflects the perspective of its time, could benefit from a more contemporary look. Phillips's *The Cousins' Wars* is a welcome new addition to that tradition.

---

*Some academics distinguish between nation-states and state-nations—the Grand Union would be a form of the later.

Histories from a pan-Anglosphere perspective should augment and replace the various nationalist narratives of the nineteenth and twentieth centuries, which emphasize the differences among Anglosphere nations and minimize the commonalties.

The great conflicts among English speakers, particularly the English Civil War, the Glorious Revolution and Jacobite Rebellions, the American Revolution, the American Civil War, and the Irish War of Independence, should be seen and taught not as nationalist tribal clashes but as intra-Anglosphere struggles that increasingly channeled a variety of economic, social, religious, and constitutional disputes into a series of essentially similar struggles over the spatial composition of our common Anglo-sphere home.

MEMETIC PLAGUES OF THE ANGLOSPHERE

The Anglosphere first emerged from the intermixture of Angles, Saxons, Jutes, Vikings, Celts, and pre-Celtic people in the British Isles. It was connected by Christianity to the wider civilizations of Eurasia and dragged into the political system of the European continent by its Norman conquerors. It digested and synthesized these elements, and preserved a substantially distinct social and political flavor through the Norman Conquest and ever thereafter. These characteristics (pace Macfarlane) included a greater individualism, more market-oriented relationships, a sense of political rights extending much lower in society than most other places, and a greater fluidity between class lines than other societies. The Anglosphere has also been exposed to countervailing tendencies throughout its existence. Some narratives, including the classical Whig narrative, define the Anglosphere by the struggle between indigenous traditions of openness, individualism, local rights, and political freedom versus alien invasions of closed, hierarchical, centralized, and coercive relationships. From a memetic viewpoint, this narrative is in fact a useful means of exploring the evolutionary history of the Anglosphere idea.

Extending the metaphor, we can see the emerging Anglosphere civilization as a memetic ecology, and the various intrusive ideas as memetic viral plagues.

A number of such plagues have infested the Anglosphere over time. One of these was Continental feudalism. Although preinvasion England shared some social characteristics with Continental societies, the Norman conquerors in 1066 unquestionably moved postinvasion society further toward a particular Continental set of practices. These included the idealization of the concept of a blood aristocracy inherently separated from the "common" people, and the social ideal of large landed estates protected by primogeniture and worked by bond labor. This was at odds with the Anglo-Saxon ideal of smaller holdings worked by freeholders, small estates with firm title, and social mobility between lower, middle, and upper classes. Writing in 1010, the Anglo-Saxon Archbishop Wulfstan held that "if a *ceorl* [free farmer] prospered so that he possessed fully five hides of land of his own, a church and a kitchen, a bell and a fortress-gate, a seat and a special office in the King's hall, he was worthy thereafter to be called a *thegn*." Today, one could equally say, "If a man prospered so that he possessed fully five newspapers of his own, a think tank and a gourmet restaurant, a web site and a security system, a town house and social invitations to No. 10 Downing Street, he was worthy thereafter to be called a Life Peer." The Normans extended the feudal ideal geographically farther by conquering Wales and beginning the conquest of Ireland. In these lands, previously characterized by clan- and family-based farming on shifting and changing land titles, feudal land relations adopted features of the preexisting Celtic system but retained their essential feature of lord-serf (or "tenant") relationships. In England proper, the pre-Norman attitudes of the independent yeomanry retained much of their vigor, and a running, low-scale guerrilla war of brigandage, mythologized in the Robin Hood stories, wore away at the feudal relationships.

The political impact of the Norman Conquest was enormous, centralizing further the relatively strong state apparatus built by the later Anglo-Saxon kings. However, the Norman feudal regime was at heart a medieval regime, and the Middle Ages, with its autonomous church and urban merchant establishments, and medieval constitutionalist traditions, created the seed of an emerging civil society. Thus Continental feudalism contained the seeds of its own demise in England, a process which was clearly begun by 1215 with the Magna Carta. Aside from a tradition of Westminster centralism (to which the Whig movement was a reaction), the principal harm this particular plague did to Britain was the continuation of Continental feudalism and rural peasantry in Ireland long after it had faded away in Britain. This problem was compounded by the politics of the Protestant Reformation in the British Isles, with the ultimate division between a disenfranchised Catholic peasantry, an Anglican landlord class, and a Presbyterian yeomanry in Ulster. These elements clashed and combined in kaleidoscopic fashion.

Long after feudalism ceased to dominate in England, its legacy has continued to burden the Anglosphere. Its land relations were the root cause of the Great Famine in Ireland and drove the division of the British Liberal Party over Home Rule at the end of the nineteenth century. Its effects kept the Irish Catholic population, both in Ireland and elsewhere, trapped in low-trust cultural patterns. And of course, the legacy of feudal relationships overshadowed the prospects for Catholic emancipation in Ireland, greatly exacerbated the political problems leading to the Irish War of Independence and Irish Civil War, and contributed to the ongoing problems in Northern Ireland that persist today.

Another major memetic plague to hit the Anglosphere was what we might call slaveism and the consequent creation of the First Empire. Following the Protestant Reformation, England and Spain began an extended hot-and-cold war that lasted for the entirety of Elizabeth I's reign and through much of the following century. One of the effects of this war was the enlargement of the mental horizons of the English.

As citizens became fully aware of the extent of the Spanish Empire in the New World and the extent to which New World wealth underwrote Spanish military strength, a debate arose as to how England could counter Spain's might.

It is useful to see this debate as an ideological one and to see the British proponents of copying the Iberian plantation system (the Atlantic slave trade was even more a Portuguese than a Spanish phenomenon) as proponents of an ideology.

This ideology might be called "latifundism," after the classical Latin term latifundia for large estates worked by slaves. But it is probably clearer and simpler to call it slaveism. Slaveism is more than the possession of slaves. Slaveism is an ideology that sees the prosperity and strength of the nation as coming from the ability to occupy broad areas of conquered land and convert them to large estates worked by slave labor. This was seen as the most effective way to amass a large amount of national wealth, and more important, it posited that states which did not engage in slave plantation activity would be vulnerable to conquest by states which, like Spain, did.

In an era marked by decades of genuine and justified fear of conquest by Spain, this perception was a powerful motivator. Like today's Europhiles in Britain, the English slaveists saw their Continental competitors amassing wealth and influence and underestimated their own native sources of strength and prosperity. They also harkened back to native models of bond labor ownership and serf-worked large estates to try to make slaveism seem a familiar and comfortable phenomenon.

This effort, fundamentally self-deceiving, endured and created a false equation of slave-worked plantations in the Caribbean and North America with the traditional tenant-worked estates of Southern England, a confusion which has persisted even to this day. This confusion was promoted in art and included the South Carolina planters described by William W. Freehling (who staged "fox hunts" in his swamp consisting of liveried slaves rowing boats to chase alligators) and the heart-warming (but essentially false) picture of antebellum plantation life in *Gone with the Wind*. British (and subsequently Dixie) plantation owners nevertheless kept trying to enjoy the real and imagined benefits of estate life in fifteenth-century Sussex.

Unfortunately, they continually swept under the rug the fact that the lowest serf in medieval England had more legal rights than the most privileged slave in Barbados or Charleston. Masters in England could not break up families, nor sell them entire. They could sell the estate, but the people stayed on it, in intact communities.

Estate tenants in England saw themselves as free people, with certain obligations to the lord, who in turn had obligations to them. Plantation slaves knew that they were slaves, but the plantation masters always sought real bonds of affection and loyalty such as existed in English estate life. Perhaps these were achieved at some times and in some places. But it was not until Appomattox, when most presumed-loyal slaves were happy to walk away from their plantations without looking back, that the Anglosphere illusion of slaveism was finally dispelled.

The consequences of slaveism for the Anglosphere have been great. In the short term, slaveism delivered substantial wealth to England and permitted rapid development of the Caribbean and southern North America. Some economists seek to credit England's position as fountain of the Industrial Revolution, or America's later prosperity, to the profits of the slave and plantation system. This is dubious.

If the massive accumulation of slave and plantation wealth were a major factor in the launch of the Industrial Revolution, we would expect to see Portugal and Spain leading that development. Brazil, the great slave destination of the New World, should have outstripped the United States from the start. We look in vain to the Ebro, the Douro, or the Amazon for seventeenth-century steam engines. If slaveism did have an effect, it was primarily in helping England fend off rival slaveist powers until the slavery-destroying Industrial Revolution could take off.

In the long term, slaveism has probably been the most costly of all the memetic plagues of the Anglosphere. Its principal cost may have been the American Civil War and the retardation of the development of Dixie both before and after that war. Slaveism saw the accumulation of agricultural plantation wealth as the fundamental and reigning wealth of society. Perhaps the Spain of the Armada, with its Peruvian gold and Mexican silver, did genuinely overshadow the sheep-farming England of 1588. By 1860, however, this doctrine, clung to in its final form of confidence in the ability of "King Cotton" to sway industrial England, led the last Anglosphere slaveists, the secessionist fire-eaters of Dixie, to overplay their hand badly. Thus the blinders of slaveism led to its demise. In fact, the enormous wealth being created by the Industrial Revolution empowered the Calvinist, Methodist and Quaker liberal industrialists of Manchester, Birmingham, Boston, and Philadelphia to snuff out slaveism.

The costs included the American Civil War and its human butcher's bill, the turmoil of Reconstruction and its subsequent reversal, the backwardness of the American South for the following century, and the turmoil of the Civil Rights revolution.

Whether the Civil War was fought more over slavery or Union is still debated, but it is clear that Dixie could never have won or kept its independence without grasping the nettle of slavery, and that it did indeed fight under the shadow of slaveism. Looking at the debate in Confederate politico-military circles over General Patrick Cleburne's proposal to arm and liberate the South's slaves as a last-ditch measure, it seems clear that some Southerners were primarily Dixie nationalists, and others primarily interested in defending slavery; when faced with the choice, most hesitated, and of course lost both independence and their slave property.

The most momentous consequence of slaveism has been the presence and condition of the slaves and their descendants in the Anglosphere, as African Americans and Afro-Caribbeans have come to form several of the Anglosphere's distinct cultural nations. A slave inhabits an inherently low-trust culture. In contrast, freed African Americans as early as the 1790s began to create a high-trust culture, and the visible institutions of a strong civil society first started to emerge among them at that time. The stalling, or possibly the sabotage, of this transition to high trust (a precondition of prosperity and political self-determination) is the central reality of the African-American cultural nation. Ironically, a mirror-ideology of slaveism has arisen among some African-American intellectuals, which holds that slaveism was indeed primarily responsible for the prosperity and preeminence of the Anglosphere. This mirror-slaveism, aside from some neo-Confederate nostalgia, is the principal remnant of slaveist ideology in the Anglosphere. If it serves to retard the final transition of African America to a high-trust culture, it will extract yet another toll before it finally slips into oblivion.

A third major memetic plague to infest the Anglosphere was revolutionary utopianism. The Anglosphere genius has always been that which Chilean historian Claudio Véliz characterizes as that of the Gothic fox—empirical, practical, gradual, tolerant of diversity, and suspicious of grand designs. But within our culture, we have always harbored a minority strain of temperament and thought more akin to what Véliz calls the Baroque hedgehog—theoretical, revolutionary, utopian, totalitarian, and enamored of the grand vision. Since this temperament has been a constant of our history, while the specific ideological content has changed with the times, it is probably more useful to see it as a single memetic plague, revolutionary utopianism, which mutates in form from time to time.

The first true revolutionary utopianism to take root in the Anglosphere was the Baroque Catholicism of the Counter-Reformation and the religious wars of seventeenth-century England. Looking back, this episode displayed almost all the characteristics of subsequent infestations of revolutionary utopianism in the Anglosphere. To begin with, it is important to distinguish it from the native Catholicism of the pre-Reformation English Church and the recusants, those who continued to adhere to it after the Reformation began. The pre-Reformation Church in England was privileged, lazy, and not very strict about enforcement of rules, but it was not totalitarian. Celibacy of the clergy meant no legal marriage for priests, not chastity. These easy-going traditions were carried on by segments of the Church of England. The Counter-Reformation Catholicism that was brought to post-Reformation England by returning exiles and Jesuit missionaries was quite different: revolutionary, disciplined, militant, and willing to resort to conspiracy, deceit, and violence to overthrow what it saw as an illegitimate government.

Unlike the great majority of the English in general or the recusant English Catholics, Counter-Reformation Catholics were willing to ally themselves with foreign powers traditionally hostile to England to carry out their wishes.

In dealing with Counter-Reformation Catholicism, the Anglosphere began its long history of difficult relations with militant utopianism. The reality of domestic English willing to cooperate with foreign agents out of ideological sympathy was novel and deeply disturbing. The Gunpowder Plot (1605) brought all these issues to the fore and introduced the language of ideological conspiracy to the Anglosphere political lexicon. Everything about the Gunpowder Plot and subsequent conspiracy events seems eerily familiar to modern English speakers: the charges and countercharges, the opportunists who discover the uses of false conspiracy accusations; the apologists who deny even real plots; and the shadowy actions of foreign intelligence agencies.

The best evidence today indicates that Guy Fawkes and his followers were members of a cell of English Catholic conspirators kept on the string by Spanish intelligence. The undercover approaches to Anglo-Spanish détente that arose around James I's accession to the throne meant that these people had to be kept under control, but their low-level handlers were not aware of this requirement—above their pay grade and beyond their need to know, as we would say today. Like many intelligence operations, the Gunpowder Plot seems to have been blow back—an unintended side effect of an intelligence operation gone wrong.

But don't the people and events seem familiar? Guy Fawkes was a drifting, alienated combat veteran, a true believer, and easy prey for a Spanish intelligence recruiter. But he was also a fanatic willing to take things beyond what his handlers were ready to allow. If there are premonitions of Lee Harvey Oswald, Timothy McVeigh, and possibly John Wilkes Booth in Fawkes, it is not coincidence.

The Anglosphere has not greatly changed its relation to "the enemy within" in four hundred years.

The Anglosphere nations eventually defeated the conspiracies of Counter-Reformation Catholic utopians and watched the Counter-

Reformation Catholic Church gradually evolve into an institution that could peacefully share a democratic society with its former enemies. Devout Catholic thinkers such as Lord Acton brilliantly reconciled the Anglosphere traditions of liberty with the Church's teachings. But the legacy of revolutionary utopianism and conspiracy politics has remained with us ever since. Subsequent memetic plagues included the French revolutionary idealism which found echoes in Britain and America, more among intellectuals taking postures than among actual oppressed people making insurrections, except to some extent in Ireland. However, this legacy of radical utopianism opened the way for Marxism in all its forms and varieties, which has been the greatest single version of radical utopianism to influence the Anglosphere in the nineteenth and twentieth centuries.

It is also interesting to note the way in which the Anglosphere absorbed and assimilated Marxism. Although a small, highly influential stratum of the intelligentsia in America, Britain, and the Commonwealth states adopted a reasonably pure and consistent form of Marxism or later its hybrid Marxist-Leninist form, most of the actual industrial workforce throughout the Anglosphere never became very good Marxists. The failure of the American working class to adopt socialism is legendary (the high-water mark of the movement being Eugene V. Debs's 6 percent of the vote in the 1912 election); Canadian socialism has done a little better, but not much. The success of the British and Australian Labor parties would seem to be proof of an Anglosphere predilection for popular socialism. What is less well-examined is the fact that these parties were in fact much more a product of a native Anglosphere tradition of liberal radicalism, which only adopted the tactic of state ownership of industry as part of a general egalitarian and antiestablishment sentiment.

This sentiment originated long before the First International, going back to the radical Ranters and Diggers of the English Civil War and before. Although the British Labour Party called itself socialist and advocated nationalization of industry, it was never formally defined as a Marxist Party, and it included many who saw themselves more in the tradition of the English Chartists than of the Paris Commune.

Tellingly, the leftist radicals of Britain share many characteristics of temperament with their fellow descendants in America, the nominally right-wing militiamen—traits such as a resentment of the elite and the rich, combined with a conspiratorial mentality. The abandonment of the principle of state ownership by the British Labour Party under Tony Blair's leadership was the end of an era—combined with a continued egalitarianism which has always been the true, core Labour interest.

While the Anglosphere working classes were absorbing the socialist memes from Germany and France, the leftist intelligentsia went through its own Gunpowder Plot crises, particularly after World War II, when their allegiances to Moscow as the Left's ideological homeland suddenly put Anglosphere leftists in real conflict with their birth loyalties. (The more intelligent ones had become Trotskyists, which allowed them the luxury of a radical stance while excusing their disinclination to carry water for the KGB.) For a short time, the Anglosphere, particularly the United States, replayed many of the scenes of the English Reformation and Civil War, with loyalty oaths, accusations of conspiracy (some real, some imaginary), penetration by foreign intelligence services, and confused intellectuals in exile, both internal and foreign.

In addition to Marxists, there was a small, reasonably influential group of intellectual sympathizers with forms of fascism and national socialism, including Ezra Pound and D. H. Lawrence. Although these never resulted in the creation of a significant political movement, they did, like their Marxist cousins, help undermine confidence in democracy, market economies, and the general institutions of civil society.

Today there is no one great totalitarian ideology overshadowing the Anglosphere, or indeed the rest of the world. Instead, there is a general malaise among many intellectuals and the artists formerly known as modernists. Rather than a memetic plague, it is more like an endemic low-grade fever. However, the same weaknesses that permitted the entry of totalitarian memes still exist—guilt, self-doubt, lack of understanding of the causes of poverty and prosperity or of the Anglosphere and its nature. We will undoubtedly see many of the same games replayed when some new totalitarian temptation arises. Perhaps it might even take the form of an amalgamation of the remnants of the radical Left into the radical fundamentalist movement, which would be an ironic and somewhat pathetic fate for the heirs of clergy-hating Robespierre, Marx, and Trotsky.

COMING HOME TO THE ANGLOSPHERE

For those reasons and more, this is a propitious moment in history to propose the Anglosphere network civilization as a basic identity for the members of all the nations of the English-speaking world. In a way, the English-speaking peoples have sailed under borrowed flags throughout history. As England first grew into united nationhood, the early Anglo-Saxon converts to Christianity, and then the English (and later, the Scots as they adopted English), identified themselves as part of Latin Christian civilization from that time until the Reformation. From the time of the Reformation onward, most English speakers, Anglicans and Calvinists alike, identified themselves as Protestant Christians. English speakers in general identified themselves as Christians up through the nineteenth century.

Eventually, however, the concept of "white" and "European" civilization replaced this primarily religious identification. This came partly through the influence of the Iberian slave civilizations of the New World, for, once their Indian and African subjects were converted, something was needed to justify the slaveholders' mastery over their fellow Christians. The English speakers of the Caribbean adopted these attitudes along with the plantations and slave codes they copied from the Spanish. As they settled South Carolina from Barbados, they brought these attitudes to North America, where they proved equally (and fatefully) useful.

Today, although the Anglosphere continues to be based on cultural values originating in Christianity, it is unlikely to return to an exclusively Christian identity.

The presence of substantial Jewish, Muslim, and Buddhist minorities, as well as the fact that a substantial percentage are rationalists, humanists, or of other nonreligious identities, precludes an exclusively Christian identity as a feasible option. The prospect of Muslim or Hindu nations adhering to Anglosphere institutions makes that possibility even less likely. Christian-derived values (particularly as interpreted in the Anglosphere) will always be at the core of Anglosphere values. But it seems more likely that Christians within the Anglosphere will have to make their political goal a society in which they can be comfortable and free to testify by word and example, rather than one in which they are the sole definers of values. Such a goal might not be incompatible with the Christian ideal of being in the world but not of it.

Western civilization as a primary category arose almost simultaneously with the advent of early twentieth-century theorists such as Oswald Spengler, who forecast its impending demise. Even the original German term used by Spengler, *Abendlandes* ("evening lands") and translated in English as "the West," carried with it overtones of decline. This was picked up by authors such as W. E. B. DuBois and used to advance a narrative of a declining white West and rising nonwhite East (later "North" and "South"), which in fact has not proved true.

The whole concept of the white race as a political category (as opposed to an anthropological classification) came first from the need of Christian theologians to justify the slavery of baptized Africans, and later from pseudoscientific modernism in the nineteenth century. Today it is a byproduct of political correctness.

(You can't have "black pride" without eventually creating a demand for "white pride," and the creation of a class of racially defined African Americans creates a demand for the creation of a class of racially defined European Americans.

Recognition of culturally defined African Americans as members of one of several cultural nations of the Anglosphere, by contrast, provides an identity that is at root cultural, not racial, and provides the basis of a narrative of fellow citizenship and mutual comity.)

Today there is a lot of shallow discussion about the United States becoming a "majority-minority" nation by 2050, with lesser degrees of "minoritization" of other Anglosphere nations. This ignores what is actually happening. The majority of second-generation Asians and Latinos are assimilating (despite the antiassimilationist agenda of the multiculturalists) and intermarrying. There will probably not be large, distinct, post-first-generation Asian and Latino communities in 2050, unless the forces of multiculturalism use state power to create them artificially.

There will be a lot of half-Asian (or -Latino) and quarter-Asian (and -Latino) people who will be culturally members of the prevailing cultural nations of the Anglosphere, mostly of Midland America but also of others as well. This assumes that we do not create state-funded rewards for these people to consider themselves members of their part-minority ancestral group.

The Anglosphere nations faced this problem once before, with the advent of Mediterranean and Eastern European immigrants. At the time, there was a lot of debate as to whether such people were white; it was eventually resolved by expanding the definition a bit so that even Middle Easterners such as Lebanese were considered white. (Although some Southern television stations refused to carry *I Love Lucy* at its inception in the 1950s because it depicted a "mixed" marriage between Lucy and the Cuban Ricky Ricardo.) This is not likely to happen with the half-Chinese Americans, Australians, or Canadians of the year 2020. They will socialize with the majority, think like the majority, and vote like the majority population, absent artificial incentives. Developing a stronger Anglosphere identity will help defeat those artificial incentives and offer a narrative and identity that are comfortable, natural, and inviting for such individuals.

"White" is becoming an obsolete definition of most Anglosphere cultural nations, for obvious reasons, unless a "one-drop-of-blood" definition of whiteness is adopted. It would be far better to move away from racial thinking entirely.

(I suspect that African Americans will not assimilate into any of the majority cultural nations. This is because they, unlike most other racial minorities, already belong to an old and well-established cultural nation, into which other immigrant groups continue to assimilate. The African-American cultural nation has a different challenge—completing the transition from a low-trust to a high-trust culture, a task which has been in process for a century and a half and was succeeding until it was sabotaged by declinist intellectuals, most of whom were white.)

Additionally, we must consider the possibility that Western civilization ended as a meaningful category some time ago. How long ago is a matter of debate, but it might be thought of as a process that began with the invention of printing and became particularly visible with the abandonment of fluency in Latin as a requirement for university admission. Consider that at the start of World War I, it was not unusual for French, German, and British officers (and even some enlisted men) to march off with Latin and Greek classics in their backpacks, and more than a few in the original languages. What did the soldiers of the Gulf War take for reading? Not the Iliad, for the most part.

Can we really speak of a civilization if it no longer has a common language (even for its educated classes) or reads a common corpus of literature? Despite the "cultural literacy" movement in parts of the West, we are now in a situation where only a handful of the important books read by an educated person are even translations from Greek or Latin, and only a slightly larger handful are translations from other European languages. Only specialists in these nations read even French literature in the original now.

But there is a substantial body of "classic" English-language literature, philosophy, political thought, poetry, commentary, and more, which, despite the state of education today, is alive and accessible to any literate person. People still discuss it and exchange opinions on it, within the intralinguistic boundary.

The Web will probably increase this discussion. There is now a large body of popular literature, film, culture, and music that is pan-Anglosphere in origin and enjoyment, and increasingly separate from the Continental tradition.

Additionally, the entire concept of a shared civilization among European and European-descended cultures, serving as a wider identity above national identities and excluding non-European nations, no longer appears to enjoy effective acceptance. The acceptance of Japan as a member of the developed nations or the North, while classifying nations such as Argentina, almost entirely white and European in population, as members of the Third World or the South, demonstrates the decline in use of European and non-European classifications. The EU tries to define itself as European while explicitly rejecting American or Canadian models as "un-European"—in other words, the term "European" has again become a geographical, rather than cultural signifier.

Even in small ways, the concept of a wider Western civilization is losing its meaning. When members of the various European and European-descended nations saw themselves as part of a common cultural whole, it was routine for a person traveling from one country of the West relocating in another to adopt the local form of his name in dealing with his hosts. Thus Cristoforo Colombo readily became Cristobal Colón in Spain, and we easily speak of him as Christopher Columbus in English. Giovanni Caboto became John Cabot on English shores and thought nothing of it. Today a Juan relocating to the United States resists becoming a John, even while speaking English—he does not see Juan and John as local variants of the same name, although if he is a Christian, he should.

On a somewhat more serious plane, we must wonder about the collapse of the live tradition of new symphonic music—with little being composed that is widely played much since the later works of Ralph Vaughan Williams and Benjamin Britten. This music, along with a genuinely pan-Western tradition of visual arts, once provided a shared and exclusive means of cultural communications among the nations of the West. Today, by contrast, the shared corpus of classical symphonic music is just as lively in Japan and China as in America and Europe—and equally dead. A century ago, Jean Sibelius and Bedrich Smetana composed symphonies declaring the nationhood of Finland and Czechoslovakia, respectively.

Sibelius's work was taken seriously, enough to be banned by the czar. Today, if music is banned, it is for its words. Nobody can imagine music alone speaking beyond linguistic boundaries.

Similarly, the modernist canon of art—particularly abstract art—destroyed utterly any civilizational references and therefore any possibilities of intracivilizational communication through the visual arts. Théodore Géricault could paint *The Raft of the Medusa* to protest his disgust with the French government of his day, and it could be "read" easily by any European, but only with difficulty by a non-European. Postmodernist products today have restored the ability to use visual symbols and import semantic content, but these have become by their nature linguistic-cultural-specific. They speak superficially to a shallow class of internationalists, but cannot serve as a deeper binding means of communication among members of a common civilization because there is little that is both common and distinct above the linguistic-civilizational level yet below the global (what globalization observer Thomas Friedman calls "Davos culture") level.

For these reasons, it may be a useful recognition of reality to say, "Western civilization, noble as it was in its time, has passed. Long live its child, English-speaking civilization, sibling to its fellow European and European-descended civilizations, but distinct in its identity." We would do well to heed David Gress when he points out that the concept of Western civilization was prolonged at the end primarily by the need to promote an identity to tie together the member nations of NATO while minimizing real differences among new candidates for inclusion.

This has immediate political implications. It reinforces the Anglosphere concept, of course, but it is also driving a substantial recasting of history and historical narratives. Consider slavery, for instance. English-speaking civilization abolished slavery quite early. In late Anglo-Saxon times, manumission of slaves was frequently recorded. The Normans finished the process by converting most of the existing *servi* on their new English estates to the status of serfs. Certainly by the year 1200 slavery was nearly extinct in England. In contrast, classical slavery continued uninterrupted in Spain and Portugal through the Islamic conquest and the Christian Reconquest, was introduced into the proto-Americas of Madeira and the Canaries in the early fifteenth century, and drove the opening of the maritime African slave trade before Columbus's voyage. After that voyage and the Iberian conquest of the New World, the Iberians extended the system to the Caribbean and Brazil. Of the 11 million slaves who landed in the New World between 1500 and 1888, 3 million went to the Anglosphere, and only 600,000 went to the North American Anglosphere mainland—mostly to the future United States.

As discussed previously, slavery and slave codes were an expression of an alien meme-invasion of the Anglosphere, albeit one that eventually won enthusiastic converts. In 1619, slavery was so alien to the Anglosphere that the Virginians couldn't decide whether the first Africans landed by the Dutch in that year were to be treated as indentured servants or permanent bondsmen. It took several generations for the legal categories of permanent, hereditary bondage and universal suppression of rights for free blacks to become fixed law. (Free black men who were property-holders were not deprived of the vote in Virginia until the 1720s.) The entire apparatus of permanent slavery, repressive Black Codes, and the concept of racial hierarchies were imported into the Anglosphere through the example of Spanish practices in the Caribbean. Eventually, these concepts were imported into the American mainland when Barbados planters established South Carolina, bringing Spanish-influenced slave codes with them.

Hugh Thomas records Anglosphere ambivalence about the slave trade in the early seventeenth century:

A merchant named George Thomson went out, on behalf of Rich's Guinea Company, to explore the river Gambia. He was primarily interested in gold. Thomson lost his vessel to the Portuguese, and a certain Richard Jobson . . . went to relieve him, to find that Thomson had been murdered by one of his own men. Jobson reported that the natives on the Gambia were afraid of him because their compatriots had "been many times by several nations surprized, taken and carried away." Jobson was offered slaves by an African merchant, Buckor Sano but, speaking for himself and not for the Guinea Company, he declared proudly that "we were a people who did not deal in such commodities, neither did we buy or sell one another, or any that had our own shapes." The African merchant seemed to marvel at this, and "told us it was the only merchandise they carried down into the country, where they fetched all their salt, and that they were sold to white men, who earnestly desired them. . . . We answered, 'they were another kind of people different from us.'" (*The Slave Trade: The Story of the Atlantic Slave Trade 1440–1870*)

Similarly, Sir Francis Drake, on his circumnavigation of the globe, met with communities of escaped slaves and Indians in Panama and elsewhere. He developed a plan to "roll back" the Spanish Empire through English sponsorship of slave and Indian rebellions, to be followed by a (hopefully) peaceful settlement of the liberated Americas by English colonists. On his return to England, however, he failed to promote this "Drake Doctrine" in the face of the Europhile Englishmen of his day. Instead, he argued that in order to be competitive with the European powers of their day, Spain and Portugal, England had to adopt Continental economics—in this case, African slavery, and sugar plantations.

Thus, African slavery is properly seen not as an inherent part of English-speaking civilization but as an alien graft on its values (promoted by Anglosphere admirers of other civilizations). It was eventually shrugged off by an indigenous Anglosphere ideology, abolitionism, which grew out of what was at its start a uniquely Anglosphere reading of the Bible, originally by Cromwellian Independents like Richard Saltonstall, Northern English Quakers, and eventually by Methodists and others. Similarly, any understanding of Anglosphere relations with the prior inhabitants of America or Australasia must be grounded in the wider history of contacts and conflicts between peoples of differing stages of development. Thus, it is informative to compare the Anglosphere at its best and worst with other cultures at their similar heights and depths. The Quakers in Pennsylvania, like the Jesuits in the *reducciones* of Paraguay, attempted to deal fairly with the Indians. Many others of both cultures tried at least occasionally to be fair; most did not bother or had so little comprehension of the other culture that no good came of the encounter and often much ill. The depressing conclusion seems to be that contacts between peoples at greatly different development levels always carry a great potential for catastrophe, even with the best of intentions. Certainly this continues to be the case in the Amazon and with the Indonesian occupation of Eastern New Guinea.

The Anglosphere, however, was at its best in these matters when it acted most in accord with its basic principles. Quaker culture, the source of enlightened treatment of the American Indians in Pennsylvania, was also the source (along with allied Protestant radical groups of the English Civil War era) of most of the principles on which the subsequent Anglosphere political culture was eventually founded. It demanded participation by all in all community decisions (the source of full franchise and women's suffrage), abolition of slavery, fair commercial dealing and sanctity of contract, and abolition of cruelty in public life, which was expressed in Quaker-led movements to reform criminal justice and education and to reduce cruelty to animals. Quaker radicalism was expressed not in defying Anglosphere values but in demanding that they be conceived as applying fully to women, Africans, Indians, and others. The Jesuit experiment in humane treatment of Indians in Paraguay (as humane was understood in the Iberian Baroque Catholic culture of the Counter-Reformation), by contrast, was locally successful for a while, but the values underlying it did not go on to create a free and thriving culture in Latin America, unlike the Quaker experiment did in North America.

I am willing to defend our sixteenth-century cultural ancestors relative to the Ottoman sultans, but it is absurd to judge them by the standards of the twenty-first century, as many people do today. Every post-apocalyptic film, novel, or comic book embodies a crude, third-rate Spenglerist narrative of moral decline. This "Black Legend of the Anglosphere" depicts pre-Columbian America as benign and advanced, and the West as inherently barbaric and cruel. For a century, the American press has been filled with predictions that one culture or another would soon overtake America in economic or military power, but the United States is now more predominant than ever. To say that the Second British Empire "fell" (with overtones of *The Decline and Fall of the Roman Empire*) obscures the fact that, as Robert Conquest observed, "The Afghans did not sack London." Instead, the empire was, rather uniquely among empires, transformed into a commonwealth that today is, if not what its founders might have hoped, at least a more effective institution than the United Nations. All of these petty absurdities would be unimportant in and of themselves, but taken together they add up to a climate of denigration (for the most part derived from ignorance and intellectual laziness) of the values whose fruits we all take for granted.

Thus I reject having to defend Cortez or Columbus as relevant to English-speaking culture.

Rather than celebrate Columbus Day, perhaps we should instead celebrate Cabot Day—honoring the introduction of English-speaking civilization to North America by an Italian who had previously immigrated to England.

The Singularity revolutions are raising the stakes too high for us to tolerate this ignorance and laziness any longer. We cannot enjoy prosperity without understanding the institutional arrangements and underlying cultural values that lifted our society out of the prevailing poverty of the world. The belief that this wealth was stolen from other nations obscures this understanding, as does a naive faith that these formulas can be imported instantly into nations with weak or nonexistent civil societies and made to work effortlessly. We cannot enjoy freedom and civil liberties without strong civil societies and functioning constitutional democracies.

Most important, we cannot expect to create and implement the measures needed to constrain the potential negative effects of the Singularity technologies unless we understand the link between strong civil societies and effective control regimes bounded by working constitutional law. These are the only institutions likely to constrain the hazards effectively while making the fruits of these revolutions available. The exploration of these roots and the mechanisms for approaching the hopes and fears of the Singularity are the subjects of the following chapters of this book.

3

Trust, Civil Society, Government, and Cyberspace

As Adam Smith well understood, economic life is deeply embedded in social life, and cannot be understood apart from the customs, morals, and habits of the society in which it occurs.

—Francis Fukuyama, *Trust: The Social Virtues and the Creation of Prosperity*

Social mechanisms evolve, and evolution is conservative. It rarely eliminates an existing evolved mechanism unless it is actively harmful, and it prefers to work by adapting existing mechanisms to new purposes. Thus, a fish's air bladder becomes an amphibian's lung, and a feudal parliament that evolved to resolve disputes between nobles and kings becomes an instrument of constitutional democracy. The Speaker still carries a mace into Parliament but rarely bashes anybody with it these days. Similarly, the challenges of the new era will be met by those solutions that take existing institutions and alter them enough to meet new demands but no more, merely because such is the least costly solution. Thus the sinews of a network commonwealth will likely consist of security agreements, common economic areas, and science and technology collaborative institutions. The mechanisms for such organizations originated in institutions such as NATO, NAFTA, and the European Space Agency, but will have substantially different relations to and among their member entities.

More important, these organizations, being created primarily along lines of geographic proximity and by planning elites in government bureaucracies, have little deep-seated popular support. Even the European

Union (EU), which is well down the road to federal statehood, has only lukewarm (at best) emotional support from citizens of many of its member states. Network commonwealths, by contrast, will grow from network civilizations—groups of nations and individuals with cultural and linguistic commonalities, linked together by new electronic media in a way previous linguistic communities never before experienced. As such, they have the potential to generate common narratives—identifications and unifying feelings shared throughout the commonwealth. Shared narratives, in turn, are essential for developing the genuinely popular support needed to last through the pressures that events may bring. One way to define a network commonwealth might be as a common market, a permanent alliance, and a shared narrative.

Even today, after decades of British membership in the EU, twice as many Britons report feeling closer to the United States than to their Continental neighbors. A survey by the pro-EU magazine *The Economist* even showed that more Britons felt represented by the U.S. flag than the EU flag and far more identified the United States than Europe as Britain's most likely source of help. This suggests that this book's central recommendation—a network commonwealth uniting English-speaking nations—may be more useful and more natural to Britons than is EU membership. Evolutionary conservatism argues that organizing relatively closely linked nations into a loose and flexible structure is a less costly step than organizing wide-scale, closely linked unions, but it is nevertheless capable of providing most of the benefits of the latter organization. Political evolution thus favors the network commonwealth solution.

The conservatism of evolution is demonstrated by the fate of proposals like that of author Clarence Streit in the late 1940s to create an "Atlantic Union"—a permanent federal union of the Atlantic democracies. Although this idea had real potential benefits, it also had a number of real problems, most of which have also been encountered in the process of building the EU. It is quite likely that as today's EU tries to become yet more statelike, it will run up against the same wall—it will become more of a solution than the problem warrants. (Many Europeans feel that point was reached some time ago.)

The Atlantic Union concept failed principally because it went against the principle of conservatism in evolution. Almost all of the benefits it promised could have been, and in fact were, delivered by less radical mechanisms, ones that did not impose the costs nor meet the resistance that federal union threatened. Many of these alternative mechanisms are the same institutions that now show promise to become the sinews of a network commonwealth: free trade agreements, alliance structures, and cooperative organizations. The network commonwealth is the next step in this actual evolution. It will be built from existing mechanisms, altered to fit the new circumstances and opportunities, and offered as solutions to problems as they arise.

Some theorists have argued that evolution works by "punctuated equilibrium"—the alteration of long periods of stability and only minor change, punctuated by periods of crisis and rapid change. To the extent that social evolution follows this pattern, advocates of change can exploit these periods by having templates for change at hand, giving an available solution to be adopted when crises arise. One reason why the network commonwealth is worth talking and thinking about now is that the new perspective it engenders may offer solutions adequate to meet emerging challenges of the Singularity revolutions. The more such solutions are built on familiar institutions and concepts, the more likely they are to be adopted. Thus a network commonwealth is built upon institutions and concepts such as alliances and trade agreements, but arranged in a new and more flexible manner. Since many of the crises of the transition to an Information Economy are foreseeable (even if the further Singularity crises may not be), it is worth exploring potential solutions as well.

The more the highest value in international trade shifts from natural resources, agricultural commodities, and low-tech manufactured goods to information products and services delivered via the Internet, the more lines of trade and cooperation will fall along linguistic-cultural lines rather than geographic ones.

Already, a high proportion of such trade in all English-speaking countries is with other English-speaking countries; it should be described as "intra-Anglosphere" rather than "international." Similarly, there has been an increasing trend for Spanish-language information trade (particularly in electronic entertainment) to flow seamlessly through what, by extension, we could dub the "Hispanosphere" (an elastic entity which today would have to include Los Angeles and Miami as well as Madrid, Mexico City, and Buenos Aires).

As the returns to political structures from large-scale revenue collections (income, capital, and sales taxation) decline, the economic states that once derived direct benefit from their large scale will find those benefits becoming increasingly elusive. Rising costs and falling benefits will encourage their devolution or breakup. However, there are other benefits to large-scale organization, such as mobility of productive people over wide areas and cooperative pooling for defensive or scientific research purposes. These benefits can be realized more cheaply by network commonwealth-type arrangements than by maintaining large-scale economic states. Therefore, many large political entities will recast themselves as, or see their constituent region-states join, network commonwealths.

Because of these new realities, current patterns and politics will shift, transform, and realign, restructuring themselves more on linguistic and cultural lines.

Regional cooperation not based on these types of commonalities will grow less important as the types of trade and relations they promote grow proportionally less important to advanced economies. The EU, NAFTA, and ASEAN will have seen their high-water marks of importance to the United Kingdom, the United States and Canada, and Australia, respectively. Existing free trade structures, such as the European Economic Area (EEA), can and should remain to facilitate trade in commodities such as wheat, iron ore, and low-tech manufactures such as cars and stereos. But they should not try to cast themselves as economic unions attempting to take control of their members' economies. Former Senator Phil Gramm's argument that the World Trade Organization principles require the EU to permit Britain to make a separate trade agreement with the United States, should it so desire, would be one way to give the EU a pretext for permitting such loosening without threatening the structure of the organization.

The proposal to create a free trade agreement between NAFTA and the EU (most recently raised by British Chancellor of the Exchequer Gordon Brown), to take a case in point, is fine as far as it goes (or can go). It could eventually succeed, although it may be more productive for the states of the British Isles to join from the Atlantic, rather than the Continental, side. However, it will not go far enough or create the right mechanisms for deep cooperation. New forms of common economic space must be created to facilitate the collaboration among countries that are neighbors in the information spaces of software, media, financial services, and other high-value information products.

NAFTA, the EEA, and the proposed NAFTA-EU link may ultimately have more value in the future as means of linking different network commonwealths, rather than as protocommonwealths in themselves. Thus, NAFTA's true vocation may be as the linkage between the communities of Shakespeare and Cervantes, rather than merely a means of allowing the sale of cheaper tomatoes in American supermarkets.

The economistic model of the state is eroding. This mental model, which sees the political and social world as a billiard table with each state constituting a distinct, economically autonomous and equivalent unit (an economic state, in my terms) becomes decreasingly useful. This model ignores the reality of civilizational commonalities. A network-based paradigm is more useful. In this view, human communities are seen as part of an evolved continuum or range of social organizations, with civic states as cores anchoring wider networklike associations. In this range, civilizational, linguistic community, national, regional, and local classifications have significance as lines for organizing cooperative institutions on various levels.

ONE WORLD THROUGH THE INTERNET? THE ROLE OF TRUST, COOPERATION, AND CULTURAL COMMONALITY

The issue of cultural commonalities as a factor in deep cooperation has been the subject of much confusion. We must examine it in detail, as the point is a crucial assumption of this work. Liberal theory held, as its progenitor Jefferson classically put it, that "all men are created equal." Multiculturalist theory holds that all cultures are created equally "valid." Furthermore, it assumes that any randomly gathered set of individuals from any set of cultural backgrounds can be assembled to successfully achieve any given goal as well or better than any homogenous group from any one particular culture. Multiculturalists tend to contrast themselves with past advocates of theories of racial or cultural imperial domination. Such theories have typically held that particular races or nationalities are inherently more suited for particular activities than others. A racist in the past was someone who argued that an individual of a particular racial or ethnic origin was inherently inferior, on account of his genetic background, to others. Today, multiculturalists brand as racist any argument that a particular culture has features that better adapt its adherents to succeed in a particular form of human endeavor.

The multiculturalist argument obscures reality and ignores the experience of history. Although individuals from every ethnic, racial, and cultural background have demonstrated an unquestioned ability to compete at the highest levels of endeavor in both Industrial Era and Information Era economies, they typically have done so as members of a limited number of specific cultures. The multiculturalist model denies the need for or value of assimilation—but typically, the successful individual from less successful cultures has immigrated to, been educated in, or otherwise strongly been influenced by more successful cultures. (I define a successful culture for the purposes of this discussion as one that maximizes an individual's control over his or her destiny relative to the forces of nature, human predation, and oppression. Philosophers may argue infinitely over whether a particular culture may be "superior" to another, in terms of virtue or happiness. This discussion is confined to a much more limited and demonstrable question: which cultures seems to be better adapted to the challenges of the ongoing scientific-technological revolution.) All of these conditions involve a greater or lesser degree of assimilation; typically, the more assimilation, the more success.

For the impact of particular cultural matrices on success in adaptation to advanced technological economies, the most interesting test cases are what I call "template" societies. These are societies in which a founding seed population has established a society characterized by a particular language, culture, politics, and economic structure. Most such societies have been one of the historic colonies of settlement, such as the United States or Argentina. The language and culture established are usually derived from those of the original homes of the colonists, or some regional variants thereof. Subsequently, an extended immigration coming from a wide variety of national origins arrives and is assimilated into the template society, molding itself into the larger patterns of life and activity. Although the immigrants may contribute attributes of their cultures to the overall mix, the fundamental national characteristics of the template society remain those of the seed population, as affected by further evolution.

TRUST AND CIVIL SOCIETY

One of the most important cultural norms embedded in the template is the characteristic of trust, discussed by Francis Fukuyama in his book *Trust: The Social Virtues and the Creation of Prosperity*, as mentioned earlier. Fukuyama differentiates between high-trust and low-trust societies. (Properly, this distinction should be termed one of societies with, variously, a high or low radius of trust—the size of the circles within which one can expect fair dealing and impartial treatment.) The principal characteristic of the former relative to the latter is the ability of individuals in high-trust cultures to form, freely and easily, associations and enterprises among individuals not connected by close kinship ties. Such associations are formed with the reasonable expectation that the letter and spirit of the original understandings of the association will be carried out by all parties, even when to do so may turn out to be more to one party's advantage in a specific instance. High-trust cultures are able to support rich civil societies—ones in which individuals spontaneously associate in all manners of organizations, from for-profit corporations to nonprofit community, civic, and religious organizations, in order to carry out the functions of society.

Furthermore, citizens of high-trust cultures can expect their governmental institutions to support the activities of the civil sector, through means like quick and fair adjudication of any disputes that cannot be settled privately, maintenance of public order, and defeat of coercive or fraudulent tactics. Low-trust cultures are ones in which the state becomes, by default, the principal organizing force for all civic and economic functions and the primary means by which individuals mediate all transactions beyond the family level. Typically, state employees in high-trust societies are oriented toward carrying out their functions as called for in their job descriptions, whereas state employees in low-trust societies view their situation as an opportunity to enrich themselves and their families. Hence we typically see higher rates of corruption and nepotism in low-trust societies.

An employee in a company or government agency in a low-trust society can be expected to play any situation for the gain of himself, his family, and his cronies, rather than for the good of the corporation or the state in general. Thus, in a low-trust society, bribes and kickbacks are the normal mechanisms of business and governmental relationships. This is not a breakdown of morality; rather, it is obedience to a more primitive morality, in which loyalty to kin networks is the highest value.

Businesses, political parties, and state administrations tend to function best in low-trust environments when they are under the personal control of a single, strong figure, one to whom inferiors are bound in personal loyalty relationships.

In such situations, personal loyalty limits the degree to which employees will put personal advantage over organizational interests. Similarly, strong ideological and nationalist movements in a low-trust society can generate loyalty to a state administration or enterprise, at least for some period of time. France, although possessing many of the characteristics of a low-trust society, used its strong national narrative to develop high-level state institutions that are relatively effective.

One does not bribe an *énarque*, at least directly, although an *énarque* may not hesitate to bribe a foreign official in order to sell a French arms system.

Low-trust societies find themselves trapped in a vicious circle—the greater the corruption of the state, the greater the obstacles to individuals trying to act in a high-trust manner. Rational individuals then abandon high-trust behavior and act in a low-trust manner themselves. Conversely, low-trust individuals entering a high-trust society find themselves in a virtuous circle—the more they learn to trust their fellow-citizens and their institutions, the more they prosper.

To illustrate the differences by example, in a high-trust civil society, a group of citizens perceiving some need—say, a university—in their town would first create an organization (which might be for-profit or nonprofit) to try to meet the need, and only turn to the state if those means proved insufficient. In a low-trust society, individuals would be unable to trust each other sufficiently to organize themselves to carry out any important task. If one person tried, members of other families would immediately suspect that person of scheming to advantage himself at the expense of the rest.

In low-trust cultures, strong individuals and family networks are the primary channels of effective action. Nepotism, which promotes inefficiency in high-trust cultures, becomes an advantage in low-trust cultures.

Hiring relatives provides collaborators who, whatever their competence, can at least be trusted not to steal or at least to steal no more than the amount to which custom entitles them.

In such societies, individuals can only petition or pressure the state to carry out a needed function that requires resources above the level of family enterprise.

The state either does it eventually, or it never gets done. The primary exceptions to this rule are individuals of extraordinary strength of will, who can maneuver the system skillfully enough to accomplish particular tasks.

The psychology of such extraordinary persons (successful or not) has been one of the great themes of Latin American literature, precisely because almost all great deeds in such countries have been the results of such wills. The multiculturalist critics of this book will likely accuse me of having contempt for members of low-trust cultures. On the contrary, I have admiration for the intelligence, energy, and will of many people I have known in such cultures, combined with regret that they are imprisoned in a system which does not permit them the full and highest use of their abilities.

Two sets of template societies demonstrate these processes as they affect levels of development. Fukuyama identified several particular cultures (although not exclusively) as high-trust: England, Germany, Japan, and Northern Italy. Cultures identified as low-trust included China, France, and Southern Italy. Spain and Portugal, although not extensively discussed by Fukuyama, also meet his definition of low-trust cultures (although the Catalan and Basque cultures display some high-trust characteristics).

Of the high-trust cultures, only the English engendered extensive template societies, particularly the United States, Australia, New Zealand, and (Anglo-) Canada. Spain engendered the template societies of Argentina, Chile, Uruguay; Portugal, that of Brazil. All of these template societies experienced extensive immigration, much of it from the same source cultures: Germany, Italy, Japan, Eastern Europe. The United States and Brazil also experienced the involuntary influx of Africans via the slave trade. Argentina, and to a lesser extent the other South American societies, drew a substantial number of British immigrants.

These source nations thus included both high-trust and low-trust cultures.

Template societies assimilated individuals from widely diverse backgrounds, individuals who then adopted the great majority of the cultural characteristics of the template, including the trust characteristics. At first, all of these societies prospered.

All had substantial natural resources and were able to adapt the new technologies of Machine Age agriculture to exploit those resources and to achieve a broad prosperity. Argentina and Uruguay achieved a level of prosperity essentially similar to those of Australia and Canada by the eve of World War I.

That is because agricultural prosperity in the Industrial Era could be adequately achieved by family scale enterprises, a level of organization at which low-trust cultures can act effectively. Countries like Brazil and Argentina have had most of the preconditions of Machine Age and Information Age success, including a well-educated population, adequate domestic capital, and plenty of hard-working, individually ambitious, motivated, and imaginative entrepreneurs.

Despite this, these nations continue to linger at the threshold of the "Third Gateway"—takeoff into the high-tech entrepreneurial revolution—without generating the critical mass of enterprise needed to accomplish it.

Consider the emerging high-technology entrepreneurial world in Brazil. At first, the region seemed extremely promising. The quality of the human capital was high, and there was plenty of the small-scale precursor entrepreneurial activity that seemed to presage the coalescing of a new Silicon Valley under the Southern Cross. Missing, however, was the fluidity with which new enterprises could self-assemble, determine the appropriate set of rewards, and work together.

Although Silicon Valley entrepreneurs are usually thought of as individualists, they are individualists with an uncommon ability to collaborate. Latin American template societies tend to generate individualists of an older model—more zero-sum oriented, less able to coordinate smoothly without hierarchical structures.

Many of the participants in this world were not Portuguese or Spanish by national origin. They were from the same mix of origins we think of as typically American: German, English, Eastern European, and Italian. Furthermore, most of the individuals in this world could speak fluent English and had studied or worked in the United States or Britain.

High-trust template societies accept individuals from low-trust cultures and gradually assimilate them into high-trust behavior patterns, through the virtuous circle of reward for trust. Low-trust templates assimilate individuals from high-trust cultures into low-trust behavior patterns through the vicious circle of penalizing high-trust assumptions and rewarding low-trust behavior. It starts with the first bribe solicited and accepted.

TRUST, REFORM, AND THE THREE GATEWAYS

Advocates of the One-World-through-Internet and English as a Universal Language persuasion too readily discount the fine-grained cultural and institutional factors that affect the ability to progress in the Singularity revolutions. It is useful in this regard to consider the various levels of trust and strength of civil society as gateways through which a society must pass on the way to prosperity. The first gateway is the basic one of property rights and rule of law. The second gateway consists of constructing a state regime that relinquishes the arbitrary assignment of wealth to parties based on state-granted monopolies, protection, or confiscatory taxation.

The third gateway consists of elimination of social, cultural, and political barriers to fluid entrepreneurship and rapid enterprise formation.

Economists often fail to understand why favorable second gateway policies regarding macroeconomic factors (such as stabilizing the currency or lowering the overall rate of taxation) are often insufficient to spark third gateway entrepreneurship without the additional removal of nonfiscal barriers such as overregulation and corruption. Similarly, universalists fail to comprehend that it is not enough to have simply learned English to become a member of English-speaking civilization, just as North Americans traveling to Spanish America require more than a knowledge of the Spanish language to integrate themselves into Spanish-speaking civilization.

Some today maintain that the emergence of automatic translation software will render linguistic differences obsolete. It is more likely, however, that the existence of such software (which *is* likely to become available) will increase friction rather than diminish it. A good human translator is a facilitator between cultures as much as between languages. Without such intermediaries, monolingual individuals who rely on software will never understand how little has been truly understood until it is too late. To mix individuals from high-trust and low-trust cultures is to create an unstable situation. Over time, either the individuals from low-trust cultures will assimilate into high-trust behavior patterns, or vice versa.

The issue of trust is only one of many cultural characteristics that affect deep cooperation, although it is a fundamental one. As I talk about English-speaking nations or Spanish-speaking nations, I am not talking primarily about the issue of linguistic competence. Rather the language becomes a marker for a whole set of cultural characteristics, standards, expectations, and practices which foster or hinder cooperation in business, politics, and civic affairs. Nor is cooperation between different high-trust cultures to be taken as a matter of course.

The particular practices, institutions, and understandings which mark and bind relationships in high-trust cultures (which began as expansions of kinship relations, as with the practice of adult adoptions in Japanese culture) tend to be culture-specific. In order to make those practices work, an outsider must learn to understand them and integrate into such structures. Once inside, the connection can be highly rewarding, as Westerners who undergo the substantial transaction costs of establishing mutual trust relations with Japanese institutions can discover.

However, such connections will not be easy to cultivate via the Internet; the transaction costs of such interactions will create a boundary in the geographically flat information-space of the Internet.

In addition to trust, it is useful to think about the role of openness in societies. The United States, the Netherlands, Germany, and Japan are all high-trust societies. However, they vary widely along a scale measuring openness—the degree to which nonmembers may enter and be given access to the trust mechanisms of those societies. America is very open to newcomers—traditionally, those who demonstrate willingness to assimilate are rewarded with membership (although racial barriers formed exceptions in the past, and do so even today in some circumstances).

The Netherlands has always had a tradition of asylum, tolerance, and acceptance. Germany today has large numbers of ethnic Turks, speaking fluent German and educated in German schools, who have not been granted citizenship until very recently. Japan is notoriously averse to assimilation of foreigners—Koreans and Chinese have lived in Japan for generations without ever being accepted as truly Japanese. One key to why America and other English-speaking nations, like Canada and Australia, have become successful high-trust template societies while others have not is the unique mixture of high-trust and openness.

Ironically, it may well be easier for an individual from one low-trust society to integrate into another low-trust culture, providing that culture is open, than for that individual to integrate into a high-trust society. An Italian landing in Rio de Janeiro at the turn of the century needed only to figure out which officials needed to be bribed, which businessmen needed what size kickback, and with which families a marriage connection ought to be sought. All of these were familiar tasks from life in Naples. The same immigrant arriving in America, unless he confined himself to the ethnic wards of the big cities, would find the familiar home strategies to be counterproductive. Thus the ethnic wards served as halfway houses for immigrants, providing limited areas in which low-trust strategies could provide a basic living while they, or their children, could learn high-trust values from the surrounding culture, permitting them to fully benefit from the American system.

We don't yet know how the Internet will affect the interplay between high-trust and low-trust cultures. In physical space, a template is provided by the surrounding culture. Values are reinforced through the sovereign government. The Internet, however, is not a single, unitary space. It is a medium more like the ocean, on which an unlimited number of islands (discrete information spaces) can exist side by side. Each has its own template, and each can impose its own rules.

To the extent that the general Internet is a single space, it is inherently a low-trust culture. As with oceanic space prior to the nineteenth century, in which any ship might be a pirate, any random party coming to you via the Internet must be assumed to be untrustworthy until proven otherwise. Smaller subsets of the Internet, particularly virtual private networks with restricted entry, can support high-trust environments. A network for an ethnic minority speaking a little-known language, such as the Hakka language of that Chinese minority, would need little in the way of passwords to exclude nonmembers. For English speakers, assurance of higher trust must come in other ways.

There are some early indications that the Internet can serve as the medium for new high-trust communities. The experience of the Linux open-source software community indicates that people from many countries can participate in a common venture on a productive basis. As I discussed earlier, Linux is software: a newer version of UNIX, a robust computer operating system. Its development was started by a computer programmer from Finland, Linus Torvalds, on a volunteer basis, and was ultimately taken up by an extremely loose-knit, worldwide community of computer programmers, all working for free, and all coordinating themselves via the Internet.

This community was more American than otherwise, but not overwhelmingly so; it did communicate and work in English, and its members are largely from high-trust cultures. Although the effort was done on a nonprofit basis, the product has served to launch a number of successful companies making commercial software products based on Linux. Linux has been a highly successful software product, preferred by many over its rival, Microsoft's Windows NT, for server operating systems.

In a sense, working on an open-source software system is the ultimate high-trust action: you work and trust that the world will reward you for the value you create. Open-sourcing may well become a powerful part of the paradigm of the network economy. How do you characterize a person whose life revolves around work, socializing, and recreation all on the Internet? Such a person is truly amphibious and spends the bulk of his time in the newer medium. One could argue that, whatever his location in physical space, he has become an immigrant to the network civilization which harbors the activities whose values he chooses to adopt. One of the ways in which a network civilization is different from previous civilizations may be that it will find a way to extend membership to such cyberimmigrants. Network commonwealths may want to extend participation in this fashion to cyberimmigrants.

If people could download the fulfillment of all their desires from the Internet, as they do software, social groupings existing only in cyberspace—

virtual nations—could become the basis of new nations. Given that humans can at best be amphibious in that regard, existing partly in cyberspace and partly in physical space, it is likely that most cyberspace institutions will be extensions of existing or adapted entities from physical space. Trust mechanisms from physical space will be adapted to cyberspace to permit establishment of high-trust business, social, and civic relationships. High-trust cultures will likely be able to readily adapt existing networks of companies, congregations, clubs, and societies to serve similar functions in cyberspace. This process is in fact now developing. In fact, such mechanisms may be improved by the ability of cyberspace to lower transaction costs of human interaction.

Low-trust cultures will find this task more difficult. As we have seen, the principal means of accomplishment in low-trust societies are kinship relations (including founder-dominated businesses or political parties driven by the dynamism of the founder figure), and the state. Kinship relationships can of course be effectively extended via Internet. Even high-trust societies, in which extended kinship relations tend to be weaker due to their relative unimportance as economic mechanisms, may see a revival of extended family ties due to their lower transactions costs, and in compensation for smaller nuclear family sizes resulting from lowered fertility rates in advanced nations.

Institutions dependent on state-mediated relationships (primarily, government agencies, state-protected corporations, and established churches) are the principal means for achieving large-scale projects in low-trust societies. They will have a much harder time adapting to the new era. In order to adapt, their forms must evolve substantially. State entities tend to depend on their sovereign powers as a means of reducing competition, obtaining capital, and securing their economic base. The erosion of effective state economic sovereignty, due to the reduced ability to control capital and human mobility in the Information Revolution, will hit state entities particularly hard. The waves of privatization already seen in the world are not just due to the return of market theory. Rather, they are a result of the increasing inability of such state entities to remain functional otherwise in the changing world environment.

These trends will likely accelerate. Therefore, such state-dependent institutions will attempt to cooperate with one another on an international basis, as a means of remaining competitive against more market-based organizations.

Unfortunately for them, such cooperation will be problematic without the existence of a supernational authority to control their operating environment, as individual states do on a national scale. Consider the EU as an attempt to create one such authority, and its politics become clearer. Its difficulties in mediating the desires, needs, and expectations of its various members illustrate the problems inherent in such a task.

Such state-mediated organizations will come under increasing competitive pressure from networks of entrepreneurial organizations based in high-trust cultures, which can more swiftly organize, capitalize, adapt, and deploy themselves on a global basis, and likewise from kinship-based networks and founder-dominated family firms operating from bases in low-trust cultures. The primary effective state-mediated organization will be those in fields where governmental decisions have substantial bearing on competitiveness, such as the arms industry.

Also, organizations may continue to prosper if their home nation remains a stable home market through essentially voluntary support. Israel may be an example of such, if Israelis remain willing to pay higher taxes to support their government's purchases from local companies at higher than world-market prices.

ONE WORLD, MANY MARKETPLACES

Although the Internet creates the possibility of an infinite number of world-spanning networks, it is likely that most such networks will connect individuals sharing access to like mechanisms for establishing and maintaining trust. One could readily create a network linking Kenya, Guatemala, and Mongolia, for example, but that network would have an extremely limited set of uses. More likely is the definition of worldwide networks connecting English-speaking cultures, or Spanish-speaking ones, or the worldwide ethnic diasporas such as the various Chinese regional and ethnic groups.

This process can best be visualized as a series of spheres on which are traced the lines connecting each pair or group of parties connecting via the Net. Thus the Anglosphere can be thought of as a worldwide network with great densities over North America, Australasia, and the British Isles, and much thinner ones over, say, Siberia; while the Hispanosphere would be densest over Spain and Spanish America (including nodes over Los Angeles and Miami). A Sinosphere would contain many subdivisions: Cantonese and Shanghaiese networks would be dense over their home regions of China, but they would also have substantial nodes in California, Australia, British Columbia, and Hawaii, to name but a few places.

These network spheres are a new category of social organization, having some of the characteristics of nations, some of civilizations, some of diasporas, but some unique characteristics as well. They overlap with, but are not entirely coincident with, states and can coexist in the same physical space—as Los Angeles, for example, serves as a node in many spheres simultaneously. For the purposes of this book, I call them network civilizations. I define a network civilization as a set of nations, communities, and individuals bound together through language, culture, and assumptions more far-reaching than those of individual national communities. Another way of thinking of it is the next widest set of civil-society networks beyond the boundaries of individual sovereign countries.

It would be accurate, but impossibly clumsy, to term them "intra-linguistic-cultural-civic communities." Another term that could be applied is "subcivilization"—recognizing that such a community may be part of a larger civilization but is quite distinct from other members. However, this is likewise an inelegant term.

"Network civilization" as a term also distinguishes this phenomenon by insisting that these entities are bound together more by information-space than by geographic space, as were all predecessor civilizations. The English-speaking cultures of this planet are emerging as one such network civilization. Others are also emerging. I believe that these network civilizations will be the preeminent form of social organization of the coming era, as the nation was of the last. The network commonwealth will become the preeminent form of political entity by which network civilizations will be bound together, as the nation-state bound together cultural nations in the last era.

Some communities may be bound together by nonlinguistic ties, such as religion or political belief. Some speculation has been made that commercial or vocational ties may form substantial networks. This may have some truth. But I would caution that communities, to have staying power in the face of the probable challenges of the future, must be able to summon substantial allegiance from their members. Networks will empower nonstate actors such as political, religious, and social movements. These are not states but can affect states. It is unlikely that corporations will become such nonstate actors. As I have already noted, traditional corporations may end up suffering many of the same problems that governments are now experiencing in the new era of the Internet.

Throughout history, communities that could not convince or compel their members to pay taxes and bear arms have been subjugated or destroyed by other communities. Microsoft may be a globe-spanning organization with immense resources, but its ability to summon its members to kill or die for its sake is most likely quite limited; at most, it could hire a limited number of mercenaries competent to handle some, but not all tasks of the type that states by their nature must be able to undertake. The Mormon Church, on the other hand, was once able to turn its members' loyalty into state power and could undoubtedly do so again should it become necessary for survival.

The network commonwealth, like humans in the Information Revolution, is amphibious, existing in two dissimilar media and adapted to function in each.

Humans are just beginning the transition to this state, so it is not surprising that their political forms will evolve along with them, at a somewhat slower pace. Like biological amphibians, network commonwealths will function in their medium of origin and physical space, and they will interact with their predecessors, those nation-states that survive.

As biological amphibians also utilize the new medium of the land to expand their range relative to their predecessors, so will network commonwealths use the unique capabilities of their new environment of cyberspace to gain advantages that their predecessors were unable to realize. In this case, those advantages will be the expansion of common areas for trade, residence, cooperation, and defense over a wide, global scale without the costs of empire or national-scale cohesion with which their predecessors were burdened.

THE NEW AMPHIBIANS: LIVING SIMULTANEOUSLY IN CYBERSPACE AND THE PHYSICAL WORLD

I previously alluded to the new, "amphibious" nature of persons immersed in the Internet and its economy, and the culture and institutions in which they participate.

Here, I will discuss the way in which that amphibious nature of Internet societies transforms the relation of people to physical space in unexpected ways. The essence of this transformation is the separation of physical space from information space.

Physical space is space as humans have always experienced it. Persons in different parts of physical space must transport themselves to a common location in order to interact; and they must transport goods to a common location in order to share them. Trade, war, and all other physical interactions among dispersed populations have always required physical transport. Physical space is measured in kilometers or miles; distances thus measured remain unchanging. For the purposes of considering the effect of technological change on society, we can also think of transportation space, which measures the distance on the planet surface in terms of the time and energy needed to transport people and goods across that space. Similarly we can define information space, as being measured in the time needed to transport information across the same space. Transportation space changed little in size for the great bulk of human existence. Only as changes in technology and social organization began to accumulate did transportation space begin to shrink.

Some human functions have not required physical presence to accomplish, or at least to initiate. Once people learned to encode information in symbolic form by writing, the symbolic medium, whether a clay tablet, a *quipu*, or a letter, could transport that information more cheaply and easily than people. Thus, a trade, a war, or a marriage could be negotiated by letter and from a distance, although consummation still required travel. In this way, information space was born as a thing separate from physical space.

At first, information space was not very distinct from physical space, because the symbolic media still needed to be physically carried from one spot to another, at rates maybe only slightly faster, and usually no faster, than the physical transport of the goods and people they represented. Postal relay systems permitted kings and emperors to move select bits of information faster and more reliably than their subjects could, an advantage they enjoyed and were loath to share.

For almost all of history, one of the key characteristics of governments has been that they enjoyed more, better, and faster access to information than those they governed, whether it be an Inca emperor receiving the knotted *quipu* rope from a runner or an American president viewing a high-resolution satellite photograph.

One of the ways the Information Revolution is changing the nature of the state is via the erosion of this traditional power differential. High-resolution satellite photography, for example, has been reduced to a commodity that anybody can buy on the World Wide Web. Any two computer users ambitious enough to download a good encryption program can communicate in better secrecy than much of the United States government. In the past few years, even defense and intelligence planners have begun to realize that they could adapt commercial software for many of their communications purposes to give them better capability than could be built for them by contract.

The telegraph and telephone began to make a real difference in the speed and cost at which information traveled relative to the speed and cost with which people and their goods traveled. When this happened, information space began to assume radically different dimensions from physical space. The physical globe, measured in the time it took to travel from one location to another, began shrinking rapidly. In the days of sailing ships, the world was perhaps a year in circumference, in terms of transportation space. Once the steamship and steam railway had been implemented worldwide, the world shrank to several months in circumference.

Jules Verne celebrated this progress in *Around the World in Eighty Days*, a book that electrified the readers of his day with its audacity. At the same time, the laying of the first great continental and undersea cables shrank the information-space globe to less than a day in circumference.

Even then, although the size of the information-space globe diverged drastically from that of the physical-space globe, its geography mimicked that of physical space for a long time. Telegraph and telephone lines followed roads and railroads.

Relay stations were placed in the same location as railway junctions. Undersea cables were laid out along the sea routes of the maritime empires they connected.

And the privileged access to those communications systems enjoyed by the states that created or licensed them reinforced, rather than eroded, their authority.

BETTER COMMUNICATIONS
AND THE RISE OF NATIONALISM

At first, the shrinking of information space did not realign the geography of states, but rather reinforced the emergent nationalism of the nineteenth and twentieth centuries. It did so by creating a coherent, instantaneous, but primarily one-way information-space in each nation-state. The construction of this information-space began in the late nineteenth century. The introduction of high-productivity, low-cost rotary presses allowed newspapers and magazines to be produced cheaply enough for the lower classes to read. Expanded schooling made them literate enough to want to buy them. Cheap railway transportation allowed entire nations to read the same papers on the same day. Mass daily newspapers, wire services, and mass-circulation nationwide magazines evolved to serve these new markets.

Each nation-state began to develop its own national-scale media. This became a powerful tool for overcoming local allegiances, suppressing regional dialects, and integrating dispersed and divergent populations into nation-state institutions. One of the criteria for nation-state status was the achievement of a sufficient critical mass of readers of a defined local language to support a complete set of media and educational institutions in that language. The size of the critical mass was determined in part by the cost of maintaining the production and distribution means for such media. Why, for instance, were Czech nationalists so insistent on including their Slovak cousins in a single state? Their urgency was driven partly by the need they felt for a critical mass of speakers of a common language to support these nation-building institutions.

At first, the invention of the radio had only minor effects on the pattern of point-to-point communication, mostly affecting maritime communications. The low bit-rate of wireless telegraphy, combined with its lack of privacy, rendered it uninteresting in comparison with landlines. In its one-to-many role, however, it strongly reinforced the popular nationalism encouraged by the mass print media of the nineteenth century, and carried it further. Even a mass circulation newspaper required some literacy to follow. The nationalism promoted by the popular press could be countered in part by newspapers carrying alternative points of view, such as the mass socialist press of nineteenth-century Europe. These tended to oppose hypernationalist sentiments—ineffectively, as the outbreak of World War I demonstrated.

Broadcast radio, by contrast, could be followed by the totally illiterate and could be played as an ever-present background throughout waking hours. It could even be played over loudspeakers in public places, as totalitarian states discovered. By making a uniform national information service the daily definer of reality, it permitted the state to have enormous influence over the perceptions of its citizenry. This reinforced the economic structural pressures to make the centralized economic state the primary (in some cases, the exclusive) scale of organization, even in the large-scale federal states such as the United States. Political leadership went to those who mastered the use of radio to generate and reinforce narratives; Hitler, Roosevelt, Churchill, and Mussolini all stand out in this regard.

Charles DeGaulle, after the German conquest of France in 1940, even created via radio what might be called the first virtual state, albeit a temporary one. Free France was created by a radio broadcast and kept in being at first by little more than his broadcasts. These served as a rallying point from which DeGaulle created an alternative state—a self-assembly protocol for an alternative French empire—which gradually emerged and eventually replaced its rival, territory by territory, until the Allied invasion installed it in the metropolis.

Motion pictures and television reinforced these effects further. The immersive nature of these media permitted an even more heightened emotional effect on the viewer. The increase in critical mass required to sustain a domestic cinema or television production industry encouraged centralization even more. It was quite possible, for example, to have a Dutch or Danish media industry publishing books and newspapers, and even radio; an independent cinema and television industry was for a longer time beyond their reach. With each technological innovation—sound, color, wide-screen—the size of the market critical mass increased. This was consistent with the assumptions of the era, which forecast continually intensifying centralization. Everyone assumed the need to create ever-larger states to maintain the critical mass for the essential capabilities of statehood.

It was only with the technological and commercial innovations of the late twentieth century that these patterns began to change. The first such innovation was the communications satellite, which permitted low-cost transmission of voice, text, and video. These could be either on a one-way, one-to-many or two-way, one-to-one basis, between any two points on earth. For the first time, information did not flow through channels shaped by geography. A message no longer had to be relayed through an ascending hierarchy of relays, through major hubs, and down again through a descending hierarchy. It merely needed to be beamed up from one spot on earth to a satellite, and down to its destination.

The cost of a relay from Tegucigalpa to Ouagadougou need not be any greater than that of a relay from New York to London, although the politics of the satellite and telephone world usually made it so. The Internet soon complemented these developments. Its first experimental form (ARPAnet) developed over the following thirty years into a worldwide ocean on which data could travel directly from any one spot to any other. The cheap, easy-to-use personal computer has made it possible for individuals in most of the industrialized world to create ports on this ocean in their own homes.

Meanwhile, the revolution in telecommunication costs, first sparked by communications satellites, began to accelerate. Fiber-optic cable drastically reduced the cost of long-distance calls even further, both on land and sea. The availability of low-cost communications options developed in tandem with the trend, previously noted, to decentralized and competitive solutions. Throughout the twentieth century, most communications were handled by state organizations or state-chartered monopolies, such as the U.S. Post Office and most post, telegraph, and telephone authorities, or the Bell monopoly in the United States, respectively. The first telecommunications satellites were operated by a new international monopoly, Intelsat, created for that purpose.

With the advent of low-cost communications options, entrepreneurial companies such as MCI in long-distance telecommunications and Orion and PanAmSat in international satellite transmissions began to challenge these monopolies.

Deregulation and rising productivity in telecommunications became mutually reinforcing phenomena. Lower costs encouraged more entrants, while competition ensured that cost-cutting innovations were implemented as quickly as possible.

The result of these developments has been to make the shape of information space profoundly different from the shape of physical space. Geography still determines the shape of physical space, and transportation space too, although the advent of low-cost aviation has begun to alter that for passenger travel. But the information economy is becoming the dominant matrix in which subsidiary economic sectors such as manufacturing, agriculture, and natural resources are embedded. Because of these developments, I believe that the new political structures to emerge will conform increasingly to the subdivisions of informational space and decreasingly to those of physical space.

SPACE AND POWER: GEOPOLITICS AND THE TOPOLOGY OF INFORMATION SPACE

Past political structures have been shaped by proximity in travel time and cost. In periods when land travel was the cheapest and safest, and therefore the predominant means of communication, political communities were determined by physical proximity over land and demarcated by features such as mountain ranges and rivers. When transoceanic travel was the cheapest and easiest means of travel, as in the Age of Exploration, waterborne empires such as Britain's, Holland's, Spain's, and Portugal's connected lands on routes determined first by trade winds and currents, and later by canals and coaling stations.

The disparity between the cheapness of ocean travel and the expense and difficulty of land travel in that era led to an unusual topology of transportation and communication space. To cite one example, Carolina and Virginia planters each found it easier and cheaper to communicate and trade with London than with each other. Subsequent changes in transportation and communications technology left many of the societies formed within the framework of these empires scattered and disconnected. The topology of cyberspace will increase the importance of many connections established during such periods of history, although on a radically different basis.

Now, cheap worldwide jet travel, communications satellites, and above all, the Internet are rapidly diminishing distance as a factor in political community.

The mountain ranges of the Information Era are the information barriers—our linguistic and cultural differences. The common spaces are the spaces of shared language, culture, and trust institutions.

Trade in agricultural products continued to be important in the Machine Age but was eclipsed as a key factor in world economic dominance by trade in manufactured goods. Just so will trade in physical goods continue to be important but be eclipsed by trade in informational goods. Continents and geographic regions will continue to be meaningful political arenas, but informational geopolitics will complement and eventually eclipse these considerations. Informational geopolitics will be a geopolitics not of mountain passes and mineral deposits, but of language, custom, religion, and shared values.

As warfare evolves further in the direction of information warfare, geographic proximity as a factor in force projection recedes as well. The maritime empires of the sixteenth through twentieth centuries arose and took their particular forms because of the Western monopoly on long-range, cannon-bearing sailing ships. These created the ability for even small European nations to project power around the globe and defeat local forces upon arrival.

Information warfare—disruption of an adversary's military and economic capabilities through unauthorized intervention in their information systems—can be projected across the globe for the same cost and with the same effectiveness as next door. The strength of a system's ability to withstand information-warfare attack is based on the strength of the system security, rather than physical distance from the attacker.

Network commonwealths can offer substantial mutual security to member-states even if they are widely dispersed geographically, as the combined economic and technological resources of such a commonwealth provide a greater critical mass of capabilities for information warfare. The "Grid"—the powerful military information, command, and control networks linking sensors (such as radar stations and camera drones), weapons, field units, and commanders—will be the matrix in which all military actions will take place. Creating an effective grid will be expensive, but extending one to cover a geographically distant country will be relatively cheap. Offering participation in such a grid will create a powerful incentive for joining a network commonwealth arrangement, as it will be an effective guarantee of security.

Samuel Huntington, in *The Clash of Civilizations* (1996), envisioned a future world divided primarily along "civilizational" lines. Huntington characterized the world as composed of six principal civilizations: Western, Islamic, East Asian, Indian, Latin American, and Orthodox, and assumes that these civilizational lines of cleavage will form the fundamental units of a future world power system. Huntington's classifications can and should be debated. Similarly, the more deterministic interpretations of his work can be called into question—cross-civilizational cooperation is not impossible, nor is intracivilizational conflict inevitable.

Caveats aside, Huntington's discussion of civilizational groupings as a useful way of classifying and comparing societies is a valuable contribution to current political debate. Huntington's assumptions might usefully be reframed in the light of recent experience in the emerging circumstance of a borderless economy without a borderless world; however, I believe such a reframing would not undermine his basic assumptions. Civilizations may differ, but in the emerging economy, states cannot effectively fight for either territory (Agricultural Age wealth), or markets (Industrial Age wealth). But attention should also be paid to the finer categories of classification of human societies—there is a substantial distance between "civilization" and "nation," just as there is between "nation" and "individual."

A civilizational level of classification, as argued by Huntington, makes sense in such a classification scheme. But to reduce any question to one of civilizational identity is to repeat the current mistake of seeing only the national-state level and ignoring other affinities. As the contours of information space diverge from those of physical space, the societies once defined by geographic and political boundaries will flow in new patterns. The network civilization I discussed at the beginning of this chapter is a start at describing one of these emerging patterns, one that may eclipse the older concept of civilization. Nationalism will be affected as one-way media are increasingly supplanted by two-way media. Combine this with a transformation of the assumptions on which twentieth-century economic states were founded, and the nature of states will change and give rise to new categories of political actors in the twenty-first century.

We cannot make sense of social and political events now emerging unless we understand how changes in information management and manufacturing are changing the basis of our daily lives. The Internet and information technologies will soon change the way the basic goods of everyday life are produced and sold, how we all make our livings, and how these changes affect the abilities of government.

Economic states—those whose support rests fundamentally on the ability to cross-subsidize population groups by controlling large percentages of the GDP—have been losing their power over people for the past twenty years, and they will likely lose more power as these trends grow stronger and faster. Coherent nations—civic states that are supported by cultural rather than economic cohesion—will continue to emerge as economic states break up or transform themselves.

Economic states are also usually large and centralized; civic states are often smaller and include decentralized federations of small civic states.

Still, many things that large-scale nations can do will remain desirable, and people will want to find ways of keeping them, even as those states break up or cede power to smaller units. A new form of political organization can be created to carry out these functions. The network commonwealth is the logical outgrowth of organizations that have already emerged over the past fifty years. Such organizations include, as I have discussed previously, permanent defense alliances like NATO, common markets and trade areas like NAFTA and the EEA, and organizations for cooperation in science and technology, like the European Space Agency. A network commonwealth will use building blocks such as these but will also be designed to take advantage of the network economy. Its membership will be drawn from network civilizations—groups of nations sharing common languages, traditions, and cultural characteristics, particularly in the degree of shared civil society, openness, and trust characteristics.

Unions of economic states, such as the EU, will fade as a model, to be replaced by unions of civic states—network commonwealths.

Network commonwealths will differ from existing structures such as common markets or alliances, however, in the way that their members will feel about them. The assembly of small medieval counties, duchies, and principalities into nation-states was accompanied by the growth of a new feeling of national belonging.

So too will the nations forming network civilizations begin to develop an emotional sense of membership in their network civilization and the network commonwealth on which it is built. Many people have predicted that the effect of the Information Revolution will be to create a globalized "One World" and reduce national differences to some lowest common denominator. This is wrong. Many cultural and civilizational differences will persist and form the effective boundaries of cyberspace.

In the next sections, I will discuss the specifics of what network commonwealths might be, and how they might work. I will describe what a world organized into network commonwealths might look like, and what the fate of existing international structures, such as the United Nations, might be. I will discuss one network civilization, that of the English-speaking nations of the world, and what a network commonwealth built on that civilization might look like. In chapter 4, I will consider what is at stake for you, the reader, in the creation of a network commonwealth and how it might affect your daily life. I will set forth some possible scenarios of how the emerging issues of the Information Revolution may create crises. Then, I will end by discussing how a movement for a network commonwealth may resolve these crises and guard the stability, prosperity, and freedom for ourselves and our fellow citizens in the revolutions of the Singularity.

HANSEATIC LEAGUES IN CYBERSPACE

Political forms other than centralized economic states once provided to their participants many of the services which citizens today receive. In this regard, the Hanseatic League, or German Hanse, is of interest. The medieval Hanseatic League provided voluntary links between a large number of existing and emerging cities in what is now Germany and the Baltic states. The Hanse avoided taking on any of the trappings of power, and always presented itself as a humble service organization. In fact, the provision of a number of mundane services (equivalent to those carried on today by consulates or trade ministries) comprised the bulk of its activity. It was particularly careful to deny any pretensions to sovereignty or challenge to the legitimacy of existing powers. Every one of its member cities was formally under the sovereignty of some prince or independent state.

The Middle Ages enjoyed a market in sovereignty services to a certain degree, such as is now returning. Whenever the Hanse needed state sovereignty to vest its actions with authority, it was always able to find some state willing to lend its cover, usually for a price or because its interest coincided with that of the Hanse. When it needed military force, which it used primarily to protect the activities of its members, it usually rented warships from its member cities and suggested contributions from the beneficiaries to pay for them. It usually characterized its military activities as suppression of piracy, which, given the nature of the princes of that time, was essentially true.

The Hanse was a coalition of the willing. It never required unanimity for action, nor did it act by majority vote. Those parties that felt a need to do something consulted each other and upon reaching consensus, proceeded to execute the decision, while those who remained outside the consensus disassociated themselves from it. Often Hanseatic communications would list those cities that exempted or disassociated themselves from the matter at hand.

The Hanse tolerated a high degree of ambiguity. It is still not clear to historians which cities belonged to the Hanse, or how many there ever were. (Somewhere between 180 and 200 is the consensus.) Each city was also free to negotiate its own terms of membership, which varied widely.

The only common institution was the Hanseatic Diet, which was strictly a forum for mutual discussion and the formation of suballiances to accomplish specific tasks. However, a consensus would emerge from the Diets that effectively shaped Hanseatic policy. Some cities seem not to have attended a Diet at all in the five hundred years of the Hanse's existence, though they were considered to be Hanseatic cities in good standing; most attended sporadically.

The Hanse was enormously influential for five hundred years but fell apart as soon as it ceased to be mutually beneficial to its members. The principal cause for its demise appears to have been its insistence on confining itself to German cities and excluding the rising Dutch cities from membership, giving them an incentive for rivalry; and in gradually excluding non-Germans from membership in its eastern European institutions. The Hanse gained immense strength from its flexibility. Appropriately enough, unwillingness to extend that flexibility was the proximate cause of its downfall.

Despite its limitations, we can see the seeds of civil society and its characteristic institutions in the Hanse. It had frameworks within which individuals and voluntary groups pursued their own purposes, rather than

mechanisms for mobilizing the constituent members for a "higher" purpose determined by a state elite.

It used force solely to protect peaceful activity, rather than to impose an
order on others; and it created a network of evolved institutions rather
than a uniform pattern to which all subsidiary institutions had to conform.

The Hanse flourished over several centuries, and in its time it dominated the Baltic and allied regions politically, economically, and militarily.
Yet it had no ruler, no army or navy, no commonly defined territorial limits, no compulsory powers of taxation, eminent domain, or conscription
over anybody, and no permanent employees. In fact, scholars have been
unable to agree on precisely what cities and states were members, for how
long, or even when it started or ended.

The league's most prominent historian has characterized its fluid nature:

> One of the most striking features of the history of the Hanse is the contrast
> between the breadth of its activities and the amorphousness of its structure.
> The community, made up of towns none of which was fully sovereign, did
> not even rank as a corporation. . . . It had no common institution other than
> the Hansetag (Hanseatic Diet), no permanent officials . . . no regular financial
> resources, no fleet and no army.
>
> It would be reasonable to expect that such an organism, which had none of
> the traits characteristic of a state, but which nevertheless wielded the power
> of a state, should have perplexed jurists steeped in the principles of Roman
> law. However, in the Middle Ages there is little trace of any desire to define
> the legal character of the Hansa. . . . In 1468, after the arrest of the German
> merchants in England, the Privy Council tried to justify the measure by
> enunciating the principle of the collective responsibility of the Hanseatic
> merchants. In reply it received a veritable treatise on the nature of the Hansa.
> It was neither a society (*societas*), nor a college (*collegium*), nor a corporate
> body (*universitas*), but a permanent federation (*firma confederatio*) of towns,
> owing allegiance to various princes, having no common institution—even
> the Hanseatic diet was not admitted as such—and consequently not respon-
> sible for the acts or undertakings of any of its members. (Dollinger, pp. 106–7)

Philippe Dollinger concludes his discussion as follows:

> Finally, the community was inspired by a spirit which, although based on ma-
> terial self-interest, is nonetheless worthy of admiration and respect. Indiffer-
> ent to nationalistic prejudices and even, to a large extent, to religious differ-
> ences, the Hanseatics were deeply pacific and had recourse to war only when
> all else failed. They always did their utmost, both among themselves and in
> their dealings with foreign countries, to settle their quarrels and remove their
> grievances by arbitration and negotiation. In this way they offer us a lesson in
> wisdom which we could well profit by today. (Dollinger, pp. 375–76)

The Hanse was, at heart, only a set of agreements on how its component entities should cooperate—a self-assembling organism. Its only institution was its Hansetag, or Diet, to which members could send whatever delegates they wanted.

The Diet met irregularly, whenever sufficient members saw the need to call it; made decisions by consensus, rather than binding majority vote; and funded its initiatives by subscription among consenting members rather than by forcing the minority to fund the decisions of the majority. I do not advocate or predict the imitation of any of the league's particular methods or practices, but I mention them to point out that less formal and precise forms of organization than those of contemporary economic states have proven to be highly effective in the past. Network commonwealths may revive some of the characteristics of this form of organization.

THE NEW UNDERSTANDING OF THE MARKET: RULES OF THUMB FOR INTERVENTION

In keeping with the massive present and prospective changes in the economic structure of advanced societies, there has been a gradual movement toward a more sophisticated understanding of the market economy. The increased emphasis on trust and civil society as critical factors in the success of market economies, which is reflected throughout this book, is one such understanding. Another very specific point is the new understanding of the market process, which I alluded to previously. This understanding has its roots in the works of Ludwig Von Mises and Hayek, particularly the understanding that prices are information.

In parallel, the general scientific advance in understanding chaotic, or nonlinear, systems is paying off in economics. Previously, scientists had understood that bounded systems—systems with a relatively small number of components moving in predictable courses—could be comprehended and predicted much more readily than unbounded systems. Unbounded systems are very complex phenomena; examples include weather systems, or the ecology of a bioregion.

Now we realize that unbounded systems are inherently resistant to precise prediction and can only be modeled in terms of probabilities.

A modern human economy, composed of millions of self-aware individuals each making decisions on the basis of a mix of motivations, no two alike, is one of the most chaotic and least bounded systems of all. This is why systems such as socialism, fascism, or even the regulated capitalism of John Maynard Keynes and Franklin Roosevelt, tend to fall apart, at a speed proportionate to the degree of ambition in planning—producing, at the extreme, disasters such as the East German and North Korean economies.

One would think that, armed with this understanding, the people of the world would move toward a universal laissez-faire economic system with no government intervention. Such is the logic of globalization. Perhaps in the long term, this will become a reality. In the short term, however, the world teems with a wide variety of interventionist practices, some explicitly imposed for economic reasons and others the by-product of pursuit of other political goals, such as national security, protection of national culture, pursuit of equality of condition, or just inertia and reluctance to change social arrangements. Given that interventions will likely continue for some long period, if not forever, it is worth discussing what sorts are more likely to avoid negative consequences. Given the new understanding of the market, it is possible to generate some rules of thumb for intervention. Such rules would include the following:

Avoid Self-deception

Admit that interventions have a price. The most harmful interventions are those taken on the basis of some convenient theory that purports to explain why the intervention will actually be economically productive. "Natural monopoly theory," which maintained that certain types of economic activity are "natural monopolies" and are most efficiently organized as state-regulated and state-protected monopolies, was an example.

Interventions must be admitted to be such, and it must be admitted that the intervention will have a price. The intervening state must say, in effect, "We know that this act will carry a price. We accept that price consciously for the sake of a social goal."

Admit that the Price Is Unknowable

It would be tempting to argue that interventions can be justified on some sort of utilitarian cost-benefit analysis: "We know this intervention costs a defined set of consumers x dollars, but another defined class of people gain $1.2x$ because of it, and therefore it is beneficial to society as a whole."

This is fundamentally illusory because, in a chaotic system such as a human economy, one can never tell what the true price of an intervention will be in advance. Even in hindsight, it is difficult to understand what the price of an intervention has been.

Don't Disguise the Price

It is better to make a visible, quantified subsidy payment out of tax funds than to mandate that, for example, the price of some good or service be lower. That way, only the specifically designated group will benefit, and the price will be borne by the taxpaying public in general, rather than unequally by some class of merchants and consumers. Also, it is better that the public be visibly and specifically reminded of what and why they are subsidizing, rather than have it become automatic.

Limit the Time Span of Interventions

Interventions do less harm if undertaken for specific goals and for limited periods of time. Since prices are information, price controls deliver distorted information, and the longer distortion goes on, the more information is lost. Similarly, the longer an interventionist program is run, the less obvious its price becomes, because it is mostly a matter of lost opportunities, which is a stealthy penalty.

Prefer Familiar Interventions to Novel Ones

With familiar interventions, it is more likely that the price will be understood to some degree.

All interventions have unintended consequences; but with familiar ones, it is less likely that the consequences will be truly disastrous. Citizens can more readily plan ways to mitigate the harm done by interventions if they can anticipate them better.

Try to Minimize the Opportunities for Moral Hazards

All interventions have a tendency to undermine civil society, because they offer the opportunity to benefit some people more readily through a government activity supposedly run for the benefit of all. Low-trust suspicions of private conspiracies are validated, destroying the needed social capital of trust. Pleadings for private benefit are disguised as public policy advocacy, temporary programs gain a tendency to become permanent, and specific benefits acquire a tendency to expand the benefited class.

Given these cautions, it is hard to see why any intervention might ever be desirable. Yet some will inevitably be undertaken. National security activities operate on their own, noneconomic logic. Soldiers risk their lives in a way not readily explainable by purely economic models. Societies have incentives for parents to invest effort and money in their children. Environmental issues cannot always be reduced to a simple economic calculus because the ecosystem in which we live is a separate complex system in which our technological interventions can have unpredictable (and potentially catastrophic) consequences. These factors, and many more, will tend to produce government activities inconsistent with free market ideals. Those who share this new understanding of the market have tended to use it to argue against intervention, but in the decades to come, attention should also be given to using that understanding to meet demands for various interventions, with practical rules of thumb for performing them with minimal harm.

THE ANARCHO-CAPITALIST
DEBATE AND OTHER RED HERRINGS

Recently, libertarian theory has begun to draw directed criticism. This is interesting largely as an indication that it has advanced sufficiently in popularity; nobody ever bothered in previous eras. It has even produced apostates such as the British think tank denizen and former libertarian John Gray. He and other critics of libertarian social and economic theory base critiques on the fact that all known market economies in fact rely upon some government actions; Gray and his allies then argue that this destroys the "pure" case for a society that is all market relations and no government.

Such a society has been called anarcho-capitalism. Many of the "cypherpunk" school of thought—those who believe that advanced encryption capabilities used over the Internet will erode the power of nation-states—are indeed anarcho-capitalists, seeing a purely voluntary and market-based society as the desirable result of the end of the nation-state. A small group of critics loosely labeled as "techno-liberals," including science-fiction writer David Brin and author Paulina Borsook, also have attacked anarcho-capitalism and the cypherpunk school, pointing out that most of the infrastructure of high technology, and in particular the Internet, has been the result of big government spending programs.

These critiques, however, are essentially a red herring to those who are interested in the future of nations and states in the era of the Singularity revolutions.

A debate between anarcho-capitalists and their critics has almost nothing to say about the critical issues that will occupy the rest of us. How do we balance control of potentially disastrous (but also potentially wondrous) technologies with the sort of freedoms which few contemporaries would be willing to do without?

What should be the relationship between nation and state, and what functions and limits of governments are consistent with the sort of strong civil society we now know to be essential to freedom and prosperity?

There have been great learning experiences in the last two decades—the revival of English entrepreneurism under Thatcher; the growth and crisis of East Asian crony capitalism; and the fate of the post-Communist societies in Eastern Europe and the former Soviet Union. These illuminate the debate in a new way if we open our eyes and learn from them. The point is not whether the anarcho-capitalist ideal society could ever be made to work—it is what are the practical preconditions that must be satisfied in order for such a society to work, and to be desirable to its inhabitants. (All we can say about it now is that it has not been proven not to work.) We now know that the strength of civil society is the indicator of whether capitalism on the Anglo-American model can take off—and that such strength depends on the habits, customs, and expectations of the population that makes up that society.

If anarcho-capitalism could ever be successful, it will require a civil society of far greater strength than we have known to date. Its inhabitants must be willing to turn to themselves and their neighbors to create the solutions for their problems, and must have the self-confidence to reject government-supplied solutions.

Mandatory government solutions are like a sledgehammer—massive, unsubtle, and hard to control. Voluntary solutions are like a jeweler's screwdriver—delicate, sensitive, and requiring fine control. However, some tasks are best done with sledgehammers. To develop an anarcho-capitalist society, a population must forgo the temptation to pick up the available sledgehammer and develop the patience always to use the jeweler's screwdriver instead.

We do not know for sure whether something like anarcho-capitalism would work, because it has never been tried, but I suspect that even a strong and advanced civil society would falter if anarcho-capitalism were tried today. It would be like the experience of Albania or Russia in trying to implement Anglo-American capitalism in the 1990s. It would fail not because the concept itself was invalid but because civil society was not yet strong enough and the habits and expectations of the people had not developed sufficiently to support it. Advocates of anarcho-capitalism would thus be best occupied not in undermining government but in strengthening civil society and trying to increase the level of trust among people. Being antinomians by nature, however, they tend to do the opposite today. Silly conspiracy theories and black-helicopter fantasies spread the idea that all governments are equally evil and all government personnel are corrupt and totalitarian. This cynicism has historically paved the way for fascism, not libertarianism.

Far better to note that some governments are better, more honest, and less oppressive than others—and to urge citizens to demand that their governments live up to the highest standard. If anarcho-capitalism ever does come into being, it will likely not be seen as the "end of government" but rather the ultimate triumph of civil society. It would almost certainly not be called anarcho-capitalism; most likely the forms and observances of current political states would remain, but in a much altered context.

Techno-liberals are equally irrelevant to the demands of the Singularity revolutions.

The experiences of the past century, and the advances in the understanding of society by theorists like Hayek, have created a set of questions they are not prepared to answer. The heart of modern critiques of government action informed by information theory lies in the problem of knowledge and the issues of incentives and disincentives. This perception is at the heart of the rules of thumb for interventions discussed previously; and it is at the heart of skepticism about the agenda of the techno-liberals. Anarcho-capitalists have never seen a government program they like; techno-liberals seem to never meet an intervention they don't like, or at least can't make an excuse for. Apologists such as Gray, Brin, and Borsook go even further—they will defend a bad program by pointing to the track record of a better one. But they overlook the obvious point that some programs are more effective than others. There is a fundamental difference between government agencies that spend money to fulfill their functional mandate and agencies that spend money to advance some nebulous social goal, one whose results can't be readily measured and linked to the decision to spend. A government agency that purchases pencils for its own needs can presumably judge the decision by whether the pencil does indeed write. An agency that spends money to advance the generic goal of advancement of communications tools might or might not spend it on pencils—and it would never be sure whether its money was well spent or not.

Take, for example, the favorite example of techno-liberals—the creation of the underlying technology of the Internet by the Defense Advanced Research Projects Agency (DARPA). This agency did not create the Internet in order to enable the emergence of cyberspace—it created it to make it easier for government researchers to share computer capability, and to disperse critical capacities in the face of mass nuclear attack. Likewise, the U.S. Air Force did not commission the KC-135 jet tanker to advance American commercial aviation—it did it to create a high-speed midair refueling capacity for American strategic bombers. In each case, many other benefits came from the government acting as a smart buyer for its own needs. In the case of the KC-135, it launched the Boeing 707 (the passenger version of the KC-135) and the era of practical commercial jet aviation. By contrast, projects promoting broad (and hard-to-measure) social goals—advancing space exploration, creating synthetic fuels, spurring advanced technology development—have historically spent much money that brought questionable or negligible results.

Projects that cannot be held to a strict functional requirement fall prey more to what economists call moral hazards. This is the tendency to recommend programs that expand agency size, payrolls, or influence rather than meet goals.

In more advanced cases, officials have a marked tendency to award contracts (or issue favorable regulatory determinations) to firms that might hire them for lucrative jobs after their retirement from government service. Rather than debate whether government is wonderful or terrible, it may be more useful to ask how we can either start making government avoid the many problems it has had in the past or how we can replace given government functions with effective private functions. And most important, we must strengthen civil society to make those functions work.

CIVIC STATES AND LARGE-SCALE FEDERATIONS

The previous discussion describes the rising state of the future—the civic state—as ideally small, coherent, efficient, and quasi-voluntary. These correspond economically to the "region-state" envisioned by Ohmae as the basic political unit of the emerging era. However, I do not assume that such states are necessarily fully sovereign or independent in today's sense. Some large federal states, such as the United States, retain substantial citizen loyalty and identification with the traditional narrative, even though (or perhaps because) that narrative has been disowned by its elite and governing institutions. Large federal states will continue to lose cohesion as economic states, particularly as the ability to undertake massive regional and intergenerational cross-subsidies continues to erode. However, sufficient identity and cohesion are likely to remain, so that evolutionary pressures in such federations will tend to resolve the needs of smaller, more coherent units through regional devolution to natural, historically based entities rather than outright independence.

In the United States, the expected long-term trend toward declining federal tax collections relative to GDP may drive responsibility back to state and local levels. A tendency for states to confederate to handle regional issues will accelerate as some regions seek to reserve capabilities currently handled federally, that other regions are not willing to support. Such activities need not require a constitutional amendment, as the need for such confederations was foreseen by the authors of the U.S. Constitution. In fact, there are already many bi- or multistate authorities (for example, the Port of New York Authority) that are in essence special-purpose multistate confederations. The regional confederations might conversely be described as general purpose multistate joint authorities.

This trend may be combined with a movement to divide existing large states into smaller, more coherent entities, as the population tends to sort itself into a diverse set of more coherent region-states. California's long-threatened split into two, three, or more states may finally come to pass. The states of Washington and Oregon may divide themselves into coastal and inland states. The Northwestern coastal states might link with themselves, with Northern California, and within a network commonwealth structure, with British Columbia. The inland Northwestern states might link with other Mountain West states and provinces such as Alberta.

As each region gradually implemented policies more consistent with its population's majority opinion, and hot-button issues left to state legislatures rather than federal courts, the minority opinion's migration to a more culturally congenial environment, already a permanent feature of American culture, might accelerate.

Large federal states need not disappear, particularly if they devolve gracefully rather than resorting in a bitter-end fashion to ever-more-intrusive coercive measures to uphold dissolving fiscal authority. Such bitter-end states will probably collapse. More flexible and accommodating federal states will find new functions that can be sustained in a new political-fiscal environment. Note that the civic states discussed in this work will not be such large-scale federal states, but rather the smaller units that remain inside the loosened federal structures.

COHERENT NONCONTIGUOUS STATES

Although the attributes of a coherent state include geographical cohesiveness, there are cases in which that attribute may not necessarily be needed: those in which two or more populations share a geographical region, with each population having a coherent, strongly held, but different and often mutually exclusive identity. Often in these cases one population has imposed its political authority upon the other(s) but has failed to gain the acceptance of the suppressed groups. The problematic nature of this situation can be understood readily by listing some well-known examples: Israel/Palestine, Cyprus, Northern Ireland, Bosnia, and Rwanda.

The increasing difficulty of implementing the peace processes as designed in the Middle East and Northern Ireland suggests that noncontiguous states may present an alternative solution in such situations. The peace process solution may be problematic for Palestine, in particular because the commingled nature of the territory it seeks to divide creates many issues requiring resolution. In the Palestinian case, one of the disputing parties is also the final arbiter, increasing the temptation to resort to extrademocratic and violent means to alter the equation.

The Internet economy makes noncontiguous, nongeographic solutions to these problems far more viable than in the past, because any location can join any economic network and create, export, and receive value without necessarily being integrated into the physical economy of the surrounding region. Safe passage of water, power, and cargo into the area would need to be assured. However, a noncontiguous solution will work best in situations where both populations are subject to a common legal framework that is mutually accepted and administered by a third party respected by both and controlled by neither. A network commonwealth is a potential candidate for the role of such a mediating and enforcing framework, at least in situations where the two populations share sufficient commonalities such that both merit membership in the same entity.

Northern Ireland would be a candidate for such a solution if a network commonwealth of English-speaking states involved both the United Kingdom and the Irish Republic; in such a situation, districts in the disputed areas would be permitted to vote on whether to become enclaves of the Irish Republic. So long as both the Irish Republic and the United Kingdom (or an Orange Northern Irish successor state) maintained membership in common economic space and defense arrangements, the jurisdictional issues would be manageable. Although not ideal from the standpoint of either community, it would permit Catholics to live under the jurisdiction of the Irish Republic (and participate in the new, prospering, Irish information economy) while permitting Protestants to maintain their own state authority indefinitely without fear of demographic and political submergence.

Alternatively, noncontiguous solutions in a network commonwealth framework could be implemented without creating polarized, ethnic states. This alternate approach would divide an ethnic area into a number of essentially autonomous, small-scale communities, modeled after the Swiss cantons.

Although each canton would be primarily composed of one ethnic group, the overall framework would contain civil rights protection for minorities. All would share access to wider markets, opportunities for migration, defense cooperation, and a judicial arbitration system through membership in a network commonwealth.

Gradually, economic and other nonpolitical interests would return as it became clear that neither side would be able to impose its long-term solution on the other, unwilling party.

Such noncontiguous solutions may provide the practical resolutions of interethnic and intercommunal conflicts in many parts of the world. The need for external stabilizing frameworks—"trusted third parties" overseeing common institutional arrangements—may become a crisis driver stimulating the formation of network commonwealths.

WHAT WILL BECOME OF BIG GOVERNMENT ESTABLISHMENTS?

Consider the U.S. government. The United States of America is a sovereign realm consisting of fifty states, assorted territories, and the 270 million inhabitants thereof. The "United States Government" is, in the ab-

stract, the constitutional process whereby the fifty states govern themselves. In another sense, however, the U.S. government is one of the
largest and most powerful corporations on Earth. There are two million or
so direct employees of the U.S. government, their dependents, and the
land and infrastructure directly owned and administered by it, as well as
the penumbra of contractors and their employees, whose lives are largely
governed by contract requirements (particularly where security clear-
ances are required).

The president of the United States is, relative to the United States of
America, the head of state. In that role he has substantial but quite specified and circumscribed powers. He is also the chief executive officer of the
corporation of the U.S. government, and commander in chief of its armed
forces. In that role, he has substantially greater and far more arbitrary
power over the several million persons under his direct rule. He is limited
not by the Constitution so much as by the Civil Service acts and the Uniform Code of Military Justice (for civil service and military personnel, respectively), and by primarily internally generated rules in the case of the
four thousand or so White House (Executive Office of the President) employees. Presidents have grown increasingly fond of exercising their executive power as head of the second United States. This occurs when they
become frustrated in dealing with the constitutional constraints of their
first role (as head of state), just as Britain's Hanoverian kings could turn
to the governance of their German realms for a refreshing bout of authoritarian rule whenever the frustrations of Whig constitutional monarchy
grew too exasperating.

What will happen when the enormous stream of revenue upon which
the exercise of the U.S. government's power depends becomes significantly more constrained? To some extent, the government will downsize,
spin out many functions via privatization, or devolve the functions to the
states and regional entities that are closer to the sources of taxation. However, within the federal government there are substantial centers of expertise, some of which are the best-in-class worldwide. Many of these
could not be supported at state or regional levels, as they are too specialized to merit support by these smaller bases of taxpayers.

The possibility exists that some of these centers of expertise will survive
through external contract revenues. This already has begun to happen in
some areas. The Gulf War differed from previous uses of U.S. military
power in that substantial portions of the cost were picked up by foreign
powers who benefited from the action but who had minor or no participation in the actual military action. Of course, the war was consistent with
the president's policy, but one might imagine a future in which significant
defense and security capabilities would be contracted to an "approved
list" of customers.

Such modern mercenary actions need not involve direct combat forces in most cases, as this would undoubtedly create negative public reaction. Also, such forces will not necessarily be the important form of help: access to U.S. information-war, communications, and logistics capabilities would be a more significant advantage in the typical conflict. Indeed, the Falklands War could be seen as a precursor of this trend. British forces enjoyed the logistics capabilities of the U.S. bases on Ascension Island as part of the quid pro quo for the base lease; U.S. satellite intelligence was a sort of lagniappe in this case, but it could be part of the tab in the future.

Most customers for such governmental expertise would be close to home; either the coherent region-states within the boundaries of the federal state or the network commonwealth states with close commonalities in language, culture, and legal systems. The Canadian federal government has traditionally contracted out police services in this manner. The Royal Canadian Mounted Police (RCMP) serve as a federal police, but at the same time contract their services to provincial and local authorities. Provinces may choose to create their own provincial police forces, as do Ontario and Quebec, or contract with the RCMP, as do the rest. Sheriff's offices in many U.S. counties contract services to towns optionally in a like manner.

One can imagine the Canadian federal state becoming a very loose confederation in response to ongoing devolutionary pressures, but with a few federal institutions such as the RCMP remaining largely intact. These institutions, surviving not on direct taxation, which might cease substantially, could subsist on contract revenues because the provinces still found hiring their services preferable to establishing their own institutions.

As with military services, it is unlikely that direct public contact services (such as street patrols or detective services) would be contacted because of the sensitivity of the population to the daily contact; using foreigners might create aggravation, and they would be hampered by lack of local knowledge. Back-office services, training, and analysis would be more probable targets for competitive bidding, and they constitute much of the value-added in security services.

Thus, the network commonwealth approach can provide the basis for a far more flexible framework for dealing with the issues of the Singularity while preserving many of the existing forms and institutions. In an era that is likely to be characterized by rapid and disorienting change, this would be in and of itself a benefit. The next chapter will discuss in more detail the specific elements that would make up a network commonwealth, and how they might come into being.

4

The Civic State and the Network Commonwealth

There can be no doubt that from a cultural vantage point, all these English-speaking countries are islands off the coast of Kent; the cliffs of Dover can be seen as clearly from Cincinnati as from Edmonton, Wellington, and Ballarat.... They all share, for example, a profound and irreverent distrust of bureaucrats, bureaucracy, and regulations that would be out of place in France, Turkey, or Mexico, while they exhibit a propensity to volunteer (prompted possibly by the wish to keep offers of time and energy constantly under review) that the Greeks, Paraguayans, and Hungarians would find decidedly disconcerting.

—Claudio Véliz, *The New World of the Gothic Fox: Culture and Economy in English and Spanish America*

The modernist economic-determinist paradigm that dominated twentieth-century intellectual thought tended toward brutal simplification. The world was to be reduced to as few basic elements as possible, and these were to be measured, quantified, planned, and administered. The fewer elements, the easier the planning. That which could not be homogenized was eradicated or ignored.

So it was with the taxonomy of societies and their political expressions. The paradigm of the Industrial Era led to the reduction of all political entities to two levels: nation-states and a notional universal world regime. The nation-state in this view was a curious construct—part economic state, part civic state, and part "blood-and-soil" state as envisaged by theorists such as Herder, which sought to unite all members of a linguistic group into a single ethnically defined state. Anything smaller than a nation-state was an essentially irrelevant administrative subdivision of a national government; above the nation-state, the only reality would be the universal state, whether in the grandiose form of the United Nations or the more effective form of the quiet but powerful "technical" international organizations. International forms that fell short of universality were seen as signs of failure. Regional organizations were seen as inevitably coalescing into new states, as the European Common Market would eventually become a United States of Europe, and would become in turn administrative subdivisions of a world government.

The result of this paradigm was to impoverish the language of political thought. It was as if biologists were to discard their existing rich taxonomy of kingdoms, phyla, orders, and species, and recognize only two levels of organization: individual species and the totality of the biosphere, from single-cell bacteria to whales and redwoods. Furthermore, such an impoverished taxonomy would eventually lead students to think there were not or more important, ought not to be, any similarities or affinities between any two or three species more than any other, that lions had no more in common with tigers than with lichen.

Such a biological taxonomy would be absurd. It is precisely the study of the groupings of organisms and species, and the measurement of the relative distance between various ones—the discipline of cladistics—that has been one of the most fruitful analytical tools of modern biology. Yet the extreme example noted previously is exactly the frame of reference that twentieth-century thought tended to use in discussing cultures and political organizations.

It is important to emphasize that this is an exercise in cultural classification, not biological categories. During the nineteenth and early twentieth centuries, some anthropologists attempted to construct a Linnean taxonomy of subraces of humanity. They sought a biological, rather than a cultural, division in which a person of western African origin was a "negroid" regardless of whether he lived as an integral part of a western African culture or as a native and resident of New York City. This book, however, is concerned with human societies and their political expression, which is a learned, cultural phenomenon. For the purposes of this work, a person of, say, Cantonese genetic ancestry growing up in the United States is a member of American society, of the English-speaking network civilization, and of Western civilization.

In thinking about the phenomenon of cultural rather than biological evolution, it is also important to remember that political-social evolution follows Lamarckian rules, rather than Darwinian ones. Entities may acquire characteristics during their lifetimes that are passed down to their descendants. Furthermore, self-aware entities can consciously choose to change characteristics. A Linnean taxonomy should not be taken as an invitation to draw spurious parallels with biological evolution; if a parallel example is to be sought, the closely related field of linguistic evolution is a better, less controversial example. Even those who doubt Darwinian evolution in biology seldom dispute the fact that the modern Romance languages, for example, evolved from Latin, nor do they argue that Satan planted Latin grammars in library stacks to cause doubt among believers.

THE SINEWS OF THE NETWORK COMMONWEALTH: EVOLVING NEW FORMS FROM EXISTING ELEMENTS

Network commonwealths will emerge in an evolutionary fashion, as do most viable political mechanisms, growing from, altering, and redefining institutions and developing in the era of economic states until these institutions become a new thing. When the history of network commonwealths is written, the current time will be seen not as the start of the process, but as perhaps a halfway mark in the building of the network commonwealth. The network commonwealth will evolve from several current institutions:

1. Common Economic Spaces: Trade and Transmigration

As noted earlier, common market areas for trade in goods have blossomed over the past half century, the successes sparking numerous imitations. A network commonwealth will have a set of free trade agreements as one of its fundamental ligatures. It would differ from existing common markets in focusing on facilitation of informational trade, services, and the free flow of people and interpersonal cooperation.

The mental model of the EU as a "harmonized" trade area (to use the EU's jargon for area-wide uniform standards) could be demonstrated by envisioning a group of corporations throughout Europe being able to manufacture an airplane jointly, coordinating tens of thousands of workers producing fuselages in France, wings in Germany, and tail assemblies in Spain. The mental model of a network commonwealth is demonstrated by envisioning a set of arrangements permitting a software company incorporated in Bermuda to use programmers, marketers, and financiers in California, Australia, India, and Ireland to put together a Web-based product in cyberspace and sell it worldwide. At the same time, they would enjoy adequate intellectual property protection and have the ability to resolve disputes fairly and expeditiously.

It is relevant that the harmonization needed to enable the European example took decades to create and has imposed substantial transition costs on the citizens of the member states. Most of the harmonization needed for the latter example, by contrast, already exists: common language, common software standards, and a common law and understanding of business practices. The network commonwealth places greater emphasis on creation of a common business space for information businesses than on the elimination of traditional barriers like tariffs or quotas. International processes such as the World Trade Organization are already effecting many of the needed changes in such areas. A NAFTA-EU free trade agreement, such as has been proposed, which would reduce trade barriers between those areas, could carry the process further and deeper.

In the network commonwealth, future trade will be dominated more by informational goods and services rather than by physical goods. In these areas, it is more important to avoid the creation of new barriers than to eliminate existing ones. Instead, such a trade regime would focus on resolving issues such as the different treatment of state-generated intellectual property by the United States and the Commonwealth countries. In an era in which the U.S. software industry is economically more important and generates more jobs than the U.S. auto industry, resolution of these types of issues ought to take priority. Similarly, a network commonwealth emphasis would ally Anglosphere nations, with their more open, competitive industries, in international decision-making forums such as those on radio spectrum allocation, where (for example) Britain today undercuts its own interests in the name of European solidarity.

In creating common trade and economic spaces, the highest-priority targets are agreements providing for free entry throughout the community's economic space in the communications and transportation sectors. Universal flat- or low-rate communications and fully competitive air transportation should be the goals of these agreements. Trade in physical goods may decline in absolute tonnage of goods shipped as local production in flexible, computer-integrated facilities from software developed worldwide begins to supplant bulk manufacture and export in coming decades. Thus protectionist struggles against such trade may be pointless, while nations pursuing export strategies based on low-wage manufacture may suffer disruption in turn.

2. Sojourner Provisions: The Human Element of Trade and Cooperation

I place substantial emphasis on immigration ties and "sojourner" status: a right to travel to, reside in, and do business within all the member states of the network commonwealth on an equal and reciprocal basis. The EU has effectively implemented such a status as of 1993; U.S.-Canadian agreements have moved in a similar direction. Sojourner status is important because the critical ties within a network commonwealth are not, as with the EU, hierarchy-to-hierarchy relationships between large corporations, but rather person-to-person relationships between the enterprising individuals who will create the businesses, civic organizations, and personal networks of the future.

Sojourner status is also important because the network commonwealth model incorporates a new vision of transnational personal movement appropriate to the era of Internet, cheap jet travel, and worldwide media. The Machine Age model was fundamentally one of immigration. Individuals were citizens of one nation-state and resided, worked, and paid taxes within that state. The only way to change that status was to give up citizenship in one nation, move to a new nation, and adopt residence, employment, and citizenship there. The immigrant who adopted the identity and customs of the new nation and fit himself into that structure, rarely if ever returned, lost contact with home-country media, and communicated with his previous home and family slowly through mails, or not at all.

The Network Era model of transnational personal movement is sojournership. A sojourner is one who moves from one country to another to reside and engage in economic activity, but retains his previous identity, returns to previous countries of residence frequently, and remains in constant communication with his home network. This sojourner is an essential element of transnational cooperation, making possible entrepreneurial activity on a wide scale with an extremely low cost of entry. The sojourner often serves to cross-pollinate activity from place to place, accelerating ties begun or continued via Net and Web. As humans cease to be inhabitants solely of physical space, we begin to have an "amphibious" existence split between physical space and information space. Each space has its own rules and realities, and the sojourner helps tie the two together by combining cyberspace and physical-space contact.

Existing immigration law is poorly adapted to such activity. The economic-state benefits attached to citizenship have risen to such levels during the Machine Age that an immigrant's slot becomes a valuable prize, particularly for persons from poorer countries. The sojourner does not seek to fill a citizen's slot. The immigration machinery and provisions of most of the industrialized world's economic states are designed to ration these entitlements by rationing citizenship. Sojourners face the choice of trying to fit the immigrant's slots or to abuse tourist, student, or temporary worker provisions, none of which are appropriate to their needs.

National borders create other obstacles to effective sojourning. Consider the situation among English-speaking nations. Despite the similarity in the legal, financial, and business systems of the English-speaking nations, and the transparency of credit records due to common language, it is difficult for an ordinary sojourner to obtain credit or secure loans across the borders of the English-speaking nations. At a minimum, credit checks in the United States require a Social Security number. But to gain a Social Security number is to stake a claim on numerous benefits, none of which are the sojourner's primary objective. Yet the would-be sojourner cannot renounce those benefits to get a Social Security number merely for the purposes of gaining credit status. Network commonwealth agreements could reduce such burdens with a substantial net gain to financial institutions as a result of an expansion of the common economic space.

Two types of concerns have fueled anger over immigration in almost every advanced industrial country. The first is concern over the rationing of employment and citizen-benefit slots, in which current citizens are concerned about immigrants absorbing jobs and benefits that they feel might otherwise go to them. The second concern is over the presence of large blocks of nonassimilating immigrants from substantially different cultures. It is precisely the fading of the classic immigration model that has fueled this concern, for the reverse of the coin of immigration is assimilation.

Today's immigrants have many of the same characteristics as sojourners, in that they can remain virtually in their home culture, maintaining instant communication and access to home media while residing in the host nation. Assimilation can be delayed or avoided, and host-country citizens fear the creation of permanent alien communities with incompatible values and social characteristics.

Put in economic terms, interaction with a person with substantially different values imposes "transaction costs"; the more alien, the higher the costs. These costs are particularly high when a person from a high-trust culture attempts to interact with one from a low-trust culture, or individuals from different high-trust cultures with different trust-validating mechanisms attempt to interact. Costs are felt directly—for example, when an immigrant has difficulty communicating with a native—while the benefits of immigration are typically diffuse and often hidden.

The immigrant bears most of the costs, but the host citizens bear some, and those are typically resented. Such resentment is usually directly proportional to the degree to which the native feels his "citizen's slot" is threatened. Political demagogues find it easy to exploit the gap between visible costs and hidden benefits.

Multiculturalist theories, rather than emphasizing the margin of benefits over costs, seek to declare these transaction costs equal for persons of all cultures, or even nonexistent, whereas empirical experience teaches daily that there are wide differences in such costs.

A sojourner regime among English-speaking nations, to examine a specific case, would create a reciprocal right of sojourning for citizens of the

adhering nations, permitting those citizens to travel to, reside in, and perform economic transactions in all member nations. Sojourners would not
be eligible for state benefits and would pay core taxes, but not taxes earmarked for state benefits. Thus, a Briton sojourning in America would
pay taxes supporting basic governmental functions, but would not make
a Social Security contribution nor be eligible for Social Security benefits,
unless the United States chose to include sojourners in the system on a
voluntary basis. Similarly, an American sojourner in the United Kingdom
would pay basic taxes but not support the National Health Service or be
eligible for those benefits.

Although it would be generally beneficial to permit sojourners to hold
employment, concerns about competition for formal employment slots
may create a barrier to agreement. Equally useful, and less controversial,
would be a provision permitting sojourners to conduct business, including acting as contractors and consultants. As such, they would be in line
with the emerging economic trends. They would not have political rights
in the host nations, though there is a reasonable argument for giving long-
resident sojourners who pay local sales and property taxes a vote in local
elections, as the EU does.

Most important, sojourner status would not be rationed; it would be
freely available to any applicant, subject only to a basic check for criminal
record. Misbehavior of a sojourner in a host nation would be dealt with
primarily by restitution and expulsion; similarly, need for welfare services
would be dealt with by repatriation.

Countries could remove sojourners from the competition for state benefits and insulate host citizens from potential problems caused by their
presence. They could make sojourner status depend on strict reciprocity
and ensure that sojourners come primarily from countries within the network civilization of the host nation (thereby minimizing interpersonal
transaction costs). This would deliver many of the benefits of immigration
while minimizing the commonly ascribed costs to the host nation and its
people. In fact, a sojourner program would enhance the ability of nations
to receive immigrants of the traditional variety as well, as it would increase the critical mass of individuals sharing many of the same or similar trust mechanisms relative to immigrants requiring extensive assimilation.

In many developed nations, politicians face the moral hazard of making immigrants the scapegoat of frustration with the structural problems
of transition from Machine Age to Network Age economies. Such politicians direct attention to every abuse of the "citizen's slot" access to state
benefits by immigrants and give the illusory impression that state benefit
programs would be viable if not for immigration. As fiscal pressure on
such programs increases in coming years, due to both the demographics

of aging populations and the pressures on the ability to tax, there will be a greater temptation to blame immigrants for the problems of such systems.

Sojourner status is crafted to minimize vulnerability to such pressures.

In fact, the problem is not with immigration per se but with economic-state social welfare structures and immigration policies that make immigrants liabilities rather than assets, by permitting working immigrants to bring in nonworking relatives, often extended-family rather than nuclear-family relations, who create net claims on the system. These combine with antiassimilation policies that create large masses of young people ill-equipped to obtain employment in the modern network economy, and ill-educated for the task of participation in the civic state. Civic states held together by shared memories, symbols, and narratives must extend these things to immigrants if they are to have other than second-class status, once offered, they must be grasped by the immigrants.

Interestingly, the theoretical availability of a sojourner-like status throughout the EU, young Britons and Irish have made relatively little use of it to work on the Continent. (In contrast, Britons with income streams from the Anglosphere use the status to retire in the French countryside.) Large numbers of both nations' young (and those of the other principal Anglosphere nations) come to the United States to live and work, often by abusing immigration statuses designed for other purposes. Sojourner status would turn current violators into constructive economic participants.

The creation of sojourner status may have other benefits as well. Some industrial states already exempt certain portions of their population from full participation in the economic state; the example of the Old Order Amish in the United States is perhaps the best known. Such populations are, in effect, domestic sojourners. States may find it expedient to extend sojourner status to elements of their domestic population who have principled objections to participation in the welfare state and its administrative apparatus.

A sojourner agreement would create a powerful incentive for active, entrepreneurial persons in all parts of a network civilization, particularly the young, to support the creation of the network commonwealth. It creates a direct and visible benefit to individuals from the creation of the network commonwealth.

3. Collaborative Organizations in Science and Technology

The EU was seen as the outgrowth of the European Coal and Steel Community, which evolved gradually into the European Economic Community (EEC), then the European Community. However, the EEC was only one of several strands from which the EU was woven. Also important was a group of organizations for joint scientific and technological cooperation, including the European Atomic Energy Agency and the European Space Agency.

These programs had two important functions. The first was a pragmatic one, of permitting European nations to participate in scientific and technological projects beyond their individual means. Second was the symbolic function of demonstrating that a united Europe could remain competitive in science and technology at a time when the United States and USSR seemed destined to dominate those fields.

The cooperation model for European scientific-technical organizations was, as in nearly all pan-European programs, one of top-down, negotiated relationships between national hierarchical structures. Programs are composed under the rule of *juste retour*—money is spent in each member nation in proportion to the percentage of funding it contributes. Nations benefit from these programs to the degree that their national economic and technical structures are organized in a top-down, state-directed hierarchical structure and their political systems can generate the bureaucratic and funding stability needed to properly support such programs. France and Germany are good examples of such nations; the United Kingdom has historically been a poor example, not surprisingly. The United Kingdom has tended to get the worst of the deal in most of the European cooperative science and technology programs in which it has participated.

A network commonwealth would find cooperative science and technology programs similarly useful in creating added leverage for national expenditures in those fields. Highly visible programs like space exploration would yield similar benefits in producing a visible source of pride in cooperation for accomplishment.

However, such cooperative programs would be conceived and structured quite differently from the Machine Age structures of the EU.

As with all network commonwealth efforts, its science and technology programs would seek to exploit the deeper cooperation possible among persons with similar cultural backgrounds. The universality of English as the world language of science would seem to reduce the value of network commonwealth commonalties.

However, difficulties of interpersonal communications among scientists are not the barrier to international cooperation; scientists are often capable of forming effective transnational teams. The problem lies in the way conflicts of their sponsoring states often intrude into the possibilities of further cooperation once initial work has produced promising results. Consider the invention of the World Wide Web. Although developed by two researchers (one of them English) at CERN in Switzerland, a pan-

European scientific research institution, its benefits were first and most widely reaped by Americans, who neither participated in the CERN consortium nor were present at the creation of the Web. The incompatibilities of the CERN member states and the slowness of state-to-state cooperation made it unlikely that any of the member states would be able to exploit this breakthrough, as indeed they did not. By aligning nations with similar and more compatible political systems, and by encouraging person-to-person and institution-to-institution rather than state-to-state cooperation, a network commonwealth is likelier to promote effective science and technology cooperation than international structures created on other bases.

As this example demonstrates, many of the economic benefits of public sponsorship of scientific and technical research come not from formal transfers of technology to industrial organizations, but by informal, entrepreneurial transfer.

Benefits arise from small groups of researchers leaving the formal research world to create entrepreneurial ventures based on the knowledge, skills, and insights they have gained. Pan-network commonwealth cooperative programs for scientific and technical research should blend seamlessly with the pan-network commonwealth economic environment created by trade and sojourner agreements.

To formalize the pan-network commonwealth institutions for science and technology, research agencies in the principal areas of investigation should be formed. Emphasis should be placed on the leading fields of the likely Singularity revolutions: space, medicine, biotechnology, molecular manufacturing, computer science, and other high-visibility fields such as nuclear physics, environmental studies, and oceanography. These agencies should cooperate with national and regional research agencies and universities, but should have their own budgets, staffs, and identities, funded by the participants. No attempt should be made at a *juste retour* policy, although the practicalities of the politics of funding will dictate that distribution of benefits will not be entirely ignored.

Such structures would enable creation of a set of visible programs, giving short-term results as well as long-term promise, to accelerate the process of public recognition of the network commonwealth. In the example of a network commonwealth with American participation, visible programs could include quick implementation of manned space flights with crews from a pan-network commonwealth astronaut corps and joint funding and participation in programs modeled on "faster, quicker, cheaper" space exploration pioneered by the U.S. Defense Department and NASA.

Environmental programs aimed particularly at biosphere preservation in the poorer parts of the network commonwealth (giving maximum benefit for dollar spent) would reach a different segment. Research and development areas of particular interest to a pan-network commonwealth aeronautics effort might include "shockless supersonic" technology, which exploits recent theoretical breakthroughs in supersonic travel without shock waves and sonic booms. Previously, enormous energy demands, short range capability, and need to fly at extreme altitude effectively prevented the exploitation of supersonic air transport for economic and environmental reasons.

Public outreach would include a very heavy Web presence, organized through pan-network commonwealth educational networks. Schoolchildren in all parts of the network commonwealth would be able to access Web sites and interact with high-visibility activities which are "theirs" in a way that U.S. space launches, for example, are not for non-U.S. spectators.

In general, education creates a powerful avenue for pan-network commonwealth cooperation, as the Web permits students at all levels to link directly with their counterparts in other nations and regions. Shared language, cultural values, and experiences permit the creation of a shared virtual space. A program of cross-commonwealth scholarships and student exchanges, with follow-up on Web-created interpersonal relationships, will make them more effective than traditional programs of such nature. Students in the class from which the exchange student originates can keep in touch with their classmate daily via the Web and incorporate his experiences into their lessons and daily realities, forming further relationships that sojourner provisions and other pan-commonwealth programs can help facilitate.

4. Security Organizations: Sailing with the Fast Convoy

Permanent security alliances rank high among the institutions that can evolve into building blocks for the network commonwealth. Since its founding, NATO has become more than a military alliance: it is now an elaborate set of permanent structures and institutions which have had a profound effect on the military, political, and economic life of the nations that have joined them. One need only look at the importance of NATO membership to Spain, Greece, Turkey, and now the states of Eastern Europe in stabilizing and democratizing them to see that permanent alliance structures have become one of the central building blocks of transnational institutions.

It is also instructive to note the failures in building or maintaining security alliance structures. America's unsuccessful attempts to replicate NATO's success in the Central Treaty Organization (CENTO) and the Southeast Asia Treaty Organization (SEATO) and the immediate collapse of the Warsaw Pact with the fall of Communism, demonstrate that permanent structures require substantial alignment of interests and values. Perception of immediate threats can create an incentive to join an alliance, but when the perception of threat changes (or the members no longer believe that resistance, rather than accommodation, is the effective way to meet it), that incentive disappears, and the alliance collapses.

Also instructive is the failure of all attempts to create a cooperative military structure for Western Europe outside of NATO. Despite the strong commitment to European unity among the core states, there has never been (despite past and current attempts to create such), any successful mechanism or tested commitment to a common security policy among European states. The past decade's tests of European will, from Bosnia through Kosovo to Macedonia, justify skepticism toward the idea of a common European security policy. In naming Javier Solana as the putative "European to answer the phone," the lack of which Henry Kissinger had noted earlier, the EU has tried to address this gap.

Solana can answer the phone. But when he speaks, will the European states stand by what he says?

This lack of a European security consensus stems from the substantial differences among European states regarding military and foreign policy—another reminder that deep cooperation comes from sharing deep values. Europeans (particularly if one includes the British) have no deeper consensus of values among themselves than do Europeans and Americans with each other. Europeans by themselves have been able to create no deeper cooperation than already exists within NATO. As of this writing, the latest incarnation of this effort, the "European Rapid Reaction Force," is still struggling to come together.

The Iraq war brought the problematic nature of a common European foreign and security policy to the fore. Germany and France opposed the U.S. efforts to assemble a coalition to shut down the Saddam Hussein regime. In opposing the U.S., they assumed they spoke for the EU, and for Europe as a whole. Yet the second-strongest member of the coalition was Britain, which supplied a third of the striking forces at the opening of hostilities. Furthermore, other key Western European states, most noticeably Spain, Italy, and the Netherlands, supported the American position. Worse yet, from the Franco-German point of view, the bulk of the Eastern European states about to enter the EU took the American side as well. French president Jacques Chirac observed that they had "missed a good opportunity to stay silent," a remark that did not help the cause of a common European outlook. A democratic state requires a *demos*—a population that thinks of itself as a people, and conducts a common dialogue. Europe has many democracies, but there is no European demos; thus the European project cannot create a genuine democratic consensus on the critical issues of war, peace, and security.

Just as the transition to the Machine Age made mastery of manufacturing the key to success in warfare, so will mastery of information be the key to success in Information Revolution warfare. Already, the predominance of the U.S. military is due increasingly to its superior information technology.

Information war is war directed not against persons or things but against the information that controls and affects both. That information war has become a major new form of warfare.

The great powers of the new age, to the extent that there are great powers, will be those nations that possess a high degree of Information Age literacy, a vigorous software industry, and the ability to develop the political-military doctrines to exploit its advantages.

The United States prevailed in the Machine Age because of its general mastery of machinery, its enormous industrial base, and its ability to find and give command to generals such as Dwight Eisenhower. Eisenhower and his peers understood how to use these assets to win in the face of clear German superiority in weapons, morale, and training throughout most of the war. Germans had, for most of the war's length, better tanks, planes, and guns; the United States had better trucks. America also had the only army in which almost every draftee knew how to drive, and most how to maintain and fix motor vehicles, from civilian life.

The dominant powers of the future will be those with a strong domestic software capability, potential soldiers who are comfortable with using computers, and the ability to generate political-military strategies to exploit the new technologies properly. The network commonwealth provides a means for today's economic states to minimize the loss of defensive potential as they undergo devolutionary pressures and fiscal constraints when their previous ability to divert large percentages of their GDPs diminishes. Those who can effectively implement it will retain substantially more power than those who don't.

The balance of power has already begun to change as a result of the increase in the rate of transition from the Machine to the Information Age. Powers like Russia, which dominated the Machine Age because of their ability to cover square miles with medium-tech tank battalions, have lost capability. Ironically, a power such as Britain, which had fallen to the middle rank of military capability, is once again among the top-rank powers today precisely because of its greater ability to master the cutting edge of current information-based technologies.

The centrality of information technology, combined with organizational and weapons-technology innovations, constitutes what has become known as the "Revolution in Military Affairs." The United States has already begun to consider how to cooperate with its NATO and other principal allies in using the "Grid"—the dense network of information, using

Internet-like techniques, that links information-gathering sensors, command and control centers, and weapons and men in the field. The defense sinew of network commonwealth ties will center around cooperation in the use of the Grid by the core alliance. NATO has built a series of standards, such as a common rifle caliber, making it easy for units of NATO member nations to cooperate in the field. A network commonwealth defense alliance would be built primarily around common standards in information.

TRADE, SECURITY, AND TECHNOLOGY INTERSECT: THE CASE OF ANGLOSPHERE DEFENSE COOPERATION

American policy consensus over the past fifty years has supported closer integration of the United Kingdom into European economic and defense institutions.

The advocates of this consensus have held that Britain would help articulate a voice in those institutions more closely in line with American policy than otherwise.

They believed that the United Kingdom's defense capabilities would help bolster the European bulwark against Soviet threats, and that the United Kingdom had no preferable alternatives, in particular no special economic or security relations with the United States other than some narrow intelligence and industrial cooperation. The passage of time has in some cases proven these assumptions false and in others rendered them obsolete.

Part of what led to these assumptions was the relatively low common denominator used as a criterion in assembling the Atlantic alliance, a process that was begun in haste and under pressure. A functioning market economy and a commitment to process democracy were sufficient to merit inclusion in the NATO core and the precursor institutions to the EU. Peripheral NATO members such as Portugal and Turkey failed to pass even these tests; core states included nations such as France, which experienced severe constitutional crises and serious military coup attempts as recently as 1962. We are now in a much different environment, one where the previous low common denominator is becoming increasingly irrelevant.

When the Soviet model was widely considered a viable alternative, the differences between the relatively unregulated market economies and stronger, more open civil societies of the English-speaking world, on the one hand, and the more dirigiste, inflexible, closed, and state-oriented economic models of the European continent on the other, seemed relatively unimportant. Following the collapse of the Soviet Union and other alternative models of social and political organization, these differences have become an important indicator of success in areas such as advanced information technology and other cutting-edge fields. These are areas with profound implications for defense force and defense industry capabilities.

Experience has shown that the two systems do not easily mix in areas of close cooperation. In the last decade, the English-speaking economies have relied increasingly on entrepreneurial innovation in high technology, combined with use of government purchases in defense and space markets to provide some stability and assurance that critical government needs will be met. The Continental economies have continued to rely on general industrial policy mechanisms with heavy state investment in defense and nondefense sectors alike. Increasingly, the Continental states have come to rely on pan-European consortia among state-owned firms to assure economies of scale and to provide a secure customer base for selling products in the world marketplace.

Several trends have become apparent. The militaries of the English-speaking states, the United States and United Kingdom in particular, have become increasingly information intensive and have begun to rely on the capabilities of the competitive entrepreneurial marketplace for software and related infotech products and services. Continental militaries have by and large not kept up this pace. Once, government-procured information-related systems could be assumed to be faster, more reliable, and more secure than products of the open marketplace, if not cheaper.

Today, none of those assumptions can be taken for granted. Since many of these systems are available on the world marketplace, the advantage of the U.S. military has been in its ability to adopt and integrate such products into its operations.

At the same time, the industrial policy projects of the Continental states have failed to guarantee their leadership in these key technology areas. Had that model been relevant to the demands of these fields, one would have expected the Internet and World Wide Web phenomena to have emerged from dirigiste projects like the French Minitel system (an early-model text terminal distributed to every household in France and used for telephone directory and other text delivery services) which had the advantages of early start, assured massive customer base, and long-term, stable funding commitments. Instead, the Internet, a project whose stimulus was provided entirely within the constraints of the classical-liberal model (i.e., the government buying as a smart customer for its own use in an area, defense, classically designated as a government function), surpassed other models and became the basis for all cyberspace development. Meanwhile, the Continental militaries have fallen further and further behind in information-intensive development. Analysts who have noticed this have tended to advocate encouraging Continental states to accelerate the modernization of their militaries—that is, to tell the slow ships in the convoy to speed up. However, such analyses may be overly optimistic regarding the ability of such economies to generate the entrepreneurial vitality needed to guarantee continued currency in this game. The alternative course of assembling a fast convoy deserves a closer look. The "fast convoy" approach starts with the "coalition of the willing" approach used to assemble the Iraq war coalition, but looks to a more concrete institutionalization of the allied powers.

Today, the United Kingdom stands on the brink of major decisions regarding full commitment to European integration. These decisions have substantial implications for U.S. defense and trade policies, most particularly in the future of the United Kingdom's defense industry capabilities. The British defense, aerospace, and infosec industries have struggled under a unique set of burdens since 1945.

They have been faced with ongoing force reductions as imperial responsibilities have been shed. They have experienced decline in traditional foreign markets as Commonwealth countries began to diversify their sources of supply while other suppliers, often heavily subsidized by their national governments, entered competition for defense and aerospace sales. They have faced a particularly pressing issue of talent drain to the United States, rendered easy by the commonality of language and attractive by the lower taxes and higher standard of living in the United States.

Between 1945 and 1979, the British government attempted to impose industrial policy style guidance on the industry without being able to provide the consistent funding and support independent of change of party which characterizes Continental dirigiste practice. Britain was too dirigiste to permit free market approaches to flourish and too democratic to permit industrial policy approaches to deliver their benefits. By trying to convert from one economic model to the other, while underestimating the cultural and political changes such a conversion required, Britain managed to achieve the worst of all possible outcomes.

The results have been striking. In 1945, Britain was the world leader or peer in most of the important emerging technologies of the latter half of the twentieth century: computers and programming, radar and related electronics, airframe design, jet engines, and atomic energy. Over time, Britain's leadership has been surrendered in most of those fields, although in a few it remains a peer. The United Kingdom and the United States are still the only nations supporting manufacture of an efficient, large-scale turbofan engine, for example, despite decades of technology transfer to France and industrial espionage by Russia. Much of the technique was transferred from the United Kingdom to the United States through the informal but effective technology transfer of emigration. Other technology has been transferred to the Continent through joint European projects.

The British government has attempted to combat shrinking market base and increasing capital costs of emerging defense technologies by first encouraging the consolidation of existing U.K. firms in these areas, and second, through participation in joint European programs. Although the consolidations have addressed the market scale issues to some extent, they have had the unfortunate effect of eroding the historic strength of the British aircraft industry, which was its ability to support multiple teams of designers offering competing approaches to aircraft design. The merger of DeHavilland, Vickers, and other famous firms snuffed out that creative competition and has resulted in a merged British Aerospace that seems to be less than the sum of its parts in terms of design innovation.

Now Britain, like other European countries, has come to the point where even the total consolidation of each defense sector has proven to be inadequate to maintain competitive economies of scale. Britain took its final available step in that direction in merging British Aerospace with GEC-Marconi, its principal defense electronic firm. Joint European projects have proven to be of limited effectiveness due to the high transaction costs of negotiating and maintaining the consortia structures.

The principle of *juste retour* further mandates inefficiencies.

The next step on this path will be the merger and consolidation of European defense and aerospace firms on a pan-European basis, across national borders. The merger of Aerospatiale-Matra and DASA, respectively, the two largest French and German aerospace national champions was the most recent major milestone in this process. This will be a major step in the consolidation of the EU into a federal state, as it will drive the emergence of a pan-European defense and foreign policy structure.

These developments will force both the United States and the United Kingdom to make some fundamental decisions in the near future, certainly within the next five years. There are two main possibilities, which we shall examine in turn: the course upon which events now seem to be committed, and an alternative course which has begun to emerge increasingly in discussion in Britain and which should be placed on the table in the United States and Canada.

On the pan-European course, British defense, space, and infosec companies will become acquisition targets for pan-European defense conglomerates, the core of which will be German and French companies. Integration of these major industries will put further pressure on the British government to join the European Economic and Monetary Union and to participate more fully in the creation of a pan-European security and foreign policy apparatus. Britain will then lose both effective foreign policy independence and will begin to lose the ability to maintain an all-around defense industry, a capability that has been maintained to date, although thinly in a number of sectors. One plan that has been urged is the creation of designated defense specialties, wherein each country would specialize in the development and production of certain items. This resembles nothing more than the old Soviet COMECON system (the economic arm of the Soviet Empire), under which each country was mandated to specialize in assigned sectors, such as Hungary's specialization in buses and rail equipment.

The participation of Britain in pan-European defense and foreign policy deliberations has often been defended on the grounds that Britain will be a U.S.-friendly voice in the EU representing positions sympathetic to those of the United States. This assumption merits a second thought. Britain, once it is fully immersed in a pan-European system, will become dependent on logrolling compromises with other nations for even more of its economic well-being than it is today. It will have less and less room to represent those values that it and the United States have had in common, because most of its bargaining chips will be fully committed to national economic goals in a pan-European public-goods system. Any representation of pro-American goals and policies will be both suspect and *anti-communitaire*, and also expensive in terms of bargaining chips that could better be used to obtain further public goods benefits for the British voting public.

Furthermore, Britain and the United States today are moving toward seamless transatlantic partnerships between companies in areas such as finance, telecommunications, and consumer software, and are only held back from similar moves in media and air transportation by national-ownership laws. Britain's Continental partnerships tend to be in sunset industries and those dominated by state-influenced purchasing decisions; its American partnerships are in industries marked by fully competitive, market-driven, private agents and emerging technologies.

These partnerships would be substantially curtailed and rolled back by the full immersion of the United Kingdom in pan-European institutions, both as a matter of European policy and as a practical effect of "harmonization" of British labor laws and tax rates with Continental levels.

This tendency of Britain to revert to the European mean can already be seen in the history of U.K.-EU negotiation. Almost all of the United Kingdom's bargaining chips have been expended in obtaining temporary exemptions ("derogations") to specific harmonization requirements, or temporary compromises on economic numbers (which can readily be changed later) rather than fundamental changes in the Continental way of doing things in the direction of Anglo-American openness.

Europeans sometime argue that Britain must demonstrate a deeper commitment to Europe, but the "demonstration" usually involves acceptance of irreversible changes of the very type that the United Kingdom would seek to reform.

The alternative course appears radical, but in fact it would end up preserving more of what the United States, Britain, and Canada value in transatlantic partnership today and would avoid a radical disruption of economic and security partnerships in the future. This course would require substantial reconfiguration of Britain's membership terms with the EU and the emerging pan-European security and foreign-policy apparatus. This could take the course of a bilateral U.K.-EU renegotiation, a general restructuring of the EU along looser lines (a possibility that may emerge as the new Eastern European members come to terms with the consequences of their membership), or, in an extreme case, a formal withdrawal from the EU. Although the latter is unlikely due to the inherent conservatism of institutions, any thoroughgoing reevaluation of Britain's status must be able at least to consider the ultimate step. A Britain bound by looser ties to Europe would then be free to pursue a free-trade agreement with the United States and Canada (NAFTA affiliation for Britain would be one such, but not necessarily the best possible approach) and the conclusion of an Atlantic Defense Industry Community (ADIC) agreement including the United States, the United Kingdom, and Canada. Such a community would liberalize mergers, cooperation, intra-community technology transfer, and access to government markets in the aerospace, defense, and infosec industries of all three nations, as well as defense-related areas such as air transportation. Both NAFTA and an ADIC are precursors of network commonwealth institutions and could easily serve as the nucleus for such, just as the European Coal and Steel Community served as the nucleus for the EU.

Were the United Kingdom to leave the Union and join NAFTA, it would likely lead to far more productive partnerships. The United Kingdom is already the only country in recent memory to sell a combat aircraft design, the Harrier, to an American armed service; Britain is now the only non-American full partner working with the American armed forces in the development of the Joint Strike Fighter. It is worth considering further measures to integrate the high-technology industries of North America and the United Kingdom, particularly including defense-related technologies.

During the Industrial Era, it was sensible for defense industrial planners to insist on an autonomous industrial base within national borders. When the critical defense production items consisted of thousands of tanks and aircraft, it made no sense to depend on sources of supply on the other side of a submarine-infested ocean. When U.S. industry was largely organized on a regional or national scale, requiring defense contractors to be domestic did not segregate the ranks of defense contractors into a different universe from the nondefense industrial base.

When substantial divergence of national interest separated the American and British governments, it would have been foolish to create a reliance on sources of critical defense items under the control of another government.

Today, the circumstances are quite different. An important component of defense procurement is software, which can be downloaded as easily from London or Sydney as from Palo Alto. If communication with London is disrupted, Palo Alto will probably be cut off as well. When most companies are internationally owned and internationally dispersed, requiring the defense industrial base to be U.S.-owned and operated begins to segregate those companies even more from the general industrial base, at a cost over time in creativity, capability, and efficiency. If there is an incentive to expand the scope of defense industrial activity beyond U.S. borders (which is already a reality given Canadian participation in many critical defense industrial activities), it makes sense to expand that circle slowly and carefully. The United States should continue this expansion with the countries that have the longest history of successful cooperation and genuine convergence of viewpoint, as opposed to participating in an alliance of expedience.

Experience indicates that the United Kingdom has aligned itself even more frequently and more willingly with the United States than has Canada on critical defense issues. Areas of agreement include isolation of rogue states, the application of military action, and export control of weapons of mass destruction and their delivery systems.

An Atlantic (eventually, an Anglosphere) Defense Industry Community would consist initially of the United States, Canada, and the United Kingdom.

This would be a precursor to more elaborate network commonwealth forms. One of its criteria for membership would be membership in NAFTA or an equivalent common free trade agreement. A second would be agreement on a number of basic issues regarding destination control of critical capabilities for selected technologies in manufacturing of weapons of mass destruction and their delivery systems.

The Community would provide a framework for close cooperation, including mergers, among defense-sector manufacturers, information sector manufacturers and service providers, and transportation service providers including shipping lines and airlines. American merchant reserve fleet and Civil Reserve Air Fleet provisions could be essentially merged with the equivalent British and Canadian programs. Although this could theoretically result in American assets being tapped for a second Falklands War, this is a small and rather unlikely price to pay for augmenting one of America's more pressing defense needs.

A relaxed visa regime among the Community members (a precursor to a sojourner structure) would facilitate mobility of labor among the member nations.

The treaty establishing the Community would supersede existing legislation. It would address restrictions in foreign ownership, investment, and control of companies in such industries; and it would provide for nondiscriminatory access to government procurement markets for companies of any Community member state, to the extent that companies could be determined to belong to any particular member state.

Under such a regime, the Community's defense industry would soon become as thoroughly intermixed as the North American automobile industry is today.

Although U.S. defense industry executives might object to such a provision initially, the opportunities for further merger and consolidation and the acquisition of valuable defense technologies would offset that. The financial capabilities of the London markets would powerfully augment Wall Street as a source of working capital, particularly for infosec ventures and airlines.

Furthermore, this approach has particular merits in helping prepare for the defense challenges of the twenty-first century. Such challenges might include thin-shield missile defense systems to guard against blackmail weapons from rogue states, intensively trained counterinsurgency forces for low-intensity warfare, or the systems needed for infowar and the information grid of the future.

America's most likely collaborators are in the militaries and the defense industries of the English-speaking world, as was the case in Afghanistan and Iraq.

An Atlantic Defense Industry Community linking NAFTA members is a means for achieving the levels of cooperation adequate to the tasks ahead. Infotech in the English-speaking world thrives on fluid cooperation among private companies, many of which are recent entrepreneurial ventures. Attempting to meld the torpid state-owned national champions of the continent into such a mix would create a "slow convoy" situation, in which the fastest ships had to proceed at the pace of the slowest. In policy as well, such an all-NATO defense community would be a slow convoy, forced to seek lowest-common-denominator positions in areas such as technology transfer and deployment of antimissile systems. Creating a consensus for relatively uncontroversial positions in NATO has been a delicate task in the post–Cold War environment.

The compromises needed to support united action in Kosovo were militarily questionable, to say the least. A fast-convoy solution in which

America created a framework for closer cooperation among a smaller group of more like-minded nations would avoid these burdens.

Most important, continued British participation in the EU, and participation in the efforts to create a unified European defense structure and policy, could create a situation the United States may come to regret. The Aerospatiale-Matra-DASA merger into EADS has pointed the way to the creation of a pan-European state-sponsored champion. The pressures on the British defense industry are currently driving it in one direction: immersion into this emerging pan-European entity. Once this is created, the substantial capabilities of British Aerospace, GEC-Marconi, and Rolls-Royce will effectively cease to be under the policy control of the British government, which has tended to agree in broad areas with the United States.

These capabilities, which in many cases have no peer outside of the United States, will come increasingly under the control of the emerging European political system, which the history of the Union project has demonstrated to be overwhelmingly a Franco-German system. We must question whether such a system can be counted on to remain as closely aligned with America's outlook over the next twenty or thirty years as it is today (and even today there is nontrivial divergence), particularly in a political-economic climate marked by increasing demographic pressures on the protectionist and dirigiste systems of the continent.

Looking forward, the accession of the United Kingdom to NAFTA (or a successor agreement) and the creation of an ADIC would accelerate the existing trend toward mergers, partnerships, and alliances between U.S., Canadian, and British infotech companies. It would extend them into allied defense and defense-impacted fields such as aerospace and commercial aviation. The prospect of the merger of British industry into a pan-European consortium would be effectively ended. The U.S. commercial space industry would benefit from better access to the nontrivial U.K. market for space goods and services.

The U.S. and British capital markets have always been closely linked and would become an essentially seamless market. This would create a powerful further development of existing incentives to create an Anglosphere Network Commonwealth.

WHO WILL CONTROL THE COMMONWEALTH?
POPULAR CONTROL OF TRANSNATIONAL INSTITUTIONS

Rather than replicate such uninspiring institutions as the UN General Assembly, the NATO "Atlantic Assembly," and the European Parliament, it may be more interesting to create an unprecedented institution based on the capabilities of the Net. One new Information Age institution that has captured the attention of Americans is C-SPAN, the ongoing cable broadcast of Congressional speeches. It is relevant that during the debate in the United States and the United Kingdom over war against Iraq in 2002–2003 (as well as during the Clinton-Blair actions of 1998), extensive excerpts from the debates in the British Parliament about this issue were broadcast on the U.S. evening news. It would be easy and inexpensive to create a pan-Anglosphere Webcasting and cable system to provide a sort of Hanseatic Diet in cyberspace—a "Virtual Network Commonwealth Assembly." With such a system, any parliamentarian of a network commonwealth member nation (or person nominated by a member nation) could take the "floor" and be seen and heard throughout the community, both live in real-time video, or almost-live in transcript on a Web log format (real-time) and indexed for later recall. The system could be further divided to provide for committee discussions on particular topics.

Such a virtual assembly would not have to rely on some selection mechanism to narrow representation down to only a few members for a state, region, or small nation; but it could permit a wide variety of voices to be heard on any topic. For the price of a broadcasting studio and Web feed from each national, state, or provincial legislature in the network commonwealth, this virtual assembly could become a reality.

The vast majority of all such parliamentary debate is of interest only to a few local constituents. However, the example of the transatlantic debate space temporarily created during the Iraq issue shows that there are minds and voices in all corners of a network civilization who would have an audience in future debates affecting the entire community. Like the Hanseatic Diet, such a virtual assembly would not require majority votes or taxation powers per se, because an idea, once it had gained currency within a few local assemblies, could begin to be implemented by creating open-ended programs that other bodies could join as they demonstrated their utility. There will be a need for formal decision making in some areas; these would more likely be made on a state-to-state basis as in NATO today.

A network commonwealth need not have a capital; in fact, it may be inappropriate to designate a single city as such. A network does not have a center. The network commonwealth assembly can be a "virtual" organization as previously described, although it may be appropriate for symbolic purposes to have several dedicated "floors" in real space. These places could be venues for symbolic and ceremonial events, occasional conferences, and dispersed offices for particular commonwealth functions as well. One city might be the headquarters of the security alliance, another the science and technology organization, another the economic organization, another a judicial center.

A particular issue driving the emergence of network commonwealth institutions could be the issue of constitutional control over existing forms of international cooperation. A common complaint in many nations is the lack of supervision or accountability of supernational institutions such as NAFTA or most EU bureaucracies. The tame-poodle nature of the European Parliament, due to both its lack of real legislative power, its lack of single-member districts to create a link between representative and constituency, and the lack of a common parliamentary sensibility among the members, has prevented that body from being an effective means of accountability or control. In contrast, the United States Congress was able to be effective immediately on formation, because the newly elected members of even the first Congress could draw on a common constitutional history and set of precedents from the British Parliament and the colonial legislatures modeled on it. It is important to remember that on the first day of the first Congress, some of the state legislatures had nearly two hundred years of experience as representative, constitutional institutions—far more than that of most of the EU member states today. A network commonwealth, linking nations and states with common traditions, could similarly expect a greater effectiveness in supervising its transnational institutions.

In chapter 5, I will discuss in greater detail the case of a prospective network commonwealth linking the nations of the English-speaking world. That case could illustrate a particular example of this issue. For decades, there has been a cooperation agreement linking the intelligence agencies of the major English-speaking nations. These agencies, led by the U.S. National Security Agency, have established the "Echelon" system, an elaborate system capable of eavesdropping on domestic and international telephone traffic worldwide. Undoubtedly, the transnational nature of this enterprise has aided it in eluding the control of existing legislatures.

One can imagine the confusion if the Central Intelligence Agency were under the oversight only of American state legislatures, each, like the proverbial blind man seeking to understand the elephant, getting to feel only one part of the creature. It is hard enough to establish effective oversight of domestic programs through Congress; it is little wonder that transnational cooperative programs elude supervision even more. A network commonwealth is built of the sinews already seen in existing transnational institutions—but it is completed through the addition of a nervous system and a brain as well. Deliberative institutions are the core of that brain, and the network commonwealth will not have truly emerged until they form and become effective.

COMMONWEALTH OR TRIBALISM

It is becoming increasingly evident that the economic state is a less and less viable model. As an ideal, it has faded already. People are seeking other solutions, and there is a great interest in decentralized institutions. Secession by itself is not an answer. It could easily lead to a more tribalized and trivialized society in which people would increasingly need passports, work permits, official papers and other such impedimenta to travel or trade even close to home. Breaking up large units into small units often aggravates the problem of nationalism, as we have seen in Bosnia, Chechniya, Karabakh, and elsewhere. The prevailing decentralist model in reality may not be the peaceful hippie reviving Celtic folk arts, but the skinhead brandishing the truncheon.

When a centralized economic state fails and breaks up, the unit that tends to emerge is a narrowly defined tribe. This can be seen in eastern and southern Europe, in the Balkans, in Africa, and indeed, throughout most of the world. The nations of the English-speaking world, as with other First World nations, will not be immune from these trends. Devolution and decentralization are essential paths for the coming world of the Singularity revolutions. But it is essential that devolution happen in a framework that does not allow local tyrannies to replace centralized ones.

At the same time, the ubiquity of worldwide information sources and the emergence of the ability of even small groups of nonstate actors, such as al-Qaeda to affect regional and even world politics, has meant that past episodes of state formation cannot be repeated as easily. Few states have come into being without the suppression, expulsion, or conversion to uncomfortable minority status of one or more nonconforming groups, be they ethnic, religious, or political. The ongoing unhappiness of such groups often becomes an ongoing drain on the moral and material sources of the new state, a source of dissension, disruption, and in time of war, of aid to the enemy.

Consider the former Czechoslovakia. At birth, it faced the task of integrating Bohemians, Moravians, and Slovaks into a new, synthetic Czechoslovak nationality.

It had to deal with the unhappiness of significant German and Hungarian minorities, each newly deprived of former majority status in the Austrian Empire and Hungarian kingdom from which the Czech and Slovak lands, respectively, had been separated. Its frontiers also contained Galician Poles and Carpathian Ruthenians who would rather have belonged to neighboring states.

This integration task remained unfinished by 1938, and the unresolved problems contributed greatly to the ease of Hitler's dismemberment of the country.

That dismemberment was enthusiastically facilitated by Poland and Hungary, who would shortly have their own problems with Hitler, and by significant numbers of their own minorities, including separatist Slovaks, who first realized their dream of a Slovak state under German patronage.

After 1945, the new Czechoslovak state expelled the great majority of its German-speaking minority, an act that went relatively unnoticed due to the context of the times. (Czech membership in the EU should theoretically give the descendants of those expelled the right to move back, which has created an interesting now; the Czech refusal to repeal the Benes Decrees, which expelled the Sudeten Germans, has become an irritant in Czech-German relations.) Other problems remained; one wonders how much of the participation in the Warsaw Pact's invasion of Czechoslovakia in 1968 (involving German, Hungarian, and Polish forces, as in 1938) was forced by the Soviets and how much was a sign of the reemergence of historical grudges. Upon independence from Soviet domination, unresolved friction between Czechs and Slovaks promptly led to the "Velvet Divorce" between those two nationalities.

Slovakia still faces substantial issues with their substantial Hungarian minority.

The Information Revolution has given new levels of power to such minorities.

It is not clear that a Czechoslovakia could be created today, given the power of instantaneous satellite television news to bring bloody confrontations to the world's screens. The Internet also gives minorities the power to organize, and to link themselves to communities of support in other nations. Nonviolent protest has become an art form that, when linked to worldwide media dramatization, can often defeat the plans of states which in former times would have been unaffected.

Furthermore, given the relative ease with which even small terrorist groups can cause ongoing disruption, the ability to incorporate unwilling minority populations into new states is rapidly diminishing.

Thus, a permanent, peaceful solution to the Northern Ireland situation will have to be based on the willing acceptance of that outcome by the great majority of both the Nationalist and Unionist populations. Incorporation of Northern Ireland into the Republic against the will of the Unionist population (whether a majority or minority) would be a disaster for the Republic. In today's world, three hundred hard men with a few tons of plastic explosive (and there is no lack of either in Ulster), given the tacit approval of a relatively small segment of the population, could ruin the current prosperity of the Republic. The British state, with a large budget and some of the best antiterrorist forces in the world, has been unable to defeat a comparable force of extremists on the Nationalist side; the Irish Republic, with fewer resources, could hardly do better. (It is also worth asking whether the Irish Republic really wants dozens of intransigent Unionist members sitting in the Dail.)

Similarly, although, given the general pressures toward decentralization, Quebec could well become an essentially sovereign entity within the next ten to twenty years, the same pressures render unrealistic the expectation of many Quebecois nationalists of creating a unitary French-speaking polity without substantial autonomy for minority populations. The minority populations in Quebec are sufficiently numerous, well-organized, vocal, and sophisticated that they could probably frustrate the ability of the Quebecois majority to dictate a settlement to them even without resorting to terrorist tactics.

Effective Quebec sovereignty is available for the asking, but it will entail more negotiation and compromise than some of the nationalists yet realize.

Network commonwealth institutions become important tools in this environment.

Formation of new polities, a trend which will continue to accelerate, will less and less result in the formation of classic unitary economic states, as the minorities become increasingly resistant to submersion in alien state-building projects and become more skilled at using their tools of resistance. World standards have become less tolerant of the repressive measures needed to resist them.

Negotiation and compromise will become more necessary; autonomy and entrenched rights will become a larger part of the solutions emerging from compromise.

Network commonwealths, by providing trusted frameworks for implementing and maintaining such solutions, become essential parts of the process of devolution.

NETWORK COMMONWEALTHS AROUND THE WORLD

The primary focus of this book is on the possibility of a network commonwealth among English-speaking nations. Subsequent chapters will examine that case in detail. Because Britain, and subsequently the United States, share a background of a particularly individualist culture long predating the Industrial Revolution, and for that reason experienced the Industrial Revolution and political modernity early, the English-speaking nations have tended to be in the forefront of social, political, and economic evolution. The position of the United States in the Information Revolution and the emergence of the Internet have continued this tendency. Therefore, network commonwealth structures will probably arise in the English-speaking world quite early as well.

A network commonwealth for the English-speaking community would not be the only such entity, although it would probably be the first. The Spanish-speaking world is another prime candidate for the creation of such a community, as there is a similar flow of information among Spanish-speaking nations and an increasing effort to renew common links and institutions. The French-speaking world has a similar potential, for the same reasons. In fact, France supports a substantial apparatus—La Francophonie—for pan-Francophone relations, which could serve as the nucleus for a Francosphere Network Commonwealth.

It is interesting to note that at the most recent meeting of the association of French-speaking states, Louisiana sent a delegate. This may be a precursor of a much wider phenomenon. The Portuguese-speaking world, whose center is now Brazil, may well construct a Lusosphere; the increasingly close connections between Brazil and the former Portuguese states of Africa foreshadows such a development.

The future of the EU in the Information Revolution is another interesting discussion. The impact of devolution, the erosion of state taxation power, and other likely developments is the weakening, and perhaps ceasing, of movement toward a European federal superstate. Certainly, the pension liability issue, placed in the context of a general decline in taxation levels, suggests that the EU will have to substantially reform its structures before or shortly after the liabilities become unsustainable.

Euro-optimism also fails to address the divisive tendencies in the EU. If in fact trust characteristics have a substantial impact on the abilities of political systems to interact, the lines of cleavage among the cultures of the EU nations—high-trust versus low-trust countries, north versus south, center versus periphery—may drive a dissolution of the Union. Alternatively, it may convert to one or more network commonwealths. In some ways, a EU consisting of a loose cooperative framework among several network commonwealths may be the optimal structure for the era of the Singularity revolutions. We can imagine a Scandinavian-Baltic Network Commonwealth; a Rhenish Commonwealth of Germany, France, and the Benelux countries; a Mediterranean Commonwealth; a Turkic Commonwealth; and a Danubian Commonwealth. These could all cooperate with the Anglosphere Network Commonwealth, with a Commonwealth of Independent States evolving toward a network commonwealth model to the east, and with language-based network commonwealths worldwide—to the Francosphere, Hispanosphere, and Lusosphere as well as the Anglosphere.

The heart of this option is the ability of member states to carry levels of affiliation to more than one network commonwealth simultaneously. Britain and Ireland may well be the test cases of this flexibility, as, whatever links they create with the Anglosphere, it makes sense for them to retain trade and cooperative links with Europe as well. British politicians have adopted the formula of defining Britain as a European country having a special relationship with America; it is probably more accurate to describe it as an Anglosphere country having a special relationship with Europe.

China provides a particularly interesting case, as the Chinese diaspora forms a worldwide business community whose common ties are already of significance in world trade. A network commonwealth approach may provide the only acceptable basis for common institutions linking the Sinosphere of Taiwan, mainland China, Hong Kong, Singapore, and other communities with substantial Chinese-language populations.

It can by no means be taken for granted that the large, ethnically diverse Asian nations, particularly China, India, Iran, and Indonesia, can maintain their political unity in anything like their current forms. Asia is not immune to the techno-political changes that drive the devolution of economic states elsewhere. For instance, widespread availability of the Web in the prosperous Chinese coast areas is necessary to ensure their competitiveness. Widespread use of the Web will make it easy to offer information in the local languages written in Western alphabetic characters. (These are usually called dialects of Chinese, but in fact Shanghaiese, Cantonese, and Mandarin—the so-called National Language—are at least as distinct as French, Spanish, and Italian.) As learning is much faster in alphabetic systems, the next generation may be more likely to think and work primarily in these local languages, and find Mandarin, written in characters, to be increasingly more alien and difficult. It might be the case that a Shanghaiese and a Cantonese of the next generation will communicate with each other in English rather than in Mandarin.

China, furthermore, is still a culture in search of a binding idea that works.

Despite the superficial claims for the resurgence of Confucianism (actually a highly mutated Anglo-Confucianism evolved in Hong Kong and Singapore), that philosophy, in anything like its classical form, is unsuited to the demands of a modern technological society. Communism and nationalism, represented by Mao and Chiang, have both failed. Religion of one form or another may return to take their place. Both homegrown movements such as Falun Dafa, based on martial-arts philosophy, and imported religions such as evangelical Protestantism have grown substantially in East Asia over the past two decades. It is possible that evangelical Protestantism, in either a pure or mutated form, will make substantial inroads in China over the next twenty years, as it has in South Korea, Taiwan, and Latin America. If that is the case, the evangelical drive to publish Bibles in Roman character regional languages may provide a strong impetus to their use.

"China," even without its non-Han minorities such as the Tibetans and Turkic peoples, is at least as diverse as Europe. The printing press drove the emergence of separate national languages and the decline of Latin as a common European language; the Web may drive an equivalent process in China. This, combined with the decline in available tax revenues, will greatly increase the impetus for a more devolved, network commonwealth structure for China, if not the complete disappearance of China as a centralized economic state. Kenichi Ohmae proposed a "Chinese Commonwealth" in his *End of the Nation-State*. This proposal, combined with the network commonwealth institutions described here, could form the basis of such a development.

Similarly, India, Indonesia, and Iran are all extremely diverse areas. Each current state is dominated by a large ethnic group (Hindi speakers, Javanese, and Persians, respectively) who are resented and suspected by the large ethnic minorities of those states, all of whom have strong national linguistic and cultural traditions of their own. The massive dislocations caused by the economic shifts of the next twenty years will make survival of these entities in their current forms unlikely. The recent achievement of independence of Timor from Indonesia and the persistent demands for the independence of Aceh, Ambon, and Eastern New Guinea foreshadow such a breakdown.

Just as Asia is unlikely to retain its current political, cultural, and economic forms over the next twenty years, Africa and Latin America will continue the current course of evolution. If they can ride these changes successfully, both Latin America and Africa (particularly English-speaking Africa) will come to substantial prosperity as a result.

Two trends have emerged in Latin America which, between them, may mark a permanent break with the past practices that have kept these regions in poverty.

One is the relative opening of their economies to market forces, most fully in Chile, but also significantly in Mexico, Argentina, Brazil, and elsewhere. This has begun to break down the cozy symbiosis between the political class and the economic monopolies, who have together historically dominated Latin American societies.

Observers such as Hernando de Soto, Mario Vargas Llosa, and Claudio Véliz have all written extensively, from their various perspectives, on this phenomenon.

The other is the explosive, and mostly unnoticed growth of alternatives to the Catholic Church, particularly evangelical Protestantism and the Latter-Day Saints (Mormons). The hierarchy of the Catholic Church in Latin America has contributed heavily to the perpetuation of the crony system throughout its history. When it has attempted to challenge the status quo, it has been vulnerable to the totalitarian temptation inherent in its Baroque hedgehog mentality (as Véliz calls it). "Liberation theologians" have ended up supporting Marxist solutions, which would take Latin America out of the crony-capitalist frying pan into the totalitarian fire, as happened in Cuba.

These economic and religious trends among them offer the prospect of transition to a stronger civil society and better constitutional mechanisms.

If successful, they could support a genuine transformative takeoff throughout most of Latin America. Observers have been expecting a "Chinese miracle" for several decades; it might in fact be eclipsed in the short term by a Latin American miracle. However, the failure to address trust issues adequately in Latin America has caused a backlash to the wave of market reform of the 1990s. Particularly in nations such as Argentina, macroeconomic reforms have destroyed the old employment system of the crony capitalists without sufficiently liberating the creative energies of the entrepreneurs.

The result has been the destruction of old jobs without the growth of sufficient new ones to replace them. This has caused a general economic crisis and, rather than creating impetus to carry out the difficult and nonobvious transparency reforms needed, has evoked a wave of nostalgia for the days of crony capitalism.

De Soto has recently criticized the "civilizational" school of analysis, particularly those taking after Samuel Huntington, because he sees that analysis as characterizing Latin American societies as inherently backwards, and thus incapable of self-reform. Yet this is true only of a particular reading of civilizational analysis. The very fact that some cultures have become high-trust and transparent is an existence proof of the ability of other cultures to acquire similar characteristics. After all, England in the Old Whig era of the eighteenth century was massively, staggeringly corrupt in some ways. Yet the takeoff into the Industrial Revolution, political modernity, and a particularly transparent and uncorrupt society was underway at the same time. Cultural traits are persistent, but they are not immutable. It is a question of time—can massive social changes be implemented in one political generation? Two? These are the questions that matter. What De Soto must concentrate upon is the question of exactly what pressures will be needed to overcome the cronyism and corruption of Latin American societies, and how to generate such pressures. In this, civilizational analysis has the potential to be a source of help, not of hindrance.

Africa is undergoing positive changes for the first time since independence.

Postcolonial regimes and their socialist-interventionist economics (which owed more to the bureaucratic socialism of the French and British colonial regimes than to Marx or Lenin) are declining, giving scope to entrepreneurism. The sanctity of colonial boundaries is also fading; Eritrea was permitted to secede from Ethiopia with the blessing of the Organization of African Unity—a political first, but not a last. Sooner or later some successful states will latch onto the opportunities presented by the Information Revolution—realizing that their pool of educated, underemployed, English-speaking people (so far more of a curse than a blessing) is actually a continental gold mine waiting to be turned into prosperity. South Africa—which desperately needs to expand its economy beyond its current natural-resource base to provide prosperity for its large numbers of educated nonwhites—could be the first.

The Arabic-speaking world has both a long-standing pan-Arab sentiment, and populations who have never been fully converted to the paradigm of the nation-state. There is a long-standing feeling that Arabs should be a unified people with shared institutions. At the same time, there is also a history of real differences among the various Arab nations, and a disinclination to submerge those differences into a common political entity. An Arabic Network Commonwealth could provide the essential benefits of unity without requiring the submission of the very different parts of the Arab world to a single political center. The rise of satellite television systems broadcasting in Arabic from the relatively free Gulf states (interestingly enough, former British protectorates with continued strong ties to London) has begun to create a common Arabic informational space, and has begun the undermining of local informational monopolies. Although at present stations such as al-Jezeera have played to demagogic sensibilities rather than democratic ones, nevertheless the creation of a common informational space beyond the control of local governments has the potential to bring forth other, eventually more constructive responses.

Similarly, the Turkic states—Turkey, Azerbaijan, Northern Cyprus, and the former Soviet republics of Turkic origin (Kazakhstan, Uzbekistan, Turkmenistan, and Kyrgyzstan)—offer a prospect for a Turkic Network Commonwealth. This would give institutional reality to a demographic and cultural fact, without creating a threat to neighboring states or closing the possibility of network commonwealth links in other directions. The Central Asian states with substantial Russian-speaking populations, particularly Kazakhstan, could belong to both a Turkic Network Commonwealth and a successor to the Russian-centric Commonwealth of Independent States without contradiction.

There will continue to be strong, unique, distinctive cultures which are not readily assignable to any wider civilization. In the world of economic states, such cultures often embodied themselves in nation-state form with substantial success.

How will they fare in a world in which many civic states are strongly enmeshed in network commonwealths? Although the Singularity revolution world will tend not to produce uniform, one-size-fits-all solutions, it is worth examining two special cases to think about the fate of states that are not obviously part of a wider network civilization. Japan and Israel are such cases.

The most important fact about Japan may not be what it is, but rather what it is not. It is not part of an East Asian, Confucian civilization as many superficial observers tend to assume. Here I must agree with Huntington and others who define it as a unique civilization. In the same way that the Anglosphere is recognizably rooted in Western Christian civilization, but has become something distinct, so had Japan become something rooted in East Asian Confucian civilization, but now similarly become something distinct. Just as a pan-European political institution is unsuitable as a primary affiliation for Britain, so would a pan-Asian political institution be unworkable for Japan. (History shows how Japan's own version of a pan-Asian political institution, the Greater East Asia Co-Prosperity Sphere, was unacceptable to non-Japanese.)

The other historical fact of interest about Japan is its deep, problematic, mutually stimulating century-and-a-half relationship with the Anglosphere. From Commodore Matthew Perry and his Black Ships, through General Douglas MacArthur as Shogun, to Edwards Deming and his quality-control revolution, and the impact of the Internet, the Anglosphere and its people and institutions have often been the irritant that causes the Japanese oyster to produce its pearls.

The influence has not been one-way. Japan's aesthetic, its architecture, its religions, its philosophies, its manufactures, and its emigrants have all profoundly influenced the Anglosphere, and to a greater degree than other European cultures.

This suggests that in a network commonwealth future, Japan may find its task to be balancing its historical ties with the Asian continent with its newer but also profound ties with the Anglosphere. Such a balance may be the key to maintaining Japanese independence, not so much from formal threats of conquest, but rather from absorption and submersion, particularly if Japan must begin admitting immigrants in significant numbers to counter its demographic decline.

Israel is another issue. Judaism was the original, definitive Diaspora. The creation of the State of Israel changed the dynamic of the Diaspora by giving it a center and an anchor. Zionist theory looked to the end of the Diaspora and hoped for aliyah—the "ascension" of all Jews to Israel. What has happened is different.

Jews have left en masse two of the three main historical areas of the diaspora—the Islamic world and Continental Europe. From the third, Russia, many left as soon as they were able and it is not unlikely that most of the remainder will leave within the next few decades. But at the same time Jews have increased throughout the Anglosphere, which has experienced a new gain in Jewish population. Thus, Judaism is becoming an Israeli-Anglosphere phenomenon. Like the Japanese-Anglosphere encounter, the Judeo-Anglosphere encounter has become extremely creative and productive. It is also starting to see a very high rate of intermarriage of Jews into the Anglosphere. Israel is not an Anglosphere state, except peripherally.

It suffers from a bureaucratic-socialist tradition and lack of a legal instrument as flexible as common law. But it is becoming increasingly more aligned and intertwined with the Anglosphere, particularly in high technology and defense relations. Ultimately, Israel's defense and trade ties with the Anglosphere may be folded into an Anglosphere Network Commonwealth of which Israel becomes more and more of a full member. One of the most interesting speculations is whether the need for an external stabilizing framework for Israeli-Palestinian peace, combined with the continuing Palestinian emigration to the Anglosphere, leads to the use of Anglosphere Network Commonwealth institutions as such a stabilizing framework, bringing both Israel and Palestine into its fold. Such a possibility seems distant today, but like Sherlock Holmes, the Israelis and Palestinians may someday have come to reject all other solutions, and find that the remaining one, no matter how improbable, is in fact the only possible one.

UNITED NATIONS—OR ASSOCIATED COMMONWEALTHS?

Since network commonwealths are not states, and are not intended to grow into states, there is no intrinsic reason why countries, regions, and even cities might not have overlapping and duplicate affiliations with multiple commonwealths.

In cases where a common legal tradition is used, it may be necessary for one commonwealth's standards to take precedence over others for particular purposes.

Two legal systems cannot exist in the same space without such precedence.

However, it is also in the nature of such organizations that there be multiple levels of affiliation—some closer, others more distant. Many cities today serve as links between one linguistic world and another. Miami, for example, is a bridge between Spanish and English speakers, Hong Kong is a bridge between English and Chinese, and Los Angeles links all three. The United States might have a primary level of affiliation with an English-speaking network commonwealth, but a secondary affiliation with the Spanish-language commonwealth (and others, such as the French, as well). Puerto Rico may have its own separate affiliation with the Spanish-language commonwealth.

What is the future of the United Nations and its technical organizations (World Telecommunications Union, etc.) in the era of the Singularity revolutions? (Distinctions must be made between the Security Council, the General Assembly, and the technical organizations, each existing in a different political reality.) The General Assembly's primary function is now as an international endorsement of sovereign statehood. The Security Council must parallel actual lines of power to be effective. The problems of the future will be in deciding where actual power lies. Should the EU have membership? Should NATO? As network commonwealths emerge, should they have representation?

The United Nations may evolve into the "Associated Commonwealths," as network commonwealths become most important actors at the global level. The interplay of too many nations becomes too complex (and too divorced from realities of power) for stable political system. The United Nations had approximately fifty-some members at founding, has about two hundred today, and could have substantially more in five to ten years. This expansion would paralyze the existing structure, to the extent that it is not paralyzed already. The General Assembly may remain as a largely symbolic function, a sort of global House of Lords. UN technical organizations may come under supervision of the Security Council, as their functions become too important to remain under supervision of the General Assembly. In a network commonwealth world, the United Nations, or its successor, would be a lower-profile organization, which would probably be a good thing.

Too much has been expected of the United Nations, given its internal contradictions.

There is only the thinnest level of consensus among UN member-states regarding what is good, desirable, or possible, and much of the consensus that does exist is not shared or supported by the citizens they purport to represent.

Many of the functions it now supposedly carries out would be better carried out by network commonwealths closer to the people and problems they address.

Reducing the responsibilities of the United Nations may eventually enable it to discover a balance between the available means and the desirable ends, rendering it more useful and restoring to it more respect.

5

The Anglosphere as a Unique Civilization

L'Angleterre en effet est insulaire, maritime, liéc par ses échanges, ses marchés, son ravitaillement, aux pays les plus divers et souvent les plus lointains.
[England is indeed insular, maritime, and tied by its exchanges, its markets, its supply, with the most diverse and often most remote countries.]

—Charles DeGaulle, vetoing British membership
in the Common Market, January 14, 1963

The American Constitution is not self-sufficient but exists embedded in a wider unwritten constitutional tradition of custom and common law shared with Britain and the rest of the Anglosphere. This tradition has evolved in a remarkably stable fashion from the Middle Ages and arguably earlier. Such stability and continuity is a rare phenomenon among modern nations. One example of that common tradition is the Anglo-American constitutional attitudes about the military, which has been a significant factor in our common history. More fundamental, and one with significant practical consequences is the Anglosphere legal tradition of the common law. This is one of the most important commonalties among Anglosphere nations. A business lawyer from any common-law nation can understand the basics of any other common-law code. The differences among American states, English law, and Canadian and Australian codes mean that most Anglosphere lawyers already have a feeling for the variability among the different codes. He or she will know the basic outlines of the problem before he begins work and is used to talking with lawyers expert in the codes of other common-law jurisdictions.

(Scottish law is an outlier, being more a fusion of common and Roman civil law, but still recognizably familiar.)

Common law is an evolved and emergent phenomenon. It was not designed but emerged from the sum total of the great number of cases and experiences of many people in many situations over many centuries. Its basic mechanism is case law and precedent—it can operate independently of statute authorities or lawmakers, if needed. In this, it differs from the Roman or Continental law used in Europe, Latin America, and many other jurisdictions. Continental law is entirely derived from the edicts of the government—originally the sovereign, more recent legislatures. Since the resolution of disputes arising from human interactions is an unbounded or open-ended problem (meaning that one cannot reliably foresee all the likely outcomes of such interactions), it is the sort of problem that is typically better addressed through evolved and emergent mechanisms. This is even more true as the pace of technological progress accelerates, making outcomes even harder to foresee and rendering designed systems of statute law and regulation more quickly obsolete.

An Anglosphere Network Commonwealth could be a means to offer a Commonwealth-wide dispute resolution system based on common-law principles and precedents. More immediately, it is the underlying basis of much of the common business practices of the Anglosphere. Large law firms are becoming increasingly trans-Anglosphere, to a substantially greater degree than they are merely international. Most American law firms establishing European practices choose England or Ireland as the first place to locate an office, for both the common language and the similarity of legal systems.

Common law is the oldest and deepest level of shared practice in Anglosphere constitutional systems. However, there is another substantial layer of common constitutional practice that we all share. This is roughly describable as the Whig constitutional settlement of 1688, established between the Revolution of that year and the founding of the United Kingdom in 1707. This settlement draws on an older constitutional tradition established by English jurists running through William Blackstone, Edward Coke, and to Henry of Bracton before them. Prior to the settlement of 1688, however, this tradition had to contend with ambitious monarchs holding to different interpretations of English constitutionalism (inevitably more favorable to royal prerogative) and with more modern waves of Continental absolutist theories. Such theories range from the Counter-Reformation to the later Bourbon centralization theories that the Stuarts envied. The Whig settlement marked a turning point in the treatment of rights in the English-speaking world, in transitioning from a particularist medieval view of rights as specific negotiated property of given classes of persons (as in Magna Carta) to something that is nearer to a more general concept of inherent right, as articulated by voices such as Sydney and Milton. The English Bill of Rights established the basic concepts of freedom of speech, religion, and property, while the settlement constitution established the supremacy of Parliament over the monarchy. The English monarchy had not been absolute, in the Continental sense, since at least Magna Carta—the powers of the monarchy had been bounded even before then by the traditions of medieval constitutionality. But the settlement made England a constitutional regime of limited government, a "crowned republic" according to the sneers of Continental absolutists, if not yet a democracy.

American freedom is unambiguously the result of this constitutional settlement.

All the Founding Fathers were clear on this—Jefferson spoke for them all when he said, "I innovated as little as possible." Those areas where American practice differed were primarily ones where triumphant American Whigs were able to implement reforms long sought by the more liberal and radical Whigs in Britain but which they were unable to implement there. Some, such as fixed terms for the legislature and reapportionment of electoral districts, were reforms instituted in the Cromwellian Constitution but undone at the restoration. Others, such as judicial review, were principles upheld by Coke and Blackstone and which were successfully established in America but not adopted in Britain.

Of the differences among Anglosphere nations, such as judicial review, most are due to branching interpretations of fundamentally common principles. Now, judicial review is coming into Britain through the back door, in the form of EU law. Britons should ask themselves whether they would rather have a fundamentally alien concept of rights imposed by treaty or whether they would prefer a concept of rights more in tune with their constitutional roots.

Since the settlement of 1688, Whig forces and their successors in Britain have had to continue the battle with Continental centralism and its local adherents in all its various forms. These have ranged from the mercantilist imperialism of George III and Lord North, through the state ownership and central planning of the twentieth-century Laborites, to the European Union Social Chapter signed by the Blair Labour government in 1998. The demise of the explicit Whig tradition, with the passing of the classic Liberal Party, has meant that most radical social critics have been Marxists (or, in the interwar period, fascists such as Mosely).

Being reflexively anti-American, they have avoided the possibility that the common constitutional tradition implemented in America might be a source of options from which Britain might choose. However, the collapse of the Marxist project has meant that at least some antiauthoritarians have begun to rediscover that common constitutional tradition. Author Jonathan Freedland, a left-wing journalist, published the controversial *Bring Home the Revolution* in 1998, in which he pointed out that a Britain that implemented many of the reforms advocated by constitutional reform advocates would more closely resemble America in many ways. His point, essentially valid, disturbed many of his colleagues.

The present is a time of unusual constitutional ferment throughout the Anglosphere. The fundamental constitution of the United Kingdom is being called into question by devolution, separatism, and reforms such as the various proposed reforms of the upper chamber and of the electoral system. The Canadian Constitution is being challenged by both Quebec separatism and the growing tensions between the Canadian West and the majority of the population in the East. Australia examined some fundamental constitutional issues in its 1999 referendum on becoming a republic, in which the monarchy, although a minority preference overall, won over any of the particular versions of republic on offer. New Zealand has undertaken an experiment with proportional representation. South Africa is settling in to a new constitution in which majority franchise is only the most publicized of its changes; now that the excitement of transition is past, the task of settling down to governance in the face of major challenges suggests that the constitution will be tested in the coming decades, perhaps severely. And the United States has, in facing the challenges begun by the September 11, 2001, attacks, entered a new cycle of weighing constitutional protections against the exigencies of war. This cycle brings echoes of similar challenges in the era of the Civil War, the turmoil of 1918–1919, World War II, and the early Cold War.

A network commonwealth is not merely a set of economic or military arrangements between governments. It will not emerge unless feelings of common ties and interests emerge among the citizens of its members. These feelings grow out of experiences, but also out of common values. Although the surface politics of the different Anglosphere nations have many differences, the underlying structures come from the same sources. British reformers are seeking to embed the European Convention on Human Rights in the British Constitution, but this is a charter with shallow roots, not based on deep common values.

An Anglosphere Network Commonwealth could generate a common restatement of basic rights with an eight-hundred-year tradition underlying it. It stems from the Magna Carta, through the English and American bills of rights, the Gettysburg Address, and the Civil Rights movement, but above all on the long tradition of juries acquitting victims of state power and ordinary citizens standing up for "what's fair" in day-to-day life. This is the essence of strong civil society. The Anglosphere has the longest and most consistent tradition of it, and it is strongly embedded in our institutions. It is the source of our freedom, our strength, and our prosperity. When those values have been negated in practice, practice has been best corrected by appeal to them rather than to alien values or abstract theories. For all these reasons, it is the firmest foundation available on which to build any broader cooperation.

Citizens of today's nations are descended from people who were once subjects of various scattered principalities and duchies. At some point in history, they began to feel that a larger realm equally or better embodied their values and claimed their loyalties. In the case of Americans, this happened long before the American federal government had more than the most rudimentary common economic institutions—when the average citizen hardly ever saw a federal employee other than those of the Post Office. Network commonwealths will become more than abstract economic institutions when they begin to develop these common feelings as well. Those based on genuine commonalties will feel this sooner than those linking people who have little in common. The Anglosphere has a particularly rich history of commonalties on which to build.

THE ANGLOSPHERE
CONSTITUTIONAL TRADITION AND WAR

The Anglo-American constitutional tradition is an evolved system of practices designed to limit arbitrary government and prevent the state from overwhelming society. As war has always promoted the encroachment of state on society, mechanisms for controlling the use of military power, while permitting effective defense, have been one of the core issues of Anglosphere constitutional politics.

The Anglo-American constitutional tradition includes centuries-old mechanisms used to prevent executive abuse of the war-making power. These have served to prevent the inevitable small-scale, limited-purpose uses of military force overseas from escalating into major wars without obtaining the consensus of the populace as to the necessity and desirability of that conflict. These mechanisms have included three principal checks: the first was the requirement that new overseas conflict be financed by explicit authorization of higher expenditure; the second, the tradition that soldiers sent to war overseas be volunteers enlisted explicitly for that conflict; and the third, and most important, that, with only a few stated exceptions, substantial land forces not be maintained in peacetime. All of these traditions had been eroded in the United States throughout the wars of the twentieth century, a process culminating in 1947, when unification of the War and Navy departments into a single Department of Defense effectively erased the third of those checks. The

United States has experienced the consequences of that loss ever since. The United Kingdom has followed a parallel course.

Anglo-American tradition had always held that the executive, whether Crown or White House, could not engage the country in war without presenting to the populace, as represented by the legislature, the reasons for the war and obtaining approval. These checks and balances came in several forms. One was the raising of funds earmarked for the conflict, in the form of appropriations and special levies approved by the legislature, and subscriptions and loans volunteered by the financial community and general public. A second was the response of the people to a call for military volunteers, in the form of voluntary enlistment and a willingness of the militias to respond to a call for mobilization. The third was the traditional sentiment in both England and America against maintaining a large standing army, or even a military establishment, in time of peace.

One of the less-noticed effects of the adoption of universal suffrage has been the erosion of the importance of nonelectoral means of expressing popular assent or dissent. In the traditional Old Whig system of the eighteenth century, the franchise was not the only, or even the most important, means of gauging popular will. As Linda Colley's work *Britons: Forging the Nation 1707–1837* (1992) demonstrated, forms of expression such as petitions, assemblies, "loyal addresses," and resolutions of the organizations of civil society—guilds, beneficial societies, etc.—were monitored as carefully by politicians as opinion polls are today.

This is why the English and American bills of rights went out of their way to expressly protect them. Enlistment rates, militia units' legal contestation of mobilization of their units (or absence thereof), rates of subscription to war bonds, and other voluntary acts have been similarly important gauges of popular consent to major wars.

All of these safeguards have effectively been greatly eroded by the experience of twentieth-century wars. The fiscal check on war making has been circumvented by several developments. The first was the sheer scale of the military forces and budgets maintained in peacetime with the onset of the Cold War. This permitted the executive to deploy a substantial part of these forces in overseas combat without increasing the level of appropriations, simply by "reprogramming" existing levels of spending. The budgetary aspect of the constraint was alleviated by the inflationary potential of the establishment in the United States of the Federal Reserve System and the income tax in 1913. The subsequent extension of income taxation (with automatic withholding, which made it harder to refuse tax payment as a means of protest) to almost all taxpayers began during World War II and continued at the start of the Cold War. This has the unanticipated (but not unexploited) effect that any increase in the rate of inflation thus increased the total revenue available to the government, through the mechanism of "bracket creep"—the larger paper value of salaries pushed taxpayers into higher and higher levels of progressive taxation.

The second protection was removed through the reinstitution (at the time of the Cold War ramp-up) of military conscription—"Selective Service"—with no restriction on the assignment of conscripts to overseas service or combat service.

Traditionally, the response of volunteers to a call to arms was one popular check on ambitious executives. George III was compelled to hire Hessians to fight the American colonists partly because most English were loath to volunteer to fight Americans, whom they considered their own flesh and blood—and this tradition has persisted in the Anglo-American countries. (The Revolution has been characterized as a "war between the English and the Germans—which the English won.") During 1939–1945, Canada would not send conscripts against their will to the European fighting. Unwilling conscripts kept at useless make-work in Canada were dubbed "zombies." The United Kingdom did not attempt to conscript in Northern Ireland even at the most desperate hour in 1940, because it did not want to challenge tradition by forcing service on a partially unwilling population.

The third protection was perhaps the most subtle—so subtle that it could be abolished without general awareness of what was lost. This was the Anglo-American tradition of maintaining no standing land forces of any great size in time of peace, requiring the executive power to go to the people to justify any proposed war. The practical expression of this safeguard was the evolution of the armed forces into organizationally distinct navy and army establishments.

In medieval times, there was no concept of a national army. The permanent military power of the monarchy consisted of the king's personal bodyguards and men levied from the king's personal estates. In time of war, the king would call on the nobles and burghers of the realm to provide the men and equipment that they were bound by tradition to make available. Usually, this call would not be answered automatically, or without limits, but rather after a negotiation over why, how many, at whose expense, and for how long. One of the original functions of Parliament was to provide a forum for such negotiations.

Between the reign of Henry VIII and the Stuarts, however, the English state underwent substantial centralization and took on many of the characteristics of the modern nation-state. The English navy began its evolution from the typical medieval levy of chartered and armed merchant ships into the structured professional force that became one of the best-organized state entities of the modern era. In contrast, the English army maintained much of its medieval flavor, even as Continental states began to create centralized, trained, and permanent bodies.

Under the Stuarts, it was still a mix of royal bodyguards, militia, and feudal and tribal (highland Scots) levies. Regiments raised in wartime by colonel-entrepreneurs were business ventures funded in expectation of loot. The English Civil War created a crisis in this system. The republican forces created a well-trained standing army of the Continental type, called, appropriately, the New Model Army.

The history of the New Model Army validated all the fears of standing armies and concentration of armed power in government hands. It intervened in politics and created a threat-in-being which greatly aggravated the totalitarian tendencies of Cromwell and his Commonwealth. In the end, the desertion of General George Monk and other key military leaders proved the final undoing of the Commonwealth, and so reinforced the lesson that the hand that controls the gun, controls the state. Much of the political effort of the Restoration was devoted to preventing the concentration of power that the New Model Army represented. Britain, the United States, and the British colonies followed the subsequent military model through 1914.

This model was based, fundamentally, on the militia system. The "general militia" was defined as the armed populace of the country, organized on a county-by-county basis. Those who trained regularly and were pre-organized into units having a dedicated function in wartime were known as "select militia." In time of war, this militia was to form the core of the army, along with the royal bodyguard regiments and any additional new regiments raised specifically for that war. Permanent peacetime military forces were viewed with such suspicion, constitutionally, that even select militia training was opposed by most Whigs throughout the seventeenth, eighteenth, and nineteenth centuries.

There were several important exceptions. It was recognized that specialized bodies of military experts could not be trained up quickly in emergencies, but would have to be maintained in time of peace. Artillerymen were the most obvious example; fortification engineers were another. To maintain this expertise, specialized bodies such as the Royal Artillery and Royal Engineers were established and maintained.

Note the terminology. Contemporaries, ignorant of the constitutional purpose behind the Anglo-American military structure, idly wonder why the British Air Force and Navy are termed "Royal" while the Army is merely the "British Army."

This terminology is not a piece of historical trivia: it reflects and illustrates a specific constitutional point. "Royal" forces are permanent forces of the state, maintained even in peacetime.

The Anglo-American tradition is fundamentally a civil tradition—the people, in general, are seen as the country and society, while the state is seen as a distinct construct, the agent, rather than the master, of the whole.

Thus, the army, based on the general militia (that is, the armed populace) and volunteers in wartime, is seen as belonging to the country rather than the state. Similarly, common law is seen as emanating from the people rather than the Crown or state, and the jury system is seen as an expression of popular will rather than a creature of government. In the United States, where Whig theory was most thoroughly implemented, the resources of the earth are traditionally seen as belonging to the people both jointly and individually, rather than to the state. (Thus, the rights of citizens to stake mining claims or hunt on public land but not on federal reservations.)

Therefore, while the British Army is not a "Royal" force, those parts of it that historically had to be maintained in peacetime are. Examples include the artillery or engineers: Royal Artillery, Royal Engineers, and so on. The Royal patronage of various individual regiments comes originally from their origin as the personal bodyguard of the king—the Coldstream Guards, Horse Guards, and the like. Another force of troops maintained in peacetime was the category of "guards and garrisons"—troops manning forts at home and overseas. This category constituted most of the nonspecialist peacetime standing forces maintained by the British military from the Restoration until the post-1918 era.

Since it was recognized that maintenance of the freedom of international commerce and other necessary functions of government might require small-scale exercise of military force, one standing land force was earmarked for that purpose—the Royal Marines, maintained as an adjunct of the Royal Navy. The navy was ever landing small parties of marines to deal with pirates or piratical small tyrants, especially in areas such as North Africa, the Caribbean, and Southeast Asia (all of which, for that matter, remain troublesome nests of piracy to this day). An examination of the use of the Royal Marines, and subsequently the U.S. Marines, demonstrates how the structure of the armed forces under the Anglo-American civil constitution historically served to create an effective barrier to the abuse of the war-making power. Small-scale interventions have been, and will probably continue to be, an inevitable adjunct of the functions of a large country with worldwide trade and maritime activities. The need to deal with organized ideological-religious terrorist groups, larger than gangs but smaller than states, makes it all the more likely that small-scale armed expeditions will be an ongoing feature of contemporary affairs.

Traditionally, intervention using the navy and marines could be done on the initiative of the executive without the explicit sanction of Parliament. When the problem became too large and army troops had to be raised (since there were so few permanent troops, to send any overseas almost always implied raising them), the Crown was required to go to Parliament for an authorization for troops and funds. In the course of this process, the goals and objectives of the conflict could be thoroughly debated, and the costs and benefits to the country weighed. The subsequent call for volunteers and appeal for subscriptions and loans gave the country an additional opportunity to demonstrate its enthusiasm or lack thereof for the conflict in question. The bias against standing armies was so great that the term "British Army" was not used in official language, like acts of Parliament during peacetime, until 1745. (Appropriations for existing forces were earmarked for "guards and garrisons.")

Nor was a permanent administrative structure permitted—military affairs were administered by a "Secretary at War" (a non-Cabinet administrative position—literally, a secretary and three clerks) until 1845, when the position was upgraded and retitled Secretary of War.

This tradition was carried over intact to America. Much of the political development of the American colonies took place in the immediate aftermath of the English Civil War and Restoration. The militia system had been established from the start—the frequent conflicts with the precolonial population kept the need and the occasion for exercising the system fresh in colonists' minds. Militia officers such as young George Washington saw graphic evidence (firsthand at Braddock's defeat in the French and Indian War) that the militia were often superior militarily to regulars in the context of North American warfare.

During the Revolution, the Continental Congress authorized the creation of a force of trained regulars—the Continental Line. After independence, this became the nucleus of the regular U.S. Army. However, the Founding Fathers were keenly aware of the history of the English Civil War and, as good Whigs, agreed wholeheartedly with the tradition of avoiding standing armies and relying primarily on militia. The episode of the Society of the Cincinnati—an association of ex-officers which strayed too far toward political activism for Whig sensibilities—served to reinforce the concerns over the intrusion of a permanent army into politics.

The resulting American military establishment was a continuation of the British tradition of avoidance of a permanent standing army and reliance on militia.

Two cabinet departments were created—the department of the navy, which maintained the fleet, dockyards, and marine corps, and the department of war, which maintained the small peacetime army (the American equivalent of "guards and garrisons"—almost all standing forces were stationed on the frontier). The war department supervised the elements, such as artillery and engineering, which must be maintained and trained on an ongoing basis.

Notice again the semantics. Why was the army's department the department of "War" while the navy's was titled the "Navy"? Was not the navy also involved in war? The point, now lost, was that the navy was intended to function in peace as well as war, while the army was expected to exist (except for its few necessarily permanent functions) only in time of war. Traditionally, nomenclature distinguished between the permanent and wartime land forces themselves. Permanent, peacetime soldiers, Regular Army, were members of the "U.S. Army"; wartime volunteers were members of the "Army of the United States." Rank in the latter did not automatically translate into rank in the former. The frontier posts of the American West were filled with lieutenants and captains in the Regular Army who had been colonels and generals in the Civil War Union Army; courtesy required the delicate task of addressing them by their higher title, while treating them as their Regular ranks dictated.

The old fort of West Point was turned into an engineering school (the first and, for decades, the only such in the country) to provide the specialists needed to maintain these functions. Unlike European military academies, which concentrate on teaching the methods and history of war, West Point was created as, and until recently remained, an engineering school. In fact, for much of its first century, West Point functioned more as a polytechnic school on the model of the French Grandes Écoles— a Republic-wide resource for technical talent. West Point graduates often found themselves loaned out to private railroad or other civil engineering projects, and in fact, many did not pursue a military career at all after graduation.

In his *Essay on Civil Disobedience*, Henry Thoreau used the example of the marine standing guard at a navy dockyard to illustrate the idea of rigid, automaton-like, unquestioning obedience to higher authority. He used this example because it was the only one familiar to Americans of the day. To the average American, soldiers meant militiamen, who were notoriously nonautomaton-like, electing and recalling their own officers and subjecting themselves to combat service and discipline only for short, specified periods of time—three months was a common period.

When Robert E. Lee, as a colonel in the U.S. Army, was assigned to put down John Brown's rising at Harper's Ferry, he commanded U.S. Marines from the still-used I Street Barracks in Washington. These were the only trained men under arms immediately available to the federal government at that time and place. When South Carolina seceded from the Union, it took several months for fighting to begin. This was partly because there was a minimal federal presence in the state (in common with all states then). It was not until the need arose to resupply Fort Sumter (a garrison, and one of the few federal installations in the state) did state and federal forces collide.

This entire tradition was gradually overturned, both in the United States and Britain, between the end of the nineteenth century and the beginning of the Cold War. This change was consistent with the rise of Industrial Era modernism. Its paradigm called for the treatment of war, as with all other elements of life, as an exercise in planning and control. Constitutional considerations were seen as irrelevant obstacles to the path of rationality. A unified military establishment, making the most rational choices of weapons and tactics for any situation, applying military power in a graduated, controlled manner as if it were steam or electric power, was the ideal of the modernist paradigm applied to war.

The sum total effect of these changes has been to endow the executive, both in the United States and in Britain, which experienced parallel changes, with a great ability to enter into conflicts of substantial scale without having to go to the nation for approval. In Korea and Vietnam, this ability led to committing large numbers of troops without obtaining the commitment of the nation to an extended conflict and to the sacrifices that commitment required. Furthermore, they encouraged the micromanagement of conflict by the executive, subjecting forces to ill-considered constraints for vague and often flatly wrong political considerations. Throughout the Anglosphere today, we dismiss the Whig bias against standing armies as merely an inefficient anachronism, and we ignore the constitutional arguments against them. Juries and due process could be called inefficient as well. Yet we tolerate the inefficiency in return for the protections these institutions give us.

Similarly, history demonstrates that there is a very good reason for the Whig arguments for militia-based defense and their abhorrence of standing armies. Just as jury trials provide a safeguard against abuse of prosecution, so does the institution of popular defense provide a safeguard against arbitrary war. In view of current events, it is hard to say that the need for obtaining broad and explicit consensus for significant military commitments has been rendered obsolete.

The above discussion does not constitute an argument that this tradition could effectively be revived, given the need to deal effectively with the issues of preparedness for conflict, which have been demonstrated to be real in the most dramatic of fashions. I only note that preparedness and need for restraint of arbitrary war making remain conflicting requirements of a democracy. Having allowed the old mechanisms to wither, we must consider new means of redressing this balance.

It is not clear to what extent this element of common Anglosphere constitutional tradition could be revived. In both major Unions, the old structure, and more important, the popular sentiments behind them, have eroded almost to the point of invisibility. Yet, the post-Vietnam reform of the military recognized the value of mobilization of reserves and militia as a means of engaging the consensus of the nation. The legislative debate prior to commitment of forces to Iraq, in America, Britain, and Australia alike was no mere rubber-stamping exercise. That episode did perhaps illustrate the value of an actual declaration of war: after the former regime loyalists mounted their campaign of continued attacks on Coalition and Iraqi targets, some American senators who had supported the preconflict resolution started to protest that their aye vote had not really been meant to approve of a war; had the vote been for a formal declaration of war, it would have been hard to claim that its meaning had been ambiguous.

FIVE CIVIL WARS: UNION AND SECESSION IN THE ANGLOSPHERE

If we were to view the English-speaking world through the metaphor of a family, it would be one whose fights always turn into arguments over the arrangement of its living space. Other families, such as the French speakers, have tended to fight over who gets what place at the dinner table (economic issues) or how family decisions were to be made (social revolution). However, the French have accepted the sanctity of their hexagonal house, with the minor additions such as Nice, since the First Republic. Attempts at incorporating outlying possessions (as in Algérie Française) gained favor among politicians, but never resonated at a fundamental popular level, as the Algerian case eventually demonstrated. Losers and winners in family fights among English speakers withdrew to their partitioned portion of the house, each set up as they saw fit; French winners and losers continued to live together, however unhappily.

English speakers, however much they dispute economic, social, or moral issues, have tended to express these differences by spatial composition or decomposition of their regimes—union and secession—rather than regime decomposition—replacing one constitution with another. Thus, the English Civil War saw Cromwell create a unitary state for all Britain, tearing down the walls between England, Scotland, and Ireland. The Restoration marked change by restoring the walls. The Revolution of 1688 created the conditions for partially tearing down the walls by a carefully negotiated Treaty of Union (1707) with Scotland, leaving autonomy in essential areas such as religion, education, and law, but letting Scots dine at the big table with the English. The subsequent Jacobite rebellions drew most of their support from Scots who opposed this deal and wished to restore their own house. The Stuart pretenders failed by placing theological and dynastic ambition—their insistence on being restored to the throne of all Britain—over a more achievable appeal to Scots secession, which might have worked. Clearly, they had spent too much time in France.

The American colonists watched the British experience with Union carefully.

They proposed dealing with the numerous social and economic issues that had arisen with new Union proposals of their own, offering a similar deal: autonomy in local institutions, sometimes with a place at the table of an imperial parliament.

When these proposals were rejected, American Whigs triggered a series of political crises, increasingly violent, leading to outbreak of a civil war in North America, which, through the logic of the vicious cycle by which conflicts expand and worsen, led to adopting the language of secession in 1776.

The American War of Independence, like the other Anglosphere wars of definition, was one name for many things: a civil war, a war of union and secession, and a social revolution. All of these elements were present in the previous (and subsequent) intra-Anglosphere conflicts. Unionist forces (Crown troops and American Tories) failed to suppress the separatists, thanks in part to French intervention.

(American secessionists, in turning to the French, were merely reviving a long-standing Anglosphere tradition, as practiced by the Scots for centuries, and as recently as three decades previously. Both the Scots and Irish sought a balance against the preponderance of English power within the Anglosphere.)

The Anglosphere house became permanently repartitioned; the American secessionists decorated their new house with neoclassical decor, adding a Roman façade to its English Whig country-house structure. (Southerners particularly liked the Roman analogy because it seemed to add the sanction of classical precedent to their increasingly challenged practice of slavery.) The defeated party of the civil war withdrew to Canada, which seceded from the larger American structure.

They continued to furnish this new home in the Tory style, while they offered to the French colonists a deal similar to the Scots—autonomy in their own church and legal institutions, and a brokered place at the big table.

The independence of America ended the brief structural unity of the Anglosphere, which lasted only from 1707 to 1776. It led to a substantial shakeup of the British Isles, including the United Irish Rising of 1798, which in turn led to the Act of Union with Ireland in 1801. That act formally added Ireland to the British political home and ultimately, to the Anglosphere. (Ireland as a whole became a majority-English-speaking nation only in the midnineteenth century, although some areas had been English speaking for centuries.) But because the deal did not deliver to the majority Catholic Irish a reasonable place at the table in sufficient time, it contained the seeds of its own undoing, as will be seen.

The American experience firmly entrenched the custom of fighting over partition of living space, even when the dispute originally broke out over other issues. Thus when economic, social, and moral issues arose in independent America over slavery, Dixie Southerners looked to the experiences of the War of Independence as their model for solutions. Another series of growing crises, breaking into violence in Kansas and at Harpers Ferry, led to a conflict that was (like the Revolution before it) simultaneously a war of secession, a civil war (particularly along the Dixie-Midland Border and among New Ulstermen), and a social revolution.

This time the Unionists won and the Secessionists lost, among other reasons because they failed to obtain outside intervention. The American house would not be divided in two.

The most recent intra-Anglosphere conflict has followed the same pattern, although since it is usually clothed in the garb of national liberation, the similarities have been disguised. The Irish had been promised their place at the table by the Act of Union of 1801, but this was not delivered until far too late. Catholic emancipation was delayed for three decades and critical land reform for seven—and, given the Great Famine and other events, it proved too little, too late. Irish interests responded, like good Anglosphereans, with a proposal of spatial recomposition—Home Rule. Unlike previous American cases, the spatial recomposition issue was not only the predominant issue, it was essentially the only issue, as land reform blunted the principal economic driver long before the spatial composition crisis came to a head.

The "Irish question," like the independence or slavery questions in America, developed over a period of decades. First it dominated and then restructured the political parties of the United Kingdom. It culminated in a series of armed crises, resulting in a conflict that was both a war of secession and a multilayered civil war. This included, as in the American cases, secession within secession. (In the Irish case, Ulster from the united Irish polity, just as West Virginia—populated by descendants of Ulstermen—seceded from Virginia.) The Easter Rising, the Anglo-Irish War, and the Irish Civil War, followed by the current long-term, low-grade conflict in Ulster, created a partially resolved situation still marked by continuing violence over spatial composition demands. Although the Irish republicans redecorated their newly separate political home with plenty of green paint, the underlying architecture—the legal and parliamentary system—remained thoroughly Anglosphere, which is perhaps fitting for a nation that generated such a significant amount of the literature and poetry of the English language. Creating the Irish Republic in its current form was a task of nation-building launched by a group of what were in essence Edwardian British gentlemen and women, and whose example set the pattern for a series of reinventions (or inventions from whole cloth) of nationhood, including Gandhi and Nehru's invention of the modern Indian state.

From this history, we can see that a recurrent pattern has emerged in An-glosphere political culture. The scripts of union and secession have been re-inforced with each conflict, to the point where the parallels now occur au-tomatically to each side. The telltale events leading up to a definitive crisis include realignment of political parties, churches, and other civil-society in-stitutions into new spatially defined patterns or growing polarization of at-titudes. This experience suggests that we may be seeing portents of emerg-ing compositional crises in Canada and the United Kingdom. These portents include the rapid volatility of the Canadian party system in the past decade, and particularly the emergence of sectional parties such as the Reform Party and the Bloc Quebecois. In Britain these portents would in-clude the decline of the Conservative Party in Scotland, and the surge of the Scottish Nationalists to challenge the Labor Party in Scotland.

Much of the extreme political conflict in English-speaking nations to-day seeks a spatial definition. White and black separatists in the United States, diehard "white homeland" and Zulu separatist proponents in South Africa, the Irish Republican Party (IRA) and some Ulster Protestant militants in Ireland, Scottish and Welsh nationalists, and separatists in Canada (both French and Westerners) have all adopted the language of secession. These potential spatial-resolution crises are brewing today, and in each of them, familiar phenomena are seen. These include increasing identification with a different spatial definition of regime and realignment of political and social organizations along spatial lines. (Only one politi-cal party in Canada now has an effective presence in every province; and no British political party has a parliamentary presence in all four parts of the entire United Kingdom.)

Looking back on this history, it is not surprising that Continental Euro-pean and Marxist ideas of revolution, almost always expressed in regime-composition terms, have never found a natural home in any English-speaking nation. Since 1789, France has had five republics, two empires, two monarchies, and miscellaneous directories, consulates, and so on—but its territorial boundaries are today only slightly different from those of 1789. The United Kingdom has had the same Constitution (much evolved, but built on English roots even older) since its founding in 1707; the United States still operates under the Constitution of 1789, also much evolved, but also very much rooted in the same underlying principles as that of Britain. The borders of both Unions, however, have changed nu-merous times. Thus, it's worth noting that France responded to a spatial-composition crisis—the Algerian Revolution in 1958—with a regime-recomposition solution, the transition from the Fourth to the Fifth Republic. In comparison, Anglosphere nations reacted to regime-composition crises such as the Navigation Acts, the slavery issue, or Irish Catholic emancipation with spatial-composition solutions.

This history has significant implications for the discussion of the network commonwealth. I anticipate substantial dislocation as a result of economic, social, and political changes driven by the transition from manufacturing to information economics. In the Anglosphere nations, disruptions leading to extreme pressures will likely polarize on spatial-decomposition (decentralist/centralist) lines. Patterns established in the past will influence future developments, if for no other reason than that people self-consciously imitate historical models. The network commonwealth offers an opportunity to accommodate and stabilize these pressures and to deal with secessionist issues with a minimum of economic, social, and political dislocations. In particular, the strength of the network commonwealth is its ability to transmute secessionism to decentralism.

For resort to secessionist language and sentiments does not mean that a situation will inevitably result in civil conflict or the emergence of new fully independent states. The other factor in predicting the outcome of secession is the strength of civil society in the country at issue. Just as a breaking of the strands of civil society across a nation is an indicator of secessionist (or at least decentralist) tendencies, civil society also has the power to generate new ties drawing societies together again. The transformation of the Canadian Reform Party from a Western-based protest movement with separatist tendencies to a national party, the Canadian Alliance, which subsequently merged with the rump of the old Tories for a new Conservative Party, is an example of civil society as a self-healing organism. If this trend continues, it argues that Canada will more likely opt for a decentralist solution than a separatist one.

Network commonwealth solutions in regard to the Anglosphere are thus presented in the language of spatial recomposition. This language is more familiar and less threatening to English speakers than the language of regime recomposition. These aspects will permit the Anglosphere nations to emerge from the crises of transition with strengthened economies and political systems more able to respond to the challenges of Singularity than those who remain bound in the rigid economic-state structures of the Machine Age. Thus the Anglosphere nations will be more able to retain and defend their core political values, without resorting to their dilution in lowest-common-denominator regimes such as the EU or the United Nations.

PRESERVING THE NATIONAL
VOICE IN A DECENTRALIZED WORLD

Some, particularly in less populous nations such as Canada, may object to greater freedom for informational goods and services. Such critics have objected in the past on the grounds that such freedom could threaten the existence of their artists and media as a distinct national voice. This concern may always have been overrated; Dixie has had its own distinct voice for centuries, despite losing its bid for national independence and sovereignty. Any three of Dixie's good writers have done more for the Southern national voice than three decades of subsidy and protection for the Canadian voice. What actually threatens such art and letters is the current structure of information industries—book and music publishing, broadcasting, and motion picture distribution—which create bottlenecks for access to the public.

New technologies, like low-cost computerized film editing, Web logs, open-source Webcasting server software, and new channels, especially the Internet and World Wide Web, promise to destroy those bottlenecks and lower the barriers to entry in all arenas of the information business. This would create direct artist-to-market channels beyond the control of governments or economic concentration. To the extent that a "distinct national voice" requires the government to control its media, this disintermediation will doom any such national agenda, short of isolationist measures rivaling North Korea's.

With its relentless thirst for novelty and diversity, the open market for information should provide a ready welcome for the smaller and more independent voices in the English-speaking world. Thus, a Canadian artist would no longer have to choose between emigration to London or Hollywood, or dependence on Canadian government subsidies and protections. Instead, the option of staying home and selling to a trans-Anglosphere marketplace would be an attractive alternative.

This would be far more stimulating and supportive than the subsidies currently given to mediocre artists through government programs and protections.

It is increasingly futile to view each nation within the Anglosphere as the private domain of a local artistic and intellectual elite. This may be a particularly painful realization in those countries that have only recently attained much in the way of an independent identity in literary and artistic fields. However, it is more realistic to see the Anglosphere as a common informational space with multiple poles of attraction.

London, New York, and Los Angeles today constitute such poles. They will probably continue to be important in times to come on account of their existing infrastructure and critical mass. But the lowered transaction costs and consequent lowered cost of entry into the information stream caused by the network economy means that many other poles can come into existence, or change in importance.

Author Jonathan Freedland has contrasted the decentralization of America with the traditional centralism of the United Kingdom. On the other hand, the movement toward independence of Commonwealth nations was also a development of decentralization and one of history's more successful models of it. The future of the Anglosphere is essentially a model of decentralization; in that environment, it is unlikely that small national voices will be threatened by the larger nations.

THE ANGLOSPHERE'S HISTORY AS
THE HISTORY OF ITS CULTURAL NATIONS

Decentralism in the Singularity environment requires an understanding of the underlying civic units upon which states are built. The history of the Anglosphere may best be understood as the story of the relationship among such units—its constituent cultural nations. Much of the history of the British Isles can be viewed as the struggle between the differing cultural nations that emerged from the local regions. This strife was especially evident between the densely populated, high-productivity agricultural regions of southeast England and the less dense, poorer (until the Industrial Revolution), more pastoral regions to the north and west. The political nations of the British Isles—England, Wales, Scotland, and Ireland—are each built from several cultural nations variously combining or separating: the southeast of England typically dividing against the north and west of that country, as in the English Civil War. Further divisions include the Lowlands versus the Highlands of Scotland; North versus South Wales; and the Ulster Orange cultural nation versus Gaelic-identified Ireland. After various formulas were tried, including a unitary state of the isles under Cromwell, and separation under the Stuarts, a United Kingdom was constructed, settling at least the constitutional issues of Britain (excluding, eventually, Ireland) for the next three centuries.

Their descendants in the colonies of settlement continued this pattern. New England supported Cromwell in the English Civil War and Virginia, the king. It was the rare convergence of the interests of each of America's four founding cultural nations of that era that permitted the American Wars of Independence to result in successful secession. Expelled Loyalists from each region resettled in Canada.

They were joined by Scottish Highland immigrants and together formed a new cultural nation there. Defending its independence by arms in 1812 perfected the narrative of the new entity and gave its citizens their distinct identity.

AMERICAN CULTURAL NATIONS AND THEIR HISTORIES

I have derived a set of designations for the cultural nations of America synthesized from Fischer's analysis in *Albion's Seed* and by Joel Garreau's discussion of North American regions in *The Nine Nations of North America* (1981). I shall discuss these designations and books in a subsequent section of this chapter. However, briefly, Dixie refers to the lowland, plantation Southern United States. New Ulster refers to the highland areas settled by the Scots-Irish (or British Borderers, to use Fischer's term). Greater New England refers to the five New England states and the northern tier of states settled by their emigrants, from upstate New York to Oregon and Washington. Midland America refers to the population originating in the Middle Colonies of Pennsylvania, New Jersey, and New York, and spreading westward to California; and African Africa for the African-American population spread among the black districts of the rural and urban South and the urban communities of the North and West.

In this section, I present a brief survey, to demonstrate to the reader how a cultural-nation perspective influences the understanding of Anglosphere history.

This field deserves extensive research, reviewing past histories written from political-state perspectives alone (or occasionally a regional perspective) and retelling the stories with an eye to including a cultural-nation perspective as well.

Prior to America's independence, each cultural stream expressed itself primarily through its religious and related cultural institutions, and where that stream was in a majority, in colonial legislatures. New Englanders were the most coherent, expressing themselves through the Congregationalist Church, related institutions like Harvard University, and their colonial legislatures. Midland Americans expressed themselves through the Society of Friends (Quaker) and other churches, and the legislatures of the Middle Colonies. Dixie Southerners expressed themselves through the legislatures of the Southern colonies and through Anglican vestry associations—the Anglican Church not being self-governing except at the local level. New Ulstermen were a political minority in every colony and had few means of political self-expression; a handful of delegates in Southern legislatures, for the most part. This lack of political power led them to open revolt several times, as in Bacon's Rebellion and the Regulator Rebellion. The Presbyterian Church (initially, and eventually various Baptist, Church of Christ, and other denominations) was their primary means of cultural expression.

African Americans, of course, had no coherent political voice, as the great majority were enslaved and had no chance at either political or religious organization. Slave revolts and escapes to Indian territories were the principal means of resistance. A small handful of emancipated African Americans were active from the start in the fledgling abolitionist movement, most affiliated with Quakers and Congregationalists. In the late eighteenth century, the first African-American church, the predecessor of the African Methodist Episcopal Church, was founded in Philadelphia. Although Africans and their descendants had been in Anglo-America since 1619, the African-American cultural nation (as opposed to simply an ethnic category) did not emerge as a distinct entity until the end of the eighteenth century. Ethnic groups have customs and dialects; cultural nations have institutions.

Independence itself was the product of a rare alignment of the interests of all of America's then-existing cultural nations. The increasing centralism and interference of George III and Lord North's attempts to rationalize the empire along Continental bureaucratic lines irritated the mercantile interests of New England, the planter interests of Dixie, and the nascent industrial interests of the Midland colonies.

It raised religious antagonism among New Ulster Presbyterians and New England Congregationalists alike.

Although Loyalist sentiment was strong in the Midlands and parts of the South, the ineptness of George, North, and their appointees gradually lost the battle for the hearts and minds of the colonies. The Continental Congress and the Committees of Correspondence created forums for members of each cultural nation and region to achieve workable compromises and form cross-regional alliances. The discovery that it was easier to negotiate with each other than with London, despite differences, made the American Union possible.

Following independence, the interests of the original nations diverged despite the achievement of a federal republic carefully designed to balance their interests. New Ulstermen, denied control of any state in which they resided, first turned to insurrection in the Whiskey Rebellion, dabbled in secessionist plots, and then turned to westward settlement and federal politics with considerable success, as the presidency of Andrew Jackson demonstrated. Dixie Southerners, frustrated by their increasing minority status in the Union, began to adopt a conscious identity as a Southern nation and began to dream of secession to turn cultural nationhood into political nation-statehood. Their first attempt was strongly suppressed by New Ulsterman Andrew Jackson.

Soon, elements of the New England nation became committed to abolition of slavery. The New England stream of settlement became a hotbed of abolitionism.

Incidents, organizations, and activities stretched from Boston through upstate New York, northern Ohio, Michigan, and Wisconsin. Gradual emancipation in the North created a class of free, educated African Americans. They formed the first institutions of their emerging cultural nation, particularly independent churches such as the African Methodist Episcopal Church and other denominations, mutual assistance societies, schools, and politically oriented organizations, particularly on issues such as abolition.

They then forged an alliance with New England ideologues and Midland pragmatists, who realized that expansion of slavery blocked the rational extension of the Midlands free agriculture and industry.

The American Civil War began as a war between hard-core New England abolitionists and hard-core Dixie nationalists. New Englander John Brown and his African-American allies fired the shots at Harpers Ferry; and South Carolinians fired at Fort Sumter. The escalating violence drew in the other cultural nations, at first gradually, then with increasing commitment. Midland Americans were lukewarm about abolition, but fervent about preventing expansion of slavery. Furthermore, they had increasingly been establishing their domination over the United States as a whole, financially, politically, culturally, and finally militarily. New Ulstermen were divided; they had no great love of slavery and were not attracted to Southern nationalism. They detested the lowland Southerners who controlled most of the states they inhabited and were more eager to gain independence from Charleston or Richmond than from Washington. African Americans had nothing to lose and everything to gain by wholehearted support of the war.

Little wonder, then, that Americans have been unable to agree even on a name for the conflict. For the Dixie nation, it was the War for Southern Independence: an attempt to turn a cultural nation into a political nation-state. They were hampered by the presence on the territory claimed by the Confederacy of two other cultural nations, one, the subjugated New Africans, almost entirely opposed or indifferent to the project, and the other, New Ulster, bitterly divided. New Ulstermen in West Virginia seized the opportunity to gain independent statehood; and others further south, such as East Tennessee, hoped in vain for the same.

Other New Ulstermen, however, saw Northern invasion as an invasion of their home; such men formed some of the strongest units of the Confederate armies. No neat lines divided one cultural nation from another; In the intermediate zones of the South, there were people of primarily Ulster backgrounds who were small-scale slave-owners, and who supported secession; higher up the mountain, their cousins formed Union army units even in Alabama.

For Midland Americans, who increasingly identified with the United States as a whole, it was for many years just "the Rebellion," and eventually the Civil War. Civil War was an extremely accurate description for New Ulstermen and those on the border between Midland America and the South. There, brother did literally fight brother. New Englanders had less loyalty to the Union in abstract.

They had contemplated secession at the beginning of the War of 1812, and abolitionists had proposed secession as a response to the Fugitive Slave Act. Their terms of alliance with the Midlands, essential to victory, enshrined the war for the Union as a part of their ideology; secession disappeared from the lexicon of New England. However, consider the words of the "Battle Hymn of the Republic"—like Cromwell's troops, they had no doubt they were the army of the Lord.

Since the Civil War, Americans have confined the struggle between their cultural nations to political and cultural means, for the most part. The increase in strength of civil society and the spread of genuine democratization tended to reduce the prospect of actual armed conflict. The emergence of the Foundry—the industrial, immigrant-based communities in New England and the Midlands—as at least a transitory cultural nation, brought a substantial amount of low-level violence in the form of labor unrest, endemic between 1888 and 1936. Typically this set Foundry immigrants against militiamen and police drawn from the older Midlands or New England population of the surrounding country and towns. And the long-term struggle of the African-American cultural nation to emancipate itself from slavery, defend itself against attacks, build up self-sustaining institutions, and transform itself from a low-trust to a high-trust civilization has broken into low-level violence many times.

However, it is in the history of parties and ballots that the conflict among the cultural nations of the United States is best found. The Republican Party from the Civil War to the New Deal could be defined as an alliance between Midland America and Greater New England, with much of New Ulster and African America as dependent allies. New Ulstermen and African Americans controlled most Southern states during Reconstruction, but only with the aid of federal military occupation. Dixie whites organized an effective guerrilla resistance through organizations such as the Ku Klux Klan. In alliance with the Foundry-based Democrats of the North, they ended Reconstruction and negotiated a withdrawal of troops in 1877. At this point, the African-American cultural nation was effectively disenfranchised as a political nation until emigration to the North eventually restored to them some political and economic power.

Elections between 1877 and 1936 were contests between the political parties of America's cultural nations. Republicans controlled Greater New England; the Democrats held Dixie and the Foundry. Republicans enjoyed dominance of Midland America in normal times, and parts of New Ulster. National elections were contests to sway Midland Americans to abandon their natural Republicanism and vote Democrat. Greater New England originated two major radical social projects, women's suffrage and Prohibition, during this time, winning the support of Midland America permanently for the first, and temporarily for the second. Prohibition split New Ulster (heirs of the Whiskey Rebels, after all) from the Republicans and engendered massive passive resistance from the Foundry, New Ulster, Dixie, African America, and much of Midland America.

Progressivism can be understood as an alliance between Greater New England and the upper class of Midland America (the ancestors of the Manhattanites).

This system mated clean-government politics and the defense of the traditional American high-trust template through the Americanization of immigrants, with a social program of improving conditions in the industrial system, a platform with strong appeal to the industrial workers of the Foundry. This alliance sought expression in Progressive Republicanism and Teddy Roosevelt's Progressive ("Bull Moose") Party. However, the bulk of Midland America and Greater New England rallied to conventional Republicanism with Harding and Coolidge, and Progressives were left politically homeless until Franklin Roosevelt's New Deal.

Franklin Roosevelt accomplished a sweeping realignment of American politics by renegotiating American politics. He held on to his base in Dixie, improved his control of the Foundry and New Ulster, swung African America over to his side, and made the Democratic Party the majority party of Midland America and Greater New England. The emerging Manhattanite culture provided the ideological, cultural, and artistic narratives to support the assumptions of the coalition.

These accomplishments sealed Democratic control of Congress and the presidency for much of the next fifty years. So long as this alliance could be held together, Democratic Party control of the politics of the United States was a political given.

The Roosevelt coalition was doomed by the unresolved conflicts of the various cultural nations and their interests and by the increasing breakdown of the economic assumptions underpinning the Roosevelt agenda. Underlying much of it was an issue of identity. Until the Civil War, the various cultural nations could not agree on a common national identity or character, beyond the minimalist narrative defining the right of the United States to independence from the United Kingdom. After the Civil War, a national narrative essentially drawing on the Midland and Greater New England national cultures was synthesized. Dixie accepted the military verdict and membership in the political entity. However, it guarded its separate cultural nationhood even more fiercely, creating the narrative of the Lost Cause. Twenty thousand Confederate exiles even created a colony in Brazil that clung faithfully to its unreconstructed Confederate narrative. (Ironically, these unreconstructed Rebels over several generations intermarried with the part-African Brazilians around them, perhaps indicating the Dixie nationalism was for some fundamentally cultural, rather than racial, after all.)

The New Deal circles around Franklin D. Roosevelt understood that such a situation was unstable. Unresolved, it undermined the Progressive project of transforming a loose federal republic into a centralized economic state based on the Western European model. The New Dealers' intention was to create a general national culture, narrative, and identity, loosely drawn from the Midland American culture but incorporating other elements as well. Its intellectual and cultural core would draw on the modernist project of utilitarian, mechanistic liberalism. John Dewey would guide education; Sigmund Freud and Margaret Mead would underlie a modernist theory of family relations; J. M. Keynes and Kenneth Galbraith would guide economics; and modernist art, literature, and theater would guide and educate mass taste. Coordinating this would be a strong central government, guiding the economy, eradicating regional differences, and assimilating all minority cultures into a new, modernized, and homogenous economic state. Unified in this fashion, the United States would, through a Wilsonian project of world governance, realized through the United Nations, guide the cultural evolution of the world.

This strategy at first seemed to succeed brilliantly. War always tends to centralize and unify states. World War II brought Americans from all its cultural nations closer together, as millions joined the services or migrated for war work.

Intermarriage among members of different cultural nations increased dramatically.

The children of the Foundry ethnic immigrants and, eventually, African Americans both enjoyed a higher status than before and greater acceptance as "real Americans." The Manhattanite intellectual culture merged with the commercial filmmakers of Hollywood to pour out a heavy stream of work supporting the Rooseveltean narrative.

By the end of the war, the promoters of Roosevelt's project looked back in satisfaction on what appeared to be a unified economic state with a homogenous national culture, or at least one heading rapidly in that direction.

In retrospect, this was an optimistic interpretation of a high-water mark in history, rather than a way-station on a path to more of the same. Americans, in keeping with centuries-old Anglosphere tradition, had only bought into centralism, planning, and control as an emergency, wartime measure. Absent a threat, they demanded lower taxation, less control, and the end of the military draft. The Cold War provided a rationale for reinstating many such controls, but most Americans had deep reservations regarding the rest of Roosevelt's project. These reservations led to the election of Eisenhower in 1952, reestablishing the Republican ability to gain a majority of Midland America and Greater New England. Dixie began to experiment with alternatives to the Democratic Party, giving electoral votes to J. Strom Thurmond over Harry Truman in 1948, and splitting the vote between Stevenson and Eisenhower in 1952. Eisenhower, a Midland American, abandoned the more extreme aspects of the New Deal project and tried to return to the cultural, if not the political-economic status quo ante Roosevelt.

Although this satisfied many Americans, the Manhattanite cultural elite, energized and committed to the Rooseveltean project, suffered throughout the eight years of Eisenhower and prepared for its return to power. Kennedy and Johnson offered a new chance to restore the Roosevelt coalition and put America back on the track toward its goals. Kennedy returned the Democrats to office by mobilizing the essential base of the coalition, but just barely. He failed to make gains in Midland America and accelerated the long-term defection of Dixie from the centralist agenda.

During the Kennedy and Johnson administrations, the Manhattanite cultural elite also began to lose the integral connections to its original Midland American roots. Once, it had served as the cultural and intellectual elite of Midland America and Greater New England, in close alliance with the financial and political elite and therefore, of the nation. This combination was known as the Eastern Establishment by some. As the Rooseveltean project collapsed, this alliance broke down; and the financial elite began to distance itself from the political-cultural elite. Simultaneously, the local financial elites of the southern and western parts of the country, deriving from other cultural nations and enjoying new wealth, began supporting decidedly non-Rooseveltean political and intellectual causes.

Carl Oglesby documented the early phases of this process as the "Yankee-Cowboy War" in his book of that title.

The Goldwater candidacy began to shift the Republican Party to a new alignment—one which established a base in Dixie and the western regions of Midland America, and fought the Democrats for the bulk of Midland America, Greater New England, and New Ulster. Ultimately, it would challenge the Democrats for control of the Foundry vote, although that would not fully bear fruit until Reagan's candidacy in the presidential race, and the 1994 elections on the congressional level.

When the Manhattanite elite lost its organic connection with any major segment of the country, this in turn increased its dependency on its connections with the federal bureaucracy. Thus, it became increasingly committed to greater control of society by government. Its principal allies were those who benefited directly from increasing such control. They became increasingly dependent on an alliance with African Americans. That cultural nation, subjugated to the Dixie political system for so long, looked to the federal government as the only power which could override the Dixie system and provide them with self-determination. The civil rights movement accomplished its most important goals, obtaining the vote and ending de jure segregation, and in return remained a faithful ally of the Manhattanite wing of the Democratic Party.

However, the 1960s brought the fundamental collapse of the Rooseveltean project, just as its most powerful and astute proponent since Franklin Roosevelt himself gained power. Lyndon Johnson tried modernizing the Rooseveltean project and pushed it to its limits. This effort destroyed the project by showing the limits of its assumptions.

A phenomenon of the Machine Age, the Rooseveltean project assumed an inevitable social trend toward greater centralism, greater homogenization, more effective scientific management and planning, and more effective social control. Instead, the Information Age brought decentralization, diversification, the collapse of large-scale planning as a model, and massive public reaction against social control.

Keynesian planning brought stagflation, and McNamara's rationalization of the military (through abolition of the traditional system of consensus for foreign military expeditions) brought defeat in Vietnam. Increasing technological progress brought entrepreneurism rather than dominance of big corporations. Social planning brought social devastation in the housing projects. Expanded "multiversities" brought rebellion on the part of students. Social experimentation and the collapse of neighborhood policing brought suburban flight and the depopulation of the cities by blue-collar and middle-class whites alike.

African Americans discovered their alliances costing them more and more and bringing them less and less. Seeing the Rooseveltean project collapse, they clung to busing and affirmative action as the remnants of their reward for supporting that project. Increasingly, younger African Americans turned to cultural separatism. Meanwhile, the increasing general racial tolerance in America made it possible for some African Americans to, in essence, assimilate into other American cultural nations, particularly the Midland American stream. This had never been possible before, given racial barriers. This had a complex effect. While permitting individual African Americans to prosper, it began to deprive the African-American cultural nation of the natural leadership that had historically headed its fight to make itself a high-trust, open culture with a strong civil society. Thus, the higher profile of entertainers conveying the postures of the prison-derived black street culture, who began to be seen as representations of an "authentic" African-American culture.

There are interesting parallels to the development of the New Ulster cultural nation. Because there was no racial barrier to assimilation into the surrounding cultural nations, individuals from the poorly educated, impoverished areas of Appalachia had a long history of seeking a personal solution to poverty by emigrating to one of the neighboring areas and adopting its accent, clothing, habits, and educational credentials. This created a constant drain of the sort of individuals who might have aided a transition to a high-trust cultural environment had they remained behind.

The impoverished areas developed a culture similar to that of the lower segments of African America, based on enthusiastic religion competing with the appeal of illegal substance trafficking (of moonshine, in this case) and the prison culture that accompanies it. Heroes have included preachers, politicians, military figures, entertainers, and successful criminals.

The United States consists of a gradient of cultural nations ranging from high-trust cultures with strong civil societies to low-trust cultures with weak civil societies.

It is one reason why the United States, despite being in general a high-trust nation with a strong civil society has, when ranked statistically with other nations, results more consistent in certain ways with a medium-trust culture. If a statistical model were constructed that could measure each cultural nation on the criteria used in radius-of-trust surveys, we might find the high-trust cultural nations (particularly Greater New England and Midland America) ranking very high on the world scale. Similarly, the low-trust cultural nations would rank quite low, in some cases at Third World levels, especially if external transfer payments were subtracted.

As the decentralization of large states continues, the transfer-payment system within large mixed-character states like the United States may come under increasing strain. Welfare reform in the United States reflects the differing cultural values toward transfer payments in the various cultural nations. High-trust, strong civil societies typically have generous transfer-payment systems, either through private charity or government action, but these have historically been viewed as either temporary payments for persons in occasional hardship or payments to persons who genuinely are unable to care for themselves, such as persons with permanent, severe disabilities. In low-trust societies, any transfer payment, under any pretext, is seen as loot that is properly captured from society at large and transferred into the personal or family pocket.

The existence of a large class of persons who have accepted transfer payments and have built a multigenerational way of life around those payments represents a conflict between high-trust and low-trust values. The continuation of these payment streams partly reflects the emergence of a federal bureaucracy as a social class in and of itself, capable of lobbying effectively for its own self-interest.

In other words, open-ended entitlement systems have lasted so long because they have benefited the class of persons who administer them, not for any effect on the persons who have received the benefits.

Thus, it is not surprising that the U.S. welfare reforms of the mid-1990s took so long to accomplish. It represented the breakdown of the historic alliance between the Manhattanite intellectuals, the African-American political leadership (although most welfare recipients were not black, such transfer payments formed a substantial part of the income stream of African America), and the Democratic Party. This was accomplished by the Republican capture of both Midland America and Dixie in the 1994 and subsequent congressional elections.

Despite the perception of some that America is becoming culturally homogenized, its political and social development continues to be overwhelmingly a result of the contentions and clashes of its cultural nations. The racial factor has disguised much of this influence. African Americans have tended to think of their cultural nation as forever identical to the black population in America. This belies the fact that there are sizable numbers of persons with African genetic background who are not part of the cultural nation (particularly Spanish-speaking Latinos of African ancestry, and many recent immigrants from Africa) and some persons with primarily non-African genetic backgrounds who are part of the New African cultural nation. In past times, this discrepancy was minor and could be effectively ignored. Now and in the future, however, the discrepancy will grow, and there will be a growing number of Americans with partly or primarily African backgrounds who will not consider themselves members of the African-American cultural nation.

Furthermore, African America has a unique and distinct relationship with each of the other cultural nations in America, which are also ceasing to be overwhelmingly European in genetic origin. It is essential for African Americans to understand the differences between the Dixie, New Ulster, Midland American, Greater New England, and Manhattanite attitudes, because individuals from each cultural nation have a substantially different set of attitudes and expectations regarding their relationships with African Americans. At the local level, African-American political leaders have often been quite adept at understanding the mentality of the particular cultural nations they encounter.

Intellectuals, who tend to create grandiose universal categories of "whiteness" and "blackness," ignore such differences to the detriment of understanding.

A conscious cultural-national perspective would permit a more realistic course of action for members of each cultural nation. African-American activists, if they absorb the lessons of this analysis, would concentrate on a strategy of achieving more local sovereignty for African-American communities and could use their political power and influence to improve the trust characteristics and civil-society mechanisms of that nation. Midland Americans should become more self-aware and understanding of their distinct culture, of which they are today no more aware than are fish of the water in which they swim—and realize that other cultural nations do not share all the aspects of this culture. Greater New Englanders should give up on moral reform of the rest of the nation by coercive mechanisms.

This has almost always created more in costs than it has delivered in benefits.

Instead, they should concentrate on creating successful examples within their own states. They should explore cross-border cooperation with Anglo-Canada, with which in many ways they have more in common than with the rest of the United States. The Southerners of Dixie must work out through one or another means their relationship to the African Americans with whom they share their land. More than in any other region, some mutually acceptable form for sharing power needs to be negotiated. Until this issue is resolved, African Americans will continue to depend on their alliance with the federal bureaucracy to protect them against the exercise of Dixie majority power. This alliance will frustrate any attempts of Dixie to reclaim autonomy, whether such autonomy affects their relationship with African America or not.

One of the principal issues in relations among the cultural nations of America is the differential among trust levels and the resulting fallout with regard to education, interpersonal violence, and willingness to abide by the law. High-trust and low-trust populations can intermix only with difficulty. A state can encompass multiple low-trust cultural nations, although it will likely be neither very prosperous nor very free. Most multinational empires in history provide examples. A state can encompass multiple high-trust cultural nations, and if done wisely, can be both prosperous and free—Switzerland is an example, although one of the few. A state that includes high-trust and low-trust cultural nations is inherently unstable.

Either the low-trust cultural nations will become high-trust cultures through assimilation or self-transformation, or the high-trust cultural nations will gradually lose their trust characteristics. The other pattern seen historically is encapsulation—either the high-trust or the low-trust cultural nations will create legal and social barriers around the other. This works for a time, but eventually breaks down. If the encapsulated culture has higher trust characteristics than the majority culture around it (which typically make it a market-dominant minority), it will provoke envy and confiscatory politics. If the encapsulated culture is low-trust in a general high-trust society, it will be a poor and powerless minority whose better-educated and more farsighted members will fight to break out of the encapsulation.

Thus, the most desirable solution for America and the other Anglosphere states requires a dual strategy of encouraging and accommodating both the assimilation of individuals from external cultures to the trust standards of the high-trust cultural nations and the self-transformation of the existing low-trust cultural nations into high-trust ones. The goal must be a vision of the United States as a Grand Union of cultural nations, all drawing from the fundamental Anglosphere ideal of a free, rights-based, strong civil society. This vision requires the minimization of public goods—of politically allocated prizes to be fought over by the respective cultural nations. This is one of the keys to Switzerland's successful federalism. It requires the curtailment of the Greater New England and Manhattanite penchant for utopian social projects and cultural reconstruction forced upon the Union by law. This has the added benefit of minimizing the number of people sent to prison for violation of the various prohibitions, as the prison environment is the most sure way of reinforcing low-trust norms in a person. It requires the revitalization of a genuinely federal system in which relatively few issues are addressed at the Grand Union level and each cultural nation can apply its own appropriate solutions at the state and local levels. This is not far from the original vision of the American Constitution, and that is no coincidence.

THE RELATIONSHIP BETWEEN
CULTURAL NATIONS AND NATION-STATES

Cultural nations are the raw material of nation-states, but there is no guarantee that any cultural nation will become a nation-state—nor is such a transformation always a desirable thing. As we have seen, North America contains many cultural nations, none of which correspond to any existing nation-state. The Canadian federal state contains at least two cultural nations, the Anglo-Canadian and the Quebecois, and arguably others. ("French-Canadian" is not synonymous with "Quebecois"; Acadian French in the Maritimes and elsewhere originated in a different region of France, and Acadians speak a different dialect, and have their own narrative, traditions, and history.)

The Canadian state narrative was traditionally based on that of the Anglo-Canadian cultural nation, with French-Canadians as autonomous minorities having relatively little influence on the state's actions. The Trudeau project destroyed the close identification between the Canadian state and the Anglo-Canadian cultural nation, eradicating its symbols and narratives. The synthetic identity offered as a replacement has failed in its purpose. In particular, it failed to realize its goal of creating a Canadian national identity, symbolism, and narrative that was equally acceptable to English- and French-speaking Canadians. As a result, Canada's locus of coherence has been drifting downward to the cultural-national and provincial levels.

Anglo-Canada, leaving apart the entire issue of Quebec, is interesting to the question of cultural-national identities relative to nation-state boundaries in North America, because of the five original English-speaking streams of settlement it is the only one which has enjoyed control (rather than merely periodic turns at leadership) of a political state. Consider, as a thought experiment, a North America in which the Articles of Confederation failed to bind all thirteen of the independent colonies into a single Union or induce them to cede their western claims. Instead, imagine the four cultural nations as defined by Fischer (the New England, the Midland, the lowland South, and the Scotch-Irish sections) each formed a confederation of their own and expanded westward along the actual historical lines of settlement.

The result could well have been four additional North American nations aligned, as is Canada today, along east-west corridors of transportation. We would see a New England nation-state reaching from Portland, Maine, to Portland, Oregon.

Midland America would stretch from New York and Philadelphia through the Midwest to California. The Scotch-Irish nation-state beginning at the Appalachians would stretch through Texas and Oklahoma. A Dixie nation-state, coterminous with the zone of plantation agriculture, would control the arc of the coastal South from the Chesapeake to the Mississippi, and probably have expanded southward into the Caribbean.

Each of these nations would have its own history, its own culture and dialect, its own heroes, and its own institutions, as each does today. In addition, each would have a legacy of border wars and conflicts with its neighbors. Each would have created its own set of national cultural institutions with an agenda of increasing internal coherence by sharpening the differences with its neighbors and deemphasizing their common heritage.

The Canadian state has long used tariffs, protective legislation, and nation-building institutions like transcontinental railways, the Canadian Broadcasting Corporation, the National Film Board of Canada, and "Canadian Content" regulation in the media to enhance the sense of Canada as a cultural nation distinct from the American republic. (These measures were aimed almost entirely at the Anglo-Canadian population, as the French population never had any danger of being assimilated.) Just so, our hypothetical American nation-states would have used similar mechanisms to establish each as a nation-state, as distinct in the eyes of the world as Australia, Canada, and New Zealand are today.

Even absent this hypothetical alternate history, each of the cultural nations of the seaboard has consciously worked to project its influence westward in the same fashion that the Canadians had striven to project their culture; they merely had to work with fewer and weaker tools. Certainly most of the early trans-Appalachian transportation projects—the Baltimore & Ohio Railroad; the Chesapeake & Ohio Canal and later, Railway; the Pennsylvania Railroad; the Boston & Albany Railroad; and the Erie

Canal, to name only the most successful ones—were consciously created by regional elites and governments to assure their ability to project their own section westward. The transcontinental railroad was delayed by fighting between Northerners and Southerners over which route was to be built first; Jefferson Davis, as U.S. Secretary of War, pushed for the Gadsden Purchase to assure that the southern route could be built. The Oregon Trail was promoted by New England clergy to assure the perpetuation of New England culture and religion on the Pacific coast. Much of the fighting over permitting slavery in Kansas was a fight over which cultural nation would get to colonize the area.

If we could project yet a different alternate history, one in which Canada had become part of the United States in the midnineteenth century, it is easy to imagine the Eastern Canadian elites and state governments backing the Canadian Pacific Railway and still working to ensure that they populated the Canadian West.

CULTURAL NATIONS IN ACTUALITY: NORTH AMERICA

Let us discuss, in more detail, the distinct cultural nations of North America.

These today possess much more reality than is generally recognized; and they strongly affect the culture, politics, and economics of the continent. Many commentators are beginning to identify regions as becoming increasingly important as social, economic, and political actors in the coming era. If regions will be the important actors of the future, it becomes critical to ask what exactly is a region, and how will it be defined.

The continuity of cultural-national values can be seen every day. A few years ago, officials in Texas considered their heretofore-ineffective anti-littering campaign.

The Greater New England states had run effective campaigns using advertisements featuring cartoon owls admonishing readers to "Give a hoot, don't pollute." Texas had tried using similar campaigns. The preachy, admonitory tone of these ads, so effective in Greater New England, completely alienated Texans.

After rethinking the issue, public authorities created a highly effective series of advertisements, featuring country-music stars, sports heroes, and other popular figures epitomizing toughness and machismo. With defiant looks, they issued the challenge "Don't Mess with Texas!" The ads succeeded by appealing to personal honor and local pride, both of which were strong features of the Dixie, New Ulster, and Mexican root cultures of Texas, rather than the shame, guilt, and moralism of Greater New England.

Cultural nations, unlike nation-states, are indistinct, and much more prone to changing, merging, or diverging over time. Fischer defines four

North American founding streams of immigration from the British Isles. The cultural nations derived from these streams serve as starting points. (This elaboration is my own construction, and I do not claim to represent the views of Fischer.) I add Anglo-Canada and the African-American nation as equivalents. I would identify several other regional groupings as actual or potential cultural nations. For several of them, I have adapted terminology from Joel Garreau's *The Nine Nations of North America*, but have altered somewhat his definitions.

My list of current cultural nations in North America includes those descended from the four founder populations identified by Fischer, including the westward stream of communities heavily influenced by them, and adds several others. I define them as follows:

The *Greater New England* stream of settlement includes the five classic New England states, plus the band of rural and county-town settlement stretching across upstate New York, northern Ohio, Michigan, Wisconsin, Minnesota, the Dakotas, Montana, Oregon, and Washington. Utah counts as a unique culture but one recognizably derived from New England culture. (Mormon prophet Joseph Smith's life trajectory, from Vermont through upper New York State, northern Ohio, and Illinois, is a veritable roadmap of New England's path west. Cooperation and coherence, hallmarks of New England's concept of "ordered liberty" as noted by Fischer, can also be seen as elements in Mormon culture—see for instance Wallace Stegner's *Mormon Country*. For that matter, if one wanted to experience what life in a colonial Puritan New England village might have been like, in a social sense, living in a small Mormon town in Utah might be the most relevant modern parallel.)

Greater New England's original core culture was heavily influenced by the German immigrants in Michigan and Wisconsin and by the Scandinavians in Minnesota, the Dakotas, and the Pacific Northwest. Germans and Scandinavians, being from high-trust cultures themselves, reinforced the high-trust characteristics of the original New England culture.

This entire band of settlement stands out in American history for the honesty of its politics, the coherence of its communities, and its adherence to the New England ideals of "ordered liberty" as discussed by Fischer—in other words, a strong, religion-based, civil society. Contemporary environmentalism, which has come to serve as a philosophy of life (or in some cases religion) for many in the Pacific Northwest, demonstrates many features of New England Calvinism, with its emphasis on personal example, moral persuasion, and public shaming of nonconformists. Even the Puritan adherence to "sadd colours" of dress lives on in the natural earth tones preferred by Greater New England environmentalists. One almost expects Cascadians to subject energy wasters to the ducking stool or a day in the stocks. Abhorrence of compromise, regardless of consequence, is another

Puritan feature embodied in today's Green movement: notice that the nationwide level of support for Ralph Nader's Green Party candidacy in 2000 faded drastically in the final days of the election, except in Greater New England.

The Southern, or (pace Garreau, *Dixie*) band of settlement corresponds to the Virginian seed population described by Fischer, and their descendants, moving westward in parallel with the Carolinian and Georgian seed populations, who similarly came from predominantly Southern English origins. It constitutes, in essence, the lowland South including all of the Chesapeake tidewater area, coastal Carolina and Georgia, north Florida, lowland Alabama, the Mississippi Valley up to southern Illinois, Louisiana, and east Texas. Dixie was the area of plantation agriculture; the nonplantation highlands more properly belong to New Ulster, a separate cultural nation as we shall discuss. As previously noted, African Americans may be more usefully thought of as a distinct cultural nation sharing the Southern region, as well as in Northern and Western urban enclaves— a population that might be thought of as New Africa. African America and Dixie, although they partly overlap in the territories they inhabit, worship at different churches, vote for different parties, attend different schools, and belong to different civic organizations. In defining cultural nations, narratives, symbols, and identities are important signposts. African Americans vehemently reject the narratives, symbols, and identities that have been for the past century and a half the strongest bonds of the Dixie cultural nation. It is exactly the conflict between Dixie Southerners and African Americans in the South over the use of Confederate symbols and narratives in public life that illustrates the impossibility of projecting a Dixie cultural nation including all residents of the South. The term South can only refer to a geographical region inhabited by several cultural nations. The term Confederacy refers to a specific political entity existing between 1861 and 1865. It might be useful to reserve the term Dixie to denote the current and historical cultural nation of the lowland white South, as I have done here.

The settlement stream of the Scots-Irish, called (more accurately) British Borderers by Fischer, constitutes what is often called Appalachia, and its westward extensions. I suggest referring to this cultural nation as New Ulster, as I have done here, on the model of New England. In addition to the classic Appalachian counties (extending into western and central Pennsylvania and upstate New York) it includes the Ozarks and parts of Oklahoma as well.

Cultural-national boundaries being indistinct as they are, it is easier to map out the areas that are definitely not part of a different cultural nation, leaving a map with a number of core areas separated by zones of intermixture. One such way of defining the New Ulster core area from that of

Dixie is the absence of plantation agriculture. Another way is to map the areas of the South that opposed secession in 1861, and in many cases, raised troops for the Union. (For every five white southerners that fought for the Confederacy, one fought for the Union; most of the latter were New Ulstermen.) Much of Texas is primarily descended from this stream as well, but Texas has been so influenced by other populations, including the Mexican, that it should probably be considered a derivative culture, as Utah is a derivative of New England. This stream also has heavily influenced southern New Mexico, rural Arizona, and the Central Valley of California.

Of Fischer's four, the stream deriving from the Quaker settlers of Pennsylvania is at once the most successful and the least well defined, because it went on to engender the predominant culture of the United States. I call this the Midland American stream of settlement, after the linguistic dialectical term. It is also the basis of what is often called Middle America. England has lacked a distinct identity and voice since it was effectively submerged into the broader category of Britain, just as Russia lacked a distinct identity and voice while it was submerged into the identity of the Soviet Union. Similarly, the Midland cultural nation has lacked identity and voice, because it has so successfully dominated the United States as a whole.

Today, it can best be mapped by defining what it is not—it is not greater New England, nor Dixie, nor New Ulster, nor Texas, nor any of the dispersed cultures of African America, MexAmerica, nor the industrial-urban culture of the Northeast that Garreau called the Foundry. It has no flag, no anthem, and no narrative save that of the United States itself. Regional assertion in the other parts of North America may eventually give rise to a Midlands identity, just as resurgent Scottish nationalism has reignited a specifically English nationalism. More likely, specific regions of Midland America will develop a stronger identity of their own; Midwesterners have always had a strong regional pride.

Garreau is a well-known proponent of regional analysis of North American culture. I will shortly discuss his proposed regional divisions, which he also terms "nations," and their relation to the cultural nation scheme used in this book. Some of his identified regions are, in my view, more of the character of cultural nations. One he calls the "Foundry." This is basically the Northeastern United States minus New England, but including the industrial Great Lakes area and industrial Ontario.

This region's previous colonial-era English population was overlaid with waves of immigrants from Southern and Eastern Europe, and later African Americans and Scots-Irish from the southern states.

It acquired a heavy social reliance on industrial employment and a culture dominated by blue-collar institutions and taste. It is worth considering the Foundry as a distinct cultural nation in North America, but not as defined by Garreau. Like the African-American cultural nation, it should be thought of not as geographically distinct, but rather overlaid on the Midland states, and spilling into New England and New Ulster.

Over the last century, the rural and nonindustrial-town populations in those areas remained quite distinct from the Foundry population, which has remained until recently very urban. In these towns, the Foundry population has belonged to different churches, spoken with different accents, worked at different occupations, voted for different political parties, and belonged to a different set of voluntary institutions than the inhabitants of the surrounding countryside. One way to map the populations, for example, would be to examine the voting records between roughly 1880 and 1980; those districts that voted heavily Democrat were of the Foundry.

Those that voted heavily Republican are of another cultural nation (usually Midland America, but occasionally New Ulster or New England) that still dominated the countryside.

It now appears that the Foundry is gradually assimilating into Midland America. The phenomenon of the Reagan Democrats—blue-collar ethnic populations, traditionally Democrats, who voted heavily for Ronald Reagan—demonstrated an assimilation of the Foundry into the Midland American political system, although it's not clear whether it will carry to its ultimate conclusion.

Intermarriage between the Foundry population and Midland Americans has greatly increased within the past several generations. This trend has accelerated particularly as Catholic-Protestant antagonism softened, a result of Second Vatican Council changes and a more general social trend toward alignment of Catholic and evangelical Protestant social and political interests, as a result of which Catholics are generally perceived as less distinct than previously. Greater geographical mobility, white flight, and the growth of the suburbs of the cities of the East and Midwest have among them commingled the formerly distinct Foundry population with the Midland Americans and Greater New Englanders from the surrounding countryside, further completing assimilation.

The decline in industrial line employment has led the new generations of Foundry youths to enter information and service professions in droves, where they mix with Midland Americans and lose or mute their distinct identities. Ironically, it was the Manhattanite liberals setting the agenda for the Democratic Party (which once relied on the Foundry as the core of its political support) who destroyed the principal autonomous political institutions of Foundry life. Now in decline are the craft union locals, the blue-collar school district boards, and the urban ward political machines—vitiated in the name of busing and affirmative action. Foundry political activism, to the extent that there is such a distinct animal, is now directed more into the right-to-life movement and the National Rifle Association, where they come further into conflict with the Manhattanites and Greater New England neopuritans, and closer into alliance with Midland America. Thus the Foundry may merely be a transitory stage in the assimilation of yet another group into the Midland American stream.

Another region Garreau dubs MexAmerica; which he defines as the United States-Mexican border area extending from south Texas to southern California and including the Mexican border states as well. He sees this as a transborder region incorporating the Mexican, Anglophone American, and other minority members as well. Although I believe that the transborder region as a unique sociocultural entity is real, I also feel that its limits are confined much more closely to the border region itself. Perhaps we might define it roughly as those areas south of Interstate Highways Eight and then Ten eastward from the Pacific (including the bulk of the old Gadsden Purchase) to Texas, and in that state the region south of the Nueces River. We might thus also describe it (a bit floridly) as "Gadsdenia-Transnueciana."

Even in this region, there are heavy overlays of other cultural nations, particularly the Midland American stream, the African-American nation, and others. San Antonio, Albuquerque, Tucson, and San Diego are unquestionable centers of this nation, as are Tijuana, Hermosillo, Monterrey, and Ciudad Juarez, but Phoenix and Los Angeles contain only enclaves of it. Even these cities contain strong enclaves of other cultural nations.

Garreau also describes a nation he terms The Islands. This consists of the greater Miami area, the islands of the Caribbean, and the north coast of Venezuela and Colombia. Although these areas have many strong mutual ties, and taken together could plausibly be considered a common economic region (one of Dellamaide's "superregions" perhaps), it would make more sense to consider them several separate cultural nations. Its principal divisions might be the bilingual Spanish–English-speaking nation defined by the triangle joining Miami, Caracas, and San Juan; the English-speaking Afro-Caribbean nation, with the smaller French, Creole, and Papamientu-speaking communities interspersed as enclaves.

Garreau also makes the point that Manhattan (not New York City as a whole, the rest of which belongs to the Foundry and African America) and Washington, D.C., are unique entities which fall into none of his regional classifications. I concur but would also expand upon his point. Both Manhattan and Washington serve as centers of dispersed, nongeographic cultures that may evolve into (or have already evolved into) distinct entities (although less than cultural nations) in their own right. Manhattan was formerly the capital of the United States in all but the political sense. It was once the unquestioned center of the financial, intellectual, informational, and cultural networks in the United States and much of the world. It has lost this centrality in many of these fields and, under the impact of disintermediation, will likely continue to fade in almost all those in which it still exercises primacy. However, it is still and will always be a significant node within those networks, and remains the capital of the northeastern United States. It is also the center of a particular mind-set, sensibility, ideology, and school of thought, appropriately expressed in publications such as the *New Yorker, New York Times,* and *New York Review of Books.*

This mind-set is characterized by a number of received ideas, including multiculturalism and the nebulous set of attitudes generally described as political correctness, now predominant in academia and its penumbra in the media and entertainment worlds. Although this mind-set has failed to gain more than a surface adherence in the cultural nations of America, it is accepted in a geographically dispersed set of insular communities scattered across the United States and in fact the English-speaking world. It could be described as the Manhattan Archipelago (or more facetiously, the Starbucks Archipelago), with islands in Takoma Park, Maryland; Berkeley, Santa Cruz, and Santa Monica in California; and various university towns, fashionable urban neighborhoods, and resort retreats favored by the glitterati throughout the Anglosphere. A similar mind-set is shared in concert in Islington and the offices of the BBC and the CBC, the *Toronto Globe & Mail* and the *Sydney Morning Herald.* Far from refuting the concept of the Anglosphere as an analytical framework, the very coherence of this pan-Anglosphere intelligentsia demonstrates its validity, as the opinions of Noam Chomsky and the products (one hesitates to call them works) of Michael Moore are replicated throughout.

Although the mildly leftish liberalism of the Clinton era was at the time thought to be the ideology of the Information Age, this is not the case. The great bulk of the workforce of the Information Age in areas such as Silicon Valley or Seattle tend to be libertarians to a greater or lesser degree, usually expressed in "moderate" Republicanism or centrist Democratic adherence. Citizens of the Manhattanite Archipelago tend to be economically dependent on the centralized nation-state, usually at second- or third-hand, and act as a rather ineffective cheering section for the enhancement of its powers, due to their insistence on deconstructing positive narratives for support of those states. As their sources of funding dry up in the coming decades and as positive narratives generated elsewhere replace theirs in the cultural nations of the Anglosphere, it is likely that many of the Manhattanites will gradually be assimilated into other cultural nations. In this role they will have to adapt to the production of more serviceable narratives.

Similarly, Washington, D.C., is not merely an autonomous city-state, but rather is the center of the other major nongeographic identity in the United States.

As discussed previously, the U.S. government, in the sense of the body of civil service workers and the career military, has begun to take on an identity and life of its own. Other Americans judge success through a combination of complex factors; federal employees talk of the GS or SES grades of bureaucratic rank. Although relatively small, it is disproportionately influential because of the current dominance of the federal government over American life.

It's worth considering whether members of this group consider social engineering approaches more plausible than other Americans. This may have had a role in persuading government decision makers and their academic allies that such measures could be successfully imposed on the population at large. They ignore important differences. The government subculture being voluntary in composition, it automatically sorts for people more willing to accept its norms and values, and can expel or marginalize nonconformists.

For example, many noncommissioned officers in the U.S. Army resisted Truman's order of desegregation in 1948. The military response was to tell them "obey or get out." Many got out; the rest got the message that compliance was essential to having a career in the Army.

This federal community has achieved some noteworthy accomplishments.

As noted more and more, it is the only part of American life that has assimilated substantial numbers of African Americans from their own cultural nation, and that experiences substantial integration of blacks and whites not just in workday situations, but in after-hours socialization as well. This has been accomplished by creating a strong cultural pole of attraction with its own strongly espoused narratives (particularly in the military), rewarding those who adhere to it, withholding rewards from deviants, and, as noted, expelling those who do not respond to this incentive system. Future trends may see the federal culture become a true nongeographic entity, or as the size of its workforce shrinks, its members may gradually realign themselves with various cultural nations. Recently the Army changed its long-standing policy of triennial rotation of location, to permit soldiers and their families to stay longer in one place. This step eases the pressure against local assimilation, one of the things that tended to make the military more of a closed culture.

Finally, new cultural nations continue to emerge from time to time. Southern California is an outpost of the American Midland culture, with strong enclaves and influences of MexAmerica and African America, but also large influxes of internal migrants and immigrants from a wide variety of cultures. The popularity of multiculturalist theory among those in control of government, educational, and media institutions has hindered the assimilation of these newcomers and encouraged the continued fragmentation of the common culture of the region. However, this is not likely to continue, if for no other reason than its degradation of the governability of the area, which if continued will eventually undermine its economic attractiveness and viability. As Fukuyama notes in *The Great Disruption* (1999), social order seems to be an emergent phenomenon of human beings. When it is broken down (usually by outside assault or other abnormal developments) a new order capable of generating social coherence eventually arises.

The current high intermarriage rates among whites and second-generation Asians and Latinos (which are more likely to accelerate rather than diminish) will also tend to encourage assimilation of the resultant population into a new Anglosphere cultural nation. This will most likely be constructed on the general template of Anglosphere values, but with specific features stemming from these admixtures.

Previous examples of this process are demonstrated by the admixture of Scandinavian features to the New England-derived cultures of Minnesota and the Dakotas, or the eastern and southern European influences in the Midland-derived Foundry.

Asian values such as the respect for education and entrepreneurship based on hard work fit well into the existing Midland and Greater New England cultures; hybrid cultures based on such admixtures have good prospects for success.

The high level of immigration today offers the possibility of other new cultural nations coalescing in North America. If they do, they will likely form on fundamentally Anglospheric templates. Cultural groups that cannot assimilate to some extent are unlikely to establish sufficient workable relations with the other cultural nations of North America. They would not be able to generate the economic success and internal institutions necessary to rise above a status either as foreign sojourners with only an economic relationship to the country, or as a servile underclass.

Another viewpoint frequently advanced is that the modern media are so homogenizing the United States that regional cultural distinctions are being eradicated entirely: the "McDonaldization" and "Wal-Marting" of America. I believe that, although these forces are present and are impacting cultures, each culture is responding in a different fashion. The real, underlying differences between cultural nations of the Anglosphere are expressed in religious, political, and social choices, which remain substantially diverse among the cultural nations, and in fact may be diverging even more. McDonald's may serve the same hamburger in Dallas as in Portland, but those who serve the food and those who buy it will react in different fashion to similar stimuli, as the example of the "Don't Mess with Texas" campaign demonstrates. Web log author Glenn Reynolds recounted an experience of being in a serving line in a Taco Bell franchise in Knoxville, Tennessee, in which he remarked to a recent Salvadorian immigrant next to him that the food in the chain must not seem very authentic. The Salvadorian responded that is was indeed authentic—in fact, it was indistinguishable from the food at the Taco Bell in San Salvador. Thus "authenticity" in this era has become a sort of luxury commodity imposed by external categorization: to the Salvadorian, Taco Bell's recipe was just one more way of making a taco.

The reality of the cultural nations of North America, and the rest of the Anglosphere, is something which requires far more study than it has received.

The sociologist Seymour Martin Lipset, for example, has devoted a lifetime of investigation of the differing cultural values of the United States and Canada, and has consistently found a substantial difference—a "Continental Divide," to appropriate the title of one of his works on the topic. However, I believe his use of nation-state boundaries to define his categories has made his results problematic.

A number of fragmentary survey results suggest that a comparative sociological study of the cultural nations of the Anglosphere would find that the divergence among them is not articulated along existing nation-state boundaries.

Rather, our principal sociological divisions transcend intra-Anglosphere demarcation lines. Consider the famous "red-state/blue-state" map of the U.S. election results of 2000, and even more so the same map broken into county-by-county results, and even more in dividing each side's winning counties into close wins and overwhelming margins of victory. By doing so we see a midcontinental armature of socially conservative sentiment, the "Republican L," with hard-core leftist support confined to the great urban cores of the coasts, while a wider swath of moderate Democrat support showing up in the northeastern quadrant of the nation, and the west coast. One might actually term the urban cores blue, and the softer areas "purple," for there is a substantial social-conservative contingent mixed in the old states of the Northeast. This purple zone extends up into the eastern and western bastions of Anglo-Canada, the zones that alternate between moderate Liberal and moderate Tory votes. The red swath of continental social conservatism also extends up into the prairie provinces of Canada, particularly into Alberta, and also extends down through the Anglo-Caribbean islands, where Christian religiosity results in public stands in favor of the death penalty and against same-sex marriage in roughly the same percentages as do the red states to their north. In fact, if black-majority states were to emerge in the American South, their politics might resemble that of the Anglo-Caribbean fairly closely.

Just so, the blue and purple zones of the North American coasts could be extended east and west fairly readily. Social surveys indicate that the greatest values and attitude gap in England is that between the greater

London area and the rest of that kingdom; London's responses match Manhattan's fairly closely, while the rest of England's are quite close to the purple zones of the American and Canadian east. Similarly, Australian and New Zealand values and attitudes for the most part resemble those of the North American west coasts, also, outside of the very liberal urban areas, in the purple zone. Britain does not have the extensive red-state zone that North America sees—Northern Ireland is the closest analogue, while Queensland is the closest Antipodean equivalent to a red state.

Rather that seeing the Anglosphere as divided into nations with substantially different values and attitudes, as does Lipset, it is perhaps the other way around—that there are a number of sociological zones throughout the Anglosphere with internally consistent social attitudes, and the different responses from each nation depend on how much of one zone or another lies within a particular set of borders. Britain has a major metropolitan area that forms a tenth of its population, while Ulster forms less than 2 percent; America's major metropolis forms less than 3 percent of the total population, while its Ulster-descended population is partial ancestor to a quarter of the nation. Much of the political difference between the United States and United Kingdom lies in these statistics.

This Anglosphere kaleidoscope of constantly remixing several sets of attitudes and values, in different proportions in each corner of the network civilization, produces a spectrum of outcomes. Lipset compares political values of the United States, Canada, and Britain against each other, as a whole, and discovers a continuum of "American" to "European" political values, with the United States at one end of the continuum, Continental Europe at the other, and Canada and Britain occupying intermediate positions. I believe that if this continuum were to be mapped along cultural-national lines, one would find a much smoother continuum, with different North American and British Isles cultural nations occupying points scattered along the scale. England, for example, is significantly less inclined to European integration than Scotland; and further differences exist between North and South England.

CULTURAL NATIONS ELSEWHERE IN THE ANGLOSPHERE

No other Anglosphere nation experiences the same complex intermingling of cultural and political nations occupying the same territory as does the United States, with the exception of South Africa, which is not a core Anglosphere nation. This is due to the relatively recent formation of these nations, their small population, and the relative homogeneity of settlement. Australia and New Zealand each form distinct nations, each relatively homogenous in the origins of their settler populations.

There are no distinct, separate cultural nations in Australia except the aboriginal nations. There is a single, relatively homogenous Australian dialect and population, and aside from the effects of policies inspired by multiculturalist dogma, immigrants have assimilated well into that culture, by world standards.

The Australian nation is both a cultural nation of the Anglosphere and a political state.

There are definite regional distinctions within the Australian cultural nation, however, particularly between the Golden Crescent or Boomerang areas of New South Wales, South Australia, and Victoria and the peripheral areas of Queensland, Western and Northern Australia, and Tasmania. These regional distinctions are making it more difficult to sustain a common polity given differing attitudes regarding economics, gun control, and other issues. These will more likely drive toward decentralization of the existing state, than to separation into different sovereign entities.

New Zealand is even more coherent and forms a relatively undifferentiated cultural nation. The Maori people form the single significant exception. New Zealand is likely to remain a coherent nation-state, although Maori country may eventually acquire more sovereignty in an autonomous formula. If Australia decentralizes far enough, it may make sense for New Zealand to become a member of the resulting confederation. As discussed elsewhere, there will be strong drivers for both Australia and New Zealand to join an Anglosphere Network Commonwealth; such a common external framework will permit both nations to adapt to the conditions of the emerging Singularity economy with relatively little trauma.

REGIONS, CIVIC STATES, AND SCALE

Some form of civic state will be the fundamental social building block of the network commonwealth. Such civic states will cohere at the level where the locus of coherence falls under the fiscal and political pressures for decentralization. These civic states will tend to be regions that possess ecological, economic, and cultural coherence. They will usually be built upon existing nations or fundamental constitutional units, such as American and Australian states, the U.K.'s kingdoms and provinces, or Canadian provinces. They will be smaller than Ohmae's region-states or Delamaide's emerging superregions of Europe and will probably sustain larger regional structures at those scales. Ohmae and Delamaide describe regions of 10 to 30 million people. I suspect this is on the large size of what is necessary to maintain true coherence, and the fundamental blocks will be more on the order of 1 to 5 million. It may be worthwhile to think of

Ohmae's region-states, or superregions, as being the next order up from coherent regions (call them, perhaps, supercantons, or canton-states). The fundamental unit would have most of the properties of the civic state, whether it was fully sovereign or not.

Complex megapolitan areas, such as Los Angeles and New York, may become region-states, formed on a confederal basis from several canton-states existing in the same geographic area. The primary purpose of such region-states would be to tend to infrastructure and environmental issues, and coordinate law enforcement; most social issues would be decided at the canton-state level.

The French scholar Jean Baechler has argued that political power systems tend to organize themselves into stable systems with a limited number of true actors, due to the difficulty of organizing multilateral relations among more than a certain number of actors. He has argued that this number, historically, has shown itself to be between five and ten significant actors. The great power system of early modern Europe, for example, usually had between those numbers of players, usually closer to five than ten.

In multilevel relationships, like federal systems, having more than a manageable number of sub-federal units tends to tip the hand toward federal power.

When the United States was comprised of thirteen states, of which only five or six were of significant size, the states could form a power system to balance the federal government. Now that there are fifty, the federal government has predominated.

Canadian provinces, despite having less theoretical sovereignty, balance the Canadian federal government more effectively.

Permitting American states to divide themselves until the new emerging states have populations on the order of 1 to 5 million citizens would result in a substantial multiplication of state units, perhaps to 100 in the United States, assuming an average of 2.5 million per newly defined state. Baechler's logic, combined with the inherent trends toward decentralization discussed earlier, suggests that on the order of ten confederations of such states might emerge, with perhaps ten members apiece. Given that most issues would be resolved at the canton-state or regional levels, the federal government would tend to restrict itself more to foreign matters, working more closely with the allied nations of the Anglosphere Network Commonwealth.

Some Europeanists express a hope that the nation-states of Europe will dissolve into their constituent regions, to the point where only two real levels of power remain in Europe: that of the regions and that of the European federal state in Brussels. Some might wonder whether it would also be the fate of an Anglosphere Network Commonwealth to see the dissolution of the Grand Unions into a Grander Union of all Anglosphere cultural nations, a sort of Anglosphere federal state. I believe this is un-likely in the era of the strong civic state.

The loyalties and identities of the Grand Unions of the Anglosphere—particularly the United Kingdom and the United States—are strong and have created a reality of their own. Consider Texas—it might seem an im-probable unit, made up as it is of Dixie Southerners from their cotton and sugarcane plantations in east Texas, ranchers of the High Plains in the north, and Mexicans in the Rio Grande Valley. In many ways, Texas *is* an improbable unit. Yet it persists in generating great loyalty, loyalty undi-minished by Texas's equally fervent participation in the United States.

Just so, I suspect that the creation of an effective Anglosphere Network Commonwealth, along with resurgence of strong local civic states, will not undermine the strong narratives and loyalties of the existing Grand Unions.

6

The Anglosphere Century

The gods send thread for the web begun.

—Greek saying engraved on the lintel
of Andrew Carnegie's home.

The concept of a network commonwealth linking the Anglosphere nations is distinct from previously proposed models of English-speaking cooperation. It would not seek to create a united English-speaking state. It would not be based on the concept of an "Anglo-Saxon Race," popular during earlier areas promoting English-speaking union: on the contrary, it sees many of the diaspora networks common to the Anglosphere as threads that can serve to network these nations together. It recognizes that the English language and cultures derived from our common Anglosphere values are today borne by people of all races and origins.

It would not be based on Cecil Rhodes's vision of a common British and American elite, or on the twentieth-century vision of the Anglo-American "special relationship."

This was a vision of a northeastern American, white, British-descended elite within the United States and a British elite within the empire cooperating in the ruling of their respective political communities. Such dominance has faded as the leadership of the elite has faded. Previous visions were often ones of London and New York jointly ruling an Anglo-American empire. Today, New York no longer rules west of the Alleghenies nor does London rule beyond the core United Kingdom. A network commonwealth, as a network rather than a hierarchy, experiences power and influence as dispersed to many nodes throughout its fabric. New York and London remain nodes—and very influential ones. Neither city nor its historical elite can expect to rule, individually or jointly, a network commonwealth—they can only influence it.

A common political structure for the Anglosphere, however loose, could not have emerged at any earlier historical moment. Although there is a long history of conceptual frameworks for uniting all English speakers in a common political home (a reality for only sixty-nine years, from 1707 to 1776), they have all failed.

Most important, they failed not by historical happenstance, but because they were unable to resolve the principal underlying contradictions of unity. These have always been issues of dominance, representation, control, and benefit. These issues have been uppermost because previous concepts of unity were always cast in state forms, whether unitary or federal, and always carried the threat of domination by one nation and its ruling elite over others. At all times, some communities continued to see (often accurately) their best interest served by independence rather than unification.

1776: DIVERGENCE AND THE END OF THE FIRST EMPIRE

It is useful to examine previous projects for Anglosphere collaboration, their partial successes and failures, and consider why a network commonwealth approach in the current environment might be more likely to succeed today.

The British Isles were unified in a series of steps starting with the English Acts of Union with Wales, the Act of Union with Scotland, and the Act of Union with Ireland. In each case the expansion of the core English state was made by integrating the local elite and giving them representation in Parliament and the national bureaucracy, while promoting the primacy of court English over local languages and dialects. These measures were largely successful in Wales and Scotland. (The latter nation retained autonomy in important national institutions such as law, education, and the Church.) The measures were relatively unsuccessful in Ireland, due in part to the reluctance to include the majority Catholic population in the civil life of the United Kingdom and to reform the archaic land system until late in its political history. Wales and Ireland also experienced substantial inflows of English-speaking colonists. These became part of the national fabric in Wales, and the earlier, pre-Reformation waves in eastern Ireland formed a hybrid Anglo-Irish culture that eventually became the core of the current Irish republic. In fact, the small towns of eastern Ireland may be the best approximation of what England might have been like had the Reformation failed there—an English-speaking Catholic-majority culture.

The American colonies provided the first movement counter to the progressive incorporation of all English-speaking and bordering peoples into the United Kingdom. Colonists, left largely autonomous until the restored Stuarts began imposing their Continental ideologies of centralized autocracy, had created a series of self-governing representative states. In the colonial view, they owed allegiance to King-in-Parliament, being good Whigs. However, to them, "parliament" in America was split between the colonial assembly, for all but imperial matters, and the Westminster Parliament, which was seen as having authority only over the latter, issues such as imperial defense and trade. (And most colonists weren't too happy about the trade restrictions.) All nonimperial matters were seen as having devolved to the colonial assemblies, permanently. It was in the question of the permanence of devolution that the problem lay.

Strains in questions of sovereignty and authority led to competing models of pan-Anglosphere political unity. The King's Party in Parliament, led by Lord North, was influenced by Continental ideals of enlightened despotism and promoted a model of permanent supremacy of the central power, with autonomy only as permitted by London. English Whigs such as William Pitt the Elder and most Americans, preferred the old model, which saw colonial legislatures as permanently devolved entities. To the centralists, power had been only leased to the colonies, and could be rescinded. To the colonists, autonomy had been a permanent part of the deal, part of their incentive for undertaking the perils and hardships of colonization.

Benjamin Franklin, among other more prescient Americans, realized that neither the old model nor North's new model would resolve the conflicting needs of imperial unity and colonial autonomy. Franklin experimented with constitutional formulas providing for an imperial parliament in London with American representation (drawing on the recent, successful model of the Scottish Act of Union), combined with substantial local autonomy. Adam Smith and many others on both sides of the Atlantic supported the concept (Smith viewing with equanimity the prospect of voting control gradually passing to the American side), but it fell upon deaf ears at the ruling levels of power. Equally unsuccessful were Crown Union models that would have preserved the King as head of state in the colonies, but removed any role for the Westminster Parliament.

With the failure of Franklin's model, and of the subsequent attempt by George III and North to impose their model by military force, the last serious attempt to create a unified state encompassing all English-speaking people failed. The American Revolution was, in essence, a constitutional crisis leading to civil war, ultimately resolved by successful secession leading to territorial partition. The Anglosphere, which consisted at that time of the British Isles, Atlantic North America minus Quebec, and the

Anglophone Caribbean, was sundered by the loss of the middle of the American side. This left Canada and the Anglo-Caribbean as isolated fragments, dependent on Britain and flooded with highly polarized Tory political refugees, the losing party of the civil war.

Both parts of the Anglosphere subsequently diverged in political, social, and economic development, each half evolving in a different direction by its respective experiences and challenges. Britain and its colonies developed in response to the Napoleonic challenge, the Industrial Revolution, and the creation of the Second Empire. The United States grew through Continental expansion and settlement, the resolution of the slavery issue (again by a constitutional crisis leading to civil war and a secession attempt, this time unsuccessful), and a more delayed entry into the Industrial Revolution. A nationalist ideology in the United States, influenced by the growing secular religion Continental European nationalism, lead to the promotion of a separate national identity (with measures such as Noah Webster's promotion of a distinct American spelling standard) and the self-conscious creation of a distinctly American literary voice, such as Longfellow's attempt to create an American mythic poetry in *Hiawatha* and *Evangeline and the Acadians*. Ironically, the idea that English literary models were somehow a foreign importation that needed replacing, was itself a foreign importation from alien models. These trends led to a historical narrative that interpreted the American experience as one of inevitable progression to a distinct emergent nationhood; incorporating the Turnerian myth of a unique culture forged in the crucible of the American frontier, and the political creation science myth that saw the Philadelphia Constitution as a unique creation without antecedents, rather than the Whiggish exercise in adapting British constitutionalism that it actually was.

CONVERGENCE IN POLITICS:
THE DILEMMA OF THE SECOND EMPIRE

Divergence of American and British culture seemed natural and inevitable.

Indeed, had the steamship, telegraph, powered presses, and subsequent means of rapid mass communications not emerged, American and British culture could well have continued divergence to the point where American and British English would be languages as separate as are Dutch and Afrikaans today.

However, the rise of cheaper, easier, and more effective communications starting in the later nineteenth century ended the process of divergence and began a new process of convergence. By the 1880s, the transatlantic voyage was sufficiently safe and convenient enough that the wealthy elite of Britain and the United States could readily visit with each other and interact, intermarry, and find profitable business to transact with each other. After a century of hostility and divergence, Americans and Britons began rediscovering the advantages of common language, institutions, and culture. Additionally, Americans began interacting with the broader world, and Britons became aware of the rise of powerful new industrializing rivals, particularly Germany. The industrialization of the Great Lakes region, and the dependence of both America and Canada on unhindered use of the lake route for iron-ore transport rendered the idea of an Anglo-American war, and the cost of preparations to adequately defend the Lakes region, unattractive and eventually unthinkable. The Rush-Bagheot agreement on Great Lakes disarmament become the cornerstone of a de facto Anglosphere entente in which naval estimates began to be made on the implicit assumption that American and Britain would never fight.

The American and British elites became increasingly more susceptible to the attraction of a like-minded ally with whom cooperation came more easily and naturally than with more alien powers. Furthermore, social and political convergence was driven by modernization in parallel. George III was in fact the last British monarch who attempted direct governance. The reaffirmation of Parliamentary dominance, and the franchise expanding Reform Bills, combined with the expansion of the franchise in America in the Jacksonian era, meant that by the late nineteenth century, both nations had become industrial constitutional democracies. As such, they no longer represented substantially opposed philosophies of governance, particularly in contrast to other national systems. This awareness led to both the sentiment of the "special relationship," which bore fruit in the winning alliance of World War II, and the less fruitful concepts for reunification of the Anglosphere in some form of federal empire or state.

The memory of the American secession hung as a constant shadow over the rise of the Second British Empire, particularly in regard to the colonies of settlement such as Canada, Australia, and New Zealand. This led to a search for federalist solutions at three levels. The creation of the Canadian and Australian federations showed its application in resolving questions of regional governance.

The search for a federal solution to the governance of the British Isles led to the Irish Home Rule proposals which dominated British domestic politics for a half century, the subsequent autonomy of Northern Ireland, and the now-unfolding autonomy of Scotland and Wales. Finally, a federalist answer was sought to the problem of governance of the empire itself.

History has shown that the British infatuation with federal states was an overgeneralization from American success. Several federations failed quickly, such as the West Indian Federation and the Federation of Rhodesia and Nyasaland. The Malaysian Federation suffered the secession of

Singapore, immediately, due to ethnic politics, but has succeeded in a less multicultural version.

India and Canada seemed like successes but have been showing their strains lately; South Africa was problematic from the start, and in the end the empire chose a unitary solution there, also ultimately unsuccessful. The post-apartheid government has now chosen to experiment with a federal form, but with only weak provincial powers. Only Australia has been to date an unqualified success as a federal state.

Examining the record, it is clear that federal states are not a panacea and cannot substitute for social coherence if such a state does not emerge by reasonably organic means. Generally speaking, federations which arose primarily through internal demand in the constituent states have done better than those imposed from above.

Successful federalism is that which is voluntarily adopted by strong civic states, where it is merely the highest level of uniting a rich structure of association starting with free individuals at its base. What is less well understood is that a civic state itself is in reality a network of federations, starting with the federation of individuals into families, associations, partnerships, companies, communities, and states. The stronger the underlying consensus, the more successful will be the federation at the top level. What is disastrous is papering over genuine deep differences with federalist formulas in a manufactured state solution.

A long series of schemes for imperial confederation, whose by-product was the concept of British Commonwealth, ultimately foundered. No formula was able to offer a binding form of government for the entire empire. The formula needed to be, at the same time, representative in nature, effective in creating a governing consensus for needed economic and military actions, and yet autonomous enough to satisfy the desires of strongly developed distinct cultures for national self-determination.

In particular, neither the "encapsulated" alien colonies of settlement such as Quebec and the Boer states, nor the politically subjugated but intact civilizations like the Indian states, the Malayan states, and the Arab nations bought into the narratives and justifications of empire except among relatively small classes of people with direct interest in its success. Finally, no federalist formula was able to resolve the issues of local economic interest with imperial preference—the concept of the empire as a protected common economic area.

In the long run, the inability to create a state form to resolve the quandary of a democratic empire was resolved by turning its successor, the (once-British) Commonwealth of Nations, into a nonstate form that survived due to its amorphousness. It survives as a collective description of a group of common institutions, created by the empire, which were sufficiently useful to all participants so as to be voluntarily perpetuated. It is those parts of the empire that remained when the compulsory element was entirely removed.

It is much less than some of its founders hoped it would be. Reading works like Nevil Shute's *In the Wet* (1953), it is possible to glimpse the hope that the assemblage of so many disparate civilizations into a cooperative entity could survive the end of the imperial, compulsory element and evolve into something new and creative, and a significant actor on the world stage. Still, it has survived, and continues to thrive in its diminished form, so much so that nations with only the most tenuous ties to the empire are now considering joining. More interesting is the fact that the president of the Republic of Ireland has even begun to speculate publicly about rejoining in the wake of the Good Friday peace agreement, though whether that will become reality remains to be seen.

POTENTIAL ROADBLOCKS TO AN
ANGLOSPHERE NETWORK COMMONWEALTH

It required the transformation of the British Empire, the denouement of the Cold War, and the end of the "American Century," combined with the advent of a network civilization, before a project for the linking of the Anglosphere could be contemplated. Yet all these things have come to pass. The convergence of the Anglosphere is already becoming a reality in its component cultures. The nature of that convergence, and the political opportunities that it presents, are what matter now.

For the past two centuries, the United States, the United Kingdom, and the other primarily English-speaking nations could not develop stronger, more distinctive common means of cooperation than the loose ties of the Special Relationship or the Commonwealth of Nations. Despite the shared values and interests, there have been a number of fundamental obstacles to any stronger relationship. These roadblocks slowed and limited the development of the Special Relationship, and made any thought of a British-American confederation a nonstarter in the court of public opinion on both sides. Chief among these roadblocks were the following:

Ireland

Simply put, there was the refusal of a varying but never insignificant segment of the Catholic Irish population whether in Ireland itself, or in America and the Commonwealth, to accept the incorporation of Ireland integrally into the United Kingdom. There was a constant struggle to reverse that act, the consequence of which was that a large and influential sector of the American electorate was automatically hostile to any close cooperation with Britain. This opposition contributed substantially to the delayed U.S. entry into World War I, and prior to Pearl Harbor, into World War II. Additionally, the Irish grievance against the empire created an ongoing resistance both in Ireland and throughout the Commonwealth against the attempt to use the monarchy and its emotional symbols as a binding element for the Commonwealth. Australian republicanism always found support in that country's Irish population.

The independence of Southern Ireland in 1921 alleviated this grievance to some extent, but the ongoing trauma of the unresolved conflict in Northern Ireland still represents a rallying point against any proposal for closer Anglo-American ties. For this reason, the full realization of an Anglosphere Network Commonwealth will require a permanent settlement of the Northern Ireland situation in a form acceptable to the large majority on both sides. At the same time (although this is a subject requiring substantial discussion elsewhere), the institutions of an Anglosphere Network Commonwealth may offer the external stabilizing institutions to permit a mutually acceptable solution to the Northern Ireland situation.

Racial Attitudes

Both the United States and the British Empire, even in the late nineteenth century, were substantially multiracial entities. They had also both evolved to a political philosophy of broad manhood (and eventually universal) suffrage. Yet in the American South until 1965, and throughout much of the empire, effective suffrage was not extended to nonwhite segments of the population. Any formula for political unification of the English-speaking world in those years would have had either to exclude many or all nonwhites from voting, or be effectively imperial (permitting some nations to make decisions for others). It might permit nonwhites to vote, which would have resulted in a nonwhite electoral majority if India participated. The issue of free movement of people, with the right to exercise political rights throughout the resulting political entity, was perhaps even more incompatible with then-current racial attitudes in the long run. Each of these solutions, therefore, was problematic.

Today, changing racial attitudes, along with a looser concept of cooperative ties, have removed this objection. A network commonwealth, although it assumes an inclusive representative government at the civic-state level, operates on the principle of a Hanseatic-style coalition of the willing at the commonwealth level.

Thus majority rule is not an issue. In feudal times, people identified, and society divided, along lines of title and status. After the Reformation, identity and social division focused on sectarian religious identity. During the Machine Age, economic class was seen as the principal division. Toward the end of the twentieth century, an identity politics of race and ethnicity arose. Now as the Singularity approaches and the economic state is in eclipse, the rapid transformation of demographics (partly enabled by the decline of racial barriers) will bring civilizational identity to the fore. A concept of an Anglosphere network civilization has the opportunity to eclipse past racial divisions, making the racial diversity of the Anglosphere an incentive to rather than a barrier against pan-Anglosphere institutions. The diaspora networks of Indian, Hong Kong Chinese, and other immigrants throughout the United States, the United Kingdom, Canada, and Australia may be unifying threads for the Anglosphere.

The Empire

The conflict between British imperial and American national interests was the underlying source of almost all high-level conflict between American and British governing elites in working out the basis for Anglo-American cooperation throughout the heyday of the Special Relationship.

Fundamentally, Britain was bound to rank protection of the empire and its interests second only to the safety of the Home Islands themselves. For America, imperial interests were suspect at best, and many times directly opposed to American interests. Full cooperation between the United States and the British Empire would have resulted in America defending British imperial interests without sharing proportionately in the benefits thereof.

Subsequently, during the era of decolonization and the Cold War, America, desiring to expand and consolidate its sphere of interest (as part of a larger strategy of consolidating an anti-Communist superpower bloc under its leadership), frequently found itself opposed to Britain's perceived need to act in protection of residual imperial interests. The Suez fiasco was perhaps the most egregious and painful example, but the trend has persisted. (Although the Suez episode was also much aggravated by specific circumstances: had Churchill remained in government just a year longer, or had Macmillan rather than Eden been prime minister, or had someone other than Dulles been American secretary of state, the entire situation would likely have been handled much better.) The Grenada episode rankled even so pro-American a leader as Margaret Thatcher. The Falklands War caused a severe internal dispute in the American government between Cold War hegemonists and the adherents of the Special Relationship. (Although it is instructive to note which party won out in the end.) More recently, America's lukewarm support of the Commonwealth strategy of sanctions toward apartheid South Africa caused continued strains in its relationship with members of that organization.

In discussions of the Anglosphere concept, there has been some criticism from the British right which seems to arise from lingering resentment of the Suez incident, or rather the inherent issues of a declining British ability to act independently at that time that caused Suez to arise. This experience is brought up to support the argument that the Anglosphere nations are like the Greek city-states of antiquity; although allied in culture, they often experienced divergent and even opposed national political interests. Yet what the Suez example demonstrates is the inadequacy of the Special Relationship model for Anglosphere affiliation. Nation-states often experience conflicts between short-term national needs and long-term civilizational interests. A completely informal relationship tends to result in the latter being sacrificed to the former; a federal state model tends to sacrifice the former to the latter. A network commonwealth solution is an attempt at a more balanced relationship between these two valid needs. And it is instructive to remember that the inability of the Greek city-states to create a successful political form uniting them against alien civilizations ended in their conquest by outsiders and the enslavement of their intellectual class.

Europe

Both the United States and the United Kingdom have sacrificed ties with each other, and in Britain's case, with the Commonwealth as well, for the sake of particular interests in Europe. The past thirty years of British history have encompassed a period of political and cultural schizophrenia that has created ongoing unresolved tensions in its national life and identity.

Opposing the trend toward British participation in Europe has been the increasing convergence of Anglosphere culture, combined with Britain's ongoing indecision over the nature of its relationship to Europe.

Since World War II, Britain has seen the emergence of common European institutions as a challenge, dilemma, and opportunity, in various admixtures.

Challenge, because the Continental states at first attained faster growth and greater prosperity through the creation of the common economic area, and also because France and Germany were seizing the leadership of Europe through their economic and political contributions to European unity.

Dilemma, because the constant temptation to join the common effort came at a high price of abandonment of overseas ties and domestic distinctness and autonomy.

Opportunity, because many of Britain's lasting military, financial, and industrial strengths created a dream in the mind of certain Britons of their seizing leadership of a common Europe.

Europe offered a different mix of challenge and opportunity to the United States. NATO, rather than the EU, was the arena of decision, and there the United States was preoccupied from 1948 through 1992 with a single, overwhelming issue: the prospect of a massive Soviet invasion on the Central European Front. To counter this, U.S. plans had to center around the maintenance of a large armored force with appropriate air cover in Germany.

The Bundesrepublik, with its large conscript army, had to be the centerpiece of American diplomacy and strategy. As the joke put it, NATO was a device for keeping "the Americans in, the Russians out, and the Germans down."

Britain, in this situation, could only be a secondary interest, a partner in patrolling the North Atlantic to ensure that American convoys could cross in wartime and an unsinkable carrier for American aircraft offshore from the continent. Thus, both Britain and the United States had strong interests in Europe, and for each, the geopolitical realities demanded that Germany and, to a lesser extent France, remain the primary partners in the central instrument of cooperation.

These realities have altered substantially over the past decade without a corresponding alteration in the political strategies of either nation. Despite a widespread feeling that new solutions and arrangements are called for, neither Americans, with regard to NATO, nor Britons with regard to both the EU and NATO, have generated a positive alternative vision.

In particular, the widespread uneasiness about further European integration, especially regarding monetary union, which continues to emerge from diverse regions of the British political spectrum, suggests that an Anglosphere Network Commonwealth could be an attractive alternative direction.

I shall discuss further on the emerging debate over the Anglosphere alternative to full British immersion into the increasingly integrated European superstate. For now, it is enough to note that the search for alternatives may prove to be one of the strongest drivers for the emergence of an Anglosphere Network Commonwealth.

POSTIMPERIAL IDENTITY QUESTIONS IN THE COMMONWEALTH STATES

The United States and the United Kingdom each pursued their own concept of national interest. Those Commonwealth states (principally Canada, Australia, New Zealand, and South Africa) that did not (like the Indian states) have an innate, common historical and civilizational identity to which to return, were each set adrift to redefine their identities in the postimperial era. An attempt to define each in terms of British Commonwealth membership fell short, as that organization was too amorphous, its institutions insufficiently relevant to core need, and its identity too tenuous to serve as the principal element of social identity as had the British Empire. In order to maintain the breadth of its imperial legacy, the Commonwealth sacrificed the depth of its institutional potential for cooperation. Furthermore, most of these countries had strong minorities who objected to the heavily British and monarchist orientation of the Commonwealth: the French in Canada, the Afrikaners in South Africa, and to a lesser extent the Irish and other republican-minded elements in Australia. The architects of the Commonwealth had hoped the role of the Crown and the Royal Family, the Union Flag, and imperial heraldry and titles would serve as a common symbolism and identity. This had its negative side, in that these minorities were at best indifferent and at worst actively hostile to such symbols.

Each nation subsequently embarked on a project of national redefinition, of seeking a new national story, and in most cases deliberately distanced themselves from British Commonwealth connections and institutions. How these projects unfolded, and how they bear on the usefulness of a network commonwealth solution, are discussed in detail further on.

THE AFRICAN SPECIAL RELATIONSHIP: AMERICAN AFRICANS, THE CARIBBEAN, AND AFRICA

The prospect of an Anglosphere Network Commonwealth presents an interesting and unique set of opportunities for three of the leading populations of African descent in the world: African Americans, English-speaking Afro-Caribbeans, and the African Anglosphere, particularly South Africa. These constitute the largest groups of educated, prosperous, and politically engaged persons of African descent in the English-speaking world, and ones with a particular self-identity as African rather than primarily as members of specific tribes or nationalities. This pan-African identity is a legacy of slavery and the struggle for emancipation and rights in the former two cases, and of the struggle against apartheid in the latter.

Tribal identifications are significant among most South African blacks; but the need for unity in the antiapartheid movement has resulted in the last several generations of educated blacks becoming accustomed to a multilayered identity, as tribal members, as blacks, and as South Africans. Similarly, African Americans are accustomed to multilayered identities as blacks, as Americans, and other identifications.

Caribbean blacks are accustomed to multilayered identifications as citizens of their unique island communities (a strong identity typically underestimated by outsiders), as blacks, and as English speakers. The latter is seen in, for example, Anglo-Caribbean solidarity with Belize and Guyana against Hispanosphere claims, or for that matter Anglo-Caribbean solidarity on the Falklands crisis against Argentina.

These three populations have dominated the dialogue among people of African descent in the English-speaking world, and will probably do so for the foreseeable future. Their prominence in music, art, literature, and sports ensures that their voices and images will continue to be heard and seen. The Anglosphere Network Commonwealth offers a means of economic, interpersonal, and political linkage among these disparate and separated communities and their outposts in Britain and Canada.

As discussed previously, African Americans have the distinct identity and shared experiences to support nationhood, but they are territorially dispersed and very enmeshed in the wider interracial communities around them. They neither desire to integrate so completely in the general population as to erase their identity (even if that were possible), nor, except for a small and unrealistic minority, undergo the trauma of territorial separation, population transfer, and secession needed to become a traditional nation-state (even if that were possible). African-American identity seems to demand a third solution. As noted previously, African Americans have not tended to assimilate into other American cultural nations, historically because of racially based barriers to such assimilation, and partly because, as a consequence of that separation, they already belong to an American cultural nation of their own. With the growing cultural acceptance of intermarriage, this may change somewhat. Some African Americans, particularly long-term military veterans, seem to be assimilating into Midland America. But I suspect that a core New African cultural nation will persist indefinitely, particularly if it evolves to complete its high-trust transition.

At the same time, African Americans and Afro-Caribbeans have technical, business, and political skills of value to South Africa; South Africans can particularly provide the link to Africa that their cousins in the Diaspora have been seeking.

African Americans who travel to Africa often end up unable to establish the close connection with African society they look for, because the local societies are still overwhelmingly tribal-based; only in South Africa is an African identity not entirely tribal or superficial at all present.

The network commonwealth ties of informational, interpersonal, and institutional cooperation could become particularly important tools enabling the African-descended populations of the Anglosphere to create an international community.

In keeping with the multilayered identities of the Information Age, this community would be tied both to the existing national communities of these populations and to wider identities, both African and Anglosphere.

EMBEDDED CULTURES, NATIVE NATIONS, AND PAN-ANGLOSPHERE MINORITIES

Like African Americans, there are many other distinct communities within the English-speaking world who may find the network commonwealth a more comfortable means of resolving the economic, cultural, and political issues of their status than current nation-state theory offers. Because of the rapid process by which the English-speaking people irrupted into North America, Australia and Oceania, and southern Africa, native English-speaking populations live side by side with a wide variety of native peoples and other settler populations. They have been incorporated into Anglosphere polities, along with the descendants of slaves and other plantation labor. (The British Isles themselves retain such encapsulated native populations still speaking Welsh and Gaelic.) Some retain their original language and political autonomy, and constitute a large majority of the population in their area. Others are primarily or entirely English speaking, constitute a minority even locally, and have no distinct political entity under their control.

Most fall somewhere in between on most counts.

The network commonwealth offers a means for many of these populations to maintain meaningful links to other populations while still maintaining substantial integration into the existing nations in which they are immersed. Hispanic communities in the United States will maintain ties with the emerging Hispanosphere. Polynesian populations immersed in the United States or New Zealand can develop meaningful ties to each other and to the independent island nations of similar background. These will most likely be in English, given the fact that none of the Polynesian languages are mutually intelligible. Native Americans in the United States and Canada, Aborigines in Australia, and others will likely continue to evolve toward greater political autonomy, which will continue to fall short of absolute independence and nation-statehood. Again, network commonwealth institutions can offer external ties of significance to these communities, helping to resolve situations such as tribes divided by the U.S.-Canadian border—as U.S.-Canada integration deepens, communities lying on both sides of the border find it easier to maintain and deepen ties.

However, the efficacy of a sovereignty solution is conditional upon resolving the trust issue. Most aboriginal cultures are traditional low-radius-of-trust, kinship-based societies that treat any public transfers as loot (as do many of the low-trust ethnic communities that receive multiculturalist subsidies). This pattern continues to encourage social pathologies such as alcoholism, low educational attainment, and violent lawbreaking in aboriginal communities. This constitutes an ongoing strain on the wider political and social structure, while generating a counterpressure for discontinuance.

Just as African Americans need to seize control of their cultural-national narratives, so do aboriginal activists in Canada, the United States, Australia, and New Zealand need to orient their struggle toward making a similar transformation of their nations to high-trust, strong civil societies. (There are some examples of success, particularly the historical Cherokees.) Sovereignty for aboriginal nations can only be a solution to their political and social problems if it is combined with such a transformational movement. Given such a movement, essential sovereignty can provide a successful basis for integration into a wider Anglosphere civilization while retaining many unique cultural characteristics. Failing such a transformation, sovereignty becomes a sham, just a different formula for welfare—based this time on a form of regulatory arbitrage, and as such, revocable at will by the larger state.

Given a resolution of the trust issue, either by assimilation in the case of immigrant minorities, or transformation in the case of aboriginal cultures, many of the "tribes," in the larger sense of ethnic groups maintaining a coherent identity, may play a unique role in binding the Anglosphere together. It may be an irony that if Cecil Rhodes's ambition of closer ties among English speakers is realized, it may well be the descendants of Chinese, Vietnamese, Greek, Italian, African and other non–Anglo-Saxon immigrants who will provide many of the sinews of these person-to-person links. Most Americans of British descent long ago lost the direct human links to their cousins in the British Isles, although new ones are forming as costs of travel and communication decrease.

In contrast, many first- and second-generation immigrants in the English-speaking world have live ties with their cousins who have been scattered among the English-speaking nations by the vagaries of immigration and refugee policies.

Flat-rate world communications and cheap jet travel will keep those ties alive.

The human-to-human contact of a network commonwealth will ultimately lead to its own new generation of human links. The growing number of intra-Anglosphere transpacific and transatlantic marriages can help foster a pan-community identity based on a rediscovery of common values.

WHAT'S AT STAKE: USES OF
THE NETWORK COMMONWEALTH

An external framework drawing on a common constitutional tradition might be welcomed to stabilize a situation where a larger union is devolving power to its constituent nations. South Africa, Canada, the United Kingdom, and the United States, among others, are all experiencing such pressure to devolve power. Even absent any explosive crises, the cultural commonalties of the Anglosphere nations will continue to create pressure to deemphasize existing alignments and rebuild ties among the cousin nations. A generation of membership in the EU has not deepened the affections of the British people for its continental partners nor improved the ease of cooperation between them. Rather, the continuing divergence of Britain from the continent in demographics, business and commercial structures, public policies, and defense structures and capabilities renders the continentalization of Britain as quixotic a goal as ever.

As the economics and politics of the Information Revolution grow, Anglo-continental divergence will accelerate rather than slow down, exacerbating political strains.

The 1999 European Parliament elections in Britain may be a foreshadowing of these tendencies. Although the Labour Party had won an electoral victory of historic proportions in the general election of 1997 (and would win even bigger in 2001), it suffered a humiliating defeat at the hands of the Euroskeptic parties. Detailed examination of the returns shows that this was not merely a partisan victory of the Conservatives. The small United Kingdom Independence Party, which advocates complete withdrawal from the EU, broke through to representation for the first time, doing so in areas that had been Liberal, rather than Tory strongholds.*

Some observers took Blair's and Labour's victory in 2001 as evidence that the Euroskepticism of William Hague, then-leader of the Conservatives, had become a spent force in Britain. However, close analysis of the election results and opinion polls indicates that Labour won despite its pro-Brussels views, rather than because of them. In fact, the British public is more Euroskeptic than at any point since entry, and now opposes joining the single currency by a large margin. Approximately as many people favor complete withdrawal from the Union as favor remaining in it.

---

* In the June 2004 European parliament elections, this trend accelerared, with UKIP winning a quarter of the vote. Euroskeptic parties won among them a majority of the vote.

It is clear that if Europe had been the foremost issue on the minds of the electorate, the Tories would have done far better. There is also the fact that many British voters are highly Euroskeptic but would never vote Tory for reasons of family tradition or other strongly held opinions. The potential for the emergence of a Euroskeptic electoral alternative of the center-left in Britain may be the most significantly underappreciated factor in the future of British politics.

Euroskepticism in Britain is leading to increased attention to alternatives.

Renewed Anglosphere ties are the most logical of such. The Euroskeptic movement, now that it is gaining momentum and discovering its independent voice, is coming to realize that so long as the EU can be presented as "The Future," their opposition retains the taint of small-minded, foot-dragging negativism.

Their opponents do everything possible to encourage this image. But the idea of a unified Europe built around the "European Social Model" is itself an old, tired idea, discredited by facts. The network commonwealth concept provides an alternative goal that can be honestly portrayed as looking to the true future.

Nor has the aftermath of the Iraq war necessarily played to the benefit of Europe. Significant portions of the Labour Left, the Liberal Democrats, and the leftist media establishment (particularly at the British Broadcasting Corporation) vocally opposed British participation in the war, and supported the Franco-German positions of nonparticipation in the coalition. Subsequent events, including the failure to (as of this writing) locate stockpiles of weapons of mass destruction on Iraqi soil, and the questions arising from the suicide under pressure of a central weapons expert, have left more of the British public uneasy about the Blair government's actions in the war, but this has not translated to any increase in pro-European sentiment among the public.*

Throughout the Anglosphere today, there are considerable factions of the public dissatisfied with the status quo. Both the Clinton and Bush presidencies have seen a sizeable and vociferous portion of the public expressing strong dislike for the administration and a willingness to believe even extreme theories of malfeasance, from right-wing Clinton-haters suspecting that the Oklahoma City bombing was a provocation by the White House, to leftists who suspect the Bush administration of complicity in the September 11 attacks. For every citizen who supports such visible indications of alienation, there are hundreds or thousands who are skeptical of the claims of their political elite and open to positive, future-oriented visions. Many of these people, whether or not they can define it

---

* A large majority of the votes in the June 2004 elections also went to parties supporting the Iraq war.

precisely, seek something fundamentally different that they cannot articulate precisely. What they seek is a self-affirming, culture-affirming, and
nation-affirming narrative that can serve as the basis for constructing (or
reconstructing) coherent civic states.

Such a positive reconstruction of civic statehood will require a rejection
of the Black Legend of the Anglosphere and a restored vision. This vision
can be negative, or it can be positive. The Anglosphere vision of our
emerging new network civilization may have for many of these people
the power to transcend the current protest politics of the marginalized
and bring them into alliance with the emerging economic winners of the
Internet economy, who are equally poorly served by the bitter-end politics
of the Machine Age. For when they look "back" to "archaic" Anglosphere
values such as individual rights, rule of law, personal responsibility, minimal government, and communities of mutual trust—in short, classic civil
society in its strongest form—they are also looking at the necessities of the
world of the Singularity.

However, the network commonwealth will be useless if it is generally
perceived as something created by an elite and forced on the citizens. The
reaction to NAFTA is an example of such a perception. Although it delivers many benefits, NAFTA is distrusted because of its reputation as an entity created by technocrats and planners in the capital cities, subject to no
visible accountability or control. Similarly, the EU has generated massive
distrust and suspicion in the United Kingdom, for similar reasons.

Furthermore, eventually relationships such as NAFTA and the EU will
undergo severe stresses. The communities formed by these agreements
will experience trial by fire in some form or another. Citizens in each
member nation will be called upon to undergo some sacrifice for the sake
of the wider community, sacrifices that may be perceived as falling more
heavily on some nations than others. Nobody will make sacrifices for the
sake of a bloodless set of trade arrangements built around a lowest-
common-denominator set of values, except on the narrowest calculations
of eventual self-interest. The English-speaking nations have this in common: the values which have been most effective in rallying their citizens,
time after time and in the face of great challenges, are those shared in
large part by all citizens. The Anglosphere possesses the raw material to
serve as the basis of a network commonwealth that can become a tough
and serviceable instrument of community self-interest, one in which each
nation and all of its citizens can participate with less compromise of its
core values than any other imaginable combination.

We see this dilemma to some extent in the Iraq war and its aftermath.
Common values and a vision of shared long-term interests had much to
do with the prompt support of Britain and Australia to the American response to September 11. Yet Tony Blair was forced to articulate his justifications for British participation in that war, the terms of his own ideology,

specifically liberal internationalism. This forced him to focus on the weapons issues and the UN process to the exclusion of the many other reasons for moving against the Ba'athists. And when the time came to move toward closer ties among the allies, America responded with a less-than-generous free trade agreement with Australia, because domestic politics trumped international gratitude. This again demonstrates that although the Anglosphere is built on common values and good feelings, it must take on some institutional forms to assure that long-term civilizational interests will not invariably be sacrificed to short-term domestic politics.

To move from an abstract appreciation of the network commonwealth opportunity to the concrete implementation of its institutions will require the generation of new narratives, symbols, and heroes, not to replace current national ones, but to place them in a wider context. Current transnational institutions have gained only the indifference, at best, and more usually the hostility of the citizens of their member nations. Citizens will give only limited support for transnational institutions based on economic mutual interest or abstract idealism; they might vote for them, but they dislike paying for them and have yet to be seen to die for them.

An Anglosphere Network Commonwealth will only come about following a change of perspective and as a result of the successful generation of these narratives and symbols. Heroic and exemplary narratives are based on experiences of mutual struggle for common goals. As a start, the very great cooperation among Anglosphere nations in the antitotalitarian wars of the twentieth century, in which no Anglosphere nation ever fought without the help of at least one other English-speaking power, offers substantial real experience within living memory as a point of departure.

To be effective, a network commonwealth in the Anglosphere would have to develop in concert with the great trends now emerging throughout the English-speaking world. Such a movement would have to create from among the various existing nations a shared sense of common values and interests that can serve as the emotional underpinnings of a serviceable community for the challenges of the future.

Higher Paychecks and Lower Prices

There are only a few ways to increase prosperity. One is to increase productivity through technological progress—to create more goods and services per hour of time worked, by using improved devices or materials. Another is to reduce waste or inefficiency in production, through better organization. Yet another is to reduce political parasitism—to stop the wasting of labor and capital forced into unproductive activities through government mandates. All of these have been pursued more and more through the last few decades. The fourth method is through expansion of the scale of the market. This can happen through natural population growth, immigration, or expansion of the economic area in question. Historically, the latter has been done through conquest and annexation.

Common markets are an attempt to deliver the same benefits through voluntary cooperation and harmonization. Current common markets, however, have either failed to accomplish true economic integration, thus minimizing benefits, or have imposed large costs in the name of harmonization. In an information economy, harmonization has a substantially different meaning. Network commonwealths have the potential to deliver substantial real benefits at the pocketbook level without the large costs that an aggressively harmonizing structure like the EU has imposed.

Financially, what is at stake is the creation of a market area almost 50 percent larger than the United States (counting here only the core Anglosphere nations), inhabited by a large population of well-educated, productive people with significant purchasing power, having a minimum of adjustment issues. Costs of goods for Britons, Australians, and others would fall sharply almost immediately; for Americans, they would fall gradually as the increased scale of production began to take effect. Real wages throughout the area would rise as the stimulus took effect.

For Americans, Britons, and other Anglosphere nations, "international" mergers are usually intra-Anglosphere mergers, particularly in cutting-edge fields like transportation, communications, and electronics. A network commonwealth would accelerate this process, making the firms yet more competitive in the world marketplace.

Freedom of Movement: A Bigger Home in a Smaller World

The English-speaking people are by nature mobile people. The fact that the people of the British Isles have poured out of their small islands and made themselves at home in so many far corners of the world testifies to their footloose nature.

Americans famously, but Canadians and Australians as well, feel at home in their continental spaces. They have always regarded as a fundamental oppression any abridgment of their freedom to pack up wagon or car and move on. In the small world of the Information Revolution, there will be no new frontiers to open until the day outer space can be colonized. Elbow room is a psychological necessity.

A reciprocal set of agreements permitting free movement of peoples throughout the Anglosphere would be one of the most appreciated personal benefits of a network commonwealth. Young British and Irish citizens have the right, through the EU, to travel and work in any other EU nation (at least in theory). Yet more go through the bureaucratic barriers to try a spell in the United States or Canada. Many Americans would enjoy the chance to try Australia without running the full-fledged immigration gantlet. Today, each of these people must act as an immigrant, when a sojourner's status might satisfy their needs. In the era of cheap flights around the world and cheap communications back home, this is realistic. Politics has not caught up with reality.

"When Free Men Shall Stand . . .":
Proven Allies in a Dangerous World

An Anglosphere Alliance would be formidable in almost any likely alignment of world politics. The Anglosphere nations have maintained a preeminent military-industrial-scientific capability. Their lead will continue for some time to come and is actually increasing in many ways, as Anglosphere nations dominate information technology and other emerging Singularity technologies. The United States and the United Kingdom are still, for example, the only nations capable of producing effective high-performance turbofan engines and possess much of the world's advanced aerospace capability. Increasingly, scientific and technological capabilities are the central factor in military strength; in such matters, an Anglosphere alliance would be, and be likely to remain, second to none.

Proponents of the "Revolution in Military Affairs" theory base their outlook on an understanding of the effects of information technology on warfare.

Recently, they have begun to realize that Britain, for some decades generally perceived as a medium-rank power, is in fact the only power other than the United States that has effectively integrated the lessons of that revolution.

As a consequence, British forces, although small, are the only NATO forces that can fully and effectively collaborate with American forces in the field—a capability proven once again in Afghanistan and Iraq. American defense analysts have concentrated on bringing the rest of NATO up to speed, but the deep structure of Continental European society itself frustrates such efforts.

To create a Machine Age military, it was essential that recruits know how to read, operate machinery, and adhere to Machine Age standards of behavior.

Peasants raised in traditional societies were at a disadvantage—and peasant societies did not have the factories and railroads needed to put their own armies in the field. Today, industrial societies structured around hierarchical corporations, strict control of information flows, and risk-averse social narratives are at a similar disadvantage as opposed to Information Age societies with entrepreneurial cultures, recruits accustomed to navigating information networks, and risk-taking social narratives.

Rather than waiting for Continental societies to transform themselves, American and British defense planners will eventually have to form the "fast convoy"—a closer defense relationship among those powers with similar demographic, cultural, and economic profiles. Such a fast convoy strategy could become a driver for an Anglosphere Network Commonwealth.

CONTROLLING DANGERS, MAINTAINING FREEDOMS: CONSTITUTIONAL TRADITIONS AND THE TECHNOLOGIES OF THE SINGULARITY

The Singularity will be a race between hope and fear. As discussed in chapter 1, some people are already expressing deep misgivings about the threats of the Singularity.

Others have responded by proposing universal controls that would inevitably lead to a static and totalitarian global society. These measures would probably not be implementable if attempted. Once people understood what the outcomes would be, there would be massive resistance. On the other hand, if such measures were implemented, it is possible, although not likely, that a situation would be established that was stable in the short term.

However, such a solution would not be metastable—that is to say, it would not stand up to the pressures of multiple generations and their experiences.

The control route is at heart a route of prohibition. Like all prohibitions, it cannot succeed through the application of state force alone; it must be supported by a broad segment of society as well. Thus, at root, prohibition depends on the widespread adoption of the narrative supporting the bans. Consider alcohol prohibition in the United States. It was adopted as the result of a century of social activism in the United States, centered in Greater New England, which had created a successful and widely believed narrative that stressed the genuine and readily-documented social costs of alcoholism. It proposed that banning alcohol by law would be effective in eliminating alcohol production and consumption, and thus eliminate the social costs of alcohol abuse. Resistance to prohibition was attributed entirely to the economic interests of the "saloon lobby" and a handful of relatively fanatic alcohol abusers. (There are interesting parallels to the narratives of the antigun movement in the United States today.)

Although this narrative was accurate in its depiction of the social costs of alcohol, it was highly unrealistic in characterizing the opposition to the proposal as rooted in economic interests and personal fanaticism. It was also highly unrealistic in its estimate of the social costs of attempting to enforce prohibition, and in the degree of success the state was likely to encounter. Existing statewide and local experiments in prohibition were also mischaracterized, with failures attributed to the lack of broader-scale enforcement.

A mere thirteen years of alcohol prohibition, despite numerous legal loopholes (homemade wine and beer remained legal, for example, and individual consumption was not punished—the status that was called "prohibition" for alcohol would be considered semilegalization if applied to, say, cannabis today) demonstrated the substantial social costs of the policy. Despite the fact that the social costs of alcoholism were somewhat reduced, the general public rapidly rejected the narrative of prohibition; so much so, in fact, that after repeal the culture generally rejected even the valid parts of the prohibitionist narrative. It took several generations for awareness of the social costs of alcohol consumption to return to the accurate perceptions of the immediate preprohibition era.

The prospect of a worldwide regime imposing severe controls on new technology development, with the attendant dislocations, costs, and disappointments, will likely (even if successfully imposed) erode its base of narrative acceptance over time. Certainly, within a few generations at most (and much sooner in all likelihood) substantial factions of the population, starting with descendants of those who rejected or only weakly accepted the narratives to begin with, would constitute a protechnology underground. Military or economic competition would create incentives for parties to stretch or bend prohibitions; corruption of the guardians enforcing the prohibitions would be a constant threat.

Eventually, the cracks in the structure would probably cause it to fall (in my estimation, likely in a matter of decades or years). It would be typical if the supporting narrative for the controls were rejected utterly, rather than critically—the baby would be thrown out with the bath water. Even a sensible and effective level of control would probably be rejected.

Ultimately, the hazards of the Singularity technologies would return, this time without the prospect of a reasonable trade-off of risk and reward.

Effective control of phenomena in complex modern societies must always be a trade-off of costs of the ability to control versus the potential toll of the risks faced, discounted by the probability of the events contemplated. Overreaching destroys the fragile consensus for support of controls; implementation of successful controls requires understanding the mechanisms by which civil society validates, accepts, and permits the enforcement of curbs on otherwise acceptable economic and technological behavior. Any attempt to create an effective system for mitigating the hazards of the Singularity must learn from the successes and failures of strong civil societies in that area. The Anglosphere's history is particularly rich in instructive examples of both.

COMMON LAW AND COMMON MARKETS: HARMONY WITHOUT HOMOGENIZATION

Higher rates of trade, travel, interaction, and human interchange typically create new commercial disputes among citizens of several political entities. Currently, decisions of each sovereign entity are final, for good reason. There is no acceptable framework for judgment that citizens of more than one entity readily accept as a basis for fair judgment. Thus, a contract between parties in more than one jurisdiction must specify a prevailing law under which disputes may be adjudicated.

Existing transnational legal regimes and their pseudoconstitutional underpinnings, such as the World Court and the UN Declaration of Human Rights, are a poor substitute for the court system and common-law tradition of any functional English-speaking democracy. Nor is the European Convention on Human Rights, which aspires to be the constitutional fount of the EU, any better as a substitute.

Under the network commonwealth model, a very attractive benefit might be a jurisprudence system providing an alternative for resolving contract and property disputes involving disputants from two or more member states of the community.

Common law is a particularly appropriate basis for such an effort, as it is based on precedent and requires no statute-making body to create new law. A "general common law" could emerge as a nonmandatory effort undertaken by an ongoing colloquy of jurists from the various federal, national, state, and provincial levels of the member nations, which would restate and affirm the fundamental common-law principles as a basis of jurisprudence. Contracting parties from different common-law nations adhering to the treaty could then have the option of specifying it as the ruling law in contracts among themselves.

General common law would require no new adjudication or enforcement mechanism: parties could specify it as the ruling law in contracts, and defendants in civil actions might have the option of choosing a trial under its rules in existing courts. Such a jurisdiction would be particularly appropriate for Internet-mediated contracts, as it would be seen as an understandable code that would have a neutral flavor between parties of different nations. Existing courts operating within existing procedures would make decisions. Decisions would be enforced by existing police forces, so there would be no feeling of alien intrusion. (I can readily imagine the English preferring such a common-law-based system to the arbitrary pan-European code or Corpus Juris, lacking juries, presumption of innocence, and habeas corpus, which is now being promoted as part of European unification.)

Appeal would be through the normal chain of appeals in each nation. However, the process would differ in two ways from existing jurisdictions: rather than refer to statute law for guidance, the courts would refer only to precedents and to specific provisions of the treaty instituting the general common law. Second, courts in any nation adhering to the treaty would take note of precedents under general common law set by courts in other adhering countries. The treaty would specify, where precedents had grown apart in the various jurisdictions, which precedents would prevail and become the point of departure in general common law.

Thus, general common law would become a polycentric system of law growing from familiar roots, but more immune from interference from legislative interests, and thus more objective. If circumstances arose that rendered the trend of general common-law decisions truly unpalatable to the majority of citizens of the adhering nations, the treaty could be amended or supplemented by consent of the signatories. This remedial action would be available, but used far less often than legislative action.

The final say, of course, would be up to the people. As a voluntary option, general common law would never get started unless sufficient parties found its jurisdiction to be superior to the existing national jurisdictions. A pan-community common-law civil practice might emerge from this and become the preferred jurisdiction for a wide variety of international contract relationships among citizens of member nations.

Although it would be preferable to begin this process with civil jurisdiction, it might be desirable to extend it to criminal jurisdiction in some cases, particularly involving offenses between citizens of the various member nations. Ultimately, some of the emotional cases involving citizens of different nations (which will inevitably increase as contacts and exchanges increase) might be more satisfactorily handled in a neutral jurisdiction and tried under a code derived from the basic underlying common law.

THE ANGLOSPHERE DEBATE

In the past few years, the idea of closer ties among the English-speaking, common-law-based nations has begun to emerge again in the field of public discourse. Samuel Huntington mentioned the possibility of a "civilizational" alliance of English-speaking nations (curiously, minus the United Kingdom) in his *Clash of Civilizations* but did not elaborate on the concept. In the summer of 1998, publisher Conrad Black (now Lord Black of Crossharbour) raised a stir, particularly in the United Kingdom, in a speech proposing that Britain leave or downgrade its EU ties and join NAFTA. This proposal has taken on a life of its own and has been edging further toward the political mainstream ever since.

A number of American, Canadian, and British political figures have begun to speak openly about this option. The now-retired U.S. Senator Phil Gramm became an ardent proponent of British NAFTA membership. Blair government figures have began to react to such talk with alarm, with then-foreign minister Robin Cook, a strong Europhile, dismissing the idea as "barmy." Yet studies of the economic impact of such a move (by British economist Patrick Minford and others) have made it clear that, even discounting the likely effects of a continued acceleration of the technology-driven entrepreneurial revolution, such a trade linkage makes sense.

Gramm introduced a new twist to the argument, one that helped bring the concept further into the mainstream of debate. He began to focus discussion on the prospect of an associate NAFTA membership for the United Kingdom without requiring a full U.K. withdrawal from the EU. Gramm pointed out that although EU rules forbid separate U.K. membership in NAFTA, such provisions themselves should be in contravention of General Agreement on Tariffs/World Trade Organization (GATT/WTO) rules. Gramm effectively reframed the question to one of whether the EU will continue on its present course toward a monolithic, inward-looking, protectionist federal state with a sense of rivalry with the United States. In such a case, the requirements of the Singularity revolutions, as well as common sense, suggest that the United Kingdom is well out of it. If, on the other hand, the EU takes a different course and develops a "variable geometry" approach that allows members to participate in various EU aspects to their taste, and doesn't stand in the way of U.K. membership in NAFTA, then this would be a different and more viable EU. In effect, it would be an EU that has many of the attributes of a network commonwealth and can serve as a link among other network commonwealths. Reid Buckley, writing in *National Review*, raised the possibility of an Anglosphere-Hispanosphere joint free trade area including both Britain and Spain. Such a development would be entirely consistent with the logic of the network commonwealth approach.

A series of memos within the Blair cabinet, leaked to the press in July 2000, indicated that Blair had already decided, contrary to public statements, to move to deeper European integration and adoption of the European single currency.

Polls, however, showed that support for the euro and the EU in general had continued to fall in Britain to lower and lower levels. They also showed that the only argument that carries any weight with the British public is that Britain's EU membership makes Britain more attractive to American investment.

Blair began using such arguments heavily by mid-2000. Since that date, Gordon Brown, Blair's chancellor of the Exchequer, has raised periodically the concept of a U.S.-EU free trade agreement entirely eliminating industrial tariffs, to the horror of the Franco-German axis.

And thus the debate has begun. Increasingly, the idea of creating tighter cooperative institutions among the English-speaking nations is being seen by more and more people as being in all of our best interests. The sharp dividing line of the Cold War era between free and unfree nations no longer fits reality very well. Now there is a gradient of societies, as measured in the strength of their civil societies. The English-speaking nations are at one extreme of that gradient. This would seem to call for a set of wider spheres of cooperation, with the strongest civil societies in the innermost sphere and progressively looser cooperative institutions as one goes outward. Concepts such as linking the United Kingdom into NAFTA while retaining trade and cooperative links to the Continental European states, lead naturally toward a network commonwealth architecture—and serve to turn the EU itself more toward a network commonwealth-type structure, to the advantage of all, particularly the new entrants in Eastern Europe.

One of the signs of vigor in the debate is the multiplicity of approaches to intra-Anglosphere linkage now emerging. United Kingdom membership in NAFTA (or some other free trade arrangement with the United States and Canada) is, of course, only one path in one particular dimension—trade ties—of all the various strands that are binding the Anglosphere together. Such a scenario may come to pass in any of a number of scenarios; perhaps through British withdrawal from the EU, or perhaps through membership in NAFTA while challenging the validity of the Treaty of Rome strictures against such multiple affiliations. NAFTA membership has the merit of being understandable and simple. The NAFTA agreements already exist and can be studied and debated with certainty. Still other scenarios are possible, and given the dynamic trade environment, they may be the most appropriate ones by the time the issue will be acted upon.

For example, John Hulsman and Gerald O'Driscoll of the Heritage Foundation have proposed that the United States create a free trade area that would automatically be open to all nations that meet certain verifiable standards of democracy, openness, and lack of economic barriers. Members would agree to specific measures for tariff and trade-barrier eradication, but would be liable to no other obligations or controls. Their study makes it clear that almost every core Anglosphere nation would qualify immediately for membership, and many of the rest could with a

relatively minor amount of internal reform. In the long run, such a proposal might be more practical than a nation-by-nation negotiated entry
into NAFTA.

The fact that there would be no "Anglosphere" test as such for membership is no reason for Anglosphere advocates to reject such a proposal.
The concept of an Anglosphere Network Commonwealth is not based on
the idea of creating an English-speaking trade fortress or on keeping non-
English speakers out of Anglosphere institutions. An Anglosphere Network Commonwealth is a coalition of the willing; it is also a coalition of
the able. In other words, states that can tolerate free trade are welcome
within a free trade coalition. However, closer ties, such as a project for a
polycentric common-law regime or some of the sojourner arrangements
for free exchange of populations, may require the member nations to have
a common-law system or be characterized by widespread use of English
as a first or daily business language. The set of institutions that will, when
taken as a whole, define the Anglosphere will probably not have identical
member lists; it is certain that some of the members of each institution
may not all be English speaking.

Meanwhile, alternative visions of Anglosphere unity continue to
emerge, including radical approaches. In his 1999 book *Reflections on a
Ravaged Century*, the eminent British historian Robert Conquest wrote a
chapter discussing the increasing relevance of the mutual associations of
the English-speaking world, as opposed to the centralist model of the EU.
The chapter culminated in a call for an Association of English-Speaking
States; such an association could easily fit the definition of a network commonwealth as I have described it.

In April of the same year, English historian Paul Johnson published a
radical essay in *Forbes* magazine proposing that Britain, Canada, Australia, and New Zealand become states of the United States. His argument
was that these nations are the most natural partners for each other, far
more than the nations with whom they are currently allying themselves.
In particular, as an Englishman, Johnson sees his country's effective
choices as narrowing down to inclusion in an EU federal superstate, or
joining with the only other effective counterweight, the United States. Put
in those terms, it is clear that unification with the United States is the
preferable option.

Although I find such a proposal intriguing in an intellectual sense, I
suspect that to bring so many new states into the Union would alter it so
much, and require such radical decentralization, as to turn the United
States itself into a sort of network commonwealth. The political barriers to
such a solution would be formidable, particularly given issues such as the
fate of the monarchy in nations where, as in Britain, parts of Canada, and
New Zealand, it continues to play a significant emotional and cohesive

role. There is a substantial "Fifty-First State" literature in Canada, Britain, and Australia, mostly satirical, but a perusal of it indicates that the concept continues to have a certain persistent appeal in some quarters of those countries. It is also clear that most of these authors have no deep understanding of the American federal system and usually underestimate the amount of autonomy the Union would afford their nations. (Just as one example, there would be no barrier to Britain retaining its National Health Service (NHS) as a state-run program; it would actually gain economically by being reimbursed by the U.S. Medicare and Medicaid programs for care provided to the elderly, the disabled, and the poor, provided the NHS could pass an external audit to HCFA standards, which is not a foregone conclusion.) It might be interesting to perform a study of such issues as a thought experiment. Britain's place in the EU, and the relative merits of the various options, ranging from full immersion in a federal European state to withdrawal and non-EU alternatives such as NAFTA, have thus become hot topics of discussion.

However, all treatments of such options to date have tended to assume that whatever Britain's options were, they were essentially binary—either in the European Monetary Union (EMU) or out, either in a European federal state or not. But in reality, Britain's options do not divide this way. Britain's future must be seen as a range of options, divided into many overlapping categories. Furthermore, not all options become available at any one time—some require prior conditions that may or may not arise.

Rather than being presented as a pair of options, Britain's future should be seen as a decision tree or flowchart, with a number of branching options and critical decision points at different junctures.

In such a decision tree, it would be worth examining incorporation into the American Union, primarily because it is the symmetrical counterpart to incorporating Britain into a European federal union. That position has a number of prominent advocates in British politics. At a minimum, the British voter should be able to compare and contrast all the options. In such a range, it could be seen that an Anglosphere Network Commonwealth (which would be less binding than current EU membership), is not the opposite of Eurofederalism, but rather a moderate position. A network commonwealth arrangement would not be inconsistent with retaining continued cooperative ties with Europe.

All of these proposals continue to elevate the idea of ties among English-speaking nations as the natural evolution of international ties. None of them have taken into consideration, except in the most superficial fashion, the impact of the Information Revolution or of the changing nature of statehood. I believe that these trends, and the prospect of the network commonwealth, make the choices even clearer and easier. It is now evident that the states of Continental Europe are avoiding and resisting necessary fundamental choices regarding the direction of their societies and economies. The people of England have at least begun the process of change.

The people of Ireland believe, and the people of Scotland hope, that they can avoid these difficult choices. However, Ireland's current prosperity is based on an anomalous and advantageous arrangement with the EU which the nation's small size and previous poverty have allowed them to retain; the recent (as of May 1, 2004) and future contemplated entry of poorer states into the Union will erode their ability to sustain their advantageous situation. The startling and unpredicted referendum defeat of the Treaty of Nice in June 2001 by the Irish electorate may mark the first step in a new, realistic assessment of its situation.

The achievement of a devolved Scottish Authority has currently (as Blair had hoped) taken the wind out of the sails of the Scottish independence movement. Once free to orate on the hypothetical glories of Scottish independence, the Scottish Nationalist Party has become bogged down in the complex issues of day-to-day governance and in the process has lost some of its glamour in the eyes of Scottish voters. However, this process had happened long ago in Quebec without permanently extinguishing separatist sentiment. In both Scotland and Quebec, it retains the adherence of a core of voters, and may reemerge as political conditions continue to evolve. In both cases, the robustness of civil society in both Unions suggests that further decentralism, rather than formal independence, will be the ultimate development of these situations.

Similarly, the bloom is off the East Asian rose, and the Australians and New Zealanders who saw their future as lying in integration into that region may be having second thoughts; if not, they ought to. The implications of the impending implosion of the Indonesian state for Australia's security should increase even more the value of ties with the civilizational family to which they naturally belong. Certainly Australians noted that it was the United States, Britain, and Canada that joined them most promptly in committing forces to the Timor crisis in 1999.

Moreover, the Bali bombing by radical fundamentalists, aimed at both the non-Muslim Balinese and Australian tourists, was motivated by Indonesian resentment at Australian support for Timorese secession, a favorite cause of the Aussie Left. Those leftists have tended to view world politics as an essentially consequence-free arena for the outward projection of the drama of their inner convictions; some may yet deduce that their actions have consequences in the real world, some of which may require making choices among real-world options. Of these, support for the agenda of radical Islamism may not (as in Timor and Bali) bring the results they claim to desire.

Anglo-Canadians have grown increasingly tired of the never-ending drama of Canadian unity. They, too, have seen the increasing value of outside ties. At the same time, enough Anglo-Canadians fear submergence in the United States that they tend to oppose any deepening of the NAFTA structure. For them, a network commonwealth would restore the traditional balance between the American and Commonwealth poles of attraction. Ironically, bringing the United Kingdom or Australia and New Zealand into a network commonwealth would increase the ability of Canadians to accept closer cooperation with the United States, precisely because it would be placed in the context of a less one-sided relationship.

MOVING TOWARD AN ANGLOSPHERE NETWORK COMMONWEALTH

A network commonwealth emerges from perception of reality, awareness of opportunity, and demand for implementation. These are the tasks of any movement for a network commonwealth.

Perception of reality means that citizens of English-speaking nations must begin articulating what they already understand instinctively: that there tends to be more in common among themselves than among peoples of more disparate cultures. Awareness of opportunity comes when this perception of commonality is translated into specific opportunities for deeper cooperation among these nations, to their mutual advantage. Demand for implementation comes when awareness of opportunity leads to support for concrete moves to create formal common institutions, organizations, programs, and capabilities.

Thus, a movement for an Anglosphere Network Commonwealth begins by spreading public awareness of a positive alternative to current identities, policies, and solutions that have not retained their appeal. Having raised awareness, it proceeds by seeking particular problems, and movements to address those problems, and presenting specific alternatives based on the network commonwealth approach, at times when those alternatives are sought. It moves to implementation by serving as the seed crystal around which broader movements and institutions form. The sum of these institutions becomes the foundations of the actual network commonwealth.

DOING THEIR PART: LEADERSHIP AND THE EMERGENCE OF THE NETWORK COMMONWEALTH

Each nation in the Anglosphere has the capability of offering leadership toward the forging of a network commonwealth. The United States particularly is the magnet of the English-speaking world. An offer for sojourner status, more open markets, scientific and technical cooperation, and permanent security alliances on a strictly reciprocal basis, as part of a movement toward a network commonwealth, would give great impetus toward such a trend. Particular historic moments will offer themselves. At some point in the next five years, the United Kingdom must face a decision to integrate itself inextricably into a common European structure or to look outward again.

Britain joined in the first place because there appeared to be no equally attractive alternative. If by that time the concept of an Anglosphere Network Commonwealth had become established, it would have been a viable option for Britain, one that could be weighed and compared to the prospect of being forever the third-ranked entity in a European superstate. The willingness of Britain to move toward such an association would create a counterpart movement in the United States. The impetus toward association would then play its part in the calculations of the other nations as well.

It is not my intent to predict specific political events. Other crisis points in other nations may catalyze the motion—perhaps a secession crisis in Canada, perhaps a unity crisis in South Africa, or for that matter, in the United States. I speculate on the prospects for several such crises in the subsequent section, not as an attempt at a prophecy but to provide some scenarios for point of illustration. The task of a movement for a network commonwealth is to advance awareness, change categories of thinking, prepare private institutions, and put forward unique solutions. Typically, states do not undertake large changes in the absence of crisis. It is at the turning of eras, and in the crises that such times generate, that new paradigms come to the fore.

An Anglosphere Network Commonwealth can provide the needed alternative to supplant the functions of the economic state. The time for such entities is fading.

Emerging technologies, and the social changes and convergence they are driving, offer the possibility of creating something new and old, different yet familiar, as the next stage of evolution of the vigorous, dynamic, and freedom-seeking culture created by the English-speaking peoples.

DEVOLUTION AND THE NEVERENDUM
IN SCOTLAND AND QUEBEC

Canada and the United Kingdom both have substantial established secession movements. Quebec has already held two referenda on the matter (leading to the popular sobriquet "Neverendum"), in the most recent of which a majority of the approximately 80 percent of Quebecois who are ethnically French voted for secession.

Its secessionist government, subsequently reelected by a narrow margin, has vowed to reintroduce the referendum, though not immediately. If they live up to their promise, and the referendum were to succeed, problematic issues of subsecession and dissent will be opened by the English-speaking Quebeckers, and the Indian and Inuit (Eskimo) inhabitants of Quebec.

Scotland held its first Assembly elections in May 1999. Neither Labour nor the secessionist Scottish National Party (SNP) were able to gain a clear overall majority. The SNP had stated its explicit intent to call for a referendum on independence if it gains a majority. They have not backed down from this position. Although a dead letter at this moment, a secession referendum is possible within the coming decade, depending on events. Although it is highly unlikely that the government of the United Kingdom would resist a democratically decided Scottish independence by military force, the issue would not be as clear-cut as some imagine. There is some potential for subsecession (particularly in the Orkney and Shetland islands, with their distinct traditions, and claims to offshore resources which would compete with Scotland's), and likely, a substantial Unionist element who would push for a federative solution short of declaration of a stand-alone Scottish state.

The situation is further complicated by the underlying assumption of Scottish secessionists that England would remain a member of the EU after Scotland seceded. They count on the EU to provide a common stabilizing framework to mitigate many of the issues of secession. But as the 1999 European Parliament elections indicate, there is a strong streak of Euroskepticism in England, far stronger than in Scotland. Scotland's secession would strengthen both English nationalist sentiment and the Euroskeptic position in England.

These could well result in England's withdrawal, in turn, from the EU. The prospect of having to clear customs when crossing the Anglo-Scottish border might dampen enthusiasm for full Scottish independence.

Whether Quebec secedes or not, western Canada has a powerful impetus to secession. It will always be out-voted in the eastern provinces, whether Quebec is counted or not. Its economic models, orientations, and opportunities are different from those of eastern Canada and are often hindered by eastern domination.

The Canadian Supreme Court has decided that a province may, by holding that a democratically created mandate for secession, require the federal government to hold negotiations in good faith to such an end. This principle will be as binding for an Alberta voting to secede as it would for Quebec. Western secession, rather than Quebec's, may be the ultimate result of that decision and the parallel Clarity Act, by which the federal Parliament set forth a process for secession.

The issue of western Canadian secession and the wider issues of unity and secession in strong civil societies are interestingly illuminated by the evolution of Canada's political right over the past decade. The collapse of the Progressive Conservative Party in western Canada and its replacement there by the regionally based Reform Party was a classic example of the sort of breakdown of nationwide institutions that precedes civil crises.

Yet the next chapter, the forming of the Canadian Alliance between the western Reformers and a faction of dissatisfied Progressive Conservatives in eastern Canada, demonstrated the self-repairing aspect of civil society networks. In a society with weaker civil characteristics, the break in parties might have sparked an accelerating downward spiral of social fissures. Instead, compromise in pursuit of political viability began to knit the fabric together again. This in turn led to the subsequent development, the unification of the Progressive Conservative rump with the Canadian Alliance to form a new Conservative Party of Canada, spanning English-speaking Canada, and more competitive than any Right party since the late 1980s.

Given the self-repairing nature of civil societies, which militates against outright secession, there may be more of a focus on gaining "essential sovereignty"—autonomy on most or all major issues—than on outright independence for Scotland, Quebec, and other historically-submerged nations. This differs from the current levels of devolution gained by Scotland, for example, in that their powers would not be revocable at will by the higher level. Instead, sovereignty would be recognized at the national level (e.g., Scotland, Quebec, or even sovereign cantons at a more local level) and certain powers would be delegated to a federal or Union-level administration. Such "essentially sovereign" nations might even have independent international ties (as does Quebec today, and did Norway before its final independence from Sweden) and membership in international organizations.

Meanwhile, membership in external stabilizing frameworks could reassure antisecessionist minorities that they would not be abandoned to a hostile majority, and that their own rights of autonomy could not be summarily abandoned.

In fact, developments in the Canadian example have demonstrated the point that, faced with similar drivers for decentralism and secession, strong civil societies tend to bend and adapt, while political units with weak or nonexistent civil societies break apart. "Effective sovereignty" solutions are a means of achieving that flexibility.

Nevertheless, by forming a new party with ties across the Canadian Anglosphere, the Conservative Party of Canada has begun to create what has been missing in Canadian politics—the basis of an interlocutor for the Anglo-Canadian nation, capable of negotiating seriously with the Quebecois. The electoral logic of Canadian politics will tend to lead eventually to the possibility of a historic deal between such an interlocutor and Quebecois who have in past times supported separatists. The previously described "effective sovereignty" model would form a viable model for such a solution.*

Scottish politics since the inauguration of the devolved Assembly have likewise diminished the likelihood of outright independence for Scotland. Unlike the Canadian case, England has never denied that Scotland constitutes a "distinct society" within the Union. A more likely final outcome will be a further reworking of the Grand Union. The three-hundredth anniversary of the Treaty of Union in 2007 might be a suitable occasion for its inauguration.

AFRICAN AMERICA: THE STALLED
TRANSITION TO HIGH TRUST

In many respects, the African-American community is now at a crossroads. Many have the feeling that they have tried everything and nothing has worked. In the economic environment of the future, no solution depending primarily on the use of federal-level government to transfer substantial sums of money into their community, no matter what justification is offered, is likely to work. The community has played its electoral card over and over again for the Democratic Party, and the payback has been calculated by party leaders to a fine degree. That payback hasn't amounted to much, and the sum will more likely decline than increase.

A cultural-national analysis suggests an intermediate path that may place African Americans on the winning side of history for the first time since 1865.

Identity as a part of a distinct, historic cultural nation, one which has been a constituent part of the American Grand Union from the beginning, tells a story that is both distinctly African American and also truly American. The Anglosphere story is the final piece of the puzzle.

Some black nationalist narratives emphasize America, or European civilization generally, as a uniquely evil slaveholding culture. But this is disingenuous on several levels. Mediterranean civilization was the source of the Atlantic slave trade, and Brazil was the overwhelmingly central participant in that trade. If slavery were the source of American wealth, Brazil's wealth should greatly eclipse it.

---

* The June 2004 federal elections in Canada came near to such a possibility: no party won a majority, and the conservatives and Bloc Quebecois could almost jointly command a majority. Had the Liberals not gained a larger plurality, the temptation of a Tory-Bloc deal would have been strong.

The Anglosphere is the civilization that eradicated slavery in its home territory, and eventually worldwide. It is also the medium for linking African Americans with the other advanced African civilizations of the planet. The devolution of the American economic state into a federation of civic states built at more local levels provides scope for an African-American activism aimed at gaining essential sovereignty for its communities.

It may require the achievement of this essential sovereignty to permit the African-American community to complete the one task that will finally eradicate the legacy of slavery with its poverty and dysfunction. That is to complete the task of conversion of African America from a low-trust to a high-trust culture. Looking back on the writings of such disparate figures as Frederick Douglass, Booker T. Washington, Martin Luther King, and Malcolm X, it is clear that they all understood the distinction between low-trust and high-trust cultures. They understood that the conversion was both possible and essential in order to ensure the prosperity and rights of their community regardless of how it was defined.

In the past, this conversion was defined as "education," "uplift," "civilizing," "organization," or "awareness"—but deep down, it amounted to the same thing.

The debate between Washington and DuBois, for example, was essentially a foreshadowing of the "economics or politics" arguments about East Asian development—must economic development come before political democracy, or is political democracy an essential part of economic development? There are some interesting, unexplored parallels between the problems encountered by Southern (and particularly African-American) society during Reconstruction and the problems encountered by the newly free peoples of the former Soviet Union over the past decade. In each case, a people completely stripped of civil-society institutions was propelled into formal process democracy, while being forced to try to adapt outside models to fill the gap. In both cases, opportunists created corruption of a level that would have swamped substantially stronger civil-society institutions.

Over the succeeding century, recovering from the failure of Reconstruction, substantial parts of the African-American nation were able to create an authentic high-trust culture through their control of autonomous schools, universities, churches, businesses, unions, and political organizations—the stuff of civil society.

This achievement was endangered by loss of control of the national narratives, which began in the 1960s when outside forces—white liberal media and multiculturalist intellectuals—began glorifying the low-trust remnants in the African-American community at the expense of the natural high-trust leadership.

Primarily, this was because the high-trust leaders were too independent and were resistant to manipulation. Most African Americans do not yet understand how or why this happened.

Previously, I stated that the control of perception is essential in achieving political reform. The battle for completion of the historic task of converting the African-American cultural nation to a high-trust culture depends on recapturing control of the narratives of that nation. Currently, low-trust narratives promoted by white entertainment-company executives and neurotic Manhattanite intellectuals seeking the thrill of the exotic have crowded out the historic narratives of African-American cultural-national voices. The Information Revolution offers a possible means of undercutting this dominance by permitting independent entrepreneurs to promote a high-trust message with a cultural-national analysis, bypassing the established media. By adopting a Singularity strategy of promoting decentralism, essential sovereignty within a network commonwealth framework, and pursuit of high-trust cultural initiatives and narratives, African-American activists have the possibility of rejoining the winning side of history, aligning themselves with other decentralists, Singularity entrepreneurs, and the other high-trust nations of the Anglosphere. To date, this has not happened (to the extent that the Web and other alternative media have been used in the African-American community, it has been to promote marginalized conspiracy theories and other intellectual manifestations of alienation) but the potential is there. Sooner or later some young African Americans will start asking themselves where they can find a strategy that can actually deliver results.

Another model for the African-American task is the Meiji Revolution in Japan. After Japan was opened to the outside world, forward-thinking Japanese, led by the Meiji emperor, realized that they had to transform its unique culture to deal with the world challenge. They broke the power of their warlord class, and told the samurai warrior class to stop swaggering around making general nuisances of themselves, and to do something useful. The samurai responded by turning their energies to becoming the core of an entrepreneurial class which quickly transformed Japan into the world's first modern, non-Western world power. A "Meiji Revolution" for African America would break the power of its drug lord and corrupt city boss classes and force its would-be warriors to put down their guns and turn their energy and attention toward economic development, while telling their hip-hop praise-singers to turn their considerable talents toward generating positive narratives.

PROSPECTS FOR THE ANGLOSPHERE

Visualize the Anglosphere nations as a series of adjacent fields, and see the network commonwealth concepts and incipient institutions as seeds broadcast into all of the fields. As they are cast, we cannot tell which ones will take root and grow.

But we know that where they do take root, they will propagate further, spreading new seeds into the neighboring fields, sooner or later to blossom in them all.

The following discussions are presented within a time frame of approximately twenty years. I expect that a network commonwealth may have emerged by the end of that period. This was not an arbitrary choice. It is the span of one generation. Within that time, baby boomers (having matured subsequent to the high-water mark of the United States and United Kingdom as economic states in World War II) will have been the dominant generation holding political and economic power. The next one, the "X" generation, will be in the middle ranks of society and on the threshold of power, and the generation now in school (the first generation to have grown up on the Internet) will be in the universities and creating the ferment in arts and software. (Such generational patterns of response are explored at length by William Strauss and Neil Howe in their book *Generations* [1991]. This work lays out a somewhat deterministic but interesting theory of generational patterns in Anglo-American politics.)

The following section discusses the prospects for movement toward a network commonwealth solution in the principal nations of the Anglosphere, considering the various civic-state issues of identity, nationhood, devolution, international affiliation, and economic drivers of the beginning of the Singularity era. It is a snapshot of some of the major issues that may give rise to movement toward the solutions presented in this book.

CANADA AND *LE PROJET TRUDEAU*

Canada, of all the states in the Anglosphere, is closest to the crisis point of its identity issue. It has had substantial identity issues throughout its history, and these have been aggravated by its division among French-speaking, English-speaking, and other populations; by its small population spread out over an enormous physical distance; and by its proximity to a much larger, economically more dynamic English-speaking state. In recent times, the limited cohesion of the Canadian polity has begun to diminish even further.

In the mid-1960s, Canada committed itself to what we may call the Trudeauvean project—the search for a distinctively Canadian identity and national symbolism which would be neither English nor French, dependent on neither the United States nor the United Kingdom, and acceptable to all Canadians. The shock of the October 1970 kidnapping and murders of then-British trade commissioner James Cross and then-vice premier of Quebec and minister of labor Pierre Laporte caused many

Canadians to regard the status quo as unsustainable, and led them to lend at least tacit acquiescence to the project.

The project was successful in a negative sense. It deconstructed the existing Canadian identity—the Anglo-Canadian dominated nation-state with its Union Jack-based flag, the Anglo-triumphalist "Maple Leaf Forever" and its narrative starting with Major General James Wolfe on the Plains of Abraham and running through Vimy, Dieppe, the corvettes of the Battle of the Atlantic, and D-Day. It failed, however, to create a new Canadian identity that summoned a common emotional space shared by a strong majority of English and French Canadians alike.

Pierre Trudeau did not seem to realize that you cannot commission a national identity from an advertising agency, nor that devotion to the universalist values of the United Nations is thin gruel for a people raised on the traditions and history of the English-speaking people. If there were such a thing as "universal meta-class values," as some observers contemplate, Trudeauvean Canada would be the closest thing to a state attempting to use such as its binding values. The results have not been overwhelmingly impressive. Rather than the basis of a coherent nation-state, the officially sanctioned Canadian nationality has all of the distinctiveness of an airport transit lounge, with snow.

The Trudeauvean project started when Quebecois independence was a mere fringe movement; after thirty-five years, it has come to the point where a majority of ethnic Quebecois voted for secession. Secession may come, or, more likely, an essentially sovereign solution may prevail in the end. However, the Trudeauvean project will have failed. English-speaking Canadians will be seeking a redefined identity again in the wake of that failure. Today, Canada faces devolutionary pressures with a variety of drivers. The following are the most prominent:

- Taxation and competitiveness pressures. The international economy is already creating strong pressures on the high Canadian tax rates, as smart young Canadians move to other parts of the Anglosphere. Exacerbating this is the growth of a world-connected entrepreneurial sector in British Columbia and other parts of the west, which can most easily flee from high taxation.

  There will be greater pressure to tax western natural resources further to pay for eastern social services, with greater resistance on the part of the west. Hydro-Quebec's James Bay projects (on Cree Indian lands), a major revenue producer for that province, will become one of its more reliable sources in the future, which will make Cree Indian threats of counter secession from Quebec economically sensitive.
- Multiculturalism and native autonomy. Canada has gone further down the path of multiculturalist deconstruction of national identity

than has the United States or Britain. Yet it is subject to the same relentless demographic and economic forces that are eradicating the
closed communities on which multiculturalist political structures
seek to base their power. At the same time, a strange version of the
concept of aboriginal autonomy has given Canadian Indian tribes
rather more autonomy than their American counterparts, while continuing to funnel public goods into them in the form of welfare and
development funding.

As noted previously, sovereignty for aboriginal communities can
be a long-term solution only if those communities develop more
high-trust cultural forms.

Canada's current system works against such transformations, and
thus works against genuine long-term sovereignty for aboriginals
and creates an ongoing irritation to the general body politic.

- The next Quebec referendum. Until a stable, long-term resolution of the
Quebec issue is achieved, it will overhang Canadian politics and the
Canadian state. The threat of secession has not gone away but has
merely exhausted itself for a while. Canada already has paid higher
rates on its government securities than it otherwise would because of
the uncertainty factor. These uncertainties leave unclear important issues such as the formulas for splitting the debt in the event of secession.

From this perspective, separation would be preferable to a never-
ending uncertainty, as it would then permit each part to make firm
plans and finance them over the long term.

On the other hand, other secession-related issues, such as subsecession within Quebec by English-speaking or aboriginal communities, will not be resolvable with simplistic formulas. In the end,
there is a bias toward reverting to the status quo. The issues involved
in dividing an advanced and complex civil society like Canada are
far more complex than those of dividing a less complex (because of
the suppression of civil society under Communism) society such as
the former Czechoslovakia. Thus, in the long run, the solution that
deals with the greatest number of valid secessionist concerns without
actually requiring secession may prove to be the most attractive.

QUEBEC AND THE NINE PROVINCES:
TWO NATIONS AND TWO NETWORK CIVILIZATIONS

Paradoxically, the growth of a strong Anglophone Canadian identity
(emphasizing current English-speaking orientation, rather than British-
Isles origin) is probably the key to a successful negotiation of an
essential-sovereignty solution for Quebec and the rest of Canada. If the
"nine provinces" (a more elegant term than ROC, as in the "rest of

Canada") regain a sense of their own identity as a distinct cultural nation of the Anglosphere, they will also gain the self-confidence to negotiate an essential-sovereignty deal with Quebec with which both parties can live permanently. Part of this self-confidence must come from a
difference in attitude from the past—one that says, "We can be happy
with a mutually acceptable formula, or we can be happy as an independent nation of the Anglosphere." A certain class of Anglo-Canadian
has always worried that without Quebec, there is no justification for
Canadian nationhood. In fact, Anglo-Canada is a distinct cultural nation of the Anglosphere and has as much justification for independence
from the United States as does New Zealand from Australia (or conversely, as much justification for a movement toward a union of the two
nations). Anglosphere institutions would give Anglo-Canada almost all
of the economic benefits it might derive from union with the United
States, with almost none of the costs. Thus an Anglosphere identity for
the nine provinces, and immersion into the emerging Anglosphere institutions, could actually become the key to a workable solution with
Quebec.

This involves a return to the so-called Two Nations analysis, which, although discredited among Canadian intellectuals, does have the merit of
being true. An Anglosphere Network Commonwealth could provide the
external stabilizing framework for an Anglo-Canadian political entity
based on the nine provinces and the autonomous English-speaking communities within Quebec. An essentially sovereign Quebec, plus the autonomous French-speaking communities within the nine provinces, could
readily belong to many of the common economic structures of the Anglosphere, along with many of the cultural structures of the emerging
Francosphere.

The nettle the Anglo-Canadians must grasp is the relinquishing of the
Trudeauvean vision. The nettle the Quebecois must grasp is the relinquishing of the French Republican model of the unitary, centralized state.
Instead, they should look to a more successful, prosperous, and freer
Francophone state in Europe: Switzerland. Reconstructing Quebec on a
Swiss confederal model, thus permitting English-speaking areas (or Cree-
speaking areas) to become highly autonomous cantons with their own external links, would release the Anglophone residents of Quebec from their
roles as hostages to the Trudeauvean model of Canada and status as per-
petual clients of the Liberal Party. A convincing commitment to this model
could detach enough Anglophone votes to put an appropriately crafted
sovereignty initiative over the top at the polls. Interestingly enough, Quebec is in many ways a stronger civil society, with a more dynamic entrepreneurial sector, than France. An essentially sovereign Quebec, recon-
structed on a Swiss model and affiliated with both Anglosphere and
Francosphere institutions, might emerge as a pole of dynamism within

the Francosphere and an important link between the two network civilizations.

BRITAIN: SCOTLAND AND THE WEST LOTHIAN QUESTION; THE EURO AND THE WESTPHALIAN QUESTION

Although most are accustomed to thinking of England, the United Kingdom, and Britain in almost interchangeable terms, they are quite distinct entities. England is a twelve-hundred-year-old kingdom with enormous cultural coherence. Britain is an island comprising three distinct nations with substantially separate identities.

The United Kingdom is a hybrid quasi-federal state (including part of Ireland) only a little older than the United States, which will see its three-hundredth birthday in 2007. As discussed previously, the United Kingdom, as a political state, has intermittently had substantial coherence problems, and the last intra-Anglosphere war developed over one of the weaker compositional elements that had never been adequately resolved, namely Ireland. Furthermore, inadequacies in the resolution of that conflict have led to renewed stress on the unity of the United Kingdom, both in the continued Unionist-Nationalist impasse in Northern Ireland and the example of Irish independence for Scotland and Wales.

These strains have been increasing, with the resultant loss of coherence in the United Kingdom becoming increasingly visible over the past decade, just as the post-September 11 events in the United Kingdom also demonstrated the weakening of coherence via the multiculturalist narrative as homegrown radical fundamentalists rejected allegiance to the British political community. Effects of the emerging information economy will exacerbate those trends as pressures on cross-regional and cross-generational subsidies grow greater. As such pressures grow, political leaders in the United Kingdom will face the choice of further integration into EU institutions designed to shore up state control over the economy, like tax, pension, and currency-control harmonization. Alternatively, they will adopt a strategy of adapting to the information economy, which will create new stresses on the now-problematical consensus for membership in the EMU and the EU.

The election of a Scottish Assembly in 1999 and the promise by the Blair government of a referendum on entry into the EMU* have created two starting points for further compositional crises in the United Kingdom. Since the beginning of the Scottish Home Rule debate, the "West Lothian Question" has become a staple issue. If voters in the Scottish district of

---

* And, as of spring 2004, the prospect of a referendum on the new, even more centralizing European Constitutional draft.

West Lothian can vote on Scottish issues through home rule, in which English voters have no say, why then do they have the right, through their expanded Labour majority in the U.K. House of Commons, to affect the vote on English domestic issues? In other words, if Scotland has home rule, why not England? And what then becomes the province of the Union Parliament, and what of the national parliaments?

The EMU creates an even more problematic "Westphalian question": all citizens of the United Kingdom would be profoundly affected by membership in the EMU, which centralizes the making of monetary policy in the European Central Bank in Westphalia. Thus, the referendum on joining the EMU, assuming it ever happens, becomes critical to the future of all Britons. (Heavy anti-EMU majorities in polls have led Blair to postpone the referendum for one Parliament's life, and likely another as well.) What happens if, as it may well, England votes against membership by a thin majority, while Scotland produces a sufficiently strong majority for membership that their vote pushes Britain into the "yes" column? This would be perceived as "Scotland forcing England to join EMU"—a move that would be particularly resented after Scotland acquired autonomy for its own affairs.

These issues would also be played out against an economic background in which England's booming information economy, increasingly tied to that of the United States, becomes threatened by EU "harmonization" policies on taxation, regulation, and employment. These have already destroyed England's industries in areas such as art sales (which moved en masse to New York when the United Kingdom was forced to raise its value-added taxes on art sales to uncompetitive levels). Meanwhile, Scotland, more oriented to old Machine Age industries that pin their hopes on EU protectionist and cross-subsidy measures, feels that they have less to lose and more to gain from EU and EMU membership.

Furthermore, the European question must be examined in light of recent British political developments. There has been a sea-change in British politics within just the last few years, one which raises the prospect of network commonwealth solutions as an item on the British political agenda within the next few years. As such, it is worth examining in some detail. It has begun with the question of an outward orientation as an alternative to British membership in the EU exclusive to other relationships, a debate that has now begun in earnest. Other issues, such as international defense-industry mergers, will drive the changes as well.

The sea-change began to work primarily after Blair's electoral landslide in 1997. Blair immediately moved to ratify the EU "Social Chapter," which committed the British to a more Continental, interventionist role in the workplace and community. He also placed membership in the EMU on the agenda, although, since it would require a national referendum to implement the change, he did not put replacing the pound with the euro at the top of his list of priorities.

The adoption of the euro would have more than economic significance. Once adopted, it would become extremely difficult for Britain ever to effectively withdraw from, or substantially alter its relations with, the EU. Membership in EMU would be the true, probably irreversible commitment to the immersion of Britain in a European political system.

The more Conservatives came to realize this, the more uncomfortable they became. John Major, the last Tory prime minister, had after all led Britain into the Maastricht Treaty, which turned the European Community into the EU, and accelerated its progress from an economic community to a quasi-federal European state. The concessions he had obtained from Brussels in return have turned out to be, for the most part, dead letters. However, under Blair they saw that, far from guaranteeing that Britain could never fall into the hard-Left socialism of Old Labour, it was locking Britain into the Third Way interventionism of New Labour—and that the Third Way was taking an increasingly Continental flavor.

When Tory leadership passed to William Hague after the 1997 electoral debacle, the old Europhile Tory faction, which had fallen out of touch with the sentiments of the party rank-and-file, began to be eclipsed by the younger, rising, new Euroskeptic contingent. Soon outright advocacy of EMU membership became a marginal position in the party. As a result, the Tories entered the 1999 EuroParliament elections with a strongly skeptical message about entry into EMU, although not openly rejectionist. It advocated waiting through the then-current parliament and the next before considering a referendum to join EMU—dubbed the "wait and see" position. Blair's position was pro-euro in tone but more cautious in actual fact—creating five "economic tests" which the euro would have to pass before Labour would move to a vote on adopting it. Britain's third party, the Liberal Democrats, had an enthusiastically Eurofederalist leadership and went in with a "join immediately" stance.

Three novelties marked these EuroParliament elections: the first, a change from "first-past-the-post" (simple plurality vote) elections to proportional representation by party list. The second, the creation of the "Pro-Euro Conservative Party" by renegade Europhile Tories, which fielded candidates for every seat at stake, a number being high-profile Conservative figures. Third, the fielding of a strong slate by the United Kingdom Independence Party (UKIP), a relatively new minor party whose platform is unconditional and full withdrawal from the EU.

Throughout the campaign, marked by a vigorous assault on euro-phoria by Hague and a lackluster, distracted defense by Blair, media-driven expectations forecast a diminished margin of victory for Labour and some Conservative gains, tempered by the possible defection of substantial segments of the Tory vote to the Pro-Euro Conservatives. If the Pro-Euro Conservatives gained a substantial fraction of the vote, pro-euro elements in the Tories could then ask for Hague's head on a platter, and return the party to Europhile leadership. Substantial press attention was lavished on the Pro-Euro Conservatives; the UKIP gained relatively little press, and what was given to it concentrated on the issue of how much of the anti-euro Tory vote would be split off.

The results confounded the pundits. The Tories defeated Labour decisively—the only Tory victory in a long string of defeats both before and after that occasion. The UKIP won 3 seats of the 87 at stake (with the anti-euro Greens winning another; firsts for both parties). And most telling, there was a complete shutout for the Pro-Euro Conservatives: approximately 2 percent of the vote nationwide (compared to 6 percent for the UKIP) and no seats whatsoever, despite their lavish media attention. Following the defeat of Europhile Kenneth Clarke in the 2001 Tory leadership race by Euroskeptic Iain Duncan Smith, the bulk of the pro-euro Tory rump joined the Liberal Democrats. An analysis of the election returns shows that the new change is not merely a matter of shifts within the Tory Party. The Tory vote seemed to consist of the loyal Tory core—few defected to either the UKIP or the Pro-Euro Conservatives, and a respectable percentage turned out, but relatively few voters from other parties crossed over to them. The poor Labour showing reflected not a defection from Labour ranks to Tories, but abstention—the great bulk of Labour loyalists stayed home or went fishing. One of the most interesting bits of analysis indicated that much of the UKIP vote came not from hardcore Tories, but from dissatisfied Liberal Democrats, particularly in the districts that elected their three members of the European Parliament.

This indicated that, rather than British opposition to the EU being limited to hard-core remnant Tory Colonel Blimps, it is in fact an underrepresented and growing sentiment, and that only a deep dislike of the Tories by many British voters prevents it from being expressed more strongly. If the sea-change spreads, it will take the form of more voters abandoning the leaderships of the Liberal Democrats and Labour, not necessarily for the Conservatives, but for whoever can offer a newer, positive paradigm beyond the now-almost-forgotten Third Way. Ideas have only a limited time on the public stage once they take power; if they do not catch fire, they can quickly be replaced by a newer one that does.

Since 1997, the political climate of Britain as a whole does indeed seem to have undergone a sea-change. After the EuroParliament elections, Blair tempered his Europhile rhetoric carefully, calling immediate entry into the EMU "daft." The New Euroskepticism has gained in respectability, shifting the ground of the debate gradually but significantly. Entry into EMU is no longer assumed by most to be "just a matter of time." "Renegotiation" of Britain's terms of membership in the EU has entered the arena of serious debate, despite Blair's attempts to characterize it as extreme. However, as leaked Blair memos indicate, this change is entirely tactical: Blair remains committed to bringing Britain, or at least himself, to the "heart of Europe."

The 2001 national elections further demonstrated the degree of this sea-change.

Although a near record-low turnout produced very little change in the Parliamentary seat totals, polling information revealed that the Tory Euroskeptic stance was not only in tune with the voters' attitudes, it was the only major issue in which this was the case. Unfortunately for the Tories, the voters placed other issues higher on their list of concerns, while Blair's charisma, still untainted by scandal, policy failures, and internal rebellion, outshone Hague's clever but still-green style. Following the election, Tory Europhile Kenneth Clarke was defeated for the party leadership by Euroskeptic Iain Duncan Smith.

However, the subsequent period, from autumn 2001 to the end of 2003, saw a complex further shift in British politics, and the consequent decline of Tony Blair's unchallenged command of Labour, without any marked improvement in Tory fortunes. Blair's government began to suffer from a failure to deliver on their original promise of reform of economic-state services, and from the continuing overhang of the Euro referendum issue. September 11, and the run-up to the Iraq war, with the contentious issue of Iraq's weapons programs and Blair's problematic representation of their status on less-than-certain (and in retrospect, inaccurate) intelligence, all combined to leave Blair in a state in which it is "never glad confident morning again." The new and growing issue of the proposed European Constitution, which would, if implemented, take Europe and Britain much further down the federal state road, has provided yet another focus for Euroskeptic efforts.

Given this much dissatisfaction with Blair, the failure of the Tories to make headway under Duncan Smith's leadership provoked the unusual step of a challenge to his leadership even though he had not had the electoral turn at bat that tradition required. In a remarkably uncontested process, former home secretary Michael Howard, a moderate Euroskeptic but not a Maastricht rebel, was elevated to the leadership. As a result, the Tories have finally regained basic credibility as a government-in-waiting.

This sea-change in the British political setup has proceeded in parallel with a broader sea-change in the social landscape of England. The old remnants of the preindustrial, country, agricultural England—the archetypal Tory England—have continued to dwindle under the pressures of agricultural disemployment, suburbanism and rural second homes. But at the same time, the century-and-a-half-old Britain of mine and factory, terrace houses, union locals, and brass bands—the archetypal Labour Britain—is dwindling as well. In its place is the next instantiation of the Anglosphere in the Isles, largely invisible to tourists, who seek the quaint and medieval, or to visiting politicians and journalists, who tend to visit the centers of political and media power in the old urban center of London. This new England (these tendencies are observable in Wales and Scotland as well, but they are most advanced in southern and midland England) is an ex-urban culture articulated in urbanized clusters along the motorways in office parks, university centers, and quasi-rural market towns now become neither independent town nor commuting suburb, but rather nodes in a networked information production system thoroughly integrated into both the Anglosphere and the broader global economy. This new emerging system is middle class, cosmopolitan, multiethnic, well-educated, entrepreneurial, meritocratic and oriented to an equality of opportunity rather than an equality of results. Yet at the same time it continues to display the long-standing Anglosphere cultural traits, such as preferring to live in nuclear families (now adjusted to the needs of women working in the market economy), owner-occupied single-family homes with gardens, individual automobile transportation, and access to open space, preferably in a rural second home. In all of these things the English continue to be less like the Continental Europeans and more like the rest of the Anglosphere, insofar as the specific circumstances of their high-population-density island permits it.

The political loyalties of this new England are up for grabs. Frankly, none of the traditional messages of the existing political parties are automatically attractive to these people. Blair's New Labour was an attempt to move the party away from the mine-and-mill culture of its roots to appeal to this third England. Although at first electorally successful in this attempt, his government has failed to deliver the pragmatic results needed to retain their loyalties. The Liberal Democrats have done well to date because their narrative appeals to their meritocratic and cosmopolitan values, but they have fatally tied their concept of modernity to the Europeanist narrative; as the luster of that dream fades daily, that policy risks becoming more of a boat anchor around their necks, than a balloon to give them lift. Finally, the Tories have not devised a policy approach that appeals to this population while retaining the loyalties of their traditional base (a problem already frustrating Labour), although the outlines of such a policy can already be discerned in the quasi libertarian, moderately Euroskeptic stances of younger, up-and-coming Tories like Oliver Letwin and Liam Fox.

As part of the process of appealing to the newer emerging England, a new approach to Europe and Britain's external orientations must be presented by one or more of the parties. Gradually, it will be seen that Anglosphere ties and European ties are not two drastically opposed options, but rather various points on a continuum of possibilities. To renegotiate or redefine ties with Europe is to automatically open the prospect of further Anglosphere ties as part of the counterbalancing mix.

THE UNITED STATES AND THE ANGLOSPHERE: FROM POST–COLD WAR REORIENTATION TO THE CHALLENGE OF THE SINGULARITY

The change in British attitudes toward the EU invites consideration of the prospects for the Anglo-American political scene as a whole—that unique, mutually influential, twin-planet system. There is a possibility of a sea-change in America's foreign-policy orientation as well. Of what might it consist?

The developments in Britain suggest a direction. The integration of the United Kingdom into a united European structure has been part of a larger strategy promoted by the United States throughout the Cold War era. This strategy was aimed primarily at containment, and eventually defeat, of the Soviet Union and the Communist system; all other considerations were secondary. An integral part of that strategy was the creation of a structure of linked alliances with the United States at their head. There would also be an international fiscal and trade order designed to maximize general prosperity and minimize trade friction through advocacy of free trade, macroeconomic reform, and creation of regional single markets.

Throughout this period, Western Europe was the model and primary focus of such energies; first, because it was the primary target of the Soviet Union, and second, because it was the largest economic area on the planet outside the United States. NATO and the European Community were promoted as the primary mechanisms for the achievement of these goals. All other systems were in some way imitations of these models. The Cold War gave these alliances focus and motivation, but it also led to a lowest-common-denominator attitude toward alliances. At first, opposition to the Soviets was qualification enough to become an ally. Even NATO, the crown jewel of our alliance structure, at first contained Portugal and Turkey when those nations were under rather authoritarian rule.

Eventually, a minimal level of process democracy became a requirement for NATO membership. By the mid-1970s, NATO membership had become a tool for aiding the transition from authoritarian to democratic rule, as in the case of Spain and Greece. This succeeded so well that it became the model and much of the justification for NATO's eastward expansion. Once aimed at defeating the totalitarian at the gates, NATO is now primarily justified by its utility for suppressing the authoritarian within the gates.

But just as NATO accepted a lowest-common-denominator definition of democracy, the EU came to be constructed around a lowest-common-denominator definition of the market economy. This was to be expected when the "social market economy" of Germany and the dirigiste French economy were the core economies of the Common Market. The United States has spent the last fifty years pushing Britain into a united Europe in the hope that Britain would be an advocate for American causes and American values. Later, after the Thatcher reforms, Americans (and the beleaguered Continental market liberals) hoped that British participation would help turn the Continent toward a more flexible, less-regulated economic model.

By this hope, Americans were returning the favor Kipling rendered in writing "The White Man's Burden." A century ago, the bard urged Americans to enter the world of colonialism in the Philippines in order to uplift the natives, the "lesser breeds without the Law."* In return, Americans have been urging the British deeper and deeper into the European federal structure in the hopes of bringing Thatcherite enlightenment to the "European Social Model."

The experiences of the Afghan and Iraqi wars are causing Americans to take a fresh look at their foreign policy. They have begun to ask whether the multilateral alliance structures erected during the Cold War still make sense in their current forms. In answering this, it would be useful to consider the viewpoint of the New Euroskepticism flowing from across the Atlantic. The enlarged NATO, with its increasingly problematic decision-making structure, may soon no longer be seen as the central, core alliance in America's security architecture. The experience of the Kosovo war, with its delicately negotiated compromises whose limits on military actions frustrated military leaders enormously, contributed in the end to the Anglo-American decisions to avoid NATO structures in the opening of the Afghan war; although it subsequently became useful in the rebuilding of that country once liberated. Use of NATO in Iraq was not even an option, even though that country bordered on the territory of a NATO member. This set of experiences cannot but deter policymakers from using NATO as the principal vehicle for certain sets of post–Cold War tasks, particularly ones in which there is a large value gap between Anglosphere and Continental European nations on approaches.

---

* Given this, it is ironic and amusing that many Kipling scholars believe that "lesser breeds" was a reference to the Germans.

It would make more sense to define a tighter, closer set of alliances and trade agreements, based on a higher degree of sharing of common institutions, outlooks, and national profiles—the network commonwealth model. The nature of the Iraqi war coalition foreshadows the likely composition of such an alignment. In this model, NATO would continue to be important. It would be seen as perhaps the second circle of a series of concentric rings of alliances defined in terms of closeness of outlook and institutions rather than on the ordering of commitments we have inherited from Cold War history. From the experience of Eastern Europe and the states of the former Soviet Union, we have begun to understand that we can't expect too much too soon from economies such as Russia's until their structures of civil society can be strengthened. Perhaps the United States should not expect as much from unreformed Continental economies as we do from English-speaking nations, and base our trade and defense strategy on that assessment.

This New Euroskepticism applied to U.S. thinking would require reconsideration of our encouragement of British participation in the European federal project, and in the "European pillar" of NATO. James Thompson, president of the Rand Corporation, observed even before September 11 and its consequential wars the growing gap between the military structures of Europe and the United States. He noted that European forces have fallen behind in spending per soldier to the point where this gap "has left European military forces at least a technological generation behind the United States." However, he goes on to add, "Britain is the exception that proves the rule. . . . Although her forces are small, they are able to operate side by side with American forces." (The Afghan and Iraqi experiences only reinforced the fundamental validity of this observation.) This reality proves the rule in the original sense of that phrase—it tests it. And in this case, what it demonstrates is that thinking of Britain as a "European" state is out of date.

In trade, the New Euroskepticism would consider a radical step that would electrify British politics. The problem with this debate has been the lack of concrete alternatives. As William Rees-Mogg, writing in the (London) *Times* observed, people like to vote "Yes." So long as the argument has been "Shall we participate in the European Union, or stay out?" it has been possible for Europhiles to characterize the "No" party as backward-looking reactionaries who will cause Britain to miss out on an opportunity. An active offer of some form of free trade affiliation from an American president would create a simple two-column comparison table—North Atlantic trade versus the EU. North Atlantic trade will likely look very attractive in comparison, particularly since, in reality, accelerated North Americans integration would not require Britain to forego much if any of its European business.

Beyond Britain, the Anglosphere strategy promises to place U.S.-Canadian, U.S.-Australian, U.S.-South African, and eventually possibly U.S.-Indian relations on a new and refreshed basis, for similar reasons.

Retreating from the no-longer-serviceable vision of a broad but shallow Cold War coalition, the Anglosphere concept emerges as the only post–Cold War strategy (and even more, pre-Singularity strategy) that can serve to redefine alliances and interests on a long-term sustainable basis.

SOUTH AFRICA: WHAT FORM OF UNION?

South Africa is one of the greatest challenges and the greatest opportunities in the building of an Anglosphere Network Commonwealth. It is the greatest challenge because of its history of conquest and strife, and the resultant complexity of its interethnic relationships. It is further challenged by the great poverty of the majority of its population, in sharp contrast to the wealth of its white minority. Its opportunity comes from the fact that it is a culture in flux, one that includes both a substantial home-English-speaking population and a larger one for whom English is their language of wider communication. It has a small but competent high-tech sector (developed during the sanctions era and now finding outside markets) that could be the platform for South Africa's entry into the Singularity economy. It is also a state whose political and economic future is in a great state of uncertainty, and one in which external ties offer the possibility of solution to its principal political and economic dilemmas.

Politically, South Africa's problem is to maintain domestic conditions sufficient to keep white South Africans living in South Africa and continuing their contributions to the national economy, while delivering a rapid and substantial improvement in the standard of living for the black population. Also required are the integration of educated blacks into its political, military, and commercial structures on a basis of equality. South Africa must prevent any major sector of the population from becoming so dissatisfied with the outcome that it supports political or military activities sufficient to destabilize the regime.

Economic growth cannot be maintained without the continued involvement of the white minority or without a domestic environment sufficiently stable to attract foreign investment. On top of this basic conundrum, the government must deal with the substantial rivalries and distrust between the various tribal groups and nationalities. Disintegration of the state into tribal-based entities is an ever-present possibility.

What an Anglosphere Network Commonwealth could offer South Africa is a set of international ties sufficient to calm the political and economic fears of the white minority, while expanding the economic opportunities for both black and white South Africans more rapidly than the purely domestic economy could support.

Immersion into an Internet economy defuses the integration issues of the upper strata of South Africa's limited industrial base by offering ambitious young South Africans of all colors economic opportunities outside of the traditional arenas.

Additionally, security ties between South Africa and the United States, as part of a pan-Anglosphere security organization, link the South African military.

As part of an Anglosphere strategy, South Africa would also be advised to go with the currents of Singularity economics and radically decentralize the South African federal state. With a highly diverse population and with many of the population groups at radically different levels of trust and strength of civil society, South Africa should follow the Swiss strategy of leaving relatively few public goods as prizes for low-trust groups to contend over. The government must also provide substantial autonomy for the higher-trust communities. The names and symbols of each community should be permitted to remain intact as a symbol of such autonomy. Essential sovereignty of such communities might be combined with the ability of some communities to develop stronger Anglosphere ties (and with network commonwealths of other civilizations as they emerge) than the federal state at large. One project worth contemplating is the adoption of common law in some of the communities, particularly those with a strong British Isles component, to replace the apartheid-era Roman-Dutch law. This would permit those communities to participate in the pan-common-law-based institutions as they emerge.

Such a solution would also permit South Africa to gradually expand its communal ties, as a number of its neighbors (particularly those with ethnic ties to existing South African groups) may choose to join such a decentralized federation.

AUSTRALIA AND NEW ZEALAND: IDENTITY IN OCEANIA

Australia and New Zealand have been searching for a satisfactory national identity since World War II, when it became apparent that imperial and Commonwealth ties alone were inadequate to guarantee the security of the island-continent against any powerful modern Asian state. To the extent that those ties resulted in deploying Australian and New Zealand military strength to North Africa, they actually weakened the security of those states. Rather than relying on imperial authorities in London to negotiate American aid in their behalf, Australians began a direct relationship with the United States.

The need to create and maintain this relationship naturally began to enhance the separation of Australian and British interests. Few have sufficiently appreciated the extent to which Australian pressure was responsible for Lyndon Johnson's decision to commit the United States to the Vietnam War. The U.S.-Australian-New Zealand alliance in that war, combined with British reluctance to openly support that effort, weaned Australia away from Britain even more. (The fact that many Britons fought in Vietnam in Australian and New Zealand uniforms served to emphasize that alienation rather than counter it, as that aspect of inter-Anglosphere cooperation remained invisible.)

The severing of Britain's economic ties with its Commonwealth partners as a price of European entry further strained those relationships. Today, Germans arriving at London's Heathrow airport breeze through the domestic arrivals line, while Australians who fought against the Germans at El Alamein for Britain's sake wait in the foreigners' line with the Japanese. As many Australians noted during the 1999 Monarchy referendum, "There were no bloody queues at Gallipoli; no bloody queues at Alamein."

After Vietnam, Australia, and to a lesser extent New Zealand, began a process of searching for national identity and a weakening of political ties to both the United States and the United Kingdom. The failure of empire and Commonwealth as effective primary identities led to the drive to create nation-state identities

This effort was similar to the Trudeauvean Project in Canada, but without the major driver of one-third of the nation potentially harboring separatist sentiments.

The Australian project has centered on three items. These included pursuit (partly successful) of closer trade, immigration, and political ties with Asia; searching for "native" identities and symbolism to replace the inherited imperial identities and symbolism, most dramatically, in the move toward a republican constitution. The rejection of that proposition in the 1999 referendum demonstrated not any overwhelming fondness for the monarchy on the part of Australians, but rather a growing distrust of "Chardonnay-sipping yuppies." This semimythic group was widely perceived as the driving force behind the rejection of Australia's inherited narratives of convicts, immigrants, and British identity in favor of a romanticization of the Aboriginal cultures, a "Dances with Dingoes" phenomenon similar to the periodic American romanticization of Indians.

New Zealand pursued a somewhat similar but more muted course, emphasizing Pacific/Oceania ties and identification with its Maori indigenous culture, but not as particularly focused on rejection of the monarchy. Australia and New Zealand were also drawn apart as Australia continued to place a high priority on its military alliance with the United States, from which New Zealand withdrew over an essentially symbolic issue. Conversely, New Zealand carried out a series of radical economic reforms while Australia experimented more gingerly with creating a soft landing for the economic state.

The defeat of the republic in the Australian referendum of 1999 is of interest in that many voters were rejecting not so much a republic (which continues to have abstract appeal in opinion polls), but rather the "Asian identity" for Australia and the political mind-set which is associated with that position. Whether Australia chooses a republican or monarchical constitution in some future referendum is irrelevant to the broader issue of Anglosphere convergence. An Anglosphere Network Commonwealth will necessarily accommodate republican and monarchical states equally, and cannot be built on the imperial ties, symbols, and institutions, such as those upon which the Commonwealth of Nations was intended to rest. More important is what happens when Australians and New Zealanders realize that the economic-state-building projects in which they are engaged have become obsolete before they were properly begun.

Australia and New Zealand are distinct cultural nations of the Anglosphere.

Australian and New Zealand film and literature have begun to establish a distinct national voice for each, and that is not in danger. Rather, Anglosphere convergence will sharpen those distinctions by creating a larger audience to which the voices can speak. However, the forces that drive Anglosphere convergence do now and will in the future operate relentlessly on Australia and New Zealand. They will draw inhabitants into closer and deeper cooperation with the rest of the Anglosphere, diminish the appeal of identities and ties based on physical geography (an appeal markedly lessened by the rise of radical Islamism in neighboring Indonesia) and demonstrate daily the need for and utility of network commonwealth ties for those peoples.

IRELAND: WHAT PRICE THE EU?

Issues regarding Ireland are centered around its relationship with the EU. Ireland's relationship to the Union has already changed; rather than benefiting primarily from the EU cross-regional subsidies (as was the case when it first joined) to benefiting from economic growth sparked by being a low-tax state with an educated, English-speaking workforce yet with access to the whole EU. Strains will arise as the principal European states fight erosion of their tax base due to information-economy competition from Ireland. These states will have to choose between accepting EU tax and regulatory harmonization that will erode their business base, or refusing harmonization and risking their status in the EU.

The plunge of the euro within its first year (which highlighted the difficulty of making economic policy for Dublin's infotech economy in rustbelt Frankfurt) began to engender some voices moving toward this realization.

Columnist Kevin Myers wrote in the April 28, 2000, *Irish Times*:

> How is it possible that, barring the one voice of Anthony Coughlan, we sleepwalked into membership of the euro?
>
> So we are living in a German empire, in which German economic requirements take precedence over ours. The very people [Irish Finance Minister] Charlie McCreevy was anachronistically calling "pinkos" are in charge of the most delinquently run countries in Europe, where the demands of the welfare state take precedence over the economic base which keeps it going.
>
> Morality has taken the place of supply and demand as the engine of the economy. Treasuries have been ransacked according to the principle of what governments *should* do rather than what they *can* do.
>
> And of course in the weird and wonderful world of roseate politics, governments should do everything. In France, the welfare state has turned the country into an open-air lunatic asylum. Not merely are all children treated free of charge but they receive monthly home visits by doctors, whether or not a child needs it, with a wanton distribution of drugs, homeopathic or otherwise, for shoving up their bottoms—which is, apparently, the French way.
>
> The problem is the same right across euroland: vast and flabby welfare states, double-digit unemployment, high taxes combined with low work-incentives, and a vast crisis in pension funds maneuvering on the horizon like an invasion fleet. This is what we have tethered ourselves to, and the rights and wrongs of that decision pale into insignificance beside our astonishing inability or refusal to discuss the problems ahead before we enlisted on this stricken vessel, S.S. *Euro*.
>
> It would have been possible to have taken the British wait-and-see option, but, of course, that would have offended our sense of un-Britishness, that curious quality which coexists with a desire to imitate so much of what goes on in British life. Our un-Britishness demanded that we prove ourselves more unquestionably and piously pro-euro than the British. Perhaps it was this very instinct toward un-Britishness which stifled debate. We were *good* Europeans. The British were *bad* Europeans. End of story.
>
> But of course it wasn't the end of the story. Political delinquency and economic inertia—common bedfellows—have meant that the structural reforms which everyone assumed would occur in euroland never happened. But they have been happening in Ireland, as they have throughout the common-law, anglophone world. The Irish, the British, the United States, the Canadians, the New Zealanders, have cut taxes, personal and corporate, and withdrawn the tentacles of state incompetence from their respective economies.

These criticisms were voiced at the beginning of the euro experiment, when the currency rapidly lost value; as of this writing, it has soared to a high value against the dollar, causing pain to Europe's exporters. But the basic point, which is that economic optimality is held ransom to European political demands that will always favor Franco-Germany over the outward-oriented nations like Ireland, remains equally valid. Thus Ireland is gradually awakened to the costs of Europhilia, and an emerging Anglosphere awareness can be glimpsed. The rejection of the Treaty of Nice by the Irish electorate in June 2001, marked a substantial further step in this direction. Suddenly, a new, more critical appraisal of the European project became admissible in mainstream Irish debate. If not Euroskepticism per se, it is at least a species of Eurorealism. Cabinet minister Sile de Valera, heiress to one of the most revered names in Irish politics, openly discussed her fears of submergence of Ireland in a pan-European superstate, and made the entirely sensible (and proto-Anglospherist) observation that in many ways, "Ireland is closer to Boston than Berlin."

Ireland is now in the unusual position of having a position backed by the majority of its voters unrepresented by either a mainstream political party or a major media outlet. This state of affairs creates an interesting opportunity if some of the talented and increasingly Eurorealist political figures in the Europhile major parties were to consider the formation of a Euroskeptic party of the center. That would be the only cure for the increasing democratic deficit represented by the lockout of Euroskeptic views from the Irish political mainstream.

A new generation of young information entrepreneurs will not want to see their businesses endangered, nor will they see the old subsidies (now endangered by fiscal erosion anyway) as adequate compensation. Irish finance minister Charles McCreevy, who has borne the brunt of defending Ireland's low-tax strategy to Brussels, has become more and more explicit in his observations on this reality. The EU member nations will be moving to reform their economies, but it will be too little, too late.

If, by this time, a trade area including some or all of the United States, Canada, Britain, Australia, New Zealand, and South Africa has generated a large critical mass of information business, affiliating with it will become an attractive, viable option for Ireland. The opportunity to participate in sojourner agreements will also become an attraction for Irish youth; they and information-sector businesses would likely lobby for accession to such a trade area. The large presence of the United States will mitigate traditional Irish suspicions of British domination. The "coalition of the willing" and variable-geometry approaches would permit Irish participation in many Anglosphere institutions without the need to participate in military projects, unlike membership in a federal European state. As I have noted previously, Irish opposition to the British imperial narrative has been an obstacle to Anglosphere projects in the past. But the network commonwealth's polycentric and nonhierarchical structure offers a different approach, one in which Ireland and the Irish can relate directly to the Irish diaspora and the entire Anglosphere without any mediation through London.

The Irish diaspora is such a large and important part of the Anglosphere that it would be strange if, in the long run, Ireland itself did not also participate in its institutions. Certainly, judged on a case-by-case basis, they would form a more attractive alternative to the EU.

TRADE AND DEFENSE DRIVERS
FOR THE NETWORK COMMONWEALTH

The network commonwealth, whatever its abstract merits may be, will not likely emerge as a living institution unless it provides the most accessible, least problematic, and most nearly adequate solution to a crisis great enough to cause people and their leaders to abandon the status quo. The principle of evolutionary conservatism suggests that, absent a crisis, the continuation of the status quo is the least costly, and therefore most likely, forecast. In a crisis, those solutions that modify existing institutions the least, while providing a sufficient solution to the problems at hand, are likely to prevail.

While the evolution of perceptions, symbols, and narratives is carried forward, a parallel process of awareness of specific opportunity must occur. The perceptions and symbols must emerge if the Anglosphere is to be more than a creature of accountants and diplomats. Yet it will not be more than a tissue of rhetoric unless and until accountants, diplomats, businessmen, soldiers, and scientists, and ultimately, voters, citizens, parents, and children all begin to perceive the specific and precise advantages of structures for deep cooperation as well.

I have described three such specific structures—for defense, trade, and science—in previous chapters. Others are possible as well. Those more immersed in particular fields can probably imagine them clearly. People and organizations involved specifically in trade, defense, science and technology, and related areas must begin the examination of existing trade, security, and research and development structures. They must study how they can be modified, supplemented, or supplanted by the envisioned pan-Anglosphere institutions.

A precursor to the creation of official pan-Anglosphere institutions is the formalization of existing networks of interest along pan-Anglosphere lines. Part of the reality of pan-Anglosphere convergence is the fact that one of the salient and distinctive features of Anglosphere cultures is their ability to generate civil-society institutions in great numbers: voluntary, nonprofit organizations built from affinity and shared interest to serve great and small. Many organizations formed around advanced interests demonstrate a pan-Anglosphere structure already.

For example, the National Space Society, a U.S.-based organization formed for the purpose of promoting space exploration and development, has strong Australian and Canadian affiliates, despite the fact that those nations support only modest space programs. France and Japan, despite vigorous national space programs, have no affiliates and no local equivalents. A pan-Anglosphere space effort would be a natural focus for such an organization on the transnational level.

Other civil-society organizations of the Anglosphere similarly have the capability to serve as seeds of formal government and private efforts.

In commerce, finance and investment already follow pan-Anglosphere lines far more than either purely national or universally international lines. Commercial cooperation has already far outpaced any official attempt to shape institutions to serve this reality. A pan-Anglosphere Chamber of Commerce would be a natural organization through which to promote such cooperation and to search for pan-Anglosphere solutions based in common-law practices to serve as a middle layer of solutions (between national and international law) for business issues.

Once the processes of promoting the Anglosphere perspective and spreading awareness of its opportunities has begun, the network commonwealth approach can take advantage of its ability to generate more satisfactory alternative solutions to problems. Such solutions will demonstrate that the network commonwealth framework can offer unique and preferable solutions to problems that have denied resolution to existing national or international institutions and traditional approaches. At that point, the nations, peoples, and parties of the Anglosphere will turn to such solutions, and the impetus of these forces will begin to consciously create the network commonwealth. Once these structures begin to emerge, new and wider uses will be found for them, furthering the process of institutionalization.

It is likely that the process will begin with conferences and ad hoc task forces created to deal with particular issues. Such efforts take on a dynamic of their own, once they have been found useful. Conferences turn into organizations; organizations expand their scope. Organizations turn into communities, and communities turn into permanent unions and alliances. I have envisioned a threefold set of institutions, which may have overlapping but nonidentical memberships, in commerce and immigration, science and technology, and defense. This tripartite division may not be the precise form that actually evolves. Once the sinews of pragmatic cooperation have been created and found useful, a further evolution can be expected, as ad hoc governance by meetings of heads of state, ministers, and technical experts evolves into a permanent deliberative function.

One set of precursor arrangements that an Anglospherist movement can engender is a series of conferences and joint working groups among various Anglosphere nations in specific areas, seeking specific cooperative measures that make sense in light of the commonality of institutions.

Each would seek to add an Anglosphere axis of cooperation to the existing axes of cooperation in the various national policies. Thus, America today has three principal axes of cooperation: the North Atlantic, the Pan-American, and the Asia-Pacific. Cooperation with Britain, Canada, and Australia is routed along each of these axes, respectively.

Many programs would be better run along an Anglosphere axis.

Consideration should also be given to elevating the Commonwealth of Nations in American foreign relations, with a high-level Embassy to the Commonwealth, a visible American presence at commonwealth events, and the formation of a series of Commonwealth-American working groups in various topic areas. This could be of particular advantage in improving U.S. relations with a number of nations America has historically neglected, including possibly India.

THE ANGLOSPHERE AS THE "OFFSHORE ISLAND"

In this book I discuss many of the increasingly important nongeographic factors that affect international politics in the Information Age. However, as I discussed, humans will remain amphibious, existing in both the virtual and real environments.

In the real environment, geopolitical considerations will remain significant.

In addition to the considerations I have discussed elsewhere, there is a geopolitical case to be made for the Anglosphere: the Anglosphere as the "Offshore Island" of the world. Britain was traditionally described as the "Offshore Island"—remaining detached from the politics of the continent, but always prepared to tip the balance to prevent a single power from so dominating the continent as to create a universal authoritarian empire. The Anglosphere Alliance may define its situation similarly as "offshore" from the World Island—continental Eurasia with its massive population centers. The further development of the main Eurasian powers, combined with the declining ability of economic states to commit large proportions of their GDP to defense purposes short of World War-like crises, will eventually reduce America's current capability to dominate world politics by itself. Even in the wake of September 11, we see the United States stretching itself to deal with the remnants of vanquished regimes in Iraq and Afghanistan simultaneously, while preparing to deal with the possibility of a North Korean action or a crisis in the Taiwan Straits.

Defining its tasks more selectively, the United States, as the core of an Anglosphere Alliance, may still be able to guarantee the freedom of its members and provide an effective backing for selective interventions to defeat new world-threatening authoritarian empires. An Anglosphere Alliance would be formidable in almost any likely alignment of world politics. The core Anglosphere nations among themselves have maintained a preeminent military-industrial-scientific capability, one whose lead will continue for some time to come, and appears to actually be increasing in some areas (as Anglosphere nations dominate the Internet, and hence, the military informational "Grid"). The United States and Great Britain are still, as noted earlier, the only nations capable of producing effective high-performance turbofan engines, and possess much of the world's advanced aerospace capability. Increasingly, scientific and technological capabilities are the central factor in military strength; in such matters, an Anglosphere Alliance would be, and be likely to remain, second to none. If world events continue to draw the core Anglosphere and India closer together (given India's long-term discomfort with an increasingly stronger China, and an increasing threat from radical Islamism), an Anglosphere-India combination would be extremely formidable.

In naval matters, the United States and the United Kingdom have the world's two best world-spanning blue-water navies. Their navies can operate effectively for extended periods of time in any waters of the world and expect to defeat local navies when they arrive (although the Royal Navy has come close to losing this capability through retrenchment and NATO specialization). With the termination of the Soviet Union's costly attempt to create such a navy (which was within a decade or two of realization), they are almost the only such navies, with the French being the only other candidate in the short term, and China being the most likely competitor in the long term.

A chain of island continents and island bases worldwide could be maintained on the home territory of Anglosphere nations, free of the risk of expulsion by unwilling host nations or loss through decolonization. Even the three main Coalition powers, the U.S., Britain, and Australia among themselves provide a near-global coverage in terms of bases on permanent territories. Such a base structure would give an Anglosphere Alliance a series of hard platforms for deploying very high-technology area-denying regional weapons that could effectively deny any hostile forces access to the Anglosphere's home maritime spaces.

The various nations of the Anglosphere have each their own strong reasons for adhering to such an alliance. The United States is facing pressure to reduce the universality of its commitments, combined with a certain fatigue among the populace for the extensive nature of American alliances. A primary alliance structure could focus on countries with the greatest shared values (and those that have visibly shared the burdens of our wars). It could permit withdrawal from those overseas bases offered primarily for mercenary or temporary alliance reasons and could be perceived as a positive and coherent direction in a foreign policy that has been visibly drifting on inertia since the end of the Cold War. Post-September 11 redeployments by the United States have already begun moving in this direction, in, for example, the redeployment of forces from Korea and Japan to Australia.

The United Kingdom similarly faces continued budgetary pressure on military expenditure, along with a variety of security requirements stemming from Coalition activities in Iraq and Afghanistan, NATO obligations, peacekeeping operations, Commonwealth commitments, and remnants of imperial involvement. Unlike the United States, the United Kingdom has already reached the point where it is greatly limited in its ability to go it alone on any major military commitment; its armed forces are explicitly in existence to serve as leverage in a variety of alliance situations. Many of the United Kingdom's commitments, most particularly the Commonwealth obligations, could most effectively be met by folding them into an Anglosphere Alliance, as most British-Canadian mutual obligations have effectively been folded into NATO.

Australia faces a long-term, permanent, and serious threat potential stemming from its position to the southeast of the heavily populated and underdeveloped Asian landmass. The current turmoil in Indonesia and elsewhere only reinforces the urgency of Australia's need for dependable security alliances. The geopolitical threat, which was immediate and dire during World War II, led to substantial Australian involvement in the Malayan emergency, the Malaysian-Indonesian confrontation, and the Vietnam War, and is a major driver in Australia's pursuit of alliance relationships. This motivation is similarly the natural driver for Australian membership in an Anglosphere Alliance as part of a network commonwealth. For Australia, the deeper the ties and the more permanent the alliance structure, the more certain is the ability to count on the alliance when it will be needed.

For the other, and particularly smaller, nations of the Anglosphere, the answer is more simply put. The world is becoming more dangerous for small nations, rather than safer. It will not likely improve in the foreseeable future. Participation in a network commonwealth alliance will be cheap insurance, offering much of the protection of being part of an empire at a substantially lower price.

For most such nations, such an alliance would be comfortable as well, working with nations long known.

THE ANGLOSPHERE AND THE
CHALLENGE OF THE SINGULARITY

This book started out as a look at what the Internet and subsequent technologies would do to the world economy. It began as an exercise in imagining a "borderless world" and an investigation into "the end of nation-state" and similar themes. However, my research on the issue convinced me that this was not what was happening at all. Yes, there is going to be a borderless economy in the sense that obstacles to flow of capital and technology and goods will continue to diminish. But even though this process will lead to the end of the economic state, it is not going to be the end of the nation-state, because nations—in the sense of cultures and institutions—will count more than ever in this environment.

It is significant that so many of the divisive disputes in the world today are no longer battles over economic substance, but about culture and nationhood and the symbols by which those qualities are embodied. Neither Scots nor Quebecois are motivated primarily by economic considerations to advocate secession; their arguments instead hark back to what Lincoln called the "mystic cords of memory" which define nationhood. African Americans and Dixie neo-Confederates battle over display of the Confederate battle flag. Even arguments over Britain's membership in the EMU talk more about sovereignty than theories of optimal currency areas.

The Anglo-American concept has always been what historian John Laughland calls the "civic state"—that in which statehood is based on cultural affinity, essentially voluntarily assumed ties, and a shared narrative and culture. We have that within the nations of the English-speaking world, and we have it to a large extent among the nations of the English-speaking world. The challenge now is to create the appropriate institutions to take advantage of this reality.

It is time to lay out the program for accomplishing this institutionally. The Anglosphere is where the action is going to be. We have the ability to create common institutions based on common values—common-law concepts, the rule of law, our concepts of constitutional government—which are vitally important to our happiness and success as a society. Other approaches and institutions have become increasingly inappropriate to the challenges of the twenty-first century. It is our core values and characteristics that have made us dynamic, and it is to those values that we must return.

These and other developments, along with others suggest that international institutional arrangements based on physical proximity, such as the EU, NAFTA, and ASEAN, may not be the most useful arrangements for Anglosphere nations during the coming scientific-technical revolution. Rather, a new set of arrangements, those described as the network commonwealth, would be more effective. These arrangements would concentrate on creating links between the unique strong civil-society mechanisms of the Anglosphere nations to create a common economic space, taking advantage of natural, preexisting harmonies to maximize the opportunities for reaping the fruits of the new scientific-technical revolutions.

Parliamentary democracy, rights-respecting constitutionalism, and a common-law judicial system have allowed the Anglosphere nations to weather the stresses and challenges of the Industrial Revolution better and with more freedom than the various totalitarian and authoritarian alternatives once promoted as solutions. It is most likely that these values will permit us to face and surmount the challenges of the Singularity as well. Those who succumbed to the totalitarian temptation at the beginning of the twentieth century could at least plead their ignorance in the face of uncertainty; those who succumb now can only plead stupidity.

The nineteenth century was the British Century, without a doubt. The twentieth century was the American Century. The Anglosphere nations, and their allies in all strong civil societies existing and emerging, can offer the world the benefit of their experiences and examples in the face of the challenges ahead. If the English-speaking nations grasp the opportunity, the twenty-first century will be the Anglosphere Century. This is not a prediction of conquest or domination. Rather, it is an admission that the most important phenomena of the twenty-first century will likely emerge in the Anglosphere, and their resolution will be a result of, and characterized by the nature of the Anglosphere. As the British Century brought the eradication of slavery and serfdom worldwide, and as the American Century brought the defeat of totalitarianism in all its forms, the Anglosphere Century can see the mastery of the challenges of the Singularity.

Annotated Bibliography

As I am not presenting this book as a work of scholarly research, but rather in the nature of a connected series of essays suggesting some new perspectives and their consequences, I have chosen not to insert numerical reference citations in the main text. As I do draw extensively on a range of books, and particularly upon several works I consider to be foundational to the Anglosphere idea, I have chosen to use the collective reference approach. This section is therefore divided into a "general source works" section, presenting and commenting upon the works whose relevance applies throughout the book, followed by a chapter-by-chapter reference, relating various points and arguments to works of particular relevance to that section.

GENERAL SOURCE WORKS ON THE ANGLOSPHERE QUESTION

The following books are among the principal works of scholarship and thought on which I have drawn in proposing the idea of the Anglosphere perspective; their influence underlies the entire book. My describing them as "General Source Works on the Anglosphere Question" indicates their importance to my thinking, rather than implying that their authors endorse or agree with the arguments of this work in part or in full, credit or blame for which is entirely mine.

David Hackett Fischer's work *Albion's Seed: Four British Folkways in North America* presents an effective challenge to one of the central myths of American exceptionalism: the Turner's frontier thesis. He argues convincingly that American culture exhibits great continuity from the British Isles to the New World, and that differences between American regional cultures are overwhelmingly the product of the differences between regional cultures of the British Isles. Turner's theories of a transformation through the frontier experience is effectively disproved, particularly in light of a continual evolution of the Anglosphere cultures through ongoing frontier experiences within the British ideas and subsequently.

Fischer's picture of Anglosphere continuity is consistent with the Anglosphere exceptionalism whose English roots are shown by Macfarlane to be deep, and whose overall characteristics are shown by Véliz to be wide and distinct when viewed through a comparative lens. Together, they add up to an Anglosphere culture that is persistent and pervasive over many generations, distinct throughout its history from other European-origin civilizations around it, and bearing for its time a particularly strong variety of civil society.

Francis Fukuyama's *Trust: The Social Virtues and the Creation of Prosperity* (New York, Free Press, 1995) is an excellent book for thinking about, and comparing and contrasting cultures and subcultures, and particularly about the role of high trust in successful civil societies. It builds on previous scholarly work of a more academic nature, most particularly Edward Banfield's *The Moral Basis of a Backward Society*, and the subsequent discussions of social trust, in a broader and more accessible manner.

Alan Macfarlane's work, primarily *The Origins of English Individualism* (Oxford, Basil Blackwell, 1978) is certainly one of the critical foundations underlying modern Anglosphere thought. It refutes in detail the prevailing Marxist assumption that England had been just another European peasant society before the modern era and the Industrial Revolution. Macfarlane makes a strong case for the distinctness of English-speaking civilization and its unique social mode reaching back to at least the fifteenth century, and possibly well before. This stands much Marxist and other economic determinist thinking on its head. Rather than a product of the Industrial Revolution, Anglosphere individualism may have been one of the leading causes of it.

Although *English Individualism* is a highly academic study (written in a dense academic style) that concentrates primarily on land tenure in medieval England, its implications, like those of Fisher's, are profound and have gone remarkably unnoticed in many circles that should be aware of them. Macfarlane's concluding chapter, in which he speculates on wider implications and possibilities, is an invitation to further Anglospherist scholarship that has been largely unexploited to date by thinkers other than Macfarlane himself.

Among Macfarlane's other works, *Marriage and Love in England: Modes of Reproduction 1300–1840* (Oxford, Basil Blackwell, 1986), is also of interest to the question of English, and by extension Anglosphere exceptionalism. Just as Macfarlane's work on land tenure suggests that English individualistic family patterns predated (and have contributed to the origin of) the Industrial Revolution, so *Marriage and Love* suggests that English mores on the status of women gave sex far more value outside of the role of motherhood far earlier than Continental cultures. Similarly, the view of marriage as primarily a contract between individuals rather than as a sacrament, or as a contract between families, is usually thought of as a result of the Protestant Reformation and Calvinism in particular. Macfarlane points out English law long predating the Reformation that treats marriage as an individualistic contract and, in contrast to Roman-derived Continental law, denies either a Church or a family veto on the right to marry.

Subsequent to the writing of the text of this work, Macfarlane's *The Riddle of the Modern World* became available. This is an extended discussion of what Ernest Gellner calls "the conditions of the Exit"—specifically, the exit from the cycle of the rise and fall of bureaucratic authoritarian empires caused by the linked phenomena of the Scientific-Technological and Democratic Revolutions. Written in the form of a discussion of four critical thinkers on this topic—Montesquieu, Adam Smith, Tocqueville, and Gellner—it goes into much greater detail on some of the interesting questions raised in *English Individualism* and serves as further substantiation of the general issue of Anglosphere exceptionalism.

It is also worth noting that Macfarlane and the authors he discusses in *The Riddle of the Modern World* properly place the emergence of the Anglosphere's complex social system built around individualism in the wider context of the emergence of individualism in the West in general, a process that extends at least as far back as ancient Greek civilization. A particularly useful reference on the early emergence of individualism in consciousness is found in *The Marvellous Century: Archaic Man and the Awakening of Reason*, by George Woodcock (New York, W. W. Norton, 2000).

Kevin Phillips has written in *The Cousins' Wars: Religion, Politics, and the Triumph of Anglo-America* (Basic Books) an excellent, comprehensive, and accessible treatment of the three principal internal conflicts of the Anglosphere—the English Civil War, the American Revolution, and the American Civil War. Phillips mentions the prospect for closer Anglo-American collaboration at the end of the book, but he fails to elaborate.

He is also not conversant with the issues of the Information Economy and the next likely phases of the Scientific-Industrial Revolution, and is therefore unduly pessimistic about the Anglosphere's future. He sees the fact that the Anglosphere is further into the transition than the rest of the world as a weakness (because of the decline of traditional Industrial Age manufacturing) than as a strength. This is like fearing (in, say, 1860) that the transition from sailing to steamships was going to doom British and American naval power because their advantages in timber-framing and sailmaking were fading.

Claudio Véliz, in *The New World of the Gothic Fox: Culture and Economy in English and Spanish America* (University of California Press, 1994) approaches the Anglosphere question from a comparative viewpoint, quite successfully. It would not be excessive to say that Véliz is to today's emerging Anglosphere what Tocqueville was to nineteenth-century America, the perceptive outsider who sees the forest where natives see only trees. His book is an extremely erudite and impressive survey of the contrasting natures of the "Gothic Foxes" of the Anglosphere and the "Baroque Hedgehogs" of the Hispanosphere. Professor Véliz, a Chilean who has lived much of his life in Australia, England, and America, knows both spheres intimately.

Samuel Huntington, *The Clash of Civilizations and the Remaking of World Order* (New York, Touchstone, 1996) is the canonical book on the "civilizational" analysis of the world political structure. He discusses briefly the idea of an English-speaking alliance as a civilizational-based unit, although without including the nations of the British Isles.

CHAPTER 1

Some new books appear: Ezra Vogel's *Japan as Number One* and Herman Kahn's *The Emerging Japanese Superstate* began this trend; Jean-Jacques Servant-Schreiber's *The American Challenge* (Simon and Schuster, 1979) was the European equivalent, with America as the foreign challenger.

Thinking about the Revolutions of the Singularity

five revolutions: Some interesting books describing possible Singularity breakthroughs include the work of K. Eric Drexler (*Engines of Creation, Nanosystems,* and *Unbounding the Future,* the later coauthored by Christine Peterson and Gayle Pergamit) and Robert A. Freitas's *Nanomedicine, Volume 1: Basic Capabilities* (Landes Bioscience, 1999). Less radical but still transformative visions include such works as Elizabeth McCaughey Ross's discussion of nongenetic medical advances in *American Outlook* (Spring 2000). A wild card, but again a potentially transformative one is Thomas Gold's *The Deep Hot Biosphere* (New York, Springer-Verlag, 1999), which deals with the possibility of a biogenic origin of petroleum.

Bounded and Unbounded Problems:
The Space Development Example

history of space exploration: I covered some of these topics in *Privatizing Space Transportation* (Bennett, James C., and Salin, Phillip K., Reason Foundation, Los Angeles, 1987) and more recently in the Hudson Institue's 2020 Forecast. For the story of America's early work on space transportation, see Project RAND, *Preliminary Design of an Experimental World-Circling Space Ship*, Report SM-11827, Douglas Aircraft Corporation, May 2, 1946, and especially the long-classified *Feed Back Summary Report* (Lipp, J. E., and Salter, R. M., eds. *Project*) Contract No. AF 33(038)-6413, The Rand Corporation, March 1, 1954). I am particularly indebted to the former chairman of the board of directors of American Rocket Company, Stuart Kreiger, for pointing out the importance of the latter document. He should know; he had been the team leader on Project Feedback.

Y2K as the Opposite Case: Mistaking
Bounded for Unbounded Problems

my column in *Strategic Investment* The column appeared quarterly between 1995 and 2000, in *Strategic Investment* newsletter, Baltimore, Agora Publishing.

Civil Society and the Hazards of the Singularity
Revolutions: The Case of Nanotechnology

a long, pessimistic essay William Joy in *Wired* magazine, March 2000.

Civil Societies and the Economy of the Singularity

peaceful states are peaceful because of the strength of their civic statehood The "democratic argument against war"—that that democracies do not start wars against democracies—goes back at least to Kant. Once examined, this rapidly becomes an exercise in taxonomy. Is it valid, for example, to call Britain in 1914 a democracy, and Germany not? The case for, more precisely, strong civil societies not warring on each other is strengthened by Spencer R. Weart's *Never at War: Why Democracies Will Not Fight One Another* (New Haven, Connecticut, Yale University Press, 1998). This is an important piece of research into the historical case for the "democratic argument against war." His distinctions among democracies, autocracies, and oligarchies, and research into their historical implications, is an original refinement of that argument. He mentions but does not elaborate on the fact that democracies tend to form "permanent leagues" with each other, which become important actors in international relations. Network commonwealths as I have defined them could be considered one form of such "permanent leagues."

Hobbes and Rousseau in Cyberspace

a few rich Singapores and many poor, conflict-torn Kosovos See for instance the various speculations of Thomas L. Friedman, whose *The Lexus and the Olive Tree* (New York, Anchor Books, 2000) offers a recent treatment of globalization (symbolized by the Lexus) versus cohesion of local cultures (symbolized by the olive tree) by a reasonably pro-globalization author. He has some strange quirks, however, such as seeing the European Union in its current incarnation as a pro-globalization force, rather than a quixotic attempt to graft all the little "olive trees" of Europe into one big, harmonized Euro-Olive-Tree which can then stand up to the Lexus. Contrast Robert Kaplan, whose *An Empire Wilderness: Travels Into America's Future* (New York, Random House, 1998) sees much of what is happening in the decentralization of America and the descent of the rest of the world into anarchy.

Georgie Anne Geyer's *Americans No More: The Death of Citizenship* (New York, Atlantic Monthly Press, 1996) is another regretful look at the waning of the economic state. Like Kaplan, Geyer sees the decline of the United States as a centralized nation-state, and the loss of coherence at the federal level. Although she has an acute understanding of the role of multiculturalist ideology in contributing to this decline, she fails to see the stronger economic pressures, which also undercut the coherence of the current American national state. Kaplan is more aware of the fact that the unity and coherence of the American state is a relatively transitory episode, "from (T.) Roosevelt to (F. D.) Roosevelt," and in decentralizing, America is returning to its more normal state of being.

Similarly, Michael Lind's *The Next American Nation: The New Nationalism and the Fourth American Revolution* (New York, Free Press, 1995) contains an excellent critique of the current multicultural school of politics; basically, however, he doesn't have a clue about the coming economy. He is a member of the Hold Your Breath and Stamp Your Feet school of national sovereignists: he feels that we can revert to the economic and political structure of the Industrial Era by force of political will, without addressing any of the real issues of loss of the ability of states to control such transactions. He mistakes the effect (loss of ability to control economic activities) for the cause (which he attributes to a lack of desire, or failure of will).

Other influential books along this line include William Pfaff's *The Wrath of Nations: Civilization and the Furies of Nationalism* (New York, Touchstone,

1993) and Daniel Patrick Moynihan's *Pandaemonium: Ethnicity in International Politics* (Oxford University Press, 1993).

These particularly discuss the issues of nationalism, decentralization, and devolution.

Three that have attracted attention on the question of the future of state institutions include Kenichi Ohmae's *The End of the Nation State: The Rise of Regional Economies* (New York, Free Press, 1996), Jean-Marie Guehenno's similarly titled (in the English translation) *The End of the Nation State* (University of Minnesota Press, 1995), and Walter Wriston's *The Twilight of Sovereignty: How the Information Revolution Is Transforming Our World* (Scribner, 1992).

Lord David Howell, an economist who served in Margaret Thatcher's Cabinet, has written a recent and thoughtful book on some of the same issues. *The Edge of Now: New Questions for Democracy in the Network Age* (Macmillan, 2000) covers many of the same points as this work, and from a similar perspective.

Of course one constant source of popular imagery that advances the picture of the rich Singapore/poor Kosovo future is the "cyberpunk" school of science fiction. The seminal work is probably Phillip K. Dick's *Do Androids Dream of Electronic Sheep?*, which became the source for the film *Blade Runner*, which provided much of the standard imagery of the chaotic future. William Gibson and Bruce Sterling (*Neuromancer*, in 1984, and *Schismatrix*, 1985, respectively and most notably, and together, *The Difference Engine*, 1990) explicitly generated the cyberpunk school, although Vernor Vinge anticipated many of its themes in *True Names* (1977). Neal Stephenson further refined the genre into the "cypherpunk" school, named after the nonfiction *Cypherpunk Manifesto* of Tim May (private circulation 1991, subsequently widely distributed on the World Wide Web). See Stephenson's *Snow Crash* (1992), *The Diamond Age* (1995) (to my knowledge, the first appearance of the word "Anglosphere"), and *Cryptonomicon* (1999).

Linux as a Foreshadowing of the Economics of the Singularity

A new "Theory of the Network" to supplement and update Ronald Coase's *A Theory of the Firm* (1937). Coase's brilliant work asked the simple question, "Why have companies? Why not just have a number of individuals contracting and cooperating with each other?" His answer, obvious once the question was asked, was *transaction costs*. Having to pay a support person for every letter typed, having to pay a receptionist for every call answered, would become impossibly complicated and expensive in a large cooperative enterprise. But what happens when the relationship of transaction costs to scope of effort is substantially altered by technology? For all the discredited hype of the Internet bubble, the fact remains that one of the effects of the Internet, and related technologies, is to change that relationship. We have only started to think about how that change will play out. This doesn't disprove Coase's fundamental insight in any way, but it does require rethinking some of the immediate conclusions of his 1937 article.

The Second Gateway wave of deregulation, decontrol, and privatization and the First and Third Gateway concepts are discussed at greater length in my article in *American Outlook* (Spring 2000).

CHAPTER 2

Historians such as William McNeill, David Landes, and Thomas Sowell have been generating what has been called a "macrohistorical" analysis. William McNeill's *The Rise of the West* is probably the foundational book of this analysis. The macrohistorical view emphasizes the emergence of particular entrepreneurial characteristics in Western civilization as the key to its rise. David S. Landes's *The Wealth and Poverty of Nations: Why Some Are So Rich and Some So Poor* (New York, W. W. Norton, 1998) is very good on the role of civil society in creating wealth, although taking a rather static view of free trade issues. Thomas Sowell's *Conquests and Cultures: An International History* (New York, Basic Books, 1998) is one of the best and most accessible discussions of the macrohistorical worldview. His *Race and Culture: A World View* (New York, Basic Books, 1994) and *Migrations and Cultures: A World View* (New York, Basic Books, 1996) are useful discussions of the racial and cultural issues in particular.

The debate over the relative role of culture in development is hotly contended in academia. A useful guide to this, with a tilt toward those who believe culture is a critical element, can be found in *Culture Matters: How Values Shape Human Progress* (New York, Basic Books, 2000), Lawrence E. Harrison and Samuel P. Huntington, eds. Note that it is coedited by Samuel Huntington, whose *The Clash of Civilizations* is itself a source of controversy.

Carlo Cipolla's *Guns, Sails and Empires: Technological Innovation and European Expansion 1400–1700* (New York, Pantheon Books, 1965) is worth reading for its discussion of the interplay between technology and cultural-historical development, a critical element of this type of analysis.

England, because of its position offshore from the European continent . . . England's insular situation is the starting point for almost any discussion of English (and ultimately Anglosphere) exceptionalism. Paul Johnson's *The Offshore Islanders* (Phoenix Press, 1998) is one of the more useful discussions of this point.

Some historians have begun to deny the criticality of Britain's insularity. Felipe Fernandez-Armesto's *Civilizations: Culture, Ambition, and the Transformation of Nature* (Macmillan, 2000) dismisses Johnson and other insularists rather cavalierly. Fernandez-Armesto discusses a category he has created which he terms "small-island civilizations" and argues that such civilizations have certain ecologically driven similarities. He then makes a rather unsupported leap to dismiss insularity as a factor in British exceptionalism (and further leaps to dismiss the validity of British exceptionalism, without any particular argumentation) because Britain does not fit his category of small-island civilization. Although he does not articulate it, he seems to be making an argument that only small islands can enjoy exceptionalism on account of their insularity.

Yet a very brief consideration of the counterfactual serves to dismiss Fernandez-Armesto's dismissal of British insularity and English exceptionalism. If the Channel were, by geological quirk, to be shrunk to the width of a fordable river, or eliminated altogether, it is hard to construct a credible scenario in which (to construct only the most limited of lists) Phillip of Spain, any of the various ambitious Louises of France, Napoleon, Hitler, or Stalin could not have succeeded in invading and subduing England by land, where in fact they aspired and failed by sea. Either England would have been just another Netherlands in European politics, or it would have responded by becoming another France: a fortified, centralized, militarized state with a strong standing army and all the political and sociological consequences thereof. Without admitting an unqualified geographical determinism, it is difficult to see how Britain's particular geographical circumstances have not been a significant factor in its exceptionalism.

Norman F. Cantor, *Imagining the Law: Common Law and the Foundations of the American Legal System* (New York, HarperCollins, 1997), is a good historical discussion of the Anglo-American legal system.

Common law as a significant factor in Anglosphere exceptionalism is neither sentimental nor imaginary. For example, consider this: "According to Ira Millstein, a lawyer at Yale's International Institute for Corporate Governance, market-based capitalism seems much more likely to take root in countries with a legal system based on English common law and with an independent judiciary. It seems to fare less well in countries with legal systems based on European civil law, particularly the French version of it. Common law is more flexible and quicker to adapt to change, provides stronger investor protection, and is less likely to sanction heavy-handed state intervention. But it will be difficult for civil-law countries to move in that direction, says Millstein. 'You can't just become a common-law system overnight.'" (*The Economist*, May 18, 2002, A Survey of International Finance, p. 28.)

a doctrine that survives today in the "Identity Christianity" movement. Although "British Israelites" and their contemporary offshoot, "Identity Christianity," have very long roots in English religious and political discourse, they have gravitated to a peculiar corner of the far right today. Howard Bushart, John R. Craig, and Myra Barnes, *Soldiers of God: White Supremacists and Their Holy War for America* (New York, Kensington Books, 1998) is a good discussion of the Identity Christianity movement and its relations with neo-Nazis in the United States.

Joel Dyer's *Harvest of Rage: Why Oklahoma City Is Only the Beginning* (New York, Westview Press, 1997) is an informative discussion of militias, mid-American rage, and the Identity Church movement. I find it a bit simplistic and deterministic in assigning blame to particular administration farm policies and underplaying the genuine cultural divisions between the New York- and Washington-based cultures and the regional cultures of the Plains and Mountain West. Additionally, as further information about possible cooperation between fundamentalist radicals and American white supremacists emerges, some parts of Dyer's thesis about the purely American and right-wing roots of these movements begin to seem less likely.

The Anglosphere and the New Understanding of the West

Ambivalence toward the Continental European concept of the nation-state. Adam Zamoyski's *Holy Madness: Romantics, Patriots, and Revolutionaries, 1776–1871* (London, Wiedenfeld and Nicholson, 1999) is a very useful discussion of the emergence of the respective Anglosphere (although he doesn't use the term) and Continental European concepts of the nation and the nation-state. Interesting is his account of the continual disillusionment of Continental nationalist radicals who admired the American Revolution and its supposed nationalism from afar but who discover the religious-sectarian and mercantile roots of the American republic on closer inspection. As Conor Cruise O'Brien observed in his similarly illuminating *The Long Affair: Thomas Jefferson and the French Revolution, 1785–1800* (University of Chicago Press, 1996), America and France have since the time of their respective revolutions chosen to enjoy a *mesentente cordiale* that inevitably is shattered upon closer inspection.

What's a nation? *Nationalism* (John Hutchinson and Anthony D. Smith, eds., Oxford University Press, 1994) is a useful introduction to the standard thinking on the nationalism question. John Breuilly's *Nationalism and the*

State (University of Chicago Press, 1982) is another competent review of the nationalism question from an academic perspective.

What Is the Anglosphere?

Védrine, in his book Hubert Védrine (Dialogue avec Dominique Moïsi), *Les cartes de la France à l'heure de la mondialisation* (Fayard, 2000).

Cultural Nations and Regions: What's the Difference?

the proper definition of a region is part of a debate including Darrell Dellamaide's *The New Superregions of Europe* (Plume, 1994) and particularly Joel Garreau's influential *The Nine Nations of North America* (Avon, 1981). An interesting and influential discussion, primarily impressionistic and anecdotal rather than scholarly, that divides North America into a number of "nations," based on a combination of economic and cultural factors. Garreau tends to oversimplify and to overrate economic factors while underrating cultural and historical factors. Published before Fischer's magisterial work, he seems to be unaware of the powerful continuity of the westward cultural streams originating from the settlement of North America. Despite these limitations, the book is useful in examining the fact that regional differences are extremely significant in North America.

Becoming a Self-Aware Civilization: The Anglosphere Perspective

Memetic, rather than genetic, identity The idea of a "meme" as the rough informational equivalent of a gene in cultural evolution, was first advanced by Dawkins in *The Selfish Gene* (Oxford, 1976). Substituting a cultural-evolutionary view of the Anglosphere for the social-Darwinist Anglo-Saxonism of previous visions is critical for understanding the phenomenon.

The second vision, that of Cecil Rhodes and Alfred Milner was promoted in a series of books and publications and was part of the founding vision of the English-Speaking Union, which survives today as a cultural organization. It was also the driving motivation behind the establishment of the Rhodes Scholarships. Insight into Rhodes's concept, highly racial, Anglo-Saxonist, and imperialist, is disclosed in his remarkable *Confession of Faith* (1877). A less social-Darwinist version of the second vision is found in works of later advocates such as George Catlin in works like *Anglo-Saxony*. Perhaps the last serious advocate of the second vision was James Burnham, who in *The Struggle for the World* (1947) advocated a union between the United States and the British Empire as part of a program for containing and defeating the Soviet Union. Perhaps the most lasting influence of Burnham's book was its impact on the thinking of George Orwell. Orwell's vision in his *Nineteen Eighty-Four* (1949) was of the division of the world into three contending totalitarian states, one of which, Oceania, was based on the English-speaking world and its dependencies. Orwell's geopolitical vision, represented by the political tract attributed to "Emmanuel Goldstein" in the novel, was drawn almost entirely from Burnham's work.

Churchill's *History of the English-Speaking Peoples*. A History of the English-Speaking Peoples (London, Cassell and Company, 1956–1958).

The Three Memetic Plagues of the Anglosphere

Archbishop Wulfstan quoted in *Oxford History of England*, Kenneth O. Morgan, ed. (Oxford University Press, 1984).

extended hot-and-cold war that lasted for the entirety of Elizabeth I's reign Anglo-America must properly be seen as an Elizabethan enterprise rather than a Jacobean one, even though permanent formal settlement in the territory of the future United States was not finally accomplished until after Elizabeth's death. A case could be made that Americans still exhibit more Elizabethan virtues and vices than were retained in England itself. Certainly the context of the settlement enterprise was part and parcel of the ongoing conflict with Spain and the Counter-Reformation. A useful discussion of the Elizabethan roots of both the Roanoke and Jamestown colonies is found in Giles Milton's *Big Chief Elizabeth: How England's Adventurers Gambled and Won the New World* (London, Hodder and Stoughton, 2000). This is a popular account of the first century of the Anglosphere's extension into North America, with particular regard to the political context of the founding and possible sabotage of the Roanoke colony within Elizabethan court politics.

The South Carolina planters described by William W. Freehling *The Road to Disunion: Secessionists at Bay, 1776–1854* (Oxford University Press, 1990). Freehling's work is an excellent, very thorough treatment of the run-up to the American Civil War, with particular emphasis on the demographics and economics of slavery and gradual emancipation in the prewar period. It argues powerfully that the ending of the U.S. slave trade in 1808, a result of the compromises needed to create the Constitution, was the beginning of the end of slavery in America, and that the secessionist movement was driven by South Carolina's desperate endgame need to reopen the trade or conquer other slave-bearing territories in Latin America.

Brazil, the great slave destination of the New World See particularly Hugh Thomas's *The Slave Trade: The Story of the Atlantic Slave Trade: 1440–1870* (New York, Touchstone, 1997). A very comprehensive history of the Atlantic slave trade, particularly useful for putting the Anglosphere role in the slave trade in the wider perspective—of the 11,328,000 African slaves carried in the Atlantic slave trade, only 500,000 were landed in what is now the United States; by far the largest destination was Brazil, where 4,000,000 landed.

The Gunpowder Plot (1605) brought all these issues to the fore See particularly Lady Antonia Fraser's *Faith and Treason: The Story of the Gunpowder Plot* (1997). Neither a "Popish Plot" directed from Rome, nor a useful figment of Protestant imagination, as respective partisans have charged, the Gunpowder Plot now seems to have been blowback from the shadowy intelligence underworld of the Anglo-Spanish cold war of Elizabethan times. Fraser's work incorporates substantial new evidence in this story of alienated military-veteran drifters with eerie premonitions of later events. I am indebted to Garry Wills's *Witches and Jesuits: Shakespeare's Macbeth* (Oxford University Press, 1995) for the ingenious and instructive device of imagining the circumstances of the Gunpowder Plot in the context of the political environment of 1950, with the Communists in the role of the Catholics. This device is a useful point of departure for further thinking about the continuity of Anglosphere attitudes about conspiracy.

Coming Home to the Anglosphere

The Iberian slave civilizations of the New World and their interaction with Anglosphere plantation practice, primarily in the Caribbean but also in Barbados-settled South Carolina and the Deep South Dixie states, are discussed in Thomas's *Slave Trade* and also in Peter Linebaugh's and Marcus Rediker's *The Many-Headed Hydra: Sailors, Slaves, Commoners, and the Hidden History of the Revolutionary Atlantic* (Beacon, 2001). Although I use the term *Iberian* because New World slavery was primarily a Portuguese phenomenon, Anglosphere slavery was most directly influenced by Spanish practice rather than Portuguese. By terming Iberian civilizations "slave civilizations," I am emphasizing the fact that slavery was a practice embedded in and integral to Roman law (as Tocqueville observed, "Roman law is slave law") and that the Spanish and Portuguese imperial civilizations were organic continuations of Roman civilization. In English Common Law, on the other hand, slavery and slave codes were grafted on by colonial statute. This did not necessarily make the life of the slave in the Anglosphere any better; in fact, it led to the doctrine of the slave as chattel, rather than as a human being with some rights, however limited. However, it made abolition of slavery as a whole the eventual focus of moral thinking, rather than melioration of the slave's lot, as in Spanish and Portuguese thought.

Hydra is an interesting work as part of the "Atlantic system" approach. By focusing on the underclasses usually ignored in older triumphalist histories, it shows the development of a memetic Anglosphere encompassing the British Isles, the English Caribbean, English North America, and English outposts in Africa very early on in the history of settlement. This Anglosphere, of course, communicated in the medium of an English-based Creole language and reflected Anglosphere working-class culture rather than upper- or middle-class culture. However, it anticipated and paved the way for the later broad multiclass Anglosphere later formed by mass emigration.

Theorists such as Oswald Spengler Arthur Herman's *The Idea of Decline in Western History* (New York, Free Press, 1997) provides a useful history of declinism as an ideological strain, including relatively little-known chapters of that history such as the Spenglerian basis of the thought of W. E. B. DuBois, and therefore of much African-American contemporary thought.

The concept of Western civilization was prolonged Gress's *From Plato to NATO: The Idea of the West and Its Opponents* (New York, Free Press, 1998) provides an excellent review of the narratives about the West, favorable and otherwise.

By the year 1200 slavery was nearly extinct in England *Oxford History of Britain.*

Of the 11 million slaves Thomas, *Slave Trade.*

Thomas's statistics on slaves landed by the Atlantic slave trade give the following breakdown by destination:

Brazil	4,000,000
Spanish empire (including Cuba)	2,500,000
British West Indies	2,000,000
French West Indies	1,600,000
British North America/U.S.	500,000
Dutch West Indies	500,000
Europe (including Canaries, Madeira, etc.)	200,000
Total	11,328,000

These statistics are significant not as an exercise in proportioning moral blame (which of course they do not) but in illustrating the point that the Atlantic slave trade was in Spanish and Portuguese America an organic extension of the classical Mediterranean pattern of slavery and slave-worked latifundia, but an alien graft onto an Anglosphere that, like Northwestern Europe in general, had left slavery behind in the early Middle Ages. As Tocqueville wrote, "Roman law . . . is slave law." Slave codes and black codes governing freedmen always rested uneasily within Common Law.

Free black men who were property holders were not deprived of the vote in Virginia This story, along with an interesting set of discussions about the gradualness of development of racial chattel slavery in the Chesapeake in the seventeenth century, can be found in Scott L. Malcolmson's *One Drop of Blood: The American Misadventure of Race* (New York, Farrar, Straus & Giroux, 2000.) This is an interesting narrative of white-black-Indian relations in America, including the interesting story of the gradual Africanization of Cherokee slavery (and the conclusion that slavery is more intrinsically compatible with a collective culture than an individualistic one) and the somewhat different experiences of slaves in Cherokee culture. The book's usefulness, however, is somewhat limited by the author's overgeneralization from his own experiences.

Sir Francis Drake . . . developed a plan to "roll back" the Spanish Empire This fascinating story is related in Ronald Sanders's *Lost Tribes and Promised Lands: The Origins of American Racism* (New York, HarperCollins, 1978). In addition, Sanders provides much interesting information about the key years between 1500 and 1700 as the English-speaking world attempted to deal with the phenomenon of racially based slavery and colonization of lands inhabited by other races.

not as an inherent part of English-speaking civilization David Horowitz, *Hating Whitey and Other Progressive Causes* (Dallas, Spence Publishing Company, 1999) discusses racial guilt as an aspect of political correctness, and its fruits in contemporary America from the perspective of a reformed practitioner of the art. An ironic side note about the propagation of the Anglosphere guilt narrative can be found in Tony Horwitz's *Blue Latitudes* (Henry Holt & Co., 2002) in which he traces the source of much of the negative picture of Captain James Cook and his explorations in the Pacific. That source, as related by Horwitz, was deliberate denigration of Cook's record by New England missionaries in early Hawaii, who wished to spread ill-will toward Britain as a result of competition with British missionaries.

An indigenous Anglosphere ideology, abolitionism See Fischer, *Albion's Seed*, on the role of the Quakers in England and America, and *Many-Headed*

Hydra for the broader context of English religious radicalism of the English Civil War era and its relation to abolition of slavery and other, now generally accepted, modern attitudes.

Quaker culture . . . was also the source . . . of most of the principles see again Fischer, *Albion's Seed*, on the Quakers. When calculating when women gained the franchise in the Anglosphere, the beginning of the process was not 1879 in Wyoming, or 1920 nationwide in the United States. One must begin with the institution of parallel men's and women's meetings in the Quaker congregations of seventeenth-century England, which had to reach consensus internally and mutually before a decision could be recorded.

Third-rate Spenglerist narrative See again Herman's *The Idea of Decline in Western History*

as Robert Conquest observed Conquest's *Reflections on a Ravaged Century* (New York, W. W. Norton, 2000), although primarily a reflection on the totalitarian ravages of the twentieth century (which Conquest called by name long before other, more fashionable intellectuals had to eventually admit he was right) contains a useful discussion of the history of the British Empire and its transformation into Commonwealth, in the context of which his observation on the fallacy of equating the transformation of the British Empire with the Gibbonesque concept of a fall of Rome is made. It also contains an excellent analytical chapter on the European Union and a following chapter advocating some form of Anglosphere alliance as an alternative to other forms of world organization. Conquest's history of intellectual courage, and his status as one of the first contemporaries to call for an Anglosphere alliance, surely should earn him the distinction of a Wise Elder of the Anglosphere.

Also worth reading on the question is David Cannadine's *Ornamentalism: How the British Saw Their Empire* (Penguin Books, 2001). This is another attempt to break new ground in the examination of Britain's Second Empire and Commonwealth experience. Rather than seeing the imperial project primarily in economic determinist terms as a fundamentally exploitative venture, Cannadine makes a well-argued case that the Second Empire was primarily an attempt at recreating overseas the values and social positions of the landed aristocracy that were fading at home under the impact of the Industrial Revolution. This gives further impetus to the examination of the paradox of a society that, at home, gave free rein to what Drucker termed the creative destruction of the market economy, while abroad allied itself with the traditional princes against exactly the same sort of middle-class entrepreneurs from which it drew its wealth and power at home. This paradox in particular laid the roots of revolt against the empire in India, Egypt, Iraq, and the more developed parts of Africa, while maintaining Britain's position in less-developed countries like Jordan or the Persian Gulf emirates.

CHAPTER 3

proposals like that of author Clarence Streit who was an influential proponent of a federal union of the democracies in books such as *Union Now: The Proposal for Inter-Democracy Federal Union* (New York, Harper, 1940). Ironically, Streit's work was an evolution from the work of the turn-of-the-century Anglo-Saxonists like Milner and Catlin. This evolution took the form of expanding from a concept of a core union between the United States and the British Empire, to gradually including other Western democracies, to ultimately including non-Western, nondemocratic states, the latter vision eventually resulting in the United Nations. Another variant excluded the United States from the vision and eventually led to the European Union. This evolution was partly the result of the gradual discrediting of the exceptionalism of the original Anglo-Saxonists, under the pressure of an economic-determinist view of the Industrial Revolution and emergence of constitutional democracy. Today Anglospherist approaches critique world federalism on the basis of a new generation of scholarship that revindicates the Anglosphere exceptionalism in understanding these phenomena, and again ironically now counterposes Anglospherist concepts of cooperation to world-federalist and pan-Europeanist derivatives of originally Anglo-Saxonist schools of thought.

Proposal to create a free trade agreement between NAFTA and the European Union by Gordon Brown as reported in the *Christian Science Monitor*, July 27, 2001.

One World through the Internet?

Gateways through which a society must pass This approach was discussed by the author at greater length in *American Outlook* (Spring 2000).

Trust and Civil Society

the characteristic of trust See again Fukuyama's *Trust* and Harrison and Huntington's *Culture Matters*.

Hanseatic Leagues in Cyberspace

The German Hanse See particularly Philippe Dollinger, *The German Hansa* (Palo Alto, Stanford University Press, 1970).

The New Understanding of the Market: Rules of Thumb for Intervention

works of Ludwig von Mises and Hayek Particularly for these points *The Austrian Theory of the Trade Cycle and Other Essays*—by Ludwig von Mises et al. (Ludwig Von Mises Institute, 2nd edition, 1996), and *The Fatal Conceit: The Errors of Socialism* (collected works of F. A. Hayek, Vol. 1) by Friedrich A. Hayek and W. W. Bartley, eds (University of Chicago Press, university edition, 1989).

The Anarcho-Capitalist Debate and Other Red Herrings

anarcho-capitalism A good general introduction to this school of thought would be *The Machinery of Freedom: Guide to a Radical Capitalism* by David D. Friedman (Open Court Publishing Company, 2nd edition, 1989).

techno-liberals include Paulina Borsook, author of the amusing but not very deep *Cyberselfish: A Critical Romp through the Terribly Libertarian Culture of High Tech* (Public Affairs, 2001), which is fairly typical of technoliberal critiques of technolibertarians. She and others like David Brin point out that the technology libertarians see as liberatory often has roots in government projects. Well, yes, and Columbus's voyages had roots in a mystical interpretation of the Book of Esdras. Actions often have unintended consequences.

CHAPTER 4

Space and Power: Geopolitics and the Topology of Information Space

cultural rather than biological evolution Richard Dawkins's *The Selfish Gene* (Oxford University Press, 1990) is the originator of the concept of the meme as the cultural-evolutionary analogue to the gene. It is critical to understand the ways in which cultural evolution differs from its biological counterpart.

The Sinews of the Network Commonwealth

The United Kingdom has tended to get the worst of the deal See especially Derek Wood's *Project Cancelled: The Disaster of Britain's Abandoned Aircraft Projects* (Janes, 1986).

Trade, Defense, and Technology Intersect

Continental militaries have not . . . kept up this pace See for example David C. Gompert, Richard L. Kugler, and Martin C. Libicki, *Mind the Gap: Promoting a Transatlantic Revolution in Military Affairs* (Washington, D.C., National Defense University Press, 1999); and James A. Thompson's "How a Militarily Strong Europe Could Help Build a True Partnership," in *The RAND Review* (Spring 1999). Thompson's article is particularly interesting in that he diagnoses transatlantic capabilities gaps, notes the British exception to European lagging, but concludes that the answer is urging the Continentals to close the gap. The alternative path, recognizing the gap but realigning organizational structures to adapt to the fact, is never discussed.

Commonwealth or Tribalism

a narrowly defined tribe Again, Kaplan's *An Empire Wilderness,* Geyer's *Americans No More,* Pfaff's *The Wrath of Nations,* and Moynihan's *Pandaemonium* are useful discussions of this trend. The work of Scottish nationalist and culturally homogenous state cheerleader Tom Nairn stands in contrast, particularly his *Faces of Nationalism: Janus Revisited* (New York, Verso, 1997). Written from a Scottish socialist and nationalist perspective, Nairn has interesting insights into the nature of nationalism and the future of the United Kingdom. Unfortunately, his Marxist perspective and lack of understanding of the emerging economy undercut the usefulness of his judgments. As a Scottish Marxist nationalist, he actually regrets the principal advantage Scotland has enjoyed, which was the absence of a court culture after 1707, which permitted a particularly rich civil society to spring up in that country. Although much of what he says about the small nation-state would be valid when talking about what I term a civic state, he grossly underestimates the amount of coherence (which as a Marxist he believes is generated through economics) needed to make a working civic state in a weak civil society.

Network Commonwealths around the World

The pension liability issue . . . suggests that the European Union For a timely and careful analysis of the European structural crisis, see Patrick Minford's *Should Britain Join the Euro?* (London, Institute of Economic Affairs, 2002).

as the Chinese diaspora forms a worldwide business community This story, and the parallel stories of other ethnic diasporas and the networks they form, is given in Joel Kotkin's *Tribes: How Race, Religion and Identity Determine Success in the New Global Economy* (New York, Random House, 1992). Kotkin discusses the relevance of emerging global, ethnolinguistic networks to the Information Economy. He mentions the English-speaking people, and subgroups within them, as the potential basis for new "tribes." Some interesting parallels with the Indian diaspora are discussed in Gurchuran Das's *India Unbound: The Social and Economic Revolution from Independence to the Global Information Age* (Anchor Books, 2002). For a wider study of the diaspora question today, see also Nicholas Van Hear's *New Diasporas: The Mass Exodus, Dispersal, and Regrouping of Communities* (Seattle, University of Washington Press, 1998).

claims for the resurgence of Confucianism See William J. F. Jenner, *The Tyranny of History: The Roots of China's Crisis,* for an insightful picture of China at the end of its Communist phase, and a much-needed historical look at Confucianism in practice, as opposed to the imagined Confucianism of Lee Kwan Yew and other successful de facto Anglo-Confucianists.

fact of interest about Japan Readers competent in Japanese may find the author's chapter on Japan and the Singularity in a recently published volume in that language to be an interesting further elaboration on these themes. (Not published in English.) James C. Bennett, *Tokuiten kakumei ni chokumensuru Nihon* (The Singularity Revolution Will Come to Japan) in *Chotaikoku Nihon wa kanarazu yomigaeru* (The ReEmerging Japanese Superstate in the Twenty-first Century), I. Herbert, ed., London, ed., Tokuma-shoten, Tokyo, 2002.

CHAPTER 5

the Anglosphere legal tradition of the common law Again, for a good general discussion of the history of Common Law see Cantor, *Imagining the Law.*

American freedom is unambiguously the result of this constitutional settlement. For example, see *Inventing America: Jefferson's Declaration of Independence* by Garry Wills (Mariner Books, 2002).

Jonathan Freedland . . . published the controversial *Bring Home the Revolution:* *The Case for a British Republic* (London, Fourth Estate, 1998). An interesting and controversial discussion of the British roots of America's institutions. Freedland demonstrates that the greater openness, decentralization, constitutional constraints, and popular sovereignty of the American system have created the results that many critics of the current British system say they want. The subtitle is somewhat misleading, as the book isn't about the monarchy very much at all. What he really is advocating is an end to an unconstrained executive, centralization, and certain other features of British life. It could better be subtitled "The Case for a British Limited Government," as his goals could just as easily be realized within a monarchical constitution. He is, however, very good on the subject of the common Anglo-American political roots, and the fact that most of the divergence has been a case of America implementing a British radical agenda.

Unusual constitutional ferment throughout the Anglosphere For example, see Vernon Bogdanor, *Devolution in the United Kingdom* (Oxford University Press, 1999), a good overview of the devolution process in the British Isles from a constitutional and historical perspective. Bogdanor is clear-sighted about the fact that Irish independence was the first chapter of an ongoing saga, a fact that most commentators on British devolution fail to treat adequately. Also on the United Kingdom, see Andrew Marr's *The Day Britain Died* (London, Profile Books, 2000), a discussion of devolution and the strains on the historical concept of Britain.

For Canada's issues, read Lansing Lamont's *Breakup: The Coming End of Canada and the Stakes for America* (New York, W. W. Norton, 1994), a good discussion of the constitutional dilemmas faced by Canada, or *The Patriot Game: Canada and the Canadian Question Revisited*, by Peter Brimelow (Hoover Institute Press, 1987).

See James A. Aho's *The Politics of Righteousness: Idaho Christian Patriotism* (Seattle, University of Washington Press, 1990), a reasonably objective survey of alienated opinion in the Mountain West states of America, and Jonathan Raban's *Bad Land*, a discussion of the history of Montana and the economic, political, and cultural roots of the current alienation from mainstream culture which has found roots there. Raban is superior in its breadth of observation to Dyer's previously cited *Harvest of Rage*. Since September 11 and its consequential activities, subsequent to any of these sources, there has been a bifurcation in the alienated American Mountain West right. The more moderate majority wing has become conditionally and critically supportive of the Bush administration, while the extreme fringe has adopted an antiwar, pro-Arab stance. The dividing line is fairly congruent with the preexisting line (described fairly well by Aho) between traditional constitutionalists and the racist, anti-Semitic fringe with neo-Nazi influences. The racist fringe tends to attribute the September 11 attacks to a U.S. government–Zionist conspiracy intended to impose totalitarian rule on the United States, while constitutionalists focus more on perceived failures of the federal government to prosecute the war against radical fundamentalists sufficiently vigorously. Also of interest are suggestions of a connection between the Oklahoma City bombing and radical fundamentalist groups.

The Anglosphere Constitutional Tradition and War

Linda Colley's work *Britons: Forging the Nation 1707–1837* (New Haven, Yale University Press, 1992). This is the story of founding the Grand Union of the United Kingdom. Very perceptive in understanding the tensions between the nationalisms of England and Scotland versus the emerging loyalties to the new Union. Some, like Tom Nairn, see in Colley a refutation of the concept of British nationhood, because she details the mechanisms through which the British Grand Union narrative propagated itself. However, it is not clear that the mechanisms by which Britain, as such, became something like a nation-state were much different, except in detail, than the mechanisms by which England or Scotland had become nations in the first place; the details are merely more accessible to us for being closer in time and better documented. Of interest to the military question for its portrayal of nonelectoral mechanisms for assessing consent of the population to government measures.

Much of the political effort of the Restoration Stephen Saunders Webb provides a valuable perspective (one quite different from the traditional Whig narrative) in *Lord Churchill's Coup: The Anglo-American Empire and the Glorious Revolution Reconsidered* (New York, Random House, 1995) and its two companions, *The Governors-General: The English Army and the Definition of the Empire 1569–1681 and 1676: The End of American Independence*. These together constitute a discussion of the development of the First British Empire between the Restoration and the Revolution of 1688. The uniqueness of the Whig settlement (and the degree to which the Whig settlement continued to retain useful elements of the Restoration imperial system) and the degree to which that settlement reflected an inoculation against the absolutist Continental systems requires an understanding of the restoration system. See esp. p. 270 of *Lord Churchill's Coup* re: continuity of Glorious Revolution and American Revolution and Constitution.

George III was compelled to hire Hessians The point about George III's need to hire mercenaries from the German principalities because of lack of English enthusiasm for the war was made in Phillips's *Cousins' Wars*.

The bias against standing armies was so great See Charles Messenger, *History of the British Army* (Greenwich, Connecticut, Bramley Books, 1993). A useful history of the evolution of British military structures.

The Founding Fathers were keenly aware See *1794: America, Its Army, and the Birth of a Nation* by David R. Palmer (Novato, California, Presidio Press, 1994). This is an interesting and useful survey of the military events of 1794 and their critical role in the final defeat of the British and Indians on U.S. territory, the formation of the U.S. Army, and the militia versus standing army controversy.

this tradition [the American militia system] could effectively be revived See Gary Hart's *The Minuteman: Restoring an Army of the People* (New York, Free Press, 1998). A good treatment of the Anglo-American military system, and a discussion of the prospects for restoring militias as a major element in the U.S.'s defense posture.

Five Civil Wars: Union and Secession in the Anglosphere

Other families, such as the French speakers For an interesting discussion of "spatial" vs. "regime" composition, using the contrasts of Ireland and Algeria, see Ian S. Lustick, *Unsettled States, Disputed Lands: Britain and Ireland, France and Algeria, Israel and the West Bank-Gaza* (Ithaca, New York, Cornell University Press, 1993). This framework ultimately draws on Gramsci's categories, but appears to be a useful approach that is not dependent on other more problematic aspects of that Marxist theorist's work.

A unitary state for all Britain In this era of romanticization of the nationalisms of the non-English parts of the British Isles, it is useful to recall that the history of the isles from early medieval times has fluctuated between the extreme poles of a unitary state of the archipelago on the one hand and independence for its constituent parts on the other. Nor have the existing definitions of the components always been the current ones. R. R. Davies, in *The First English Empire: Power and Identities in the British Isles 1093–1343* (Oxford University Press, 2000) provides a good recapitulation of ideologies of a united Britain long preceding Cromwell's achievement of it. Also of interest, to show that the line between the "natural" formation of England and Scotland, and the "synthetic" formation of Great Britain, is not as clear as nationalist narratives like to present, is his discussion of a five-nation model of British Isles nationality as an alternative that nearly happened, with Galloway and the Western Isles as a fifth potential nation separate in identity from Scotland. The book also gives a fascinating look at what might be called the first Anglosphere—the extension of English-speaking populations and social institutions beyond the boundaries of England into Scotland, Ireland, and Wales in the twelfth and thirteenth centuries, and their eventual melding with the local populations to form what now are the recognized nations of the British Isles. Also of interest is John L. Roberts, *Lost Kingdoms: Celtic Scotland and the Middle Ages* (Edinburgh University Press, 1997). As he depicts events, Scotland was a Celtic nation, a mixture of the Brythonic Picts and the Goidelic Celts, with heavy Viking influence. It was never conquered by England. How did it become an English-speaking nation? This book is a good discussion of the question.

Simultaneously a war of secession, a civil war, . . . and a social revolution

In addition to Phillips's extensive discussion of this aspect in *Cousins' Wars*, it is interesting to read Mark Perry's *Conceived in Liberty: Joshua Chamberlain, William Oates, and the American Civil War* (New York, Penguin, 1997). Perry provides a useful discussion of the events before and after the American Civil War from the perspective of two important figures, North and South. It is most interesting to watch the changing perceptions during the prewar period, as well as the conceptual adjustments made subsequently.

For the war-within-the-war aspect and the complex nature of the New Ulster subsecession, see William W. Freehling's invaluable *The South vs. the South: How Anti-Confederate Southerners Shaped the Course of the Civil War* (2001). Consistent with the cultural-nationalist analysis of the Anglosphere, Freehling demonstrates how the Confederacy was almost as diverse as the presecession Union, and that the various cultural nations were very much at odds with each other. This internal conflict was one of the major contributors to Confederate defeat.

Of course, Charles Frazier's *Cold Mountain* (Vintage Books) remains an excellent fictional treatment of the cultural antagonisms between the coastal Dixie culture and the New Ulster mountaineers, and its expression in the struggle between the New Ulster deserters and draft-dodgers and the pro-Confederate internal patrols that constituted, in some respects, a Confederate occupation force in the highlands. Neo-Confederates like to refer to the events of 1861–1865 as the "War of Northern Aggression"; from the viewpoint of core New Ulster, it might have been considered the "War of Southern Aggression against the Mountaineers."

Preserving the National Voice in a Decentralized World

Author Jonathan Freedland has contrasted *Bring Home the Revolution*

American Cultural Nations and Their Histories

the cultural nations of America Fischer's *Albion's Seed*, of course, is the primary source of the cultural-national analysis of American regionalism as derived from regionalism of the British Isles; Phillips's *Cousins' Wars* provides a particularly useful view of American history from this perspective.

A frequently quoted popular work dividing North America on an (almost) strictly geographical basis is *The Nine Nations of North America* by Joel Garreau (Avon, 1981). A useful text from a traditional academic viewpoint is F. M. Shelley, J. C. Archer, F. M. Davidson, S. D. Brunn, *Political Geography of the United States* (New York, Guilford Press, 1996).

Jay Winik's *April 1865: The Month That Saved America* (Perennial, 2001) contains a good discussion of the coherence issues in the early republic, and the substantial cultural, economic, and political differences among the states. He also has a useful discussion of the many secessionist episodes and threats between 1776 and 1865, which were more numerous than generally realized.

Also of interest is Walter Russell Mead's *Special Providence: American Foreign Policy and How It Changed the World* (New York, Knopf, 2001). Mead follows Fischer's quadripartite analysis of America in general, but assigns terminology for the outlook based on archetypal representative American political figures rather than the cultural-national terminology used in this work. What is here termed the Midland American pragmatic and commercial outlook he terms the *Hamiltonian* view; the New Ulster (and to a great extent also the Dixie) view, the *Jacksonian*; the greater New England moralistic view, the *Wilsonian*; and the relatively isolationist view that sees democracy as an American system not easily replicated abroad, the *Jeffersonian*. (The Jeffersonian view is the only one without an easily assigned cultural-national analogue; it has some parallels to tidewater Dixie thought, and some to Midwestern isolationism, which is perhaps the flip side of Midland pragmatism.)

A rare alignment of the interests This paragraph is a brief synopsis of the thesis of Phillips's *Cousins' Wars*.

Progressivism can be understood as an alliance In particular, the rise of the Social Gospel tendency of Protestant Christianity forged an alliance between Greater New England and Midland denominations of Protestant Christianity, fusing the moral purpose of New Englanders with the pragmatism of Midland Americans. See in particular, Robert William Fogel's *The Fourth Great Awakening & The Future of Egalitarianism* (University of Chicago Press, 2000). This book advances the theory that Social Gospel progressive Christianity was the true underpinning of the Progressive movement of early twentieth-century America, and was in itself a "Great Awakening" of religious enthusiasm equivalent to the first two waves, and the current Fourth Wave of evangelical Christianity.

A colony in Brazil Dixie's colony in Brazil is discussed in Eugene C. Harter's *The Lost Colony of the Confederacy* (University Press of Mississippi, 1988). A contemporary visit to their descendants, illuminating the gradual racial intermarriage of the colony, is included in a rather rambling and anecdotal first-person travel narrative in *Lost White Tribes* by Riccardo Orizio (Avril Bardoni, translator) (New York, Free Press, 2001).

the "Yankee-Cowboy War" in his book of that title Carl Oglesby, *Yankee and Cowboy War* (Berkley, 1977). Written from a leftist perspective, but one that looked back with something like nostalgia to the program of the Roosevelt coalition.

The increasing general racial tolerance in America See Dinesh D'Souza's *The End of Racism: Principles for a Multiracial Society* (Touchstone Books, 1996), which argues that racism should be viewed not as the casual dislike of others, or primitive xenophobia, but rather as a specific early scientific doctrine attempting to explain human variations; and that this doctrine, and the political ideologies that it engendered, have largely disappeared from the cultural mainstream of America (and from that of the Anglosphere in general). Although this change has not brought perfect intergroup harmony, it does make possible a primarily cultural, rather than genetic, understanding of interpersonal and intergroup interactions.

The Relationship between Cultural Nations and Nation-States

The Trudeau project destroyed See especially Brimelow's *Patriot Game.*

Cultural Nations in Actuality: North America

are described in Mormon culture by Wallace Stegner Compare Stegner's description of a Mormon town circa World War II in *Mormon Country* (University of Nebraska Press, 1982) to Fischer's description of New England characteristics of ordered liberty in *Albion's Seed*. Stegner is an acute observer of North American regional differences; his childhood experiences in an American family on a farm in Alberta presented in *Wolf Willow*, for example, are interesting to read as an essay on similarities and differences between Anglo-Canadians and Greater New Englanders.

the strongest bonds of the Dixie cultural nation See Tony Horwitz's *Confederates in the Attic: Dispatches from the Unfinished Civil War* (Random House, 1999) for a contemporary account of the persistence of the Confederate narrative in white Dixie and the antipathy to it among African Americans.

map out the areas *Albion's Seed* and Freehling's *South vs. the South* both are useful in localizing these criteria.

Seymour Martin Lipset . . . has devoted a lifetime of investigation See particularly his *Continental Divide: The Values and Institutions of the United States and Canada* (Routledge, 1990).

CHAPTER 6

1776: Divergence and the End of the First Empire

Franklin experimented with constitutional formulas See H. W. Brands, *The First American: The Life and Times of Benjamin Franklin* (Anchor Books, New York, 2002).

Convergence in Politics: The Dilemma of the Second Empire

Reading works like Nevil Shute's *In the Wet* (House of Stratus Inc., 2000; original publication, 1953). Shute's novel is set a generation into his future, and depicts a strong, monarchist Commonwealth that is far more unified than actually occurred, and still an independent world power on a par with the United States, but with the center of power shifting from a declining, depopulating, social democratic Britain to a vigorous Australia and Canada. He discusses issues that would be relevant in such a Commonwealth, such as the tension between role of the monarchy as a Commonwealth unifier, and its functions specific to its role in the United Kingdom, that have not become acute due to the relative unimportance of the actual organization. However, such tensions still continue to arise: e.g., as when the role of Prince Charles as a spokesman for the British beef industry, which opposed him to the interests of Australia, became an issue in the 1999 Australian republic referendum campaign. Shute's solution, the creation of an Office of Governor-General for Britain, equalizing its status relative to the rest of the Commonwealth nations, effectively would make the institution a Commonwealth monarchy rather than a British monarchy that is also head of state of some other Commonwealth nations. It is a solution that may return to view should the monarchy's role in nations beyond Britain continue.

Removing the Roadblocks to the Network Commonwealth

The Falklands War caused a severe internal dispute Sir John Nott's *Here Today, Gone Tomorrow: Recollections of an Errant Politician* (Politicos Pub,

2002) contains a frank discussion of the Anglospherist-Hemispherist controversy in the Reagan administration during the Falklands War, caused primarily by the fact that the Galtieri regime in Argentina was one of the key players in the Iran-Contra network being run by Alexander Haig.

What's at Stake: Uses of the Network Commonwealth

The continuing divergence of Britain from the Continent See for example the discussion in *Statecraft: Strategies for a Changing World* by Margaret Thatcher (HarperCollins, 2002) or again Robert Conquest's *Reflections on a Ravaged Century.*

The idea of a unified Europe built around the "European Social Model." John Laughland's *The Tainted Source* (Trafalgar Square, 2000) critiques the Europeanist narrative from a political and historical viewpoint; Patrick Minford's *Should Britain Join the Euro: The Chancellor's Five Tests Examined?* (London, Institute of Economic Affairs, 2002) examines the economic problems of the European Social Model in light of the unaddressed overhanging economic and demographic problems facing the Continental European countries. Specific case examples of the Continental European model's problems can be found in works such as Jonathan Fenby's *On the Brink: The Trouble with France* (London, Warner Books, 1998), an examination of the structural barriers in France (but useful for understanding Continental Europe in general) to entrepreneurship and high technology in general, although considered entirely in a pre-Singularity context.

The Anglosphere Debate

Conrad Black raised a stir *Britain's Final Choice: Europe or America?* (lecture given to the Centre for Policy Studies by Mr. Conrad Black [now Lord Black of Crossharbour] on the occasion of the 1998 Centre for Policy Studies Annual Meeting, held on July 9, 1998).

proposed that the United States create a Free Trade Area *The World Turned Rightside Up: A New Trading Agenda for the Age of Globalization,* John Hulsman et al. (London, Institute of Economic Affairs, 2001).

Paul Johnson published a radical essay in Forbes *Forbes* magazine, April 5, 1999.

Britain's place in the European Union The increasing moves toward federal statehood for Europe, and the continued discomfort of the British with these trends, combined with the constitutional changes of the Blair government, have resulted in a remarkable literature of self-examination in Britain over the past few years. These would include certainly Laughland's *Tainted Source*, but also Simon Heffer's *Nor Shall My Sword: The Reinvention of England* (London, Wiedenfeld and Nicholson, 1999). A discussion of the reemergence of a specifically English national identity as Scottish nationalism unravels the British narrative. Written from a conservative English viewpoint that discusses the case against a federal solution for Britain. It's Union or independence for Heffer.

More deeply cultural is philosopher Roger Scruton's *England: An Elegy* (London, Chatto and Windus, 2000). A beautiful evocation of the now-vanishing culture specific to the England of the early and mid-twentieth century. Scruton particularly shines in showing how the institutions of that time and culture made sense in their own terms, and how they have been abolished in favor of a bland modernism with its own dissatisfactions.

Peter Hitchens's *The Abolition of Britain: From Winston Churchill to Princess Diana* (Encounter Books, 2002) covers much of the same territory as does Scruton, but with a more political outlook. His narration of the process by which the death penalty was abolished in England, along with other constitutional matters, is very insightful.

Michael Wood's *In Search of England: Journeys into the English Past* (London, Viking, 1999) deals with some issues of English identity in a much different style. An interesting set of journeys to find traces of old England in the present. His examination of English late-medieval village life serves to bring some of Alan Macfarlane's points to life.

The Rotten Heart of Europe: The Dirty War for Europe's Money by Bernard Connolly (Faber and Faber, 1996) covers the political-economic case against the European Union from the perspective of a former insider.

Secession Crises as a Driver: Devolution and the Neverendum in Scotland and Quebec

Developments in the Canadian example Stabilizing frameworks: Jane Jacobs, *The Question of Separatism: Quebec and the Struggle over Sovereignty* (New York, Random House, 1980) considers Network Commonwealth-like solutions for Quebec separatism and Canadian devolution. Robert A. Young's *The Secession of Quebec and the Future of Canada* (Montreal, McGill-Queen's Press, 1998) gives a comprehensive and thoughtful treatment of the various options for linking sovereign and subsovereign entities, with implications for other states besides Canada. It's easy to advocate a "common market" or a "free trade area," as well as more elaborate unions. But each level of association has its own drawbacks and benefits. This book does a good job of setting them out.

a further reworking of the Grand Union John Kendle, *Federal Britain: A History* (New York, Routledge, 1997), gives a comprehensive academic treatment of the federal idea in British thought, in three contexts: the organization of the home islands, the organization of the empire and its constituent parts, and in relation to Britain's role in Europe. Naive in its attribution of British opposition to a federal Europe to British unfamiliarity to the federal idea. It does not seem to occur to Kendle that there might be other objections.

African America: The Stalled Transition to High Trust

began glorifying the low-trust remnants in the African-American community See *Losing the Race: Self-Sabotage in Black America*, by John H. McWhorter (Free Press, 2000).

Prospects for the Anglosphere

generational patterns of response See in particular *Generations: The History of America's Future, 1584 to 2069*—by William Strauss and Neil Howe (William Morrow and Co., Reprint edition, 1992) and their subsequent *The Fourth Turning: An American Prophecy* (Broadway Books, Reprint edition, 1998). Strauss and Howe take an insight that is not particularly original, but is certainly true: that each generation in politics reacts both against the previous generation and in response to generation-shaping events, adds an interesting and original elaboration, which is that the four distinct generations present in politics at any one time each react against each other, and go from there to an original, interesting, but somewhat problematic systemic structure they hold to be deterministic, giving a four-generation cyclic structure and analyzing all of American history in its terms. A particular strength of their analysis can be seen in their subtitle: by starting their analysis on 1584, they recognize the continuity between English and American politics, and between preindependence and postindependence America.

South Africa

radically decentralize the African federal state A blueprint for a radically decentralized South Africa was presented by South African antiapartheid activists Frances Kendall and Leon Louw in *South Africa: The Solution* (Bisho, Ciskei [now South Africa], Amagi Publications, 1986) and *Let the People Govern* (Bisho, Ciskei, Amagi Publications, 1989). Published before the end of apartheid, they called for one-person, one-vote to be implemented in a highly decentralized framework. Today their call for decentralization continues to be relevant to a still unsettled South Africa.

Index

Aerospatiale-Matra, 162, 167
Afghanistan conflict, xiii
Africa: colonization and, xix;
    devolution in, 175–76; First
    Gateway (civil society) in, 53–54;
    slavery and, 84, 96; tribalism in,
    170. *See also specific African nations*
African-American cultural nation:
    defined, 200, 215; assimilation and,
    84, 101, 220, 238–39; as cultural vs.
    racial group, 84, 100–101; history of,
    200–208; trust and, 96, 239, 263
African Americans: alternatives to
    racial identity, 84; as Anglosphere
    population, 84, 234–35, 238–39;
    consequence of protected class
    status, 100, 263; cultural narratives
    of, 239, 261–63; desegregation of the
    U.S. military, 220–21; imagined
    independent nation of, 207, 238;
    low- vs. high-trust cultural
    patterns, 101, 239, 261–63; pan-
    African identity, 238–39; political
    alliances of, 206–8; slavery and, 84,
    96
Albania, 139
Amish, 153

amphibious society, 28–29, 120, 124–26,
    285
anarchocapitalism, 138–40
Anglosphere: defined, 79–82; African
    American participation in, 84,
    234–35, 238–39; "Anglo" term, 71,
    91, 230; assimilation vs.
    multiculturalism in, 72, 100, 113,
    234–35; civil society in, 3–4, 10, 186,
    210–11, 241, 284, 288–89; civil war
    in, 93, 191–92, 195–96, 231–32;
    cultural and historical foundation,
    34–35, 89, 89–93, 288–89; cultural
    nations and, 82–83, 92, 199;
    exceptionalism, 72–74; feudalism
    and, 5, 93–94; high-trust societies
    in, 67–69; intermarriage within, 77,
    234, 241; language and, 39, 42, 75,
    79–80, 230, 257–58, 267; legal
    traditions of, 3, 72, 181–85; mass
    media and, 75–78; reconvergence
    of, 74–78, 233–34; regionalism in,
    82–88; religious roots of, 36, 93, 100,
    106; slavery and, 5, 95–97, 105; U.S.-
    British "special relationship", 233,
    235, 236–37; utopianism and, 65–66,
    97–99

Anglosphere Network
Commonwealth: alternative terms
for, 91; British Empire as precursor
to, 6; Common Law as prerequisite,
257; conditions leading to, 260–62,
284; defense alliance, 159–62,
248–49; imperial unification vs.,
231–34; intra-Anglosphere trade,
110, 242–45; NAFTA as precursor
to, 106, 137–38; as post–Cold War
strategy, 275–76; race not basis for,
70, 91, 230; Virtual Network
Commonwealth Assembly control
structure, 167. *See also* Network
Commonwealth; Network
Commonwealth examples
apocalyptic theories, 9–10
Arabic Network Commonwealth, 177
Argentina, 114, 116, 175–76
artificial intelligence, 27, 28
arts, 59, 103, 197
ASEAN (Association of Southeast
Asian Nations), 38, 112
assimilation: across cultural nations,
213, 221; African-American cultural
nation and, 84, 101, 220, 238,
221–22; cyber-immigration, 120;
ethnic neighborhoods, 119;
openness and, 118–19;
sojournership vs., 147–48, 248; state
intervention in, 100, 113, 206, 208,
221–22; template societies and,
116–17; transformation vs., 239–40;
trust and, 70–71, 116–17, 118,
147–48, 211, 240. *See also*
multiculturalism
Associated Commonwealths, 179–80
Atlantic Defense Industry Community
(ADIC), 159–62
Atlantic Union, 111
Australia: aboriginal peoples in,
238–39, 279–80; as Anglosphere
nation, 71, 80, 256–57, 279–80;
British colonization and, 233, 237;
constitutional reform in, 185; as a
cultural nation, 92–93, 223, 280;
defense, 249–50; market economy

in, 38; New Zealand and, 74, 280;
protectionist backlash movement,
242; Sinosphere connection of, 69,
123–24, 280; trust and openness in,
115–16
Austria, 71, 170
authoritarian society, 31–32

Baechler, Jean, 225
Barbados, 99
biotechnology, 17, 20–21, 25
Black, Conrad, 251
Blair, Tony, 59, 99, 241, 251–52, 272–73
Bolivia, 176
borderlessness, 2, 118, 288
Borsook, Paulina, 138, 140
Bosnia, 142, 169
bounded/unbounded distinction:
economic theory and, 13–14, 135;
indicators of unboundedness,
20–22; political disputes and, 182;
space exploration and, 13–18; Y2K
crisis and, 18–20; zero-sum oriented
societies, 116
Brazil: devolutionary forces in, 176;
Lusosphere Network
Commonwealth, 173; openness in,
116; Portugal as template for,
116–18; slavery and, 95, 106, 261;
U.S. Confederate exiles in, 204
Breadbasket cultural nation, 85–86
Brin, David, 138, 140
British Aerospace, 158, 162
British Empire. *See* Great Britain
Brown, Gordon, 110–11, 256
Buchanan, Patrick, 24

C-SPAN, 167
Cabot, John, 104–6
Calvinism, 34, 69
Canada: American Revolution and,
229; as Anglosphere nation, 80, 91,
106, 194; constitutional reform in,
184; cultural nations in, 211–13;
devolution in, 146, 266–67; export
products of, 68; Francosphere
Network Commonwealth, 174; as a

nation-state, 91–92; national culture movement (*le Projet Trudeau*), 212, 265–69; Newfoundland statehood, 74; political parties, 195; post-Imperial identity, 242; protectionist backlash movement, 246; regionalism in, 84–85; secession movement, 169, 257, 259–61, 288; Sinosphere connection of, 123–24; socialism in, 98; technological development in, 39; trust and openness in, 116, 118. *See also* Quebec cultural nation
capitalism: "crony capitalism", 33, 37, 68, 138–39, 189; Industrial Revolution and, 47–48, 53–54; Internet content as commodity, 48–49; labor and capital components of value, 26–27; market economy vs. traditional capitalism, 26–27, 47–51, 53–54, 138; natural monopolies in, 136–37; personal computer as means of production, 49–50. *See also* labor; market economy; regulation
Caribbean nations, 81, 95, 103, 207, 219, 231, 238
Catholicism: anti-slavery movement, 106; assimilation and, 220; in Ireland, 95, 142, 199–201, 230, 234; liberation theology, 176; relation to Anglosphere, 81; trust characteristics and, 71; utopian characteristics and, 97–98
CENTO, 157
CERN, 155
Chadhauri, Nirad, 7
Chechnya, 172
Chile, 176
China: Chinese Empire as model for Britain, 6; devolution in, 176–77; legal traditions in, 74; as low-trust society, 115; Sinosphere Network Commonwealth, 123–24; Western classical culture in, 102
Chrétien, Jean, 261
Christianity, 70–71, 93, 100

Church of England, 97
Churchill, Winston, 93, 127
civic states: characteristics of, 46, 288; civic social democracies, 56–58; civil society and, 33, 56, 58; criteria for survival, 54–56; devolution of federal/regional authority in, 141, 233; economic states vs., 39, 85–86; noncontiguous (shared) states, 142; prosperity narratives in, 58; role in Network Commonwealths, 223–24, 237; types of Singularity Era civic states, 57. *See also* economic states; nation-states
civil society: defined, 31; anarchocapitalism and, 138; as Anglosphere characteristic, 2, 10, 65–66, 183, 210, 244, 285, 288; characteristics of, 38; civic states and, 31, 56, 58; democracy and, 29, 32–33; entrepreneurial culture in, 33–37; feudalism and, 34, 71, 83; First Gateway as, 52–53, 117–18; individualism and, 31–32, 73; kinship (family) and, 31–32, 37; openness in, 10, 36–37, 69–70, 118, 131; persistence of, 29–30; religion and, 34, 71; self-healing capacity, 195–96; social planning and, 208; spatial composition and, 194–96; technological development and, 28–30, 33; trust and, 69–70, 72, 113–17, 131
classical-liberal civic state, 56, 58–59. *See also* liberalism
Clinton, Bill, 59
cloning, 16, 19
Coase, Ronald, 52, 55
Colley, Linda, 184
colonialism, 3–4, 72, 79, 175, 231–34, 276. *See also* imperialism
Columbus, Christopher, 103, 104, 105
COMECON, 162
Common Law: as Anglosphere characteristic, 2–3, 74, 79, 95, 181–84; commercial cooperation and, 16, 145; as prerequisite for

Anglosphere Network
Commonwealth, 252–53, 278–79;
transnational jurisdiction and,
251–52
computers: Apache server, 50; Linux
computer system, 15, 36, 49–51, 53,
119–20; Microsoft, 48, 50; Moore's
Law, 27; open-source movement,
15, 27, 49–51, 53, 119–20; personal
computers, 15, 48–49, 128; "Turing
Test", 27; Y2K crisis, 16–18. *See also*
Information Revolution
Confucianism, 9, 30, 173, 176
Conquest, Robert, 105, 253
Continental law tradition, 182
Cook, Robin, 256
Cortéz, Hernán, 105
Coughlan, Anthony, 282
cryptoanarchy, 46, 54
Cuba, 84
cultural nations: assimilation of,
100–101, 206, 221–22; as
fundamental Anglosphere
structure, 82–88, 124, 197–207,
222–23; Grand Union of, 92, 206,
224–25, 261–62; hybridity of, 221;
immigration streams of, 209;
nation-states vs., 92, 122, 206–8;
non-North American cultural
nations, 222–23; optimal size of,
224; political boundaries and,
85–86; preeminence over economic
concerns, 288; preeminence over
media homogenization, 222; region-
states vs., 223–25; regions vs.,
84–89, 216–23; trust and, 205–6. *See
also* African-American cultural
nation; Breadbasket cultural nation;
Dixie cultural nation; Foundry
cultural nation; Greater New
England cultural nation;
MexAmerica cultural nation;
Midland cultural nation; nation-
states; New Ulster cultural nation;
Quebec cultural nation
cypherpunkism, 138
Cyprus, 143

Czech Republic, 104, 127, 169–70, 266

DARPA (Defense Advanced Research
Projects Agency), 140
DASA, 161, 165
Debs, Eugene V., 99
defense: Anglosphere Defense Alliance
proposal, 162–65, 248–49, 285–86;
Atlantic Defense Industry
Community (ADIC), 162–65; B-2
bomber, 25–26; bounded/
unbounded distinction and, 12–14;
constitutional theory and, 186–89;
DARPA (Defense Advanced
Research Projects Agency), 140;
draft (selective service) system, 186;
"Grid" information network, 130,
158, 286; information technology
and, 159–60; militia system, 187–89;
in nationalist-conservative civic
states, 58; NORAD (North
American Air Defense Command),
37; U.S.-British defense alliance,
158–65, 233, 235, 236–37, 285–87;
West Point (U.S. Military
Academy), 190. *See also* war
DeGaulle, Charles, 126, 181
DeHavilland Corp., 161
Delamaide, Darrell, 84–85, 223–24
democracy: as abstraction of civil
society, 30, 33–34; economic
development and, 160, 263–64;
social democracy, 53, 57–59, 87–88;
as voluntary association, 55
Denmark, 58
determinism, 7
devolution: in Anglosphere nations,
153–54, 183–84; in the British
Empire, 231–32; cryptoanarchy and,
46, 54; cultural diversity and,
173–74; economic states vs. civic
states and, 109, 131, 140–41, 234;
limits of, 43, 109, 141; Network
Commonwealth as outgrowth of,
109, 172; privatization, 53, 121, 144;
prosperity and, 248–49; regional
competitiveness and, 141, 173,

265–67; sovereignty a consequence of, 45, 175, 266–67; tribalism vs., 170, 279

Dewey, John, 203

Dixie cultural nation, 86, 198–207, 208–9, 210–11, 288

Douglass, Frederick, 72, 84, 262

Drake, Sir Francis, 103–4

Drexler, K. Eric, 29

DuBois, W. E. B., 100, 262

East Asia: Anglosphere areas in, 82; crony capitalism, 31, 34, 67, 138–39, 131; cultural identity in, 280; devolution in, 173–74; Japan as cultural anomaly, 177; neo-Confucianism, 9, 30; as U.S. axis of cooperation, 197. *See also specific East Asian nations*

Eastern Europe, 30, 63, 72, 138–39, 156

economic states: defined, 45–46; anarchocapitalism (pure market society) and, 138–40; "billiard ball" concept, 113; civic states vs., 39, 84–85; communications industries and, 125–29; "creative destruction" (Schumpeter), 53; "cryptoanarchy" in, 46, 55; currency control and, 45; defense industries in, 159–60; devolution of, 111, 131, 169, 234; social democracy as stabilizer, 53; state-mediated relationships, 121–22; status of citizenry in, 191; tribalism emergent from, 169, 192. *See also* civic states; devolution; nation-states

economy: corporate vs. network model, 52; economic determinism, 6; entrepreneurial vs. hierarchical economy, 23–25; "follower" economies, 36–37; market economy vs. traditional capitalism, 26–27, 47–51, 54–55, 138; morality as basis for, 282; open-source movement, 28; reputation economy, 49–51; visibility of transactions, 45. *See also*

capitalism; labor; market economy; Marxism

Egypt, 237–38

Eisenhower, Dwight, 158, 207

environment, 2, 137–38, 104, 214, 226

Eritrea, 175

Ethiopia, 175

ethnicity: assimilation and, 72, 101, 114, 242–43; bridge cities, 178–79; civic states and, 56; civil society and, 31–32; diasporas, 56, 173, 178; diversity fundamental to Anglosphere, 236–37; Hispanosphere, 112, 122, 174–75; mimetic vs. group identity, 89–90; network paradigm and, 241; overstates both similarities and differences, 90; racial identity, 100–101; scientific concept of race, 147; terrorism and, 170; "white" ethnicity, 101–102. *See also* multiculturalism

European Atomic Energy Agency, 152

European Coal and Steel Community, 152, 163

European Common Market, 146

European Convention on Human Rights, 251

European Economic Area (EEA), 112–13

European Space Agency, 131, 152

European Union: British role in, 162–63, 238–39, 244–45, 176–77, 258–59, 269–73; as economic vs. civic union, 47, 109–10, 131; European Parliament control structure, 167, 244, 261; Euroskepticism movement, 244–45, 261, 274–77, 283; "harmonization" strategy, 65, 148, 162, 272, 282; "lowest-common-denominator" economic inertia, 197, 276–77, 282; as model for Network Commonwealth, 64–65, 109–12, 148; NAFTA trade agreement with, 112–13, 148; as self-assembly protocol, 61; Singularity Revolution

and, 38; sojournership in, 149–53, 248; successes and failures of, 63, 121–22, 131; trust atmosphere in, 172–73
evolution, 69, 109–11, 147
evolutionary conservatism, 110, 284

family: adult adoptions, 118; civil society and, 31–32, 38; as economic mechanism, 121; feudalism and, 93, 95; individualism and, 73; modernist concept of, 203; openness and, 118–19; trust and, 114–16, 121, 243; as voluntary association, 31; wealth and, 53
federalism, 62, 140–41, 175, 211, 225–26, 232–35
Ferguson, Adam, 61
Fiji, 56
Finland, 37, 103, 120–21
First Gateway (civil society), 49–50, 117–18
Fischer, David Hackett, 73, 38, 199, 214, 216
Foundry cultural nation, 84, 141–43, 216–17
Fox, Vicente, 176
France: civil society in, 34, 269; collaborative technology, 148, 152; defense capability of, 158, 287; degree of trust in, 115, 116; entrepreneurial barriers in, 38; Francosphere Network Commonwealth, 172; government spending, 37; modernist art, 103; as a nation-state, 92; national radio network, 126–27; NATO membership, 159; regime-composition revolutions in, 196; Rhenish Network Commonwealth, 172–73; role in European unity, 238–40, 277; socialist influences in, 99, 281–82
Francosphere Network Commonwealth, 172
Franklin, Benjamin, 232
Free Trade Area proposal, 256

Freedland, Jonathan, 184, 199
Freehling, William W., 95
Freud, Sigmund, 203
Friedman, Milton, 53
Friedman, Thomas, 103
Fukuyama, Francis, 114–16, 222

Galbraith, John Kenneth, 203
Garreau, Joel, 84–85, 199, 214, 226–27
GATT (General Agreement on Tariffs and Trade), 253
GEC-Marconi, 161, 165
General Common Law, 251–52
George III, King of England, 231–33
Germany: as civic state, 46, 56; collaborative technology, 148, 152; defense industries in, 161; entrepreneurship in, 36–38; Hanse organizations, 132–35, 167; as industrial rival to Britain, 233; relation with Czechoslovakia, 169–70; religious influences in, 71; Rhenish Network Commonwealth, 172–73; role in European Union, 232, 277, 282; socialism in, 99; trust and openness in, 116, 118
Global Positioning System, 15
globalization: borderlessness, 2, 118, 288; fundamental civilizational groupings (Huntington), 130–31; inevitable limits of, 42; "lowest-common-denominator" effect, 35–36, 132, 166, 197, 246, 276–77; market intervention and, 135–39; network civilizations, 123; New World Order, 42; "One World" prediction, 117, 132; regulation of information, 121–22; regulation of technology, 29–30, 49, 53, 127–29, 89–90; transnational currencies, 45; world government vs. cooperative civil society, 36–37, 39–40. *See also* treaties
Goldwater, Barry, 53, 204
Gramm, Phil, 112, 253
Grand Union, 92, 211, 226–27, 262–63
Gray, John, 138, 140

Great Britain: as Anglosphere nation, 80–81, 110, 244–45, 277–78; British Empire, 4–5, 6, 129, 231–35, 237–40, 277; British exceptionalism, 73–75; classical-liberal heritage of, 60; democracy in, 32, 108, 184–85, 233; Euroskepticism movement, 34, 69, 244–45, 261, 274–78, 283; governmental structures of, 234, 269; as high-trust society, 116; individualism in, 73; legal traditions of, 185–86; market vs. industrial economy, 37, 103, 160–61, 270; NAFTA membership proposed, 162–63, 253–56, 270–71; National Health Service, 23, 45–46, 257; North Atlantic Free Trade Agreement, 90; origins of aristocracy, 93–94; religious influences in, 71, 95–96; role in European Union, 162–63, 238–40, 244–45, 253–56, 258–61, 269–75; Scottish nationalism, 196, 233, 260–62, 269–70; slavery vs. serfdom in, 95, 103–4; state ownership in, 99; U.S. cultural fusion with, 76; U.S. defense alliance with, 158–66, 233, 236, 237–38, 286–88; U.S. statehood proposal, 257; Whig historical narrative, 3–4, 72–73, 93, 184
Greater New England cultural nation, 199–211, 213–14
Greece, 63–64, 126, 229
Gress, David, 69, 103
"Grid" military information network, 130, 158, 286
Gulf War, 144, 167

Hague, William, 270
Hanseatic Leagues, 132–35, 167
Hanson, Pauline, 246
harmonization, 65, 148, 162, 270, 282
Hart, Gary, 193
Haushofer, Karl, 6
Hayek, Friedrich A. von, 13, 51, 52, 135, 139
health insurance, 23, 45–46, 257

Herder, Johann Gottfried von, 73–74, 91–92, 146
Hispanosphere, 112, 122, 174–75
history: American historical narrative, 204–5; Anglosphere historic foundation, 89; ideological conspiracy narrative, 98; macrohistorical analysis, 69; Marxist narrative of, 3–4; Whig historical narrative, 3–4, 72–73, 184, 133–34
Hitler, Adolf, 30, 126
Hobbes, Thomas, 39–40
Holland, 129
Howe, Neil, 265
Hulsman, John, 256
Human Genome Project, 20
Hungary, 169–70
Huntington, Samuel, 130–31, 122, 175–76

immigration. *See* assimilation; multiculturalism; nation-states
imperialism, 4–6, 129, 231–34, 327–40, 263
India, 5–6, 82, 173–74, 233, 240
individualism, 31–32, 73
Indonesia, 105, 173–74
Industrial Revolution: agricultural production and, 25; British Empire and, 232; capitalism and, 46–47, 54–55; civil society in, 2–3; conversion of agricultural labor skills, 28; individualism and, 73; Information Revolution compared to, 11, 25, 129–30; modernist Machine Paradigm, 63–64; slavery and, 95–96; standing armies and, 192
Information Revolution: amphibious society, 121, 123–25; broadcasting vs. narrowcasting, 74–78; cryptoanarchy, 46, 55; cultural reconvergence and, 74–79, 233–34; decentralizing effects of, 39, 121–22, 128, 153, 243; defense industry and, 158–66; design-to-manufacture

process, 25–26; encryption programs, 45, 125; history of, 124–25; Industrial Revolution compared to, 11, 25, 129–30; information warfare, 130; intellectual property and, 143; national security and, 156–58; nationalism and, 125–26; open-source movement, 15, 28; political affiliation and, 221; topology of information space, 129–32, 286. *See also* computers; Internet

Intelsat, 127

Internet: basis for information economy, 26, 44; broadcaasting vs. narrowcasting, 74, 78; communications content as commodity, 48–49, 124–25; control of, 30; creation of, 140, 160; cultural network underpinning of, 118, 122; cultural reconvergence and, 74; effect on Network Commonwealth, 40; impact on civilization, 11; Internet currencies, 45; model for network civilization, 65, 122–23; One-World-Through-Internet movement, 40, 117, 132; pictographic vs. alphabetic languages and, 173; as self-assembly protocol, 61–62, 65; trust and, 120–21, 125; World Wide Web, 54, 61, 62, 125, 155. *See also* Information Revolution

Iran, 173–74

Iraq, 32

Ireland: as Anglosphere nation, 78, 80–81, 91–92, 164, 283–84; as civic state, 56, 58; European Union arrangement with, 257, 281–82; feudalism and, 4, 83; low- vs. high-trust in, 71, 94; Northern Ireland, 142, 170, 233; reunification movement, 234; secession movement, 74, 162; technological development in, 36–37

Islam, 74, 82, 130

Islands cultural classification, 220

Israel, 56, 60, 82, 142, 178. *See also* Judaism

Italy, 38, 45, 71, 116, 119–20

Japan: alleged global dominance of, 9–10; as Anglosphere nation, 82, 177–78; entrepreneurship in, 37, 38; as high-trust society, 71, 116, 118, 264; kinship in, 118; as a nation-state, 92; openness in, 118; regionalism in, 84; technological cooperation with, 44; Western classical culture in, 103

Jefferson, Thomas, 113, 184

Jesuits, 98, 105

Johnson, Lyndon, 13, 90, 102, 280

Johnson, Paul, 257

Joy, Bill, 29–30

Judaism, 82, 100, 178. *See also* Israel

juste retour policy, 152, 153, 161

Karabakh, 169

Kennedy, John, 13, 204

Keynes John Maynard, 135, 203

King, Martin Luther, 72, 263

kinship. *See* family

Kipling, Rudyard, 277

Kissinger, Henry, 157

Kosovo, 40, 144, 277

Kuwait, 32

labor: corporation-employment model, 45; labor theory of value, 3–4, 26–27, 94; labor unions, 53, 201; manufacturing and service industry, 26; sojournership, 149–52, 165, 248; use of immigrant labor, 38. *See also* capitalism; Marxism

Landes, David, 70

language: as Anglosphere characteristic, 4, 39, 44, 75, 230, 256–57, 268; degrees of Anglosphere participation and, 81–82; English-as-a-Universal-Language school of thought, 40, 117; evolutionary model of, 147;

imperialism and, 231; information economy and, 36, 68, 112, 120–21, 129, 148, 155; minority languages, 242, 256–57; nationalism and, 2, 126; network civilizations and, 88–89, 123, 131; pictographic vs. alphabetic languages, 173; reconvergence and, 74–79, 233–34; template societies and, 114; translation and, 102–3, 118, 173–74; trust and, 120–21, 150

Latin America: as Anglosphere affiliate, 82; devolutionary forces in, 174–75; Hispanosphere, 112, 122–23, 120–21; template societies and, 117; trust in, 31, 36, 116

Laughland, John, 288

Lawrence, D. H., 99

Lee, Robert E., 192

liberalism, 113, 203, 219–20. *See also* classical-liberal civic state

Liberia, 44, 83–84

libertarianism, 60, 138–40, 153

Linnean paradigm. *See* network paradigm

Linux computer system, 15, 37, 49–50, 120–21

Lipset, Seymour Martin, 223

literature, 102

Lusosphere Network Commonwealth, 172

Macfarlane, Alan, 73–74

MacNamara, Robert, 13

Major, John, 270

Malaysia, 282, 231

Manhattan Archipelago cultural classification, 205–10, 220–22. *See also* New York City

Mao Tse-Tung, 30

market economy: anarchocapitalism (pure market society), 138–40; capitalism vs., 27–28, 47–51, 54–55, 138; cryptoanarchy and, 46, 55; cultural basis for, 72–73; democracy and, 33; Network Marketplace, 54, 122–23; prosperity and, 247–48;

state intervention in, 135–38; Third Gateway (fluid entrepreneurism), 54, 117–18. *See also* capitalism

Marxism: Anglosphere utopianism and, 98–100; centralization in, 47–48; collective identity in, 31; concept of revolution and, 196; economic determinism of, 6; historical theory of, 69; labor theory of value, 3–4, 27–28, 57; "liberation theology" and, 174; open-source movement and, 49–51; social democracy, 53; Whig demise and, 184. *See also* labor; socialism

mass media, 75–76, 78–79, 125–29, 113, 223

McCreevy, Charles, 282–83

MCI, 127

McNeill, William, 69

Mead, Margaret, 203

Medicare, 23, 45–46

Mediterranean Network Commonwealth, 172–73

Methodism, 34, 95, 105

MexAmerica cultural nation, 84, 214, 218, 220

Mexico, 174–76

Microsoft, 48, 50, 120–21, 123

Midland cultural nation, 101, 195, 199–211, 216

military. *See* defense

militia system, 185–87

Minford, Patrick, 253

Mises, Ludwig von, 135

modernism, 1–2, 63–64, 91, 103, 146

molecular nanotechnology (MNT), 15, 20–22, 29, 29–30

monarchies, 59

Moore's Law, 28

moral hazards, 140

multiculturalism: assimilation and, 72, 101; deconstruction of national identity, 266–68; equality and, 113–14; immigration transaction costs, 101–2; multiculturalist ideology, 40, 220–22, 264; noncontiguous (shared) states,

141–43; trust and, 116, 243, 264. *See also* assimilation; ethnicity
music, 102
Mussolini, Benito, 126
Myers, Kevin, 282

NAFTA (North American Free Trade Agreement): British membership in, 162–63, 255–56, 272–73; European Union trade agreement with, 112–13, 148; geographical vs. cultural basis for, 68; immigration patterns and, 38; Network Commonwealth as outgrowth of, 131, 165–66, 257–58; protectionist reaction to, 246; as self-assembly protocol, 63–64; Western culture and, 103
nanotechnology, 15, 20–22, 29, 29–30
NASA, 14
nation-states: civic vs. economic qualities of, 2; civilization vs. nation, 130–31; conception of, 146; continental vs. Anglosphere conception of, 73–74; cultural nations vs., 211–13; ethnicity as foundation for, 39, 91; future of, 288; immigration, 38, 121, 150; national culture and, 59, 197–99, 212–13, 265–69, 280; national narratives, 56, 59, 203, 212, 221; nationalism, 125–26, 212, 265–68; sovereignty services and, 44–45, 132; U.N. recognition and, 179. *See also* civic states; cultural nations; economic state
National Advisory Council for Aeronautics, 14
National Endowment for the Arts, 59
National Health Service (Great Britain), 23, 45–46, 257
National Space Society, 284–85
nationalist-conservative civic states, 57, 59
Native Americans, 83–85, 105, 242–43, 259–60, 266, 269

NATO (North Atlantic Treaty Organization): Anglo-American high command of World War II and, 90; anti-Soviet origins of, 238–40, 276–77; "Atlantic Assembly" control structure, 167; geographical vs. cultural basis for, 112; importance to small nation members, 57; lowest-common-denominator membership criteria, 160, 246; member nation loyalty to, 156–57; Network Commonwealth relation to, 131, 167, 277; as self-assembly protocol, 63–64; "slow convoy" dilemma, 165–66; specialization in, 286–87; technological cooperation in, 144, 158, 250; U.S. interest in, 238–40; Western Civilization and, 103
natural monopolies, 135–36
neo-Confucianism, 9, 30
Netherlands Antilles, 44
Netherlands, The, 37, 59, 71, 118
Netscape, 54
network civilizations, 123, 237
Network Commonwealth: defined, 6, 39, 63–64, 110; as amphibious society, 121, 123–25, 286; civic state as fundamental social unit of, 224–27, 237; collaborative technology in, 152–53; conditions leading to, 40–42, 259–62, 284–86; constitutional vs. utopian structure, 40; cyber-immigration, 121; economic/cultural vs. geographical basis for, 39–42, 47, 68, 109, 289; European Union as model for, 64–65, 109–13, 148; government in, 54, 131; Greek city-state alliance vs., 238; information (vs. goods) as basis for exchange, 62–65, 68; institutional control, 167–68; institutional precursors of, 147–58; intellectual property in, 148; limits on consensus in, 62; mechanisms of transnational cooperation, 46–47; network civilizations linked by, 123,

237; nonassimilable minorities in, 142–43, 242–43; relation to Network Marketplace, 54; relations among coherent states, 61; role of government in, 54, 130, 95; self-assembly protocols and, 61–64, 132–34; socio-political organization of, 42–44; sojournership, 78, 149–52, 248; tolerance for multiple linkages in, 88; trade alliances vs., 112–13, 148–49, 246; transnational institutions vs., 247; transnational legal jurisdiction, 251–52; United Nations and, 179–80; as united state vs. separate nations, 61–62, 230

Network Commonwealth examples: Arabic Network Commonwealth, 176–77; Francosphere Network Commonwealth, 172; Hispanosphere Network Commonwealth, 112, 122–23, 120–21; Lusosphere Network Commonwealth, 172; Mediterranean Network Commonwealth, 172–73; Rhenish Network Commonwealth, 172–73; Scandinavian-Baltic Network Commonwealth, 172–73; Sinosphere Network Commonwealth, 122–23, 173–74; Turkic Network Commonwealth, 177. *See also* Anglosphere Network Commonwealth

Network Marketplace, 54, 122–23

network paradigm: civil society and, 30; civilization paradigm vs., 131; ethnic identity in, 241; as evolved social entity, 113; hierarchical structures vs., 23–25, 90, 93, 149, 152, 230, 283–84; network spheres, 122–23, 230–31; as social model, 51, 90; sojournership, 78, 149–52, 248. *See also* society

New Africa cultural nation. *See* African-American cultural nation

New Guinea, 75, 105

New Ulster cultural nation: defined, 199, 216; in American Revolution, 200; moral principles in, 213–14; political alliances of, 208–10; populism and, 85; slavery and, 201; in West Virginia, 195

New World Order. *See* globalization

New York City, 6, 141, 199, 225–26, 230. *See also* Manhattan Archipelago cultural classification

New Zealand: aboriginal peoples in, 242–43, 281; American Revolution and, 233; as Anglosphere nation, 73, 78, 80–81, 257–58, 280–81; constitutional reform in, 185; as a cultural nation, 91–92, 224, 281; postimperial identity, 240; as template society, 116; U.S. statehood proposal, 257

Nixon, Richard, 14

NORAD (North American Air Defense Command), 38

North American cultural nations: Dixie cultural nation, 85, 199–211, 213–14, 215–16, 288; Foundry cultural nation, 84, 201–4, 216–18, 222; Greater New England cultural nation, 199–211, 213–14; MexAmerica cultural nation, 50, 214, 220, 222; Midland cultural nation, 101, 195, 199–211, 216. *See also* African-American cultural nation; New Ulster cultural nation; Quebec cultural nation

North American Free Trade Agreement. *See* NAFTA

North Atlantic Free Trade Agreement, 90

North, Lord, 231–32

Northern Ireland, 142, 170–71

Northrop Grumman, 25–26

O'Driscoll, Gerald, 256

Oglesby, Carl, 204

Ohmae, Kenichi, 56, 83–84, 140–41, 174, 224–25

open-source movement, 15, 28, 49–51, 54, 120–21
openness: access to trust and, 118–19; assimilation and, 118–19; civil society and, 10, 37–38, 68–69, 118, 131; essential value of Anglosphere, 10, 68–69, 118, 131
Organization of African Unity, 175
Orion Corp., 127
Orwell, George, 5

Pakistan, 82
Panama, 44
PanAmSat Corp., 128
Paraguay, 106
Philippines, 82, 277
Phillips, Kevin, 26, 73, 92
Poland, 169–70
Portugal: Lusosphere Network Commonwealth, 172; NATO membership, 63–64, 159; Portuguese empire, 129; slavery and, 4, 95, 104–5; as template society, 116
postmodernism, 103
Pound, Ezra, 99
privacy, 45, 125
privatization, 53, 122, 144
prosperity, 59, 247–48
Protestantism: in American colonies, 199–201; as Anglosphere characteristic, 81; evangelical Protestantism, 173–74; in Ireland, 142, 196; Protestant Reformation, 94, 100; Protestant Work Ethic theory, 70–71; U.S. political affiliation and, 217
Puerto Rico, 80–81, 83–84, 179
punctuated equilibrium, 110–11

Quakers, 34, 83, 95, 105, 153
Quebec cultural nation: Bloc Quebecois political party, 196; Canadian nationalism and, 265–68; cultural narratives of, 234; language and, 75, 80–81; political boundaries and, 85, 89, 211–12, 268–69;

secession movement in, 170–71, 183, 259–62, 288

race. See ethnicity
Reagan, Ronald, 53, 217
recreation, 28
Red Hat Corp., 49, 51, 53
Rees-Mogg, William, 277–78
region-states, 224–27
regionalism, 82–89, 140–41, 224
regulation: bounded/unbounded distinction and, 181; costs and justification for, 46, 56, 135–38; of global technology, 29–30, 49, 53, 127–29, 138–39; market intervention, 135–39; Second Gateway (deregulation), 53, 117–18
religion: Christian roots of the Anglosphere, 15, 100; churches as state-mediated institutions, 121; civil society and, 69–70; Confucianism, 9, 30, 173–75, 177; cultural nations and, 199; as foundation for network civilization, 123; Islam, 130; Judiasm, 48, 100, 123; Latin American Protestantism, 174; Old Order Amish, 152; Quakers, 24, 64, 75, 84, 181. See also Catholicism; Protestantism
retirement, 14–15, 32–33
Rhenish Network Commonwealth, 117–18
Rhodes, Cecil, 230, 243
Rhodesia and Nyasaland, Federation of, 233
Rolls-Royce, 166
Roman law tradition, 74, 182, 278–80
Roosevelt, Franklin, 126, 135, 202–4
Rousseau, Jean Jacques, 39–40
Russia: post-Soviet society, 33, 42, 53, 139, 277; Trotskyism, 99. See also Soviet Union
Rwanda, 142

Santa Fe Institute, 28
satellite photography, 15
Scandinavia, 37

Scandinavian-Baltic Network
Commonwealth, 117–18
schools, 60
Schumpeter, Joseph, 53
Scotland: as cultural nation, 82, 199; as
political nation, 199; role in
European Union, 155, 257, 269–70;
Scottish nationalist movement, 196;
secession movement, 233, 259–60,
269–70, 288; Treaty of Union and,
181–82, 194, 231
SEATO (Southeast Asia Treaty
Organization), 157
Second Gateway (deregulation), 53,
117–18
self-assembly protocols: examples of,
61–62; Hanseatic Leagues and,
132–34, 167; Network
Commonwealth principles, 62–63;
voluntary pan-network
organizations, 284–85
Seminole Indians, 83–84
Servan-Schreiver, Jean-Jacques,
9–10
Shaw, George Bernard, 74
Shute, Nevil, 234
Sierra Leone, 75
Singapore, 5, 40, 56, 173, 233
Singularity: defined, 3, 11, 12;
bounded components of, 19–20;
essential values of, 246; as
precursor to globalization, 2; as
unbounded, 13
Singularity Revolution: ambitions and
expectations of, 11; civic states after,
57, 199–200; collaborative
technology and, 155–56; human vs.
technological issues, 17–18;
indicators of likely revolution,
20–22; market (exchange driven)
model of, 52; physical disability
and, 28–29; prohibition as a control
mechanism, 250–51; time frame of,
30–31, 38, 265; voluntary cohesion
vs. coercion in, 55, 59–60
Sinosphere Network Commonwealth,
122–23, 173–74

slavery: abolition movement, 4, 72,
105, 200–201; African Americans
and, 83–84, 96; classical architecture
and, 194; Dixie cultural nation and,
216; economic consequences of, 95,
263; English serfdom vs., 95, 103–4;
imperialism theory and, 3–4;
Industrial Revolution and, 11–12;
John Brown uprising, 192, 201;
racial identity and, 100; religious
roots of, 101; "slaveism" ideology,
94–96, 104
Slovakia, 103, 126, 169–70, 268
Smith, Adam, 61, 232
Snow, C. P., 21
social democracy, 53, 57–59, 87–88
social democratic civic state, 57, 58–59
Social Security, 23, 45–46
socialism. *See* Marxism
society: amphibious society, 28–29,
121, 123–24, 275–76; authoritarian
society, 31–32; conditions for
technological development, 30,
37–38; cryptoanarchy, 46, 55;
economic states vs. civic states, 39;
hierarchical structure, 90;
individual vs. group identity,
31–32; kinship networks and,
114–15, 121; memetic vs. genetic
identity, 89–90; openness in, 10,
37–38, 68–69, 118, 131; trust and,
114–17. *See also* civil society;
network paradigm
sociobiology, 6
sojournership: as alternative to
migrant labor, 222; component of
European Union, 149; component
of Network Commonwealth, 78,
149–56, 165, 248, 258, 283;
relocation transaction costs, 56, 61
Solana, Javier, 157
Soto, Hernando de, 174
South Africa: Afrikaner population, 75;
as Anglosphere nation, 80–82,
223–24, 242, 277–80; anti-apartheid
movement, 237; federalism in, 233;
pan-African identity in, 241;

postimperial identity, 240; secession
    movement in, 196
South Korea, 33, 82
Southeast Asia, 82
sovereignty services, 44–45, 132
Soviet Union: COMECON system, 162;
    NATO and, 238, 275–77; Soviet
    Republic break up, 42, 169, 277. *See
    also* Russia
Sowell, William, 69
space exploration, 12–13
Spain: degree of trust in, 116;
    development of slavery and, 4,
    94–95, 100, 105–6; English Catholic
    conspiracy and, 98; European
    super-regions and, 84; European
    Union effect on, 63–64; as NATO
    member, 156, 277; Spanish empire,
    94, 129
Spengler, Oswald, 3–4, 101, 105–6
Sri Lanka, 56
Stalin, Joseph, 30
Strauss, William, 265
Streit, Clarance, 110
subcivilizations, 123
super-regions, 84, 156
Sweden, 56, 58
Switzerland, 57, 155, 269, 192

Taiwan, 33, 82, 173
taxation: civic social democracies and,
    59; economic unions and, 281–84;
    income tax, 187; tax havens, 44;
    visibility of transactions and, 45
technoliberalism, 138–39
technological development: conditions
    for technological development, 30;
    global regulation of, 29–30, 49, 53,
    127–29, 138–39; government
    sponsorship of, 37, 139–40
Thatcher, Margaret, 30, 37, 53, 138–39,
    277
Third Gateway (fluid
    entrepreneurism), 54, 117–18
Third Way, 59–60, 257, 273–74
Thomas, Hugh, 104
Thompson, James, 275–77

Thoreau, Henry David, 192
Thurmond, Strom, 204
Tibet, 174
Torvalds, Linus, 37, 120–21
totalitarianism, 32, 97–100, 289
treaties, 17, 46–47. *See also*
    globalization
tribalism, 169, 278
Trudeau, Pierre, 212, 265–69, 280
Truman, Harry, 204
trust: agriculture and, 116; assimilation
    and, 71–72, 116–17, 118, 150–51, 211,
    243; civil society and, 69–70, 72,
    114–17, 131; cultural nations and,
    210–11; exploitation of low-trust
    status, 263–64; high-trust societies,
    38, 68–71; Internet and, 120–21, 125;
    kinship and, 114–16, 121, 243;
    language and, 117–18, 150; low-
    trust to high-trust transition, 62,
    242, 243, 262–64; multiculturalism
    and, 116, 243, 264; Network
    Commonwealth and, 39; openness
    and, 118–19; role of government in,
    114–15, 121–22, 278; slaveist
    ideology and, 96; undermined by
    corruption, 35, 115
Turkey, 156, 159
Turkic Network Commonwealth,
    177

United Kingdom. *See* Great Britain
United Nations: control structure of,
    167; globalization and, 40; legal
    jurisdiction of, 251–52; nations vs.
    commonwealths in, 179–80;
    networked co-rule as alternative,
    90; space law and, 17
United States: American
    exceptionalism, 73–75; American
    Studies university programs, 92; as
    Anglosphere nation, 80–81; British
    cultural fusion with, 76; British
    defense alliance with, 158–66, 233,
    235, 238–39, 286–88; Constitution as
    self-assembly protocol, 61, 188–90;
    defense profile, 158–66;

government of, 143–45; government subculture in, 221–22; as high-trust society, 116; influence of English civil society, 72–73; influence of English feudalism, 34; legal traditions of, 181–85, 188–90; national culture, 59, 102, 203–4, 221, 232; openness in, 118; political parties, 202–5; protectionist backlash movement, 246; Roosevelt coalition, 202–4; as Singularity Revolution site, 2; Sinosphere connection of, 122–23; slavery in, 95–96, 104; socialism in, 99; sojournership and, 150–51; as "template" society, 114–16; Whig political theory and, 186, 188–89, 192–93, 231–32. *See also* African Americans; North American cultural nations

UNIX computer system. *See* Linux computer system

Uruguay, 116

utopianism: conspiracy narratives and, 96–97; Counter-Reformation Catholicism, 98; determinist logic of, 6; intellectual malaise and, 98–111; network paradigm vs., 40, 65–66; Singularity Revolutions and, 11–12, 29–31; socialism and, 98–99

Vargas Llosa, Mario, 174
Védrine, Hubert, 80–81
Véliz, Claudio, 96, 174
Verne, Jules, 125
Vickers, 161
Vietnam War, 13, 280, 287
Vinge, Vernor, 3, 11
Virtual Network Commonwealth Assembly, 167

Wales, 80, 233
war: American Civil War, 92, 95–96, 195, 200–201; American Revolution, 92, 194–95, 200, 231–32; Anglosphere civil wars, 92, 193–94; English Civil War, 3, 92, 99, 188, 190, 193–94; Falklands war, 237; French and Indian War, 191; Glorious Revolution, 92; Gulf War, 144, 167; information warfare, 130, 157; Irish Civil War, 94, 195; Irish War of Independence, 92, 94; Jacobite Rebellion, 92, 194; Kosovo war, 40, 144, 277; spatial definition vs. regime composition, 193–94; United Irish uprising of 1798, 194; Vietnam War, 13, 280, 287; World War I, 5, 76, 126, 164; World War II, 12–14, 76, 90, 203, 236. *See also* defense

Washington, Booker T., 263
Washington, George, 191
Weber, Max, 69–71
Webster, Noah, 232
welfare, 60, 185–86, 282
Western Civilization, 101–2
Whig historical narrative, 3–5, 72–73, 93, 184, 192–93
Wilson, Harold, 90
World Court, 251–52
World Trade Organization, 40, 148, 253
World War II, 13–14
World Wide Web. *See* Internet
Wulfstan, Archbishop, 93

X, Malcolm, 263

Y2K crisis, 18–20
Yugoslav Federal Republic, 42

Zambia, 233
Zimbabwe, 81–82, 233

About the Author

James C. Bennett has been a founder or cofounder of several companies in the area of private space launch and Internet transactions and remains active in those fields. As part of those roles he has been involved in formation and implementation of technology law and policy, including serving on the Commercial Space Transportation Advisory Committee of the U.S. Department of Transportation and giving invited testimony before Congress.

He has written in a variety of venues including the *Wall Street Journal*, *Reason*, *National Post*, *Orbis*, *National Interest*, and *National Review Online*, and has been a contributor to three books on technology and society. He has been, since 1986, a founding director of the nonprofit Foresight Institute, which deals with education and research on nanotechnology, and the related Institute for Molecular Manufacturing. He wrote a weekly column, The Anglosphere Beat, for United Press International for three years. He is an Adjunct Fellow of The Hudson Institute.

Bennett is married and lives in Alexandria, Virginia, with his wife and child.

Bennett and his colleagues have formed a nonprofit organization, The Anglosphere Institute, to conduct policy research and further the concepts of the Anglosphere and the Network Commonwealth. The Institute's website can be found at www.anglosphereinstitute.org, and can be reached by mail at P.O. Box 15268, Suite 600, Alexandria, Virginia 22309-9998, USA.